WITHDRAWN
HARVARD LIBRARY
WITHDRAWN

STUDIES IN BAPTIST HISTORY AND THOUGHT

Volume 10

The Tribe of Dan

The New Connexion of General
Baptists 1770–1891: A Study in
the Transition from Revival Movement
to Established Denomination

Foreword by
Roger Hayden

'This careful study...fills a gap in our
knowledge of British Baptist history'
Richard V. Pierard

Frank W. Rinaldi

STUDIES IN BAPTIST HISTORY AND THOUGHT
VOLUME 10

The Tribe of Dan

The New Connexion of General Baptists 1770-1891: A Study in the Transition from Revival Movement to Established Denomination

STUDIES IN BAPTIST HISTORY AND THOUGHT
VOLUME 10

A full listing of all titles in this series
appears at the close of this book

STUDIES IN BAPTIST HISTORY AND THOUGHT
VOLUME 10

The Tribe of Dan

The New Connexion of General Baptists 1770-1891: A Study in the Transition from Revival Movement to Established Denomination

Frank W. Rinaldi

Foreword by Roger Hayden

MILTON KEYNES · COLORADO SPRINGS · HYDERABAD

Copyright © Frank W. Rinaldi 2008

First published 2008 by Paternoster

Paternoster is an imprint of Authentic Media
9 Holdom Avenue, Bletchley, Milton Keynes, MK1 1QR, UK
1820 Jet Stream Drive, Colorado Springs, CO 80921, USA
OM Authentic Media, Medchal Road, Jeedimetla Village,
Secunderabad 500 055, A.P., India

www.authenticmedia.co.uk
Authentic Media is a Division of IBS-STL UK, a company limited by guarantee
(registered charity no. 270162)

15 14 13 12 11 10 09 08 7 6 5 4 3 2 1

The right of Frank W. Rinaldi to be
identified as the Author of this Work has been asserted by him
in accordance with the Copyright, Designs
and Patents Act 1988

*All rights reserved. No part of this publication may be reproduced, stored in a retrieval system, or transmitted in any form by any means, electronic, mechanical, photocopying, recording or otherwise, without the prior permission of the publisher or a license permitting restricted copying. In the UK such licenses are issued by the Copyright Licensing Agency,
90 Tottenham Court Road, London W1P 9HE.*

British Library Cataloguing in Publication Data
A catalogue record for this book is available from the British Library

ISBN 978-1-84227-143-8

Typeset by A.R. Cross
Printed and bound in Great Britain
for Paternoster
by AlphaGraphics Nottingham

Studies in Baptist History and Thought

Series Preface

Baptists form one of the largest Christian communities in the world, and while they hold the historic faith in common with other mainstream Christian traditions, they nevertheless have important insights which they can offer to the worldwide church. Studies in Baptist History and Thought will be one means towards this end. It is an international series of academic studies which includes original monographs, revised dissertations, collections of essays and conference papers, and aims to cover any aspect of Baptist history and thought. While not all the authors are themselves Baptists, they nevertheless share an interest in relating Baptist history and thought to the other branches of the Christian church and to the wider life of the world.

The series includes studies in various aspects of Baptist history from the seventeenth century down to the present day, including biographical works, and Baptist thought is understood as covering the subject-matter of theology (including interdisciplinary studies embracing biblical studies, philosophy, sociology, practical theology, liturgy and women's studies). The diverse streams of Baptist life throughout the world are all within the scope of these volumes.

The series editors and consultants believe that the academic disciplines of history and theology are of vital importance to the spiritual vitality of the churches of the Baptist faith and order. The series sets out to discuss, examine and explore the many dimensions of their tradition and so to contribute to their on-going intellectual vigour.

A brief word of explanation is due for the series identifier on the front cover. The fountains, taken from heraldry, represent the Baptist distinctive of believer's baptism and, at the same time, the source of the water of life. There are three of them because they symbolize the Trinitarian basis of Baptist life and faith. Those who are redeemed by the Lamb, the book of Revelation reminds us, will be led to 'fountains of living waters' (Rev. 7.17).

Studies in Baptist History and Thought

Series Editors

Anthony R. Cross	Centre for Baptist History and Heritage, Regent's Park College, Oxford, England
Curtis W. Freeman	Duke University, North Carolina, USA
Stephen R. Holmes	University of St Andrews, Scotland
Elizabeth Newman	Baptist Theological Seminary at Richmond, Virginia, USA
Philip E. Thompson	North American Baptist Seminary, Sioux Falls, South Dakota, USA

Series Consultants

David Bebbington	University of Stirling, Stirling, Scotland
Paul S. Fiddes	Regent's Park College, Oxford, England
† Stanley J. Grenz	Carey Theological College, Vancouver, British Columbia, Canada
Ken R. Manley	Whitley College, The University of Melbourne, Australia
Stanley E. Porter	McMaster Divinity College, Hamilton, Ontario, Canada

*To my friend and brother in ministry,
the late Stuart Cook,
for his friendship, encouragement, conversation
and constant supply of books*

Contents

Foreword by Roger Hayden xv

Acknowledgements and Preface xvii

Note from the Editors xix

Abbreviations xxi

Chapter 1
Introduction 1
Literature 1
Dan Taylor 2

Chapter 2
'Essential truths': The Theological Background and Development of the Movement 6
Background 6
   General Baptists 6
   Methodism and the Evangelical Revival 8
   Theological Protest 9
The Six Articles 11
Biblicism 14
Free Grace 16
   Evangelistic Imperative 16
   Faith and Conversion 18
   Feeling with the Heart 19
The Erosion of Distinctives 20
Practical Theology 24
   Adversity 24
   Larger Hope 26
Biblical Criticism 28
Science and Secularism 30

Chapter 3
Mission or Maintenance: An Examination of the Organisational Structure of the New Connexion 36
Formation 36
Local Church Forms and Influences 37
   Yorkshire 37

The Midland Group	41
General Baptist Tradition	42
Structures	44
Church Meeting	44
Conference	45
Annual Association or Assembly	49
Institutional Development	53
Public Institutions	53
Missionary Society	56
Reorganisation	57
A Plan of Union	57
Connexional Authority	59
Boundary Concerns	61
Baptism	61
Lord's Supper	64
A New Connexion?	66

Chapter 4
'The middle sphere of life': Aspects of the Social and Demographic Background to the New Connexion

Background to the New Connexion	69
Adapting to the Age	69
A Rural Movement?	72
Rural Nature	72
Framework Knitting	73
Economic Influences	75
Hinckley	75
HINCKLEY MEMBERSHIP 1810–1840	77
Wider Effects	79
New Connexion Response to Conditions	80
Social Migration	83
Protest and Conflict	88
CHURCH RATES	88
The Temperance Movement	91

Chapter 5
The Progress of the Gospel: An Examination of the Development and Evangelistic Strategy of the New Connexion

Evangelistic Strategy of the New Connexion	96
Initial Growth 1770–1815	96
Itinerancy and Church Planting	96
Itinerancy	101
The Role of Church Members	103
Marginal Growth 1816–1840	106
Marginal Phase	106

Evangelistic Strategy 107
Sunday School and Evangelism 109
One Man Ministry 115
Stagnation 1840–1870 117
Deceptive Growth 117
Demographic Changes 124
Beginnings of Decline 1871–1891 129
Revivalism 129
The Leakage Issue 135
Institutional Church 138

Chapter 6
'Labour, poverty, dependence and anxiety': Ministry in the New Connexion 143
Dan Taylor 143
The Nature of Dan Taylor's Authority 143
Order or Orders 144
Pastors and Ministers 144
Elders and Helps 147
Deacons 148
Ordination 150
Approval for Ministry 150
Authority Conferred 152
Laying on of Hands 154
Academy 157
Concerns of Ministry 162
Income 162
Personal Relationships 165
Lay Ministry 166
Dan Taylor and John Clifford 170

Chapter 7
'Union not absorption': The Development of Discussions with Particular Baptists which led to Union in 1891 174
Early Relationships 174
Points of Convergence 176
Union of Particular Baptists 1812 and 1832 177
Mid-century Conversations 180
Crossing the Boundaries 182
Practical and Theological Convergence 182
Cautious Voices 185
Obstacles 185
No Debates! 188

The Down Grade Controversy 189
Amalgamation 190
Opposition 192
Reasons for Union 196
The Secularisation Argument 197
The Theological Convergence Argument 199
The Constituency Argument 202
The Common Agenda Argument 204
Conclusion: A Question of Identity 205

Appendixes **207**
Appendix 1: Annual Percentage Growth Rate: New Connexion, National Population and Sunday School: Table 1. 1770–1815 208
Appendix 2: Annual Percentage Growth Rate: New Connexion, National Population and Sunday School: Table 2. 1816–1839 210
Appendix 3: Annual Percentage Growth Rate: New Connexion, National Population and Sunday School: Table 3. 1840–1869 211
Appendix 4: Annual Percentage Growth Rate: New Connexion, National Population and Sunday School: Table 4. 1870–1890 212
Appendix 5: Numerical Growth of the New Connexion 213
Appendix 6: Graphs Showing Numerical Growth of the New Connexion by County 216
Appendix 7: Number of Baptisms per 1,000 Members. Age of Church by Size of Church 240

Bibliography **243**

Index **255**

Tables
Table 1: Distribution of New Connexion Churches in Relation to Village Size, 1832–1856 72
Table 2: Land Ownership Patterns 73
Table 3: Table of Occupations at Hinckley 74
Table 4: New Connexion Membership as Density of Population 119
Table 5: Comparison of Churches in Yorkshire and Lincolnshire 126
Table 6: New Lenton Membership Additions, 1864 133

Figures
Figure 1: Hinckley Membership 1810–1840 78
Figure 2: Annual Percentage Growth, 1770–1815 97
Figure 3: Development of the Barton Group of Churches 102
Figure 4: Annual Percentage Growth, 1816–1840 107
Figure 5: Comparison of Church Growth vs Sunday School, 1845–1890 110

Figure 6: Annual Percentage Growth Rate, 1841–1870 118
Figure 7: Population Density of the New Connexion, 1800–1890 120
Figure 8: Annual Percentage Growth, 1871–1890 130

Foreword

Who are the Baptists? Why are some 'General and others Particular'? Do the adjectives have any real meaning? Surely the generic term, Baptist, is enough. The story of the General Baptists of the New Connexion from 1770 to 1891 is the theme of Frank Rinaldi's book, and out of a wealth of original material come some challenging questions about the past to illuminate contemporary issues about English Baptists.

Are Baptist Christians essentially a 'movement', or more properly described as a 'gathered church', even a denomination? Rinaldi analyses the changes from movement to denomination in a clearly identified span of time and it makes fascinating reading for all concerned with mission, or 'church growth'. He traces the positive, lively, mission-concerned input of lay people within their own identifiable communities. He raises questions about the deadening effect of 'institutionalism', the shift from a 'mission' to a 'maintenance' culture, as professional 'one man ministry' began to dominate the New Connexion. At first, evangelical preaching was the major sphere of service for New Connexion lay leaders. As the 'institutional church' model came to dominate, particularly through the advent of Sunday school and other valid agencies, Rinaldi argues that the use of lay preachers becomes formalized in apposition to full-time ministry. It was 'moved indoors', until preaching was largely to the converted, not the unconverted, with serious results for church growth. Rinaldi challenges several contemporary Baptist assumptions about the crucial place of ministry in pursuit of that mission goal, not least the Richard Baxter dictum, beloved of many recent Baptist College Principals, that 'the churches rise and fall as doth the ministry'. Rinaldi's evidence goes a long way in challenging this assumption.

Rinaldi considers the pressures of secularization, the theological breakdown of Calvinism, matched by a parallel General Baptist conviction that their testimony to Arminianism had found wide acceptance, together with a nineteenth-century Nonconformist common agenda against the State Church and Anglo-Catholicism. Over the period studied he suggests the independence and protest of Dan Taylor becomes a 'desire for fusion' under John Clifford's leadership, ending in the demise of the General Baptists. Dr Rinaldi's thesis is resourced from the primary sources, and covers the New Connexion in a way that has not been attempted for a century or more, and includes a wide range of statistical information that is available for the first time.

Since 1990, Baptists who are the successors of the 1891 union of Particular and General Baptists in England have been searching for a new energizing way of being Christians together. Rinaldi's book, delayed because of his ill-health, is a doubly welcome addition to current Baptist studies, and will repay careful consideration. It could help to identify a meaningful future Baptist lifestyle, as yesterday's lessons for Baptists, through the Holy Spirit, provide some new possibilities in the twenty-first century.

Revd Dr Roger Hayden,
Bristol, 2008

Author's Preface and Acknowledgments

There are many people who deserve acknowledgement and thanks in helping to bring this work to completion: Dr. Raymond Brown who first encouraged my interest in this period of Baptist history. Dr. Michael R. Watts of Nottingham University and Dr. Douglas Murray of Glasgow University who guided my studies; Douglas Woolridge the archivist of the East Midland Baptist Archive who allowed me to plunder his resources; my good friend Graham Roberts who rescued statistical date when my computer crashed and, together with Phil John and Tim Jackson, introduced me to the mysteries of databases and spreadsheets. A special word of appreciation should go to the trustees of the Dr. Williams's Trust whose generous funding made possible the study of which this book is the product, also to the Rev. Alan Griggs, Rev. Graham Doel, Dr. Raymond Brown and Dr. Anthony R. Cross for their help in editing and preparing the manuscript for publication following my illness. Finally, I would like to thank my family who tolerated long periods of absence on my part and especially my wife, Thelma, without whose continual encouragement and support I would have never finished the study or this book.

Frank Rinaldi,
Melton Mowbray, 2008

Note from the Editors

We are delighted to see the appearance of Frank Rinaldi's study of the New Connexion of General Baptists, *The Tribe of Dan*. It is a welcome addition to the Studies in Baptist History and Thought series for a number of reasons: it is a comprehensive survey of its subject; it is the first published book on the New Connexion for well over 150 years; and it will, we hope, encourage others to pursue this much neglected stream of Baptist life further through new research. It is also particularly welcome because it has come to print despite Dr Rinaldi's poor health. In 2003 he suffered a brain haemorrhage which, having forced his retirement from the pastorate of Rothley Baptist Church and his position as the Ecumenical Development Officer in Leicestershire, also prevented him from undertaking the revision of his doctorate leading to this volume. Since he was unable to complete this revision himself, the editors of the series and Dr Rinaldi are deeply grateful to a number of friends and ministerial colleagues who have worked to bring his research to the wider scholarly community. Together they have aimed at revising the material as best they could in the realization that Dr Rinaldi, as a specialist in the subject, would have been able to revise the material to a degree that has, in the circumstances, not been possible. This study, then, is published in the recognition that it is not the work that Dr Rinaldi would have presented had he been able, but which is nevertheless a valuable contribution to Baptist history in particular and to the history of the church of Christ in general.

Professor David Bebbington,
Senior Consultant Editor, Studies in Baptist History and Thought,
on behalf of the editors.

Abbreviations

BH	*The Baptist Handbook*
CCPD	*Calendar of the Correspondence of Philip Doddridge*, ed. G.F. Nuttall
CHST	*Transactions of the Congregational Historical Society*
CQ	*The Congregational Quarterly*
CR	*Calamy Revised*, ed. A.G. Matthews
CYB	*The Congregational Year Book*
CUEW	*The Congregational Union of England and Wales*
DBI	*Dictionary of Biblical Interpretation*, ed. John H. Hayes
DEB	*Dictionary of Evangelical Biography*, ed. D.M. Lewis
DECBP	*Dictionary of Eighteenth-Century British Philosophers*, eds J.W. Yolton, J.V. Price, and J. Stephens
DHT	*Dictionary of Historical Theology*, ed. T. Hart
DMBI	*A Dictionary of Methodism in Britain and Ireland*, ed. J.A. Vickers
DNB	*Dictionary of National Biography*
DNCBP	*Dictionary of Nineteenth-Century British Philosophers*, eds W.J. Mander and A.P.F. Sell
DSCHT	*Dictionary of Scottish Church History and Theology*, ed. N.M. deS. Cameron
DSCBP	*Dictionary of Seventeenth-Century British Philosophers*, ed. A. Pyle
DTCBP	*Dictionary of Twentieth-Century British Philosophers*, ed. S. Brown
DWB	*Dictionary of Welsh Biography*
EEUTA	*English Education Under the Test Acts*, H. McLachlan
EM	*The Evangelical Magazine*
ET	*The Expository Times*
FAE	*Freedom After Ejection*, A. Gordon
GEE	G.E. Evans, *Vestiges of Protestant Dissent*
JEREMY	W.D. Jeremy, *The Presbyterian Fund, etc.*
JURCHS	*The Journal of the United Reformed Church History Society*
MURCH	J. Murch, *A History of the Presbyterian and General Baptist Churches in the West of England*
ODNB	*Oxford Dictionary of National Biography*
PNT	*Protestant Nonconformist Texts*, series editor, A.P.F. Sell
SCM	W.D. McNaughton, *The Scottish Congregational Ministry*
TSJ	T.S. James, *Presbyterian Chapels and Charities*
URCYB	*The United Reformed Church Year Book*
UHST	*Transactions of the Unitarian Historical Society*
WTW	*Who They Were*, eds J. Taylor and C. Binfield
WWW	*Who Was Who*
WW	W. Wilson, *History and Antiquities of Dissenting Churches and Meeting-houses in London, Westminster and Southwark*

CHAPTER 1

Introduction

Literature

There were a number of reasons for the choice of the New Connexion of General Baptists as a subject for study. First, they reflect an aspect of the impact of the Evangelical Revival on Old Dissent. Second, the connexional structure of the movement is distinctive among Baptists. Third, the New Connexion reflected the concerns and aspirations of nineteenth-century Nonconformity, and because of this it may be viewed as a typical example of Victorian Dissent. Finally, there has not yet been a full account of the life of the Connexion. Such treatment as it has received has centred on the Connexion's emergence in 1770 and on its union with Particular Baptists in 1891. The object of this book is to explore the history of the New Connexion of General Baptists from their origins as a revival movement through their subsequent development and evolution as an established denomination.

The first account of the Connexion appeared in the *General Baptist Magazine* of 1798. The writer, John Deacon of Friar Lane, Leicester, was the brother of Samuel Deacon, Jr, of Barton. His account views the history of the Connexion from the perspective of its Leicestershire origins. John Deacon makes no mention of the work in Yorkshire or Lincolnshire. Adam Taylor's two volume *The History of the English General Baptists* is much fuller. The first volume deals with the Old General Baptists, the second with the churches of the New Connexion. This work, published in 1818, was the standard authority, and subsequent histories drew heavily on Taylor. His work is based on histories submitted by the churches of the Connexion. *A Condensed History of the General Baptists of the New Connexion* by J.H. Wood, and published in 1847, provides a wealth of statistical information in a tabular format. The history of the Connexion has not received a great deal of attention from modern historians. W.T. Whitley, *A History of British Baptists*, gives a good account of the origins, but that aside there is only brief mention of one or two individuals and a short account of the 1891 union. A.C. Underwood, in *A History of the English Baptists* (1947), and E.A. Payne, in *The Baptist Union: A Short History* (1959), make brief mention of the emergence of the Connexion and the events surrounding the process of union, but little else. F.M.W. Harrison's MPhil thesis for Nottingham University, 'The Life and Thought of the Baptists of Nottinghamshire', is much fuller in its account of the New Connexion, but is limited to Nottinghamshire. Raymond Brown, in *The English Baptists of the Eighteenth Century* (1986), gives a comprehensive account of the background to the emergence of the connexion. The fullest account of the connexion is to be found in

J.H.Y. Briggs, *The English Baptists of the Nineteenth Century* (1994), who gives a New Connexion perspective on the events leading to the union of General and Particular Baptists, but again the concern is more with the process of union than with the New Connexion. Michael Watts' two volume work, *The Dissenters* (1978, 1995), makes a number of references to the New Connexion but there is no systematic treatment. Loren Shull, *The General Baptist Process: From Sect to Denomination* (1985), is a sociological study of the church–sect process of the American General Association of General Baptists. It will be seen from the above that there has been to date no work that has the development of the New Connexion as it primary focus.

One of the difficulties associated with the New Connexion of General Baptists is the limited amount of published material in the early period. While Dan Taylor features heavily, other early members of the Connexion are not so well represented. The connexional magazine, published under various names from 1798 to 1892, was a very rich source. Much of the material is of a secondary nature, but it contains biography, Baptist history, essays, sermons, and correspondence. Also included in some bound editions are 'Minutes of the Annual Assembly', the annual 'Letter to the Churches' and the statistical returns from the churches. The latter has been compiled into a database which is the statistical resource for this work. The *Baptist Reporter* was similar to the *General Baptist Magazine*, and was edited and published by J.F. Winks, a General Baptist, but was directed at both Particular and General Baptists. *The Freeman*, politically liberal in its views, was intended as a family paper, and covered church matters. Biographies related to the Connexion tend to be mainly of Dan Taylor and John Clifford, although there are one or two of other leading ministers. Primary source material used includes minute books of associations, churches, Sunday schools, and lay preachers associations.

The main strength of the New Connexion lay in South Yorkshire, the East Midlands and Lincolnshire. Rooted in the tradition of Independency usual with Baptists and Congregationalists, there was a tendency towards planting chapel-centred communities. This tendency and other demographic factors affected its development and distribution.

An attempt to explore the processes at work in the New Connexion as an example of the transition from sect to denomination, together with a chronological approach, was abandoned. It became evident that the Connexion should be viewed as a revival movement, an embryonic denomination, rather than a sect. The factors giving rise to the distinctiveness of the Connexion were found to be in the eighteenth-century Evangelical Revival. It is this process of transition from revival movement to established denomination that is the substance of this work.

Dan Taylor

Because of the importance of Dan Taylor to the formation and development of the Connexion a brief biography seems appropriate. Born at Sourmilk Hall, Northowram, West Riding of Yorkshire on 21 December 1738 he was by the age of five working in a coal mine along side his father. As the son of a miner, he had only occasionally attended school, but this self-taught man had a great thirst for books and knowledge. At the age of fifteen, Taylor came to faith at a Methodist class meeting. His conversion was typical of the period: there was a long period of searching which resulted in a 'greater confidence to lay hold of the hope set before him in the gospel'; he formally joined the Methodists at the age of twenty.[1] His keenness and his reading led to pressure on him to become a Methodist travelling preacher, and he was soon speaking and preaching in the local circuit.

While Taylor embraced the theology of Methodism he did not do so without question. There were points at which he differed: 'he was convinced that the New Testament gave no countenance, either by precept or example, to the scheme of discipline which that gentleman (John Wesley) imposed on his followers'.[2] During this period of unease with Methodism, four friends at Wadsworth, a small village just outside Halifax, 'occupying lowly stations in life and possessing little influence', invited him to come and teach them. 'Mr Taylor resolved to cast his lot among them; and to attempt to introduce the gospel in this dark neighbourhood'.[3] Having rejected Methodism, this group began to seek an identity for themselves. Taylor and his followers were led to an examination of believer's baptism. Reading Dr William Wall's defence of infant baptism, *History of Infant Baptism* (1705), Taylor became convinced that this was not what the scripture demanded. Conscious that no Particular Baptist would baptize him because of his theology of the atonement, he was informed of a General Baptist church at Boston where his baptism might be a possibility. *En route* there, he and one of his group stopped at Gamston in Nottinghamshire and discovered a General Baptist church. After waiting three days, during which time he was questioned by John Dossey the minister, he was baptized by Jeffries, the associate pastor, in the River Idle in February 1763. It was on the basis of this meeting, that Taylor and the group in Yorkshire styled themselves General Baptists. Seeking fellowship, he joined the Lincolnshire Association of General Baptists to whom he had been introduced while at Gamston. He attended the Association meeting at Lincoln in May 1763, where he formed a life-long friendship with William Thompson of Boston. He accompanied Taylor on his return to Yorkshire and baptized a number believers, fourteen of whom formed themselves into a church. In the autumn of 1763 he was ordained, together with Dossy of Gamston, by Gilbert Boyce, the Lincolnshire Messenger, the pastor at Conningsby. In 1765 he went as the representative of the Lincolnshire Association to the General Assembly in London, and again in 1767. He was a participant in the

---

[1] Ernest F. Clipsham, 'Dan Taylor', in Leslie Stephen and Sidney Lee (eds), *Dictionary of National Biography* (Oxford: Oxford University Press, 1921–22), XIX, pp. 405-406.

[2] Adam Taylor, *Memoirs of the Rev. Dan Taylor Late Pastor of the General Baptist Church Whitechapel, London. With extracts from his Diary, Correspondence and Unpublished Manuscripts* (London, 1820), p. 9.

[3] Taylor, *Memoirs of the Rev. Dan Taylor*, p. 9.

meeting at Lincoln in 1769 which led to the formation of the New Connexion the following year.

The role of Dan Taylor was most significant for the new movement. From 1770 to 1816 he was chairman or president of all but two meetings of the Annual Association. His name is only twice missing from the list of Assembly preachers during that period. One of these occasions was an Assembly at Taylor's church in London. He was present but 'only gave out the hymns'. In addition to his preaching, he wrote some seventeen of the annual 'Letter to the Churches'. These letters dealt with such subjects as 'The Nature and Obligation of Christian Fellowship', 'Nature and Utility of Associations', 'Early engagements between the Sexes', 'Operations of the Holy Spirit', 'Depravity of human nature', 'Assurance of Salvation' and 'The General Baptist Academy'. The Angus library catalogue lists forty-nine publications and thirteen 'Association letters'. He edited *the General Baptist Magazine* from 1798–1800 and contributed to its sequel *The General Baptist Repository*. In his writing he sought for plainness and simplicity, keeping the needs of the illiterate and 'persons of inferior capacities' in mind.[4] The letters were circulated to all the churches of the Connexion and may be viewed as official policy papers on the part of the movement. In addition to this, he officiated at thirty-eight ordinations at which he preached, either to the minister or to the church, and on some occasions to both. Adam Taylor estimates that he attended 200 conferences and delivered 'upon a very moderate computation nearly twenty thousand discourses'.[5] In addition to this he was the first tutor of the 'General Baptist Academy' at Mile End, London, from 1798–1813. Adam Taylor says of him, 'Mr Taylor was looked upon throughout the New Connexion with the greatest deference, his opinion was consulted almost as an oracle. He was consulted on difficult cases, and frequently invited to settle disputes.'[6]

Dan Taylor, the founding father of the movement, had no formal education and for most of his life he combined secular occupations with the pastoral office. The application of this self-educated man was formidable. His diary for June 1770 gives a proposed time-table: from five to ten in the morning were devotions; from ten till twelve the classics, 'or some book in Greek or Latin'; after dinner till three biography or church history; from three till eight visiting except when he was preaching. Tuesdays were set apart for literary correspondence, and Saturdays for the pulpit.[7] How this fitted into running a farm and looking after boarders at his school we are not told. His diligence meant he was well read and understood the major theological issues that confronted the Connexion. In the first few decades of the movement it was his thinking that was formative.

What made him such a representative voice in the movement? The faith he imbibed in his early days was the evangelistic Arminianism of the Methodist Revival. John Taylor records that, when the subject of election 'became the general topic of conversation in the neighbourhood he was then a warm advocate for the

---

[4] Taylor, *Memoirs of the Rev. Dan Taylor*, p. 94.
[5] Taylor, *Memoirs of the Rev. Dan Taylor*, p. 289.
[6] Taylor, *Memoirs of the Rev. Dan Taylor*, p. 289.
[7] Taylor, *Memoirs of the Rev. Dan Taylor*, pp. 49-50.

great truth that Christ died for every man'.[8] John Wesley had offered to men and women a living faith, an experience of God, a supernatural encounter, a faith orthodox in its content, but new in its form.[9] The sociologist Bryan Wilson sees a tension within Methodism; it was, he says, 'a reaction, a reassertion of religious values to new classes'. But even in this reaction, this attempt to perpetuate the old, it found itself 'already embracing much of the new spirit'.[10] The faith Taylor held, and offered, was a product of the Evangelical Revival. It centred around a secure relationship with God, that a person may discover through an act of faith, an experience as well as a belief system, something stable and secure in an age of change. In addition to his theological contribution, Taylor's physical presence helped to integrate the movement. His fund-raising tours and influence in the organization of the Connexion meant that he was known and trusted by the majority of ministers of what was, in its early stages, a relatively small group of churches. For nearly half a century:

> few cases of perplexity or doubt arose in any of the churches of the New Connexion in which he was not consulted. Few ministers settled with a people, or took any important step without first seeking his advice. When an abtruse query or important measure was proposed at the conferences it was not unusual to 'refer it to brother Taylor'.[11]

For forty-six years Dan Taylor exercised a unique authority within the Connexion and was a major contributor to its development; to this extent the New Connexion could be called 'the tribe of Dan'.

---

[8] Taylor, *Memoirs of the Rev. Dan Taylor*, p. 6.
[9] G.R. Cragg, *The Church and the Age of Reason 1648–1789* (*The Pelican History of the Church*, 4; Middlesex: Pelican Books, 1966), pp. 144, 151. W.R. Ward 'The Evangelical Revival', in Sheridan Gilley and W.J. Sheils (eds), *A History of Religion in Britain* (Oxford: Blackwell, 1994), pp. 268-69.
[10] Bryan Wilson, *Religion in a Secular Society: A Sociological Comment* (London: C.A. Watts 1966), p. 27.
[11] Taylor, *Memoirs of the Rev. Dan Taylor*, p. 308.

CHAPTER 2

'Essential truths': The Theological Background and Development of the Movement

Background

Theology was the declared issue for the formation of the New Connexion, which was formed as a protest against the theological drift of the General Baptists. In the middle of the eighteenth century Baptists in England were divided into two groups: the Particular Baptists whose theology was Calvinist in nature, holding a doctrine of limited atonement or particular redemption—that God had already determined the course of an individual's destiny and that only those who were his elect would be saved. The other group were General Baptists who believed in a general redemption—that Christ had 'tasted death for every man', no one was beyond the reach of saving grace, everyone was free to respond. These positions were well defined and clearly understood by both groups and, at the time of the formation of the Connexion, they had a history stretching back over 150 years: there was a degree of mutual acceptance and understanding between the two main groups. For them, the church was a fellowship of believers, bound to each other by friendship, forbearance, mutual support and rebuke. They had much in common, similar systems of church government, and were marked off from the rest of Dissent by their doctrine of believer's baptism.

General Baptists

The late seventeenth century and early eighteenth century saw the emergence of Socinian and Arian views, and these had a powerful impact amongst Dissenters. Socinian teaching derived from a sixteenth century Italian, Fausto Sozzini or Socinus (1539–1604) who had been associated with a group of anti-trinitarian Anabaptists at Rakow in Poland in 1580. The more radical of this group denied both the divinity and pre-existence of Christ and rejected the doctrine of vicarious atonement.[1] Generally Socinian teaching held that Christ was not pre-existent, but was merely a man, and that the Holy Spirit was a power or an influence and not the third person of the Trinity. God did not require an infinite satisfaction and sin was not a deep corruption. Christ saved men by revealing to them the way of faith and

---

[1] Michael R. Watts, *The Dissenters*. Volume 1: *From the Reformation to the French Revolution* (Oxford: Clarendon Press, 1985), p. 371.

obedience as the way to eternal life; he gave an example of true obedience in his life and death and inspired them to lead a similar life.

A major division amongst General Baptists took place in 1696, when the General Association of more orthodox churches, centred in Buckinghamshire and the Midlands, separated from the less orthodox General Assembly, which drew its strength from the south—Kent, Sussex, Essex and the West Country.[2] Leon McBeth attributes the shift in General Baptists from orthodoxy to a weak Christology as an inheritance from the Menonnites.[3] Alongside the theological issues many churches adopted literalism in exegesis, leading to a legalism in minor issues. This resulted in a series of splits which had a withering effect.[4] There was an attempt at re-union at the General Assembly of 1731. Seeking to avoid theological issues, a compromise was sought by means of a scriptural formulation that did not spell out doctrine with any precision. The Assembly resolved that 'all debates public or private respecting the Trinity should be managed in scripture words and terms and no other'.[5] They also required that any one willing to reunite on the compromise basis 'shall not be permitted to ask any question, neither shall any question be asked of him upon pain of being excluded'.[6] Thus the General Baptists chose denominational unity at the expense of doctrinal agreement. This compromise did not resolve the differences; the differences were pushed underground to resurface in a number of minor factions.

Later, Dan Taylor and the other members of the New Connexion sought to assert the divine nature of Christ and a direct connection between Christ's death and the salvation of sinners. The basis of his appeal was the teaching of the Bible. It was just such an appeal to scripture that had led some General Baptists to reject the Trinity and to embrace elements of Socinian and Arian teaching, which were the very things that Taylor was seeking to counter.

Dan Taylor, as a representative at the General Baptist Assembly's meeting in London between 1767 and 1769, became aware of the extent to which disputes and differences of opinion were tearing at the fabric of the denomination.[7] The lack of zeal for conversion was also evident to Taylor, which was one of his main criticisms of the General Baptists. The group which separated, and became the New Connexion

---

[2] Watts, *The Dissenters*, I, p. 300.

[3] H. Leon McBeth, *The Baptist Heritage: Four Centuries of Baptist Witness* (Nashville, TN: Broadman Press, 1987), pp. 152, 155.

[4] Raymond Brown, *The English Baptists of the Eighteenth Century* (London: Baptist Historical Society, 1986), pp. 21-23.

[5] McBeth, *Baptist Heritage*, p. 157. McBeth is here using the language used of the 1697 General Assembly, on which see Adam Taylor, *The History of the English General Baptists* (2 vols; London, 1818), I, p. 470.

[6] This language is that of the General Assembly's 'The Unity of the Churches' (1704), see Taylor, *History*, I, p. 477. On this attempt at reunion, see W.T. Whitley, *Minutes of the General Assembly of the General Baptist Churches in England With Kindred Records. Volume 2: 1731–1811* (London: Kingsgate Press, 1910), pp. 2, 13-14 and 32-34.

[7] J.H. Wood, *A Condensed History of the General Baptists of the New Connexion* (London/Leicester, 1847), p. 175.

did so, according to Taylor, in order: 'to preserve themselves from the contagion of what they esteemed as dangerous heresy'.[8] To some extent they are an example of Bryan Wilson's 'protest' groups that emerge in a particular period and present a challenge to the dominant grouping.[9] It is against this background of theological ambiguity that the formation of the New Connexion needs to be seen. It was, in part, a protest against the theological compromise that had taken place within the General Baptists and a desire explicitly to espouse evangelical doctrines. The extent to which 'a theology of protest' is an accurate description of the Connexion will be examined as we consider the nature of that theology.

Methodism and the Evangelical Revival

Dan Taylor sought to fuse the theology of the Evangelical Revival with that of the General Baptists and thereby gave to the Connexion its theological hallmark. His brother, John, tells how this theology was formed. At the age of twelve he and Dan encountered the Particular Baptists who were then establishing a church in Halifax. Calvinism became a topic of general conversation. John Taylor recorded that:

> As soon as I heard these men and their new religion, I made one of their congregation and attended constantly as most for several years. By going thither, I was considerably strengthened in my opinions, and was forward enough to retain and indicate them. I disputed much as well as a child could dispute with many of my companions in favour of Calvinism; but my principal antagonist was my brother Dan. He always opposed it from a child through his whole life till now: and I hope he will hold out to the end of his life to oppose it.[10]

John Taylor tells us that Dan's first interest was in Methodism, which was then in its early stages of expansion: 'My brother then was inclined to Methodism and afterwards commenced a Methodist. I was never one nor could I satisfy myself to design it. I went commonly to the public worship with them for many years. But never that I remember to any of their class meetings.'[11] The two young men would travel to hear the great preachers of the day, 'To Whitechapel, to Birstall, and Hayworth, we went often: especially when the celebrated Wesleys and Whitefield came.'[12] Thus the earliest influences on the founder of the New Connexion were those of the Evangelical Revival.

The Revival asserted the Reformation doctrines of justification by faith alone, the priesthood of all believers, the fall, or sinful depravity of man and the assurance of

---

[8] McBeth, *Baptist Heritage*, p. 162.
[9] Wilson, *Religion in Secular Society*, p. 214.
[10] Adam Taylor, *Memoirs of Rev John Taylor Late Pastor of the General Baptist Church at Queenshead, near Halifax Yorkshire (Chiefly compiled from a manuscript written by himself)* (London, 1821), p. 11.
[11] Taylor, *Memoirs of John Taylor*, p. 9
[12] Taylor, *Memoirs of John Taylor*, p. 10

faith, and this teaching was the source of activism with in the movement.[13] It was strongly individualistic in character, emphasizing a personal commitment to God through conversion, an experience which often included an emotional dimension. The fruit of such conversion was understood in terms of a personal moral and spiritual transformation, revealed by morally disciplined living, personal devotion and good works. It was this theology that Dan Taylor and his brother imbibed in their early years.

The Yorkshire Methodists thought highly of Dan Taylor. They were 'anxious that he should visit Mr. Wesley, and enter regularly into the ministry, as a travelling preacher'.[14] Dan Taylor declined, and shortly after, in the summer of 1762, broke with the Methodists over the question of authority, not being willing to submit 'to that dictatorship which Mr. Wesley then assumed over the conduct and faith of his preachers'.[15] He was invited to preach for a small group of Methodist dissidents at Heptonstall, who, like Taylor, had broken with Methodism over the question of authority. This small group of four first met in the open, and later, as winter approached, they took a house at Wadsworth. The group was soon discussing church order, and the subject of baptism arose; their appeal to the Bible led them to adopt 'believer's baptism'. Local Particular Baptist ministers refused to baptize Taylor because he taught a general atonement. However, an unknown Particular Baptist minister directed him to the General Baptists of Lincolnshire, a group of which Taylor seems to have had no knowledge prior to this. *En route* to them he stopped at Gamston in Lincolnshire where he discovered a General Baptist church and he was baptized by Joseph Jeffries, the General Baptist minister. It was the church at Gamston that introduced Taylor to the Lincolnshire General Baptists. Adam Taylor says, 'As he stood alone in Yorkshire, he was anxious to form a connexion with other ministers whose sentiments agreed with his own.'[16] Dan Taylor's contact with the Lincolnshire General Baptists came at a time when they were deeply divided amongst themselves, and harmonious relationships between the General Baptists were not to last long.

Theological Protest

Dan Taylor's theology developed in the context of debate. Most, if not all, of his work had an apologetic basis, and was written in response to a pressing need or an urgent situation. Throughout his ministry he had some form of secular occupation in order to supplement his income: 'he could never apply his thoughts uninterruptedly to a subject, but was always obliged to pursue it at detached and often distant portions of leisure'.[17] Despite this handicap, he was more than willing to enter into

---

[13] D.W. Bebbington, *Evangelicalism in Modern Britain: A History from the 1730s to the 1980s* (London: Unwin Hyman, 1989), p. 74.
[14] Taylor, *History*, II, p. 70.
[15] Taylor, *Memoirs of the Rev. Dan Taylor*, p. 9
[16] Taylor, *History*, II, p. 75.
[17] Taylor, *History*, II, p. 304.

debate. His first major conflict with the General Baptists was in 1765, and involved Gilbert Boyce who was the minister at Coningsby and messenger of the Lincolnshire Association; as he said 'I and my great and good friend Mr B. are ere long to meet at Gamston to talk upon some points wherein we differ.'[18] The points at issue were the General Baptist's adherence to what Taylor considered an over literalist approach to trivial issues, and, more importantly, Arian and Socinian tendencies amongst some of the General Baptists. An entry in his diary for 27 August 1675 tells the result of the meeting:

> I am now returned from Gamston where I have had much disputing for what I call truth. But I am surprised that, while no solid arguments are produced, wise men can satisfy themselves with impertinent quibbles. I see how easy it is to perplex when we cannot refute, the plain truth of the Gospel. Lord help me to hold fast by thy word.[19]

The concerns raised in this meeting were to result in a break with the General Baptists and the formation of the New Connexion. While no details of the controversy are given, for Taylor the main issue was the 'plain truth of the Gospel'. The teaching which could not be refuted was the preaching of 'Christ crucified as the only Saviour of sinners'.[20] The Lincolnshire General Baptists were, he felt, deficient in this area, and Taylor forcibly expressed his protest: 'It is not to be doubted, if we regard the Bible, that some of the vilest errors are, in this age, maintained by some of the General Baptists, with as much warmth and zeal as they were by any party of men in former ages.'[21] Much later, in 1793, he wrote to Gilbert Boyce, the General Baptist Messenger for Lincolnshire, explaining his reasons for separation. He argued that the atonement was 'fundamental' and neglecting to preach it would inevitably lead to decline.[22] On the way back from the meeting with Boyce at Coningsby he took the opportunity to meet with, and preach to a group of independent Midland churches linked with the church at Barton in the Beans in Leicestershire of which Samuel Deacon was pastor. He found them 'strenuous advocates' for what he considered the 'essential truths' of the gospel.[23] His suggestion that they join the Lincolnshire Association was rejected because they 'esteemed several of them highly erroneous in their creed'; no doubt a reference to the Unitarian tendencies that were present in the Lincolnshire Association.[24]

For its part Old Dissent, which comprised Congregational, Presbyterian, Quaker and Baptist churches, clung to the traditional forms and patterns, and there was a suspicion of enthusiasm associated with the Evangelical Revival. The evangelical

---

[18] Taylor, *Memoirs of the Rev. Dan Taylor*, p. 21.
[19] Taylor, *Memoirs of the Rev. Dan Taylor*, p. 22
[20] Taylor, *Memoirs of the Rev. Dan Taylor*, p. 200.
[21] Taylor, *Memoirs of the Rev. Dan Taylor*, p. 76
[22] Taylor, *Memoirs of the Rev. Dan Taylor*, p. 273.
[23] Taylor, *Memoirs of the Rev. Dan Taylor*, p. 29.
[24] Taylor, *Memoirs of the Rev. Dan Taylor*, p. 30.

emphasis of the Connexion may also be seen as a protest against the formality, introversion and lack of conversionist zeal of Old Dissent, especially amongst Baptists.[25]

The difficulties felt by Taylor, Deacon and the early preachers of the New Connexion, centred around this lack of conversion zeal on the part of the General Baptists. Given the concerns expressed by the Connexion at its emergence, a theology of protest would seem an apt description. This protest is reflected in the name they chose, 'Free Grace General Baptists', for it was this desire to offer God's grace freely to all, and their evangelistic emphasis and heart, that gave them their distinctive nature.

The Six Articles

The distinctive theology of the Connexion found expression in the 'Six Articles'. This was a statement drawn up by Dan Taylor in 1770 at the time of their separation from the General Baptists, and was the theological rationale behind the formation of the new movement. Adam Taylor, the early historian of the movement, said of the 'Six Articles of Religion' that they were not intended as a statement of faith, 'not as a perfect creed of the new party; but principally as a declaration of their views on those points which had been the chief subjects of debate, between them and their former associates'.[26] The concern of Taylor in the 'Six Articles' was to make clear the difference between the New Connexion and the General Baptists.

The influence of the Evangelical Revival is reflected in his theology. Writing to his friend Thompson at Boston, he said: 'I assure you, dear brother, that you do not seem too catholic for me in what you say about Messers Watts, Doddridge, Hervey Venn, Whitfield &c &c &c. I pray God give you and myself a large increase of Christian candour.'[27] Taylor and the founding members of the New Connexion were concerned with a restoration to 'Primitive Christianity'; in this desire, they were part of the renewal of evangelical orthodoxy that accompanied the Revival.[28]

The object of the 'Six Articles' was to 'revive Experimental Religion', which a general concern of the Evangelical Revival.[29] The Articles deal with the following subjects: the fall of man, the nature and obligations of the moral law, the person and work of Christ, salvation by faith, the work of the Holy Spirit and baptism. They are an attempt to set out the position of the New Connexion in relation to General Baptists, rejecting their Arian and Socinian tendencies; they are also a rejection of the antinomianism of high-Calvinism. In outline the 'Six Articles' are as follows.

---

[25] John A. Deacon, 'History of the General Baptist Churches in the counties of Leicester, Warwick, Derby, and Nottingham, &c Usually Denominated the New Connexion', *GBM* (1798), p. 158.

[26] Taylor, *History*, II, p. 139.

[27] Taylor, *Memoirs of the Rev. Dan Taylor*, p. 81.

[28] Taylor, *History*, II, p. 139.

[29] Taylor, *History*, II, p. 139.

Article 1: 'On the Fall of Man' holds that man, at his creation, was in a state of moral purity, with freedom of choice, capable of obedience or sinning. Thus man's subsequent sin, placed him under the 'divine curse'. Man's nature is depraved, his mind defiled and his powers weakened: 'his posterity are captives of Satan till set at liberty by Christ'.[30] Sin is universal, 'No man naturally seeks after God, but wanders from him', says a New Connexion tract.[31] What is required is a sacrifice for sin that is equally extensive.

Article 2: 'On the Nature and perpetual Obligation of the Moral Law'. This applied to the 'powers and faculties of the mind' as well as outward behaviour. Rejecting legalism, Taylor recognized there was a moral dimension in which man was accountable. This 'Moral Law' is of 'perpetual duration and obligation, to all men, at all times and in all places' and is expressed in the Ten Commandments and in the words of Christ.[32] This concern brings about a fusion between theology and ethics for the churches of the New Connexion; right living was as important as right thinking. So, said Taylor, 'as we cannot judge the hearts of men farther than their dispositions appear by their conduct, let us not be forward to determine concerning the former, without good evidence by the latter'.[33] In his statement of faith Dan Taylor expanded on this: 'The moral law requires all men to love God with all their heart, with all their mind, with all their soul and with all their strength; and to love their neighbour as themselves; this is the test of right and wrong, and the only rule of every man's conduct.'[34] It was this concern for the moral law that provided the basis for church discipline. While the Connexion was influenced in a number of ways by Methodism, there is no evidence of a stress on Wesley's holiness teaching or doctrine of sanctification.

Article 3: 'On the Person and work of Christ'. here we find a counter to the Socinian teaching Taylor found amongst some General Baptists. Taylor states clearly the union of the divine and human nature, 'in a way which we pretend not to explain, but think ourselves bound by the word of God firmly to believe'. As with the incarnation there is no attempt to explain the nature of the atonement, it is simply stated. Christ 'suffered to make a full atonement for all the sins of all men'; this is a 'compleat (sic) salvation' which is offered to men as a free gift.[35] *A Brief Sketch of the Doctrine and Discipline of the General Baptists* expands on the articles by saying that while in the death of Christ there is 'a provision made for the salvation of all', a failure to enjoy this 'must be attributed to the depravity of men,

---

[30] Taylor, *History*, II, pp. 139-40.

[31] *A Brief Sketch of the Doctrine and Discipline of the General Baptist Churches.* General Baptist Tracts (Leicester: Midland Tract Society, n.d.), p. 3.

[32] Taylor, *History*, II, p. 140.

[33] Dan Taylor, *The Respective Duties of Ministers and People Briefly explained and Enforced. The Substance of Two Discourses, delivered at Great-Yarmouth, in Norfolk Jan. 9th, 1775 at the ordination of the Rev. Mr. Benjamin Worship, to the Pastoral Office* (Leeds, 1775), p. 29.

[34] Taylor, *History*, II, p. 473.

[35] Taylor, *History*, II, p. 140.

not to any deficiency in the grace of God, or in the atonement of Christ'.[36] Taylor sought to assert the divine nature of Christ and a direct connection between the death of Christ and the salvation of sinners.

Article 4: 'On Salvation by faith'. Here, Taylor's Arminian theology comes to the fore. God's offer of grace is universal, 'this salvation is held forth to all to whom the gospel revelation comes without exception'. Man has the freedom to respond in faith and so 'we ought in the course of our ministry, to propose or offer this salvation to all those who attend our ministry' and to 'invite all without exception to look to Christ by faith'. It is by faith alone that one may be possessed of this salvation.[37]

Article 5: 'On Regeneration by the Holy Spirit'. For Taylor, we are justified, purified and sanctified by faith, and that when someone comes to believe in Jesus (adding parenthetically, 'and not before') they are 'regenerated or renewed in his [sic.] soul by the spirit of God through the instrumentality of the word, now believed and embraced'. Such action produces holiness in heart and life.[38]

Article 6: 'On Baptism'. This is an indispensable duty of all who repent and believe the gospel, it is by immersion in water, 'in order to be initiated into a church state', and is a condition for reception into a church. The article is explicit on this point 'that no person ought to be received into the church without submission to that ordinance'.[39] For the writer of *A Brief Sketch* baptism was a duty in order to 'intimate to all men that he is a disciple of Christ and intends henceforth to be obedient to his requirements'.[40]

The 'Six Articles' reaffirm traditional orthodoxy; they take a clear position on the fall, the person of Christ, salvation by faith, and express the concern of the Evangelical Revival about the salvation of the individual. The statements are a protest against the drift of theology among the General Baptists as well as the rigid Calvinism of the Particular Baptists. They are an assertion of the distinctiveness of the Connexion. In setting out the Connexion's beliefs in this way the 'Six Articles' exercised an integrative function within the Connexion; they were a kind of theological glue that bound the Connexion together.

The 'Six Articles' initially assumed the role of a test: the first Assembly of the New Connexion agreed 'that no minister be permitted to join this assembly, who does not subscribe, the articles we have now agreed upon: and that those who do subscribe and afterwards depart from them, shall be considered as no longer belonging to this assembly'.[41] However, at a conference some five years later, the 'Six Articles' were dropped as a test for fellowship due to a concern about the subscription to creeds. While no longer required as a basis for membership of the Connexion, they still expressed the theological concerns of the embryonic

---

[36] *A Brief Sketch of the Doctrine and Discipline*, p. 4.
[37] Taylor, *History*, II, p. 141.
[38] Taylor, *History*, II, p. 141.
[39] Taylor, *History*, II, pp. 141-42.
[40] *A Brief Sketch of the Doctrine and Discipline*, p. 6.
[41] Taylor, *History*, II, p. 142.

denomination. The concern about personal conversion within the movement was expressed, not just in subscription to the 'Six Articles', but in the requirement that 'every minister do, at the next assembly, give an account of his religious experience'.[42] In making this requirement the Connexion's debt to the Baptist tradition as well as its own heart are revealed. Neither Presbyterians nor Congregationalists had to confess their faith each year—they simply had to affirm the Westminster Confession. To affirm faith experimentally was a mark of Baptists only. The 'reality' of a minister's conversion experience was set alongside doctrinal affinity, testimony became a part of the distinctive theological basis of the New Connexion. It gave the movement a unity, not only of doctrine, but of evangelical religious experience. So at Market Harborough in 1831, when a new member was received into the newly formed church, 'She was unanimously received into church fellowship with us this day having first in the presence of the church made a profession of her faith and recounted the dealing of God with her soul.'[43] What the Connexion sought in this confession was, according to Adam Taylor, 'that they should have full evidence not only of the soundness of each other's faith, but of the genuineness of each other's piety'.[44] While Taylor says this of ministers, it was equally true of the members of churches. R.W. Ambler says 'the experience of personal conversion sealed by baptism lay at the heart of the New Connexion: the regeneration and renewal by the spirit of God which came with belief in Jesus'. Thus in Ambler's words, 'The essential unity of the connexion's membership was spiritual not structural.'[45]

While the 'Six Articles' were a theological reference point in the early days of the movement, over the course of 100 years they lost this position and towards the end of the Connexion's life were neglected, so that in 1881 Thomas Goadby could say that 'the discovery that there are such things as General Baptist principles' would come as a 'surprise' to some General Baptists.[46]

Biblicism

In an age of appeal to natural revelation, in which God's existence could be demonstrated, his attributes determined by examination of the universe, and man's status and destiny could be inferred from an unbiased study of his nature, the Bible was Taylor's rule and guide. He regarded it as the word of God: 'a full and sufficient

---

[42] Taylor, *History*, II, p. 143.
[43] Market Harborough Church Book, 9 January 1831. Leicester Record Office. NB/215/2.
[44] Taylor, *History*, II, p. 143.
[45] R.W. Ambler, 'Building up the Walls of Zion: The Development of the New Connexion of General Baptists in Lincolnshire, 1770–1891' (unpublished paper, delivered at University of York Conference 'Church and People in Britain and Scandinavia', 6-19 April 1995), p. 18.
[46] Thomas Goadby, 'General Baptist Principles: An Exposition', *GBM* (1881), p. 6.

Theological Background and Development

revelation of his will to mortals inspired as a whole and in every detail'.[47] As such it was to be 'our only rule in every branch of practice and faith'.[48] Dan Taylor exhorted Benjamin Worship at his ordination service at Great Yarmouth in 1775:

> This word of God, this word of truth, this word of life, you Sir, are to preach. Not the inventions and traditions of men; not even the wisest men living. Not the fancies, supposition and conjectures of your own mind, or any other person, be they ever so ingenious or plausible.[49]

It was, he said, 'the Word of God and that alone' that was to be 'the foundation of our faith and hope'. In saying this Taylor reflected the biblicism of the Revival. In 1766 Taylor set out his approach to the scriptures in a sermon, *The Faithful and Wise Steward*. The influence of the Enlightenment may be detected in terms of the role that reason had to play in interpreting the scriptures. Although reasserting traditional values, evangelicalism was itself profoundly influenced by the appeal to the reason of the Enlightenment.[50] The adoption of a scientific approach resulted in a rejection of metaphysical discussion in favour of a concentration on observation. The function of reason was to weigh up the evidences, but, as Bebbington contends, the scientific approach had a philosophical basis and was dependent on the assumption of a contingent universe.[51]

Taylor said, 'When we apply to the word of God and would clearly and faithfully handle any part of it, let us propose such queries to our consciences relating to it, as may naturally lead to its genuine sense and most natural import.' This is to be discovered by looking not only at the context of a verse but setting that in the whole tenor of scripture. Parallel readings should be compared. As far as possible one should make oneself aware of influences that condition interpretation. He suggested asking,

> Am I not influenced and led to take this sense by prejudice for or against some party, scheme or sentiments? &c were I of another party, or of no party, do I sincerely think this sense wou'd then appear most natural? Are the references naturally and fairly deduced from this sence of the text scriptural? Have I solid arguments whereby to defend both the sense and inferences deducible from it, if any should oppose them? What can be objected to it? Can I answer those objections better than vindicate them?[52]

---

[47] Dan Taylor. *A True Statement of the Leading Religious Sentiments of The New Connexion of General Baptists By a Friend to the Truth* (Dudley, 1824), p. 6. Angus Library General Baptist Pamphlets CLX 9. (This is in the main part a reprint of Dan Taylor's 1785 Confession of Faith)
[48] Taylor 'Confession of Faith'; in Taylor, *History*, II, p. 471.
[49] Taylor, *Respective Duties of Ministers and People*, p. 11.
[50] Bebbington, *Evangelicalism in Modern Britain*, p. 57.
[51] Bebbington, *Evangelicalism in Modern Britain*, pp. 58-59.
[52] Dan Taylor, *The Faithful and Wise Steward* (Leeds, 1766), p. 57.

He argued that doctrines that are held should have 'their foundation in, and be naturally deduced from some plan of Scripture'. It is not at all difficult to 'invent a figure' in order to explain passages according to our own prejudice. However, his principle of interpretation is that plain passages, 'the sense of which can't well be mistook', should 'regulate' the difficult ones. Unless this rule is adhered to, 'we shall easily be led away from the doctrines of the Bible, and the inventions and fancies of men rather than the unerring word of God, will soon be regarded as the test of faith'.[53]

Whilst he advises reading the works of the 'aged, and learned, and wise' he also says 'we ought to be very fully assured, that we have examined their argument to the bottom, and find it to have firm foundation in the word of God, before we venture to assert it for truth'. The young preacher is advised to stick close to the Bible and 'to have a thus saith the Lord for what you assert'.[54] To Benjamin Worship at his ordination he advised that he should not preach 'the mere dictates of reason or the religion or morality of the heathens, as, in any sense, a foundation of faith, or a rule of practice'.[55] He warns of the danger of going to the Bible with preconceived schemes or doctrines 'which you are determined not to break'; there needs to be a 'desire to receive further light'.[56] This is a simple biblicism, that, confining itself only to the scriptures, leaves questions unanswered and does not consider the complexities of interpretation.

Free Grace

Evangelistic Imperative

The members of the Connexion were to be living examples of the message they proclaimed; all was to be subjected to the goal of proclamation. Taylor urged,

> let our dress, our table, our conversation, and every part of our behaviour witness for us, that our sole aim and study, is, not how we may gratify our own or other's appetites and inclinations, or how we may conform most punctually to a vain world, but how all we are, all we do, and all we possess may contribute to render the truths and ways of our redeemer more available in the eyes of men, and promote his honour and interest in the eyes of the world.[57]

The sermons of Samuel Deacon the younger, pastor of the Barton church, expressed the kind of theology that was the basis of the Connexions' evangelism. There was an emphasis on understanding prior to a conversion experience.

This understanding was in two areas: first the nature of man as a fallen sinner, who had come under the judgement of God, 'and having no portion in the world to

---

[53] Taylor, *Faithful and Wise Steward*, p. 52.
[54] Taylor, *Faithful and Wise Steward*, p. 19.
[55] Taylor, *Respective Duties of Ministers and People*, p. 12.
[56] Taylor, *Faithful and Wise Steward*, p. 48.
[57] Taylor, *Faithful and Wise Steward*, p. 40.

come they must be wretched and forlorn forever'. Deacon said the judgment was retributive, 'they die and are buried, and in hell lift up their eyes being in torment'.[58] The emotional language of Deacon's sermon was echoed in a more prosaic form in Taylor's confession, where a man is held personally responsible for rebellion against God and is, as a consequence, 'exposed to his wrath as the just punishment of it'. Taylor further states that 'mankind can never be happy, till their sins be pardoned and their hearts purified'.[59]

Second, a man must know something of Jesus Christ before he can respond, and 'act faith' or believe upon Christ. 'Their', that is the preachers of the Connexion, 'previous teaching is intended to give the sinner this information, to prepare his mind that he may embrace the Gospel with readiness and Joy.'[60] The appeal is initially directed to the mind of a man, 'Yet man though spiritually dead, is a rational being; and it is as rational, ministers are to address him'.[61] Conversion was understood as a process rather than a decision in a moment of crisis: 'faith comes by searching the scriptures...faith comes by hearing'.[62] For Samuel Deacon believing implied three things: '1. A persuasion of our need of salvation, and that we cannot save ourselves. 2. A persuasion of the ability and willingness of Jesus Christ to save us. 3. A giving up of ourselves to Jesus Christ, to be saved and Governed by him.'[63] Dan Taylor, in a letter to the Lincolnshire Association, attributed the decline of the General Baptists to a lack of this gospel preaching.[64] The grounds for Taylor's assertion may be found in a letter to Gilbert Boyce, where, reflecting on the history of the General Baptists in the seventeenth century, Taylor said that the adoption of Arianism and Socinianism by some of their leaders had resulted in a division in which those who insisted that 'Christ atoned for the sins of men, and that none can be saved but through that atonement' were 'calumniated and aspersed as defective in charity'. These 'fundamental' doctrines, he continued, were treated as 'matters of indifference' and, consequently, 'they were but seldom preached; and when they were mentioned...it was rather in a way of controversy...not as the only foundation on which the everlasting all of man depends.'[65] As a result

---

[58] Samuel Deacon, 'The Christians Portion', *A Cabinet of Jewels Barton Memorial*, Vol. 1 (London, 1889), p. 25.

[59] Taylor, *History*, II, pp. 472-73.

[60] [Samuel Deacon], *A comprehensive account of the General Baptists with respect to principle and practice in which are displayed their manner of Worship, Church order and Discipline. By a Mechanic who was long conversant with them* (Coventry, 1795), (Although no author is named, I have attributed this to Samuel Deacon, on the basis of a reference in *Preacher Pastor and Mechanic*, p. 60, which refers to this pamphlet saying it was published by Mr Deacon and 'has been much esteemed in the connexion'.

[61] Taylor, *Respective Duties of Ministers and People*, p. 26.

[62] [Deacon], *A comprehensive account*, p. 54.

[63] Samuel Deacon, 'The Wells of Salvation', *A Cabinet of Jewels*, I, p. 54.

[64] Dan Taylor, 'Letter to the Lincolnshire Association', in Taylor, *History*, I, p. 484.

[65] Wood, *History*, pp. 147-48.

The gospel, the great mean of conversion being nearly laid aside, others could not possibly be converted by their ministry. And thus one church after another came to nothing; and a great number of their meeting-houses were lost or converted to other uses, in almost every part of the nation.[66]

Man's state, his need of redemption, stands first in the 'Six Articles'. He is a fallen creature and has laid himself under the curse of God. Man and his descendants 'are captives of Satan till set at liberty by Christ'.[67] Taylor's 1785 *Confession of Faith* holds before men the grace of God: 'Therefore, that salvation is not of works, but of free Grace. That all that is done for us, or wrought in us, or that we are able to do for Him, is entirely due to the free, rich and undeserved bounty of the great and blessed God'.[68] This offer of 'free grace' drew the theological boundary between the New Connexion and the Particular Baptists.

Faith and Conversion

The offer of free grace was central to the New Connexion's doctrine of the church and the gospel. They believed all men were sinners but that everyone could be saved if they had 'opened to them their ruined wretched state', and looked 'to Christ by faith, without any regard to anything in, or done by, themselves; that they may in this way alone, that is, by faith, be possessed of this salvation'.[69] Faith was understood as something active; divine blessing would come to those who 'act faith'. In his 1785 *Confession of Faith* Dan Taylor stated faith is believing the gospel; it is this act of believing that was the crucial element; 'faith in Christ and that only, or the believing of the gospel, entitles poor sinful mortals to every part of happiness'.[70] And again, 'exert yourself then, my dear friend, to lay hold upon the hope set before you in the gospel; labour to enter into the rest that remains for the people of God: in a word believe on the Lord Jesus, and thou shalt be saved'.[71] In these passages faith borders on a work. In the 1785 *Confession of Faith* faith believing is accompanied by 'repentance, regeneration and holiness in heart and life' which are 'absolutely necessary in order to prepare the soul for salvation and eternal glory'.[72]

This offer of salvation may be made to men because God wills to 'treat with mankind on a new foundation, in a way of free grace; and can now be just and the justifier of him that believeth in Jesus'.[73] The conviction that salvation was to be

---

[66] Wood, *History*, p. 148.
[67] Taylor, *History*, II, p. 140.
[68] Dan Taylor, 'Mr Taylor's Confession of Faith', in Taylor, *History*, II, p. 473. The 'Six Articles of Religion' had dealt only with the points of difference. This Confession is a fuller statement of Taylor's prepared by him for use in his church at Whitechapel.
[69] Taylor, *History*, II, p. 141.
[70] Taylor, *History*, II, p. 474.
[71] *GBR* 4 (1812), pp. 205-206.
[72] Taylor, *History*, II, p. 474
[73] Taylor, *History*, II, pp. 473-74.

Theological Background and Development 19

found in Christ alone, and that he had 'tasted death for every man', led to the frequent appeal to 'examine yourself', to 'embrace the glorious Gospel' and to 'search the divine word'; in this way a man could 'act faith' or believe.[74] Such appeals were seen as setting in process an attitude of reflection and searching that would lead, sometimes after a period of months, to an espousal of the faith.

We can illustrate this from the life of Francis Smith, a leader of the Barton group of churches and a founder member of the New Connexion. His obituary in the *General Baptist Magazine* of 1798 contains his own account of his conversion: 'but as to the precise time, scripture sermon, in which it might be said that I was converted I know nothing of it. The manner of my conversion...may be compared to a misty and dark morning which gradually becomes clearer and clearer.'[75]

Having come to faith, the believer was then led to look for 'evidences'. Samuel Deacon cites as evidences humility, a rejection of sin and a love for holiness, a love for God and his people 'at least in desire', 'delight in the word and ordinances' and a 'disposition to pray; to hear Christ's voice and to follow his directions'.[76] Failure in this area could mean exclusion from membership, which happened when the church at Packington questioned one of its members, Thomas Sharpe:

> he was desired to give the church a plain and circumstantial account of his first convictions and conversion accordingly he attempted so to do but his account of himself respecting that important matter was so foreign from what might be expected from a soul converted to God...

The church meeting concluded that 'he was assuredly an unconverted man; and therefore an improper member for a church of Christ, and as such was excluded from our fellowship, by a unanimous vote of the church'.[77] This is an indication of a firm boundary line between the church and the world and reflects an understanding of the church as a believing community.

Feeling with the Heart

To what extent did emotion and feeling, rather than reason, govern popular religious attitudes? The Revival under Wesley was intensely personal, directed at the heart rather than the head. With him, it was the experience of new birth, not reasonable

---

[74] Deacon, 'The Faithful God', *Barton Memorials*, Vol. 1 (London/Leicester, 1889); *A Cabinet of Jewels*, I, p. 77.
[75] *GBM* (1798), p. 264. For similar accounts see *GBM* (1798), p. 472; *GBR* 3 (1808), pp. 2, 57, 98.
[76] Deacon, *A Cabinet of Jewels*, p. 6.
[77] Thomas Budge, 'Records of the most Material affairs belonging to the Baptist Congregation at Melbourne in Derbyshire. Extracts from the Church Book 1774-1832. Dec 25th. 1777' (unpublished MS East Midland Baptist Association Archive).

morality, that made a man a Christian: 'God give us grace to know these things and to feel them in our hearts', said Wesley.[78]

The reasonable religion of the upper classes tended to make any form of 'enthusiasm' suspect. Witness the famous remark of Bishop Butler to Wesley: 'Sir, pretending to extraordinary revelations and gifts of the Holy Ghost is a horrid thing—a very horrid thing.'[79] But as Hugh McLeod argues, it was this very area of private revelation that appealed to the working classes for whom the supernatural was important. They could understand life in terms of a supernatural battlefield with God and the believer on one side and the devil on the other.[80] As a product of the Evangelical Revival the writers who helped shape the thinking of the Connexion shared that outlook, as the doggerel of one of the New Connexion hymns by Samuel Deacon put it:

> Expect a war within;
> It surely will be so
> For Satan, and the world, and sin,
> Oppose you as you go.[81]

They believed that God spoke directly to man through dreams and visions. This was an attractive doctrine for the poor, for here was a form of religious experience that was as accessible to the illiterate person as to the preacher, parson or educated person.[82]

The preachers of the Connexion held before men a simple uncomplicated message, their appeal was to those who were seeking a direct experience of God, and they were part of a popular religious protest and antagonism to the Church of England and to a lesser extent established Dissent. Evangelical Arminianism allowed them to take full advantage of the Evangelical Revival and gave to the movement a missionary emphasis. It perceived itself as a missionary agency in a wider culture.

The Erosion of Distinctives

One of the interesting features of Baptist life is the way in which fundamental theological differences underwent a gradual erosion and a drawing together of the two courses of Baptist church life became possible. Here we consider the extent to which external influences brought about a convergence of the theology of the Connexion and the convergence of General and Particular Baptists.

---

[78] John Wesley, *The Works of John Wesley* (London, 1830), VII, p. 105.
[79] Cragg, *Church and the Age of Reason*, p. 150.
[80] Hugh McLeod, *Religion and the Working Class in Nineteenth-Century Britain* (London: Macmillan, 1984), p. 27.
[81] Deacon, 'Cabinet of Jewels', I, p. 81.
[82] McLeod, *Religion and the Working Class*, p. 27.

The question addressed to the Methodist Conference on the admission of a preacher was, 'Does he preach our doctrine and observe our discipline?'[83] In the Connexion, although subscription to the 'Six Articles' was required in the early days, in 1775 this doctrinal requirement was set aside in favour of 'experience'; and no other specific doctrinal affirmation seems to have been required of preachers and pastors.

The erosion of differences began with the publication of Andrew Fuller's *Gospel Worthy of all Acceptation* (1785) which opened the way for a warmer outgoing form of Calvinism. Dan Taylor welcomed its publication and at the request of ministers in the Connexion took the opportunity of stating their position, in a tract published under the pseudonym 'Philanthropos'.[84] Fuller asserted the need for preaching for conversion, and the necessity of the work of the Holy Spirit in conversion, and urged the need to present the gospel with compassion to all. Fuller's position was supported by another influential Particular Baptist, Robert Hall of Leicester, who felt that 'only a belief in a General Redemption would justify an appeal to all men'.[85] According to Ernest Payne, Fuller's teaching 'provided a bridge' between the Particular Baptist churches and those of the New Connexion.[86] The day of rigid Calvinism began to wane amongst Particular Baptists.

In the opening decades of the nineteenth century there is the beginnings of a gradual drawing together of the two streams of Baptist church life. In 1812, the Midland conference of the Connexion took up a collection for the Baptist Missionary Society which had suffered a fire at Serampore. Robert Hall said of Joseph Freestone, pastor of the General Baptist church at Hinckley,

> though he exercised his ministry through the whole of his life among the General Baptists, his sentiment approached nearer to those of Mr. Baxter than the system of Arminius, nor would his statement of Christian Doctrine have given the slightest offence to a congregation of moderate Calvinists.[87]

This would seem to indicate that the theological differences between some General and Particular Baptists were not that great.

At a personal level men like Robert Hall and Joseph Goadby, Sr, of the New Connexion could exchange pulpits and enjoy a real friendship, as Joseph Goadby, Sr, said: 'Mr Hall of Leicester and family, have been at Ashby Baths; his family with whom we are very friendly, remained here a fortnight. He came several times during the stay, took his tea, smoked his pipes, etc., and preached for us. It was very

---

[83] John Bowmer, *Pastor and People* (London: Epworth Press, 1975), pp. 153, 196, 216.
[84] Wood, *History*, pp. 194-95.
[85] Underwood, *History of the English Baptists*, p. 202.
[86] Payne *Baptist Union*, p. 61.
[87] Joseph Freestone, *Memoirs of Joseph Freestone late Pastor of the General Baptist Church Hinckley: Written by Himself* (London, 1823), p. XII.

agreeable.'[88] In September 1831, J.G. Pike's son went to the Stepney Academy, a Particular Baptist college, and wrote to a friend, 'probably some staunch General Baptists may think this step of mine unorthodox, but I care less and less for the distinction between the two bodies'.[89] But the distinctions were still there and sufficiently great to preclude the involvement of the New Connexion in the formation by the Particular Baptists of the 1813 Baptist Union. However, communication had been opened up, and the loosening of the rigid theological demarcation lines meant that the two streams of Baptist life in this country were at the headwaters of that course that would end in their eventual convergence.

This growing openness allowed Particular Baptists into New Connexion pulpits. In 1845 the Ashby and Packington church invited Mr Salisbury, a student of the Bradford Particular Baptist college, 'to preach for us 6 Lords days during the midsummer vacation', and the same church in June 1861 unanimously invited E.C. Pike, who had trained at the Regent's Park College, to 'supply us for twelve months'.[90]

In 1859 Joseph Winks, addressing a special meeting called to consider the lack of progress of the Connexion, said, 'The death of the Son of God for the salvation of all men has now become a popular doctrine in our land; and not withstanding the Surrey Gardens Music Hall has resounded with loud warnings against Arminianism'. Noting the coming together he observed:

> the most useful preachers in our land now, of every evangelical party, are those who call on all men every where to repent and believe the gospel. Calvinists, or Fullerites some may wish yet to call themselves, but as one of our American visitors facetiously told us a few years ago, 'They all thrash with our machine.' Rather let us take the advice of a venerable minister of the other section of the Baptist body, who, in conversation with the late Adam Taylor, said, 'Stay where you are brother Taylor; we are all coming to you as fast as we can.'[91]

A generation had emerged for whom the distinctives of the New Connexion, the three great universals—God loves all men, Christ died for all men, the Holy Spirit strives with all men—were no longer sufficient reason for a separate identity. J.C. Pike, himself trained at the Stepney College, writing the Association letter for 1870, recognized that they were living in a very different situation from that in which the Connexion had been formed and which had dictated the need for its separate existence, and that here was now 'a much closer approximation of sentiment in reference to the

---

[88] Bertha Goadby and Lilian Goadby, *Not Saints but Men or the story of the Goadby Ministers* (London: Kingsgate Press, n.d.), p. 63.

[89] John B. Pike and James C. Pike, *A Memoir and Remains of the Late Rev. John Gregory Pike* (London, 1855), p. 206.

[90] Ashby and Packington Church Book, 11 May 1845 and 3 June 1861. Leicester Record Office N/9/1.

[91] J.F. Winks, 'The Adaption of our present home missionary system to the Accomplishment of its object', *GBM* (1859), p. 446.

Theological Background and Development

leading truths of the Gospel'.[92] For many, the thought of joining forces with the Particular Baptists was attractive. In the negotiations preparatory to union, the secretary's report in 1889 recognized the extent of the change:

> If the circumstances of those days demanded distinct institutions it is at least clear that those circumstances do not exist today. Wesleyans are now not only received to baptism, but are often gladly welcomed to communion without baptism even. A reorganisation of our congregational forces may therefore be fairly considered after the lapse of more than a century.[93]

Some churches were willing to go even further. The previous year the church at Nether Street, Beeston, Nottingham, had passed a resolution that 'the church be opened to receive into full membership members of Congregational churches'. This went much further than opening membership since it requested 'that the minister and deacons be deputed to confer with such Congregationalists with a view to further union'. Within eight years that union had been accomplished.[94] It would be wrong to think that the process of convergence was without problems. Following a report of the 1858 General Baptist Assembly in *The Freeman*, the 7 July edition carried an article in which the writer said, 'we happen to know that their exists in some parts of the country considerable misconception respecting the doctrinal sentiments of the General Baptists'. He said that the

> antagonistic creeds of the seventeenth century have undergone a sifting and an amalgamating process. Each party has adopted some of the truths that were then deemed the exclusive characteristics of the other, and the broad and well defined boundary that then separated them, has become dim.

He noted the free movement of members between Baptist churches of different persuasions: 'in many cases our ministers have passed over the boundary without a questioning of their consistency or any stain upon their orthodoxy'.[95]

So it was that, in the centenary year of the New Connexion, William Underwood, in his chairman's address, commented on changes that had occurred in the Connexion and on the fact that one sixth of their recognized pastors now came from Particular Baptist colleges or churches. He remarked that there seemed to be very little difference in theology or practice. The extensive co-mingling of ministers would seem to indicate that the ordinary church member could not tell, or did not feel that strongly about, the difference.[96]

This practical reconciliation came about not because the distinctives of the Connexion were abandoned, rather it was the movement of the Particular Baptists

---

[92] J.C. Pike, 'Our Future', letter, *GBM* (1870), p. 6.
[93] 'Secretary's Statement', *GBM* (1889), p. 44.
[94] Beeston Church Book 4, 23 September 1889, p. 108. Nottingham Record Office BP/29/8.
[95] 'The General Baptists', *The Freeman* 7 July 1858, p. 395.
[96] William Underwood, 'President's Address', *Minutes* (1870), p. 14.

towards the position of the Connexion. In 1870 John Clifford complained that the growing practice among Particular Baptists who were 'giving universal invitations to sinners to accept the gospel even where they do not allow for a universal provision for the salvation of men, has tended to diminish our interest in denominational work and institutions, and so hindered our progress'.[97]

'It is remarkable that the period of the beginning of our decline saw the last day of the fathers of our body', said Thomas Goadby in 1868.[98] This statement reflects the change that the Connexion had undergone. The protest theology of the early years, a theology which had asserted its distinctives, a theology which had required an evangelistic thrust on the part of the whole congregation, was supplanted by a more staid and less passionate strain. The distinctive elements around which the New Connexion had emerged were subsumed in a growing theological consensus and practical convergence amongst Baptists.

Practical Theology

Adversity

Theology does not remain static; it is an ongoing attempt to interpret and make sense of life in the context of a system of belief. The extent to which theology served practical ends can be seen in the way in which the Connexion viewed suffering and the life to come. The Connexion had to work out its theology against a background of war, economic depression and fluctuating trade cycles. How did their theology help the members of the Connexion interpret these events? In times of great hardship converts were urged to cast themselves on the providence of an all-wise God. The events of life were viewed as a discipline to bring one nearer to God. Following the death of Dan Taylor's daughter in June and wife in October 1794 he said, 'In passing through life, we have many fatigues, pains, cares, distresses, and dangers. But if God be in them all shall be well.'[99] And being 'much depressed in spirit by incessant labours and incessant thought and anxiety' with 'trade very low, worth almost nothing: taxes high and everything dear' (he was running a bookshop to supplement his income), he says of his troubles, 'I have not willingly allowed myself to murmur, I have prayed and endeavoured that I might reverence and justify Thee in all. O that I may do it from the heart.'[100] Eighteen years later the same spirit is still evident at the death of his third wife: 'My duty is to "be still and know that he is God"; to be "dumb and not to open my mouth because he hath done it" to him be everlasting praise, Amen.'[101]

The theology of the Revival offered to men and women, many of whom led lives of unbearable hardship, a solace, a hope that there was a larger meaning to life; that

---

[97] John Clifford, 'Secretaries' Report', *Minutes* (1870), p. 56.
[98] Thomas Goadby, 'Chairman's Address', *Minutes* (1868), p. 52.
[99] Dan Taylor, *Mrs Elizabeth Taylor* (London, 1794), p. 6.
[100] Taylor, *Memoirs of the Rev. Dan Taylor*, p. 204.
[101] *GBR* 5 (1813), p. 84.

beyond the drudgery of this world were glories of heaven and that they were a part of that. Van Den Berg draws attention to the eschatalogical dimension of the Evangelical Revival, and notes that the church, although weak and suffering, is the indicator and evidence of what God will accomplish. But this expectation provided a 'comforting background rather than a political solution'.[102] The theology of the New Dissent offered the promise of 'salvation'; it held before them a present experience of the Holy Spirit, the comforter who would be with them in times of crisis and hardship.

The Association letter for 1815 sought to address itself to the problems of famine and suffering faced by many as a result of the economic depression which was then affecting trade, especially the framework knitters of the Midlands. There was little support for radical or political solutions to the problems of the poor and distressed. In the letter 'Directions and Encouragements in Times of Temporal Distress', John Bissill adopted the view that the economic climate was ordained of God.[103] The New Connexion was part of the church which, says Elliott-Binns, 'shared in the almost universal idea that social evils, as the product of inflexible laws were inevitable'.[104] Bissill would have certainly supported that view; 'Remember', he said,

> our afflictions do not spring out of the dust, no sorrows rise by chance. Our wants may perhaps grow out of the state of this world: for God has long had a controversy with the nations: and therefore we should be careful lest we attribute all our evils to the conduct of men and forget the God who rules on high: and so lose a powerful motive to humble us before him. Let us endeavour, Brethren, to see the hand of God in his chastisements as well as in his mercies: and ascribe our sufferings to our sins and our blessing to his goodness.[105]

In a period of great social change and upheaval the members of the Connexion were asked to show self discipline and acceptance of their lot. Whilst theirs was a protest theology it does not seem to have extended much beyond the church; in interpreting the world around them the Connexion did not adopt a radical stance. What the Connexion offered was an internalized faith, a more immediate and emotional expression of the faith than was present in the older dissenting bodies. Here we have the beginnings of that privatized religion, characteristic of the nineteenth century, the beginning of that process of accommodation through which religious thinking and practice, in the form of movements, lose their impact and social significance.

---

[102] J. Van Den Berg, *Constrained by Jesus Love: An Inquiry into the Motives of the Missionary Awakening in Great Britain in the Period between 1698 and 1815* (Kampen: J.H. Kok, 1956), p. 103.

[103] J. Bissill, 'Directions and Encouragements in Times of Temporal Distress', letter, *GBR* (1815), p. 20.

[104] L.E. Elliott-Binns, *Religion in the Victorian Era* (London: Lutterworth Press, 1946), p. 262.

[105] Bissill, 'Directions and Encouragements', p. 21.

Larger Hope

A very different approach to the problem of suffering and evil was taken by Samuel Cox. Born in 1826, one of a large family, he started work in London docks at the age of fourteen. Feeling a call to the ministry he went to the Particular Baptist college at Stepney. He went to his first pastorate at Southsea in 1852, from there to Ryde in the Isle of Wight in 1856, a fellowship 'almost entirely composed of Congregationalists'. While in the Isle of Wight there are the first indications of his having 'formulated those views on the final restoration of the whole human family' for which he was later known. While there he supplied contributions to *The Nonconformist, The Church, The Christian Spectator* and *The Quiver*. In 1861 he was secretary to the committee responsible for the celebration of the Ejectment of 1662. Cox came into the New Connexion when he went to the Mansfield Road Baptist Church, Nottingham, in 1863.

Concerns about the nature of hell and future punishment had been raised by two early advocates of conditional immortality. Henry Hamlet Dobney (1809–84) who published *Notes of Lectures on Future Punishment* in 1844, first formulated conditional immortality, but played little part in the debate subsequent to that. A more important role was that of Edward White, a Congregationalist minister who also adopted a conditionalist theology in two books, *What was the Fall* and *Life in Christ*. The impact of this teaching was greater amongst Congregationalists than Baptists.

It was at Mansfield Road that Cox gave the series of lectures, later published under the title *Salvator Mundi*.[106] Cox's universalist views on hell and punishment exposed him to considerable criticism. Much later, quoting a sermon from his friend T.T. Lynch, Cox made a plea for theological freedom:

> All good Protestants claim the right of private judgement as though it were their common but exclusive possession. But though we may all claim it, and make our boast of it, we must not use it. No: you may have your gun; and it may be a good gun; but you must not shoot with it, lest you should injure your neighbour, or even yourself.[107]

Cox, who had recently been asked to resign his position as editor of *The Expositor* because of concern over his universalist theology, went on to say, 'I have been found guilty of using this gun, of exercising the right which every good Protestant asserts for himself, and many deny to their fellows and I have been warned off from a certain preserve which has long been free to me, lest having undeniably injured myself, I should injure my neighbours.'[108] The 'injury' occurred as he sought to reconsider traditional eschatology in *Salvator Mundi*. His object in writing, he says, was to

---

[106] Samuel Cox, *Salvator Mundi or is Christ the Saviour of All Men?*(London, 1877).

[107] Samuel Cox, *Expositions* (London, 2nd edn, 1891), p. 7. (Lynch, a Congregationalist, provoked a dispute, the 'Rivulet Controversy', when he published a collection of hymns in 1856.)

[108] Cox, *Expositions*, p. 7.

Theological Background and Development

encourage those who 'faintly trust the larger hope to commit themselves to it wholly', on the basis that they have 'ample warrant for it in the Scriptures of the New Testament'.[109]

Cox summed up his arguments regarding the teaching in the following way:

> (1) That as there are degrees of bliss in Paradise, so also there are degrees of punishment in Gehena (2) that as the reward of the righteous is at once retributive and perfecting, so the punishment of the unrighteous is at once retributive and remedial: and (3) That both to the righteous and the unrighteous there will be vouched safe a new and deeper revelation of the grace of God in Christ Jesus.[110]

It is this opportunity for a revelation after death that constitutes the larger hope. Cox is significant because he marks an important stage in the accommodation of doctrine to the new moral consciousness of the age. He was not content, as Bissell had been, to leave things to the devices of an inscrutable God. That was no longer adequate, for it raised questions about the very nature of God. '...but how can any thoughtful man reconcile the infliction of interminable and never ceasing anguish either on those who sinned and knew not what they did, or even on those who knew what they did when they sinned, with the love or with the very justice of God?'[111]

In 1853 F.D. Maurice had been ejected from his chair at King's College for entertaining the 'Larger Hope'. But by 1877 the members of the Mansfield Road Baptist Church, a body at least as conservative as the Governors of King's College, 'were not afraid of his "heresy"'.[112] Cox said in defence of his theology,

> We still believe in the sinfulness of man, especially our own sinfulness, but we believe that evil will finally be overcome by good. We still believe in the Atonement, that the forgiving and redeeming love of God is revealed in the life, death and passion of Our Lord Jesus Christ, but we also believe in an Atonement of wider scope, that Christ will see the travail of his soul and be satisfied in a larger and diviner way than some of our theologians have supposed.[113]

While the fear of hell may have been a contributing factor to the success of the Evangelical Revival of the eighteenth and early nineteenth centuries, by the middle of the century things had changed.[114] The church at New Lenton on the south-western outskirts of Nottingham experienced a small revival in 1864. There are some forty-three 'Experiences', or personal accounts of coming to faith, in this revival. A

---

[109] Cox, *Salvator Mundi*, Preface, p. vii.

[110] Cox, *Salvator Mundi*, p. 202..

[111] Cox, *Salvator Mundi*, pp. 90-91.

[112] Samuel Cox, *The Hebrew Twins: A vindication of God's way with Jacob and Esau* (London, 1894), Prefatory Memoir, p. xxxv.

[113] Samuel Cox, cited in Geoffrey Rowell, *Hell and the Victorians* (Oxford: Clarendon Press, 1974), p. 133.

[114] Michael R. Watts, '"The Hateful Mystery" Nonconformists and Hell', *Journal of the United Reformed Church History Society* 2.8 (October, 1981), p. 248.

fear of hell is not explicitly mentioned, and what features most strongly is an overwhelming sense of guilt.[115]

While the second half of the nineteenth century saw the traditional evangelical doctrine of hell being questioned, social dislocation, industrial and demographic changes had provided an environment in which the Evangelical Revival had initially thrived. But those same changes, based on the conviction that man was the master of his own end, undermined the other-worldly faith on which the revival drew. Cox shows the extent to which wider social and religious influences had an effect even on a conservative grouping like the Connexion. Thomas Goadby had earlier stated that there would be no 'reconstruction of theology' to allow for 'a future opportunity for repentance if this in this life be neglected; a future probation if this be abused'.[116] The New Connexion's college would not change its theology. Cox's views were strongly challenged, but he remained within the Connexion. This acceptance, if not endorsement, of Cox represented a shift away from the original stance of the Connexion and gave some cause for the theological concern which later emerged in the 'Downgrade' controversy. It may also be argued that the views represented by Cox blunted the evangelistic cutting edge of the movement, and helped to redirect energies into social concern. Although radical in his approach, Cox had sought a biblical basis for his position. But in the middle of the century, the nature and authority of the scriptures themselves were being questioned.

Biblical Criticism

Speaking as chairman of the Connexion in 1889 Joseph Fletcher saw 'A Working Theory of Inspiration' as 'one of the imperative wants of the present time'.[117] What had brought about this need for a new understanding of inspiration?

The publication in February 1860 of *Essays and Reviews* 'proved...to be a turning point in the history of theological opinion in England', says B.M.G. Reardon.[118] The impact of this publication was not immediate. The significance of the book lay not in the topics that were chosen, but in the approach which called into question the traditional methods of historical theology and biblical exegesis. The Baptist Union Committee in 1860 considered *Essays and Reviews* to be 'misrepresentation' of the scriptures and viewed 'with grief and indignation the efforts to spread these views'.[119] The *General Baptist Magazine* of January 1862 carried an article which lamented the publication of *Essays and Reviews*, seeing it as

---

[115] Beeston Experience Books. Nottingham Record Office BP.10/14/1-6.

[116] Thomas Goadby, 'England's Evangelisation', *GBM* (1877), p. 295.

[117] Joseph Fletcher, 'Our Denominational Organisation', Chairman's Address, *GBM* (1889), p. 2.

[118] B.M.G. Reardon, *Religious Thought in the Victorian Age: A Survey from Coleridge to Gore* (London: Longman, 1980), p. 321.

[119] F.M.W. Harrison, 'The Life and Thought of the Baptists of Nottinghamshire, with special reference to the period 1770–1913' (University of Nottingham MPhil thesis, 1972), p. 662.

'an evil of a most fearful kind', and one which has given an opportunity to 'certain individuals to disseminate pernicious ideas'. It called for 'earnest Christian opposition to the book'.[120]

However, amongst some General Baptists there was a measure of support for these new methods, if not the conclusions. Some Nonconformists, because of their exclusion from the universities in England, had gone to Scotland, or the Continent—Germany in particular—in order to obtain an academic theological education from which they were excluded at home. This exposed them to the new developments that were taking place in biblical criticism, especially in Germany.

While the publication of *Essays and Reviews* was viewed mainly as an Anglican affair, the implications of its approach affected the New Connexion along with the rest of Nonconformity, bringing to light a theological divide in the movement. On one side were those who stood by the traditional view of verbal inspiration, often with little appreciation of the issues involved. On the other side were men like William Underwood, Thomas Goadby and Samuel Cox, men sympathetic to the new approaches. Within the space of a very few years the Baptist colleges were being staffed by, and turning out men of much broader opinion. While Rawdon Baptist College was the most notable, the General Baptist College in the Midlands was not immune. William Underwood, Principal of the General Baptist College in Nottingham (one of those who studied in Germany), was, according to Harrison, of a 'moderate position', ready for a cautious acceptance of the validity of some conclusions of biblical criticism while not rejecting the basic elements of the evangelical faith.[121]

His position as Principal was influential. According to Harrison, 'He was an acknowledged leader in policy, an authority in matters of doctrine, an arbiter to whom everyone listened with respect when precedents were sought for, or questions of discipline came up for settlement.'[122] W.R. Stevenson was a tutor at the college with Underwood, Harrison describing him as a 'broad Evangelical'.

Thomas Goadby was Principal of the College from 1873 to 1889. He spent most of his college vacations studying in Germany at Halle, a more moderate school of criticism, and occasionally Leipzig.[123] According to R.W. Stevenson in the *General Baptist Year Book* for 1889, 'There was perhaps no non-conformist divine in England who had a fuller aquaintance with German Theological speculations and at the same time such firm reliance on "the old paths". He was a man on terms of personal intimacy with eminent Theologians in America and Germany.'[124] His main contribution was that of a translator of Heinrich Ewald (a representative of the more conservative approach in Germany), for the publishers T&T Clark, completing *Revelation—Its Nature and Truth* in 1884 and *Old and New Testament Theology* in 1888. According to Bertha and Lilian Goadby there were those who were suspicious

---

[120] 'The Defence of the Scriptures', *GBM* (1862), pp 4-5.
[121] Harrison, 'Nottingham Baptists', pp. 665, 669.
[122] Harrison, 'Nottingham Baptists', 665.
[123] Goadby and Goadby, *Not Saints but Men*, p. 243.
[124] *General Baptist Year Book* (1889), p. 66.

of his theology: 'a few of the more fossilized minds in the denomination looked upon Thomas Goadby with a certain amount of distrust, as being somewhat of a heretic. This made him a welcome advisor of young men who, in their search after truth, often leave the beaten tracks.'[125] Thomas Goadby's approach was a constructive questioning; he sought to use the methods of biblical criticism and interpretation in the defence of evangelicalism.

As we have seen, the general reaction to *Essays and Reviews* was negative. In 1857 Joseph Wallis had urged the Connexion, 'Close your ears, brethren against every communication which tends to diminish your reverence for the sacred records.'[126] It was not until 1892, after the death of C.H. Spurgeon and at the very end of our period, that John Clifford felt free enough to address himself openly to the issue of inspiration in his book *The Inspiration and Authority of the Bible*.[127] For Clifford the Bible contained the word of God. It was not its infallibility, but its 'spiritual and saving truth which compels credence and gives it its matchless power over the lives of men'.[128] The book provoked a storm of protest. Clifford was accused of undermining and even destroying faith.[129] The main issue that confronted both the New Connexion and the rest of Nonconformity in the second half of the nineteenth century was the demise of a religious *a priori*. As society and church moved further apart the accepted verities of evangelical Nonconformity were being called into question.

Science and Secularism

1859–60 saw evangelicalism in the midst of revival and Sir Morton Peto opened the Metropolitan Tabernacle for Spurgeon. But 1859 was also the year which saw the publication of Darwin's *On the Origin of Species by means of Natural Selection*.[130] In the discussion that surrounded this work the growing division between science and religion came out into the open. Darwin sought to avoid religious controversy by not explicitly extending his theory to include man. He later commented, 'Many years ago I was strongly advised by a friend never to introduce anything about religion into my works, if I wished to advance science in England.'[131]

While Darwin saw no necessary conflict between religious belief and science, a large number of Christians felt extremely threatened by the seemingly secular trend

---

[125] Goadby and Goadby, *Not Saints But Men*, pp. 242-43.

[126] J. Wallis, 'German Neology', *Letter, GBM* (1857), p. 43.

[127] John Clifford, *The Inspiration and Authority of the Bible* (London: James Clarke, 2nd edn, 1895).

[128] Quoted in Michael R. Watts, 'John Clifford and Radical Nonconformity 1836–1923' (University of Oxford DPhil thesis, 1966), p. 337.

[129] G.W. Byrt. *John Clifford: A Fighting Free Churchman* (London: Kingsgate Press 1947), pp. 97-98.

[130] For further references to the 1859 Revival see below, pp. 128-134.

[131] Quoted in Tess Cosslett (ed.), *Science and Religion in the Nineteenth Century* (Cambridge: Cambridge University Press, 1984), p. 87.

of science. *The Origin of Species* became a focal point for unease with the new science. Darwin seemed to have linked man and the lower brute creation; this called into question the nature of man's moral consciousness. Elliott-Binns argues that it was a concern for the moral dimension that provoked the response to the publication of Darwin's book. The implication was 'that sin itself was nothing more than an animal survival or an ancestral failing handed down to individuals who might outgrow it, but could hardly be blamed for its presence'. 'Thus', he says, 'the sense of sin and of responsibility was weakened.'[132]

An alternative theory and explanation of the physical world and the meaning of life was being offered to men and women, and it was a construct that seemed to have the support of demonstrable science with proven practical results. Bryan Wilson suggests that science was supplanting religion..[133] The Christian world-view was giving way to that of science. H.G. Wood says that for the scientist, religion 'is not so much a closed book, but as one that need not be touched at all'.[134]

What was the response of the Connexion? Some felt the church needed to embrace the challenge. It was the 'timidity' of the church, its 'narrowness and hardness, its controversies and divisions' rather than the 'advance of scientific thought and method' which drove away thinking men, argued Samuel Cox.[135] He was supported by another influential General Baptist, John Clifford. He argued that the church was 'afraid of science' and that it 'locks the door against enquiry'.[136] In 1868, Thomas Goadby, feeling the pulse of the New Connexion, correctly diagnosed the true source of the membership crisis that faced the movement in the late 1860s and early 1870s. For Goadby the vitals of the traditional faith were being eaten away by an encroaching secularism. Goadby saw the area of conflict as a change taking place in the nature of the faith, the areas to be fought over were 'the inspiration and authority of the word of God and the character and claims of our Lord Jesus Christ'. And he continued: 'if the teaching of ritualistic and sacramental medievalism [a side swipe at the Oxford Movement], and the dogmas of half-religious and half-sceptical philosophy have chiefly to be met, we may find it necessary to close our ranks in other forms and order than now, and enter into new combinations'.[137]

Goadby identified the problem as a change in the traditional concept of Christianity, a change identified as 'Modern Infidelity' by a writer in the *Freeman* in 1855, who observed,

---

[132] Elliott-Binns, *Religion in the Victorian Era*, p. 167.

[133] Wilson, *Religion in a Secular Society*, p. 42.

[134] H.G. Wood, *Belief and Unbelief since 1850* (Cambridge: Cambridge University Press, 1955), p. 46.

[135] Samuel Cox, *The House and Its Builder, with other discourses* (London, 1889), p. 7.

[136] John Clifford, *A New Testament Church in relation to the need and tendencies of the age* (London, 1876), p. 6.

[137] Thomas Goadby, 'Presidents Address', Minutes, *GBM* (1868), p. 50.

This is not a mere question of words or names. It points to a far deeper fact; that though Christianity be no longer regarded as the older infidelity, as a thing wholly false and bad, it is yet denied to be wholly true and divine in any special or particular sense. It is true just as science is true; it is divine just as art is divine; it is inspired just as poetry is inspired.[138]

Goadby looks to the closing of the ranks as an attempt to counter the spirit of the age. In 1889 the assembly chairman said, 'if the Amalgamation question had not come to the front, I might have been tempted to deal with the modern attack on Christianity'. He saw this attack as coming from

> Agnosticism...Higher Criticism...which makes of Moses a mosaic, which dissolves the personalities of the prophets, which makes the Pentatuch into the Hexateuch, which upsets all previous chronology, which seeks to get rid of the supernatural, which has suggested to that able writer W.S. Lilly, the question 'what is left of Christianity?'[139]

The comment reflects the extent to which the leadership of the movement was struggling with the new theology. Men like Cox, Clifford and Goadby—men who were able to wrestle with the theological issues involved—found themselves restrained by the theological establishment of which they were a part. An issue dealt with by Thomas Goadby in *Christian Theology and the Modern Spirit*, the presidential address of 1879.[140]

'Religion', according to a writer in the *Westminster Review* in 1882, 'no longer commands the absorbing interests of all classes as it did but a century or two ago. Religion has come to be regarded as a holiday suit, to be donned on special occasions and on Sundays. Practically all that is left to Religion is a shadowy belief in a Deity and in a future life.' The writer of this article attributed the decline of religious faith to four factors: 'Science, the rise of historical evidence, the separation of morality and religion, and the decline of the priesthood.'[141]

In looking to secularism as the real cause of concern, the writers identified the fundamental change that was taking place. Theology might adapt to the pressures of the age, but the forces at work were external to the church; they were a part of a national shift in values, brought about by the emergence in the second half of the century of scientific humanism and a growing secularism. Frederick Temple's Bampton Lectures of 1884, with their unquestioned acceptance of evolution, were an attempt on the part of the Established Church to embrace the new scientific thinking. But in the popular mind, such a reconciliation was not possible; a wedge had been driven between science and religion. Tyndall's presidential address to the

---

[138] J. Heaton, *The Freeman* 24 October 1855, p. 365.

[139] Joseph Fletcher 'Our Denominational Organisation', *Minutes, GBM* (1889), p. 1.

[140] Thomas Goadby, 'Christian Theology and the Modern Spirit', *GBM* (1879), p. 161.

[141] Cited by Patricia Stallings Kruppa, *Charles Haddon Spurgeon: A Preachers Progress* (New York and London: Garland Publishing, 1982), p. 363.

Theological Background and Development

British Association meeting in Belfast in 1874 set up a conflict model for relations between science and religion.[142]

The early editions of the the *General Baptist Repository* had carried articles of a scientific nature and the *General Baptist Magazine* for 1866 carried a report of the meeting of the 'British Association' at Nottingham, but increasingly intellectual concerns passed beyond the knowledge and ability of clergymen. Science developed outside the control of the religious intellectual strata, and a new professional group, scientists, came into being.[143] It was a grouping that did not feel the need to posit a theistic explanation for things.

The 'worldliness' of members and the indifference of society at large reflected the growing secularization of society. 'The mass of the population pay little attention or no regard to the Christian teaching which is within their reach; they will not go to the house of God, although they live within sight of its very doors', said J. Salisbury, chairman of the Connexion in 1869.[144] This trend indicated a decline in the perceived value of church membership, in what has been termed its 'utility'.[145] John Clifford had considerable theological insight and was probably the most influential member of the New Connexion. His presidential address of 1872 argued that Christianity could successfully meet the challenge of the new science and ethical criticism.[146] The problem was that Christianity had a decreasing sphere of influence, that it left untouched large areas of society. The evils of the day would only be addressed and changed as men were addressed and changed by Christ. The role of the church was to have a part in this transformation.

We find this theme in his 1877 sermon *The Church of Christ*. Addressing the question of how those untouched by the Christian message might be reached he says, 'the only infallible solution of the problem will be found in putting societies of Christian men and women in the midst of the people and steadily and earnestly directing their energies to the amelioration of their condition'.[147] For Clifford, the good news of the gospel, the message of the kingdom, takes on a social as well as a spiritual dimension. On another occasion he said, 'The Christian church is the first

---

[142] John Tyndall, 'The Belfast Address', in Cosslett, *Science and Religion*, pp. 172-89.

[143] Colin A. Russell, *Cross-Currents: Interactions Between Science and Faith* (Leicester: IVP, 1985), pp. 190-91.

[144] J. Salisbury, 'Christian work', Chairman's address, *Minutes*, *GBM* (1889), p. 5.

[145] Robert Currie, Alan Gilbert and Lee Horsley, *Churches and Churchgoers: Patterns of Church Growth in the British Isles since 1700* (Oxford: Clarendon Press 1977), p. 63.

[146] John Clifford, *Jesus Christ and Modern Social Life* (London: Marlborough. 1872), p. 17.

[147] John Clifford, *The Church of Christ, its work character and message: An address delivered at the dedication of Westbourne Park Chapel. Sept. 3. 1877* (London: Malborough & Co, 1877), p. 15.

but not the only divine instrument for establishing the rule of God here and now.'[148] Clifford tried to hold together the offer of free grace and the need to change society.

The New Connexion's 120 years' existence saw the most profound change in the world of theological reflection and scientific thinking. Clifford sought to meet this challenge by a fresh expression of God's concern for man in the light of contemporary need. This has been termed his 'social gospel'. It has at its heart that warm evangelical concern for the souls of men found in the 'gospel preaching' of the early leaders of the movement.[149] But its starting place and manner of expression were very different.

Towards the end of the period, falling membership rolls and increasing doubt were the order of the day. There were a growing number for whom the sciences of biology and geology were felt to cast doubt on the biblical accounts of creation, and the influence of biblical criticism undermined the authority of the biblical record. In 1881 Leicester saw the opening of the 'Secular Hall', what Malcolm Elliott calls a 'physical monument to unbelief'.[150] According to the *Leicester Daily Mercury*, reporting the opening speeches, it was the failure of the churches in terms of social concern and social injustice that necessitated the challenge of these issues by society. Elliott comments, 'There was much in the conduct of affairs at the Secular Hall that followed the pattern of nonconformist worship. Secular hymns were sung and Sunday schools held for children and the sermon was replaced by a series of public addresses often by eminent visiting speakers.'[151] One writer to the *General Baptist Magazine* saw the growing scepticism of society at large, weakening the church:

> It may not be amiss to ask, however, whether our diminished progress has arisen in any degree from the prevalence of scepticism. The presence of icebergs lowers the temperature of a great breadth of sea; and so the prevalence of scepticism in the literature of popular writers may be the means of depressing warmth and life of our churches.[152]

Although an attitude of doubt and uncertainty was generated there were other factors.[153] Improvements in housing, medicine and health had raised standards of living and improved the quality of life. This meant that men and women no longer lived as close to eternity as previous generations; the threat of death had become more distant. Industrial legislation had given large numbers an increasing sense of control over their lives:

---

[148] Cited by David Thompson in 'John Clifford's Social Gospel', *Baptist Quarterly* 31.5 (January, 1986). p. 209.

[149] Bebbington, *Evangelicalism in Modern Britain*, p. 211.

[150] Malcolm Elliott, 'Belief and Disbelief in Victorian Leicester', *The Leicester Archaeological and Historical Society: Transactions* 56 (1980–81) (Leicester: Leicester Archaeological and Historical Society, 1982), p. 92.

[151] Elliott, 'Belief and Disbelief', p. 94.

[152] *GBM* (1883), p. 257.

[153] A.D. Gilbert, *Religion and Society in Industrial England: Church, Chapel and Social Change, 1740–1914* (London, New York: Longman, 1976), p.117.

One of the effects of modern civilisation is to take the pain and suffering from our sight. We see less of the hardships of poverty than our father did who lived near it, and we can endure the thought of it less; so that there is more sentimental pity now than ever, and accordingly much less friendly and really efficacious help.[154]

The immediacy of death being postponed and the moral reaction against the preaching of hell contributed considerably to this change of climate. At the time of the formation of the New Connexion life had been precarious; it was lived either in a world of chance, in which a multitude of disadvantageous circumstances might prompt an appeal to a divine benevolence for help; or it was a world of 'Decree' where every happening was seen as coming from the 'great disposer of events'. Both of these responses posited a deity, both allowed for the supernatural. But late Victorian society did not find deity such a necessary prerequisite. Society as a whole was less interested in what the churches had to offer.

---

[154] John Clifford 'Jesus and Modern Social Life', *General Baptist Yearbook, GBM* (1872), p. 21.

CHAPTER 3

Mission or Maintenance: An Examination of the Organisational Structure of the New Connexion

Formation

On 6 June 1770 Dan Taylor met with twenty-four delegates or representatives of General Baptist churches at the Church Lane Meeting House, Whitechapel. Their intention was to separate themselves from the General Baptist Assembly then meeting in London. Six points at issue were drawn up; the concerns were not new, and were, in substance, very similar to issues that had been raised at assemblies in 1696 and 1707; they concerned the person of Christ and the nature of Atonement, and as we have already seen are fully expressed in the *Six Articles of Religion*.[1] Eighteen of those present put their name to them.[2] A deputation headed by John Brittain was sent to the General Baptist Assembly '—to acquaint them with their design of withdrawing from their connection—to assign the reason for that separation—and in a friendly manner to bid them farewell'.[3] John Brittain, pastor of the Church Lane meeting, one of the oldest in the General Baptist Assembly, headed the delegation.[4] The minutes of the Assembly record,

> The Case deliver'd by Mr John Brittain & others, was read & We are very sorry that any of our Brethren in Union with us in this Assembly establishd on the principles of general Redemption & and on Hebrews 6.1-2. should make any particular Sentements (sic) & Interpretations of Scripture a Plea for their Separation from us—We heartily wish for Union & Harmony & while we express our Determination not to make a Difference of private Opinion a Breach of brotherly love & Affection

---

[1] Taylor, *History*, II, p. 139.

[2] Taylor, *History*, II, p. 138. The eighteen who signed the *Six Articles* which were the basis of the formation of the New Connexion were as follows: Dan Taylor of Wadsworth, Yorkshire; David Wilkin of Halsted; William Thompson of Boston, Lincolnshire; John Knott, Eythorn; John Stanger of Bessels Green, Kent; John Brittain of Church Lane, Whitechapel, London; Henry Poole; Samual Deacon of Barton in the Beans, Leicestershire; James Fenn of Deal, Kent; Francis Smith and Thomas Perkins of Melbourne, Leicestershire; John Grimley of Loughborough, Leicestershire; William Smith and Geo. Hickling of Longford; John Tarratt of Kegworth, Leicestershire; N. Pickering of Castle Donnington, Leicestershire; Charles Parman from Castle Hedingham; and W. Summers of Southwark, London.

[3] Taylor, *History*, II, pp. 138-39.

[4] Whitley, *Minutes of the General Assembly of the General Baptist Churches*, p. 141.

we recommend the Complaints to a more deliberate Consideration of their present Proposal & future Conduct, leaving them entirely at Liberty to judge and act for themselves.[5]

The offer to consider the differences was not taken up; there was no going back, and so the New Connexion of General Baptists came into being.

This separation did not take place in a vacuum; the General Baptist Assembly had a history of theological dispute. The previous year had seen a violent disruption among the Lincolnshire churches; a large number of them withdrawing from the Assembly.[6] Dan Taylor attributed this wrangling to a preoccupation with theological controversy rather than gospel preaching and concluded that a withdrawal was necessary.[7] Those who bade farewell and formed the 'Assembly of New Connexion General Baptists' consisted of three convergent streams. The first, the Midland group of 'Barton preachers', came from Leicestershire. They were Independents, who had adopted 'Believer's Baptism'. Of the eighteen who formed the New Connexion they numbered eight. The other ten consisted of two groups of General Baptists: the first, a group from Lincolnshire, Essex, Kent and London, were part of the old dissenting body of General Baptists; the second smaller group was that which centred around Dan Taylor and the Yorkshire General Baptists. These made up the third founding component of the Connexion. Taylor and the Barton Independents were converts to the Baptist tradition and not products of it. Their thinking about church life was strongly influenced by Methodist structures and methods.

Local Church Forms and Influences

Yorkshire

The method of approach to the development of structure within the Connexion will be as follows: first, to consider the local church forms, the 'experience' and 'church meeting'; then regional 'Conferences'; and finally the development of a national structure in the annual 'Assembly' or 'Association'.

Dan Taylor had come to faith in a Methodist church and spent the early years of his Christian life within Methodism. When he parted with Methodism and founded his own church he modelled it along Methodist lines. Taylor appears to have divided the church at Birchcliffe into 'classes', and a person who was judged 'qualified by his piety and experience, was appointed as a leader'.[8] Taylor's classes are very similar to the class meetings which were central to early Methodism. As with Methodism lay leaders played an important role. The meetings enabled people to talk about their religious experience; they provided an important step in integrating new believers and interested people into the church, and, gave a significant opportunity for active lay participation. Dan Taylor also adopted the Methodist practice of holding 'leaders'

---

[5] Whitley, *Minutes of the General Assembly*, II, p. 141.
[6] Brown, *English Baptists*, pp. 57-70.
[7] Wood, *History*, pp. 142-43.
[8] Taylor, *History*, II, pp. 77-78.

meetings', and his own version of the Methodist Quarterly Meeting for 'discipline' every six weeks.

The experience meetings reflect the eighteenth-century concern for evidence of spiritual vitality rather than argument which, as John Briggs and Ian Sellers point out, changed the nature of church life.[9] This had been an essential concern amongst Independents and Baptists from the seventeenth century, and was regarded as a basis for membership and devotion.

The New Connexion experience meeting involved members gathering on a weekly basis in a home. The meetings were open, and enquirers were encouraged to attend if they 'wished to obtain religious knowledge'. The gathering started with singing and prayer and then,

> ...the leader declared, in a few words, the state of his own mind, as to the concerns of religion, since the last opportunity: his trials and supports, his hopes and fears, his struggle against inward and outward enemies, and his advancement or decline in the christian cause.[10]

The leader then went round the group, asking each member to give a similar statement, then he would comment and make 'such observations, and offered such advice and cautions, as the circumstances...seem to require'.[11]

Although widely adopted in Yorkshire, references to them in other parts of the country are to be found. While the establishment of something like the class system may have been Taylor's intention, the use of the 'experience meeting' was not consistent throughout the Connexion. One may cite two churches in Lincolnshire, Boston and Fleet, the former held experience meetings, the latter did not. Ambler comments, 'The cooler tone of church life at Fleet meant that it was not in tune with the evangelical dynamic of the New Connexion.'[12] Adam Taylor notes with approval the formation of five or six meetings in Nottingham, with 'two leaders appointed over each: a plan which greatly promoted the interest of vital religion'.[13] These meetings, centring around testimony, encouraged personal spiritual development and reflected the evangelical dynamic of the Connexion. But by the turn of the century, they had lost their central role and the question was being asked, 'Shall we have a meeting to talk of our experience?'[14]

J.G. Pike's Association letter *Experience Meetings* in 1822 cited 'social prayer and free communion on the great subjects of Religion' as 'those means which the Scriptures point out as instrumental to the promotion of personal piety'.[15] But the

---

[9] John Briggs and Ian Sellers, *Victorian Nonconformity* (Documents of Modern History; London: Edward Arnold, 1973), p. 2.
[10] Taylor, *History*, II, p. 78.
[11] Taylor, *History*, II, p. 78.
[12] Ambler, *Walls of Zion*, p. 22.
[13] Taylor, *History*, II, p. 249.
[14] Bourne Church Book. 2 September 1804. At Bourne Baptist Church.
[15] J. Jarrom, 'Experience Meetings', letter, *GBR* (1822), p. 28

response of the church at Melbourne would seem to indicate that the meetings were unknown to them:

> The subject of Experience Meetings was resumed and a paper was read which was drawn up at the request of the Officers Meeting containing a plan for conducting them, after some conversation on the subject was agreed the church meeting begin at 10 o'clock and that one hour be employed as an Experience Meeting as a Trial.[16]

The response was similar at Hugglescote where the choice of leaders was left to the classes, 'Though it is thought it will be best to change the class leader every three months.' Here, although called 'experience meetings', they are also referred to as classes.[17] We are not told what became of these experiments in either case. However, in the church at Archdeacon Lane, Leicester, the experience meetings were 'found very productive of unity and we trust assist our piety'.[18]

By the middle of the nineteenth century the experience meeting had undergone a change. From being a regular meeting, it had in many cases been abandoned, or had become occasional, single meetings for the giving of testimony, often in the context of mission. In 1847, the church at Archdeacon Lane concluded, 'The church consider that the meeting for experience as a general principle is for Members, but it is left to the Leaders to admit others who may be considered Christians or seeking salvation.'[19] At Market Harborough they were held monthly, and linked with 'enquirers' meetings.[20] At New Lenton, Nottingham, in 1854, they seem to have become a more formal meeting, and ten years later, the church agreed to 'arrange a 6^d tea on the first January and an Experience Meeting at the close'.[21] A church meeting at Retford and Gamston in 1844 'agreed to have Class meetings'. The reference is ambiguous and may refer to experience meetings, as in 1859 they agreed to hold experience meetings as long as they did not interfere with other meetings of the church.[22]

While the practice of experience meetings was similar to the Methodist class, their role in the structures of the church was very different. John Wesley placed great

---

[16] Thomas Budge, 'Records of the most Material affairs belonging to the Baptist Congregation at Melbourne in Derbyshire. Extracts from the Church Book 1774-1832', (unpublished MS in the East Midland Baptist Archive), 24 November 1822.

[17] Minutes of Hugglescote General Baptist Church, 1 December 1823. Leicester Record Office N/B/150/1.

[18] Archdeacon Lane Minute Book, 22 June 1828. Leicester Record Office, N/B/179/102.

[19] Archdeacon Lane Minute Book, 19 January 1847. Leicester Record Office, N/B/179/102.

[20] Market Harborough Church Book, 25 August 1831. Leicester Record Office. NB/215/20.

[21] General Baptist Church New Lenton, 25 June 1854, and 24 September 1865. Nottingham Record Office. BP/10/5.

[22] Retford and Gamston Church Book, 22 April 1844, and 4 January 1859. Nottingham Record Office BP/20/2, 3.

value on the class meeting; it was, for him, a 'prudential means of grace'; this meant that, while not demanded by scripture, it was to be embraced because of its usefulness.[23] Attendance at class was the means of obtaining a 'class ticket', which was a passport to a Methodist Society.[24] One was a member of a class first, and by virtue of that, a member of a Society.

Whilst the General Baptist 'experience meeting', described above, was thought to be right and valuable, they were not seen as mandatory, or an essential part of church structure as in Methodism.[25] For Taylor one was a member of the church in the first instance, not the 'experience meeting'. Church membership was the primary relationship and commitment; the 'experience meeting' was an expression of that relationship. The value of the 'experience meeting' lay in the way in which it extended the boundaries of the church to include any who desired to 'obtain religious knowledge' and 'engage in the cause of Christ'; it made possible the easy assimilation and incorporation of new believers.

Traditionally, General Baptists had drawn on their independent heritage and understood the nature of the church in terms of the fellowship of believers covenanting together. Taylor's use of the 'experience meeting' introduced a new element, drawn in part from Methodism and the Evangelical Revival. The church became a means of individual salvation, with the emphasis on personal salvation and experience. The tension between the outward looking missionary philosophy of the revival, and the more inward focus of the gathered churches of Independency was one that was never fully resolved.

The experience meetings gave practical expression to the importance of spiritual experience which was central to the life of the New Connexion. But these meetings did not have the 'holiness' emphasis of the Methodist class.[26] The diminishing concern about the experience meeting reflects something of the loss of evangelical fervour at the level of the local church; despite urgings from pulpit and association platforms to greater devotion.[27] Like the Methodist 'class', the experience meeting suffered from the second generation onward.[28] In 1817 the church at Bourne complained that although congregations were healthy, 'too many mind their own things more than the things of Christ'.[29] The church at Derby said, 'we want more vital piety'. At nearby Duffield, while there were 'great additions', it was feared 'the progress of inward and vital religion has not kept pace with our increase'. Gosberton complained about 'the low state of vital religion among us'.[30] At Queenshead, Yorkshire, the complaint was specific, although the experience meetings were better

---

[23] R.J. Billington, *The Liturgical Movement and Methodism* (London, 1969), p. 129.

[24] Leslie F. Church, *The Early Methodist People* (Fernley–Hartley Lecture; London: Epworth, 1948), p. 170.

[25] Taylor, *History*, II, p. 78.

[26] G.S. Wakefield, *Methodist Devotion* (London: Epworth, 1966), p. 41.

[27] J.G. Pike, 'Experience Meetings', *Letter* (1822), pp. 27-33.

[28] Gilbert, *Religion and Society*, p. 180.

[29] Bourne, Minutes, 1817, p. 5.

[30] Bourne, Minutes, 1817, p. 6.

attended, some of them were 'too much neglected'.[31] With the passing of the founding generation there seems to have come a cooling of ardour and spiritual experience.

The Midland Group

The second major group of churches involved in the formation of the Connexion was the Midland group. These churches had evolved around the Barton church: they had come into being as a result of the preaching of John and David Taylor.[32] David Taylor was initially encouraged and supported by the Countess of Huntingdon who freed him from service in order to develop his preaching. Assisted by Stephen Dixon and William Kendrick, they established groups of believers along Methodist lines. According to the *General Baptist Magazine*, the Barton churches were mistaken for Methodist churches.[33] John Deacon, one of the early leaders of the Barton group, said they 'raised a society somewhat resembling the plan of Mr Wesley'. The group that met at Nailstone also attended the parish church, as was the early Methodist practice.[34] In addition to this, they would meet together as often as convenient for the purpose of social friendship and religious instruction. According to Wood, 'In the constitution of their societies they imitated in a great measure the methodists'.[35] Small groups of believers were gathered; there was a probationary period of six months during which candidature was under review, and they were subject to the discipline of the meeting. These groups, like Methodist classes, were issued with a 'ticket'; it was by means of the 'ticket' that discipline was exercised. Refusal of a 'ticket' excluded an individual from communion.[36] The extent to which the appellation 'Methodists' was an accurate description could be questioned. The Barton preachers adopted Methodist styles of activity, preaching in the streets and fields, meeting in houses; these activities alone may have been sufficient to cause confusion. The most we can say is that the Barton movement adopted Methodist characteristics in its practice and fused it with an 'independent' theology of church government.

There were other influences at work. William Kendrick who was instrumental in establishing the church at Barton in 1745, had a chequered ecclesiastical history;

---

[31] Bourne, Minutes, 1817, p. 10.
[32] J.R. Godfrey, *Historic Memorials of Barton and Melbourne General Baptist Churches* (London: Buck/Leicester: Winks and Son, 1891), p. 11. John Taylor spent the summer of 1742 travelling with John Wesley as his companion and helper on his journey through Leicestershire and Derbyshire up to Newcastle-upon-Tyne. On the return journey they parted company after leaving Epworth. John Taylor came to Barton in the summer of 1743. He was followed by David Taylor who was a convert of Benjamin Ingham. According to J.R. Godfrey, David Taylor was also a friend of George Whitefield.
[33] *GBM* (1798), p. 184.
[34] *GBM* (1798), pp. 186, 188.
[35] Wood, *History*, p. 173.
[36] Wood, *History*, p. 173.

having been involved with Whitefield, then Wesley 'and being excluded by the latter joined the Moravians'.[37] The building, if not the theology, of the church at Barton was constructed 'on the plan of the Moravians'with rooms for 'single brethren and sisters'. Adam Taylor attributes this to the influence of Stephen Dixon and William Kendrick who had links with a Moravian church at Pudsey in Yorkshire.[38]

The Barton group of churches also held regular 'conference meetings' for the 'purpose of promoting each other's spiritual improvement' and to conduct the 'affairs of the church'. Initially these groups were under the direct control of the preachers. As Wood remarks, 'The supreme control of the societies, as long as they continued to act as one body, was placed in the weekly conference of the ministers, at which the general operations of the whole community were directed: subsequently, the private members obtained that ascendancy in the conduct of the concerns of the church to which they are certainly entitled by the principles of the New Testament'.[39]

The church had been established some twenty-five years before joining the New Connexion and had, in John Deacon's words,

> chosen the title 'Independents' not because their views either of doctrine or discipline were conformable to the generality of those that bear that name, but indeed for the same reason the Independents originally applied it to themselves: that is they were independent of other religious societies, and were determined to be under no foreign control.[40]

Two of the three groups that founded the New Connexion (Taylor's churches, and the Barton Independents) were not tied to General Baptist organisation or tradition. Their organisation and structure seems to have been pragmatic, drawing evangelistic inspiration from Methodist strategy and organisation, to which was grafted a General Baptist theology of the church as a covenant community. There was in this structure a tension between community and missionary needs.[41]

General Baptist Tradition

The nature of the Connexion was influenced by the process through which it came into being—that of synthesis—each group bringing its own contribution. The Connexion never existed in its own right, only as a composite of three disparate groups. It was the second of these groups, the General Baptists of Lincolnshire and the South, in which the Baptist ethos was strongest. Almost as soon as it was formed, the Connexion was divided into two associations: the Northern and the Southern. The former comprised churches from the Midlands and Lincolnshire, the

---

[37] *GBM* (1798), p. 226.
[38] Taylor, *History*, II, p. 16.
[39] Wood, *History*, p. 173.
[40] *GBM* (1798), p. 228.
[41] Briggs, *English Baptists*, p. 14.

An Examination of the Organisational Structure 43

latter churches from the South and East.[42] The General Baptists of Lincolnshire, Essex, Middlesex, Kent and Sussex had a long history, and prior to joining the Connexion had been members of the older dissenting body of General Baptists. The connection with the General Baptists was formative in shaping the ecclesiology of the new movement, and assimilation of General Baptist churches continued to be a feature in its development. The first fifteen years saw the following General Baptist churches come into the Connexion: Maltby (1773), Killingholme (1778), Yarmouth (1778), Kirton in Lindsey, (1779), Ashford (1782), Gosberton, (1784), and Wisbech (1785). This process of absorption was continued well into the next century. In 1831 of the 108 churches listed in the annual returns thirty-three had been established before 1770. The influence of old General Baptists was especially substantial in Lincolnshire, their old stronghold, where ten out of nineteen had foundation dates prior to the formation of the Connexion.[43]

As converts to the General Baptist position, the churches of the North and Midlands had not come empty handed; they had brought to the Connexion an ethos and style associated with the Evangelical Revival that did not always sit comfortably with the old traditions of Independency. While there was a desire for renewal in many of the Lincolnshire and southern churches, most of them were not willing, or able, to embrace the new movement. Whitley describes the London church at Church Lane as 'apathetic in their new relations'. It appears to have been a situation where the 'new wine' of Connexionalism was too heady for many of those of the old General Baptist tradition.

While dissatisfaction with the theological tensions and drift of the old General Baptist Assembly may have been the reason why some found the Connexion attractive, they were not comfortable with the evangelistic demands that membership of the Connexion entailed. Within a relatively short period of time, the southern group fell away. In 1773 the 'nature of the connection between the Northern and Southern churches was enquired into'; by 1775, there was not a single minister representing the South; in 1778, an enquiry was instituted into the reason why the southern churches neglected to associate annually. The reason for this may be in part the nature of membership within the Connexion.

In the early years the membership of the Connexion was on a personal basis, ministers being admitted even if churches were unwilling to join. Ambler contends that free movement among the churches by ministers helped the development of links based on a common emphasis and approach, and that it was this informal networking that was the basis of the New Connexion. It was the personal contacts of Taylor rather than the institution that were important. These contacts 'were based on a shared spiritual experience which came from among the churches rather than one which was imposed from above'.[44] The different spiritual ethos of the southern churches could account for their lack of commitment to the Connexion.

---

[42] Taylor, *History,* II, pp. 144-45.
[43] *GBRM* (1831), p. 56.
[44] Ambler, *Walls of Zion,* p. 15.

Structures

Church Meeting

The structure of the movement was conditioned by the nature and exercise of power within it. The Connexion placed power and authority in the church meeting. Dan Taylor describes two types of meeting: the one having a fellowship function, the other for management. He says,

> there were two kinds of stated meetings one of these was weekly. The church was divided into several branches which met together once a week, for prayer and mutual edification, by conversing on experimental and practical subjects [experience meetings]. The other was designed for the preservation of order, discipline and purity in the church generally called church meetings and less frequent than the former.

In both the women were encouraged to speak freely on every subject as well as the men.[45] It was in the 'preservation of order, discipline and purity' that power and authority were exercised.

The formation of the Connexion was, to some extent, an attempt to reassert the traditional values of Dissent in a new form. There was a debt to a variety of influences, which reflect the background and ecclesiology of its founder members. John Lee says that the New Connexion had two points of distinction: firstly, they rejected the Calvinist doctrine of election; and secondly they 'consciously organised their churches under a national association, which, while allowing virtual congregational autonomy did exercise an element of central control... Both of these features were Methodist in derivation.'[46]

The second of these observations needs some qualification. Both the General Baptists and Methodists were connexional in nature, but the Baptists had a much stronger doctrine of the autonomy and independency of the local church. According to Taylor, 'They believed, that each society was competent to manage its own concerns: and allowed of no foreign controul (sic), not even from their own conferences or association. The executive power of a church they conceived to be lodged in the members regularly assembled.'[47] The power of the members in the meeting was considerable, allowing them, on occasions, to remove ministers and officers, 'And, while they disclaimed all external authority, they were equally jealous of undue internal influence: holding their rights as church members sacred against the encroachment of their own officers.'[48] So though the churches were in a Connexion, each church within that grouping was independent. This would indicate that the

---

[45] Dan Taylor, *A Sermon Occasioned by the Death of Mrs. Elizabeth Taylor who departed this life Oct 22nd 1793 in the 49th year of her age. With a short account of her life and a description of her character* (London, 1794), p. 69.

[46] John Lee, 'Baptists in Lancashire 1831–81' (PhD thesis, University of Liverpool, 1970), p. 24.

[47] Taylor, *History*, II, p. 468.

[48] Taylor, *History*, II, p. 468.

structure of the Connexion was much more Baptist than Methodist, where there was a surrender of control on the part of the local church to the circuit. Within the New Connexion structure the church meeting was the decision-making body; although the local Conference might propose a course of action, it was ultimately a decision of the church meeting to implement it. 'What reason have we to be glad & rejoice that Conf<u>n</u> <u>can</u> <u>only</u> advise!', said the minute writer at Kegworth when Conference sent a letter to the church concerning the repayment of a loan.[49] It was the church meeting that took decisions about membership, discipline, the calling of people to ministry and outreach, indeed any matter that affected the life and witness of the church. 'At these church meetings the Pastor presides and states the business, and it is considered to be the privilege and duty of each member to give his thoughts respecting it; and the decision is generally regulated according to the majority', wrote the writer *of A Brief Sketch of the Doctrine and Discipline of the General Baptist Churches*. He further explained, 'The method here described is what is called the *Independent* form of church government, which supposes every church to have the power of regulating its own concerns, without the interference of any other person.'[50] The circular letter of 1824, 'Church Discipline', defined the purpose of meeting as, '1. To elect your officers. 2. To Raise up and call forth preachers. 3. To consider and adopt every rational and scriptural method, for the support of the truth and the spread of the Gospel. 4. To receive members into the church. 5. To censure and exclude offenders.'[51] The power of the meeting was understood to be vested in the body and not in the pastor or deacons.[52] The autonomy of the church was jealously protected, and the connexional organisation had no overriding power at the level of the church meeting.

Conference

The Connexion sought to marry this strong independence with a stressing of the interdependence of local churches upon each other. According to *A Brief Sketch of the Doctrine and Discipline of the General Baptist Churches*, 'though they hold, that every church is an independent Society, they think that in many instances, the cause of Christ may be most effectually promoted by the united exertions of churches: hence they unite in *Conferences*, which assemble several times in the year'.[53] These conferences were the distinctive feature of the Connexion; a local grouping they usually met on a quarterly basis. They need to be distinguished from the annual assembly or association. The 'Conferences' had originated as a means by which the Barton group had provided fellowship for their ministers and managed the preaching

---

[49] Kegworth Church Book, 13 July 1800. Leicester Record Office. N/B/159/1.

[50] *A Brief Sketch of the Doctrine and Discipline of the General Baptist Churches* (Midland Tract Society; General Baptist Tracts CLIV No. 6; Leicester: J.F. Winks, n.d.), p. 7. The Angus Library, Regent's Park College..

[51] *Minutes*, 1824, p. 29.

[52] 'On Admitting Members into Churches', *GBRM* (1831), p. 254.

[53] *A Brief Sketch of the Doctrine and Discipline*, p. 7.

demands of their churches. When the Connexion was formed Dan Taylor adopted this structure and implemented it in Yorkshire. The practice was introduced to Lincolnshire when W. Burgess, who had been minister at Halifax, settled at Fleet in 1791.[54]

It was the conference more than any thing else that was the distinctive organisational feature of the Connexion. Although originally designed for individual churches and their satellite preaching stations and chapels, these conferences had evolved by the 1780s into a form that began to resemble Baptist associations. In 1795, their purpose was defined as 'a company of men who meet at appointed seasons to consider the difficult concerns of the churches'.[55] In 1843, this had been broadened to 'maintain a mutual knowledge of the Churches, sympathy and friendship with them, a due care for their welfare and a readiness to assist them'.[56] They were comprised of ministers and deacons and in the later stages by delegates sent by the churches. The conference sought to resolve difficulties both theological and practical, and was a local policy making body, with a limited degree of executive power, for they met 'to consider the necessity or utility of any expensive proposition, and to represent the general opinion to several churches'.[57] The exact power of the 'general opinion' is not spelt out. So in 1815, when a proposed 'plan of Itineracy' was submitted by the conference to the churches, the church at Castle Donnington deemed that while it had 'some advantages & disadvantages attending it' it was 'on the whole impracticable', and they rejected it.[58] In addition conferences also saw to the stationing of preachers for new and ailing causes. It had been the custom of the Barton group to have a regular meeting for mutual encouragement and to fix preaching arrangements in the various causes that the church served. In this, the conference acted like a Methodist circuit meeting, but without its power of enforcement. One disadvantage was noted by an observer who said that conferences were like church meetings, 'though often more said and less done'.[59]

John Taylor gives an account of the early 'preachers' meetings and Conferences' he had with his brother Dan Taylor in the early days of their ministry:

we designed them to be regulated to have our errors corrected, to be aware of them, and endeavour to amend them in the future. This was our intention, and we found the meetings of very special benefit to us, or rather to me. I could not pretend to regulate others; but being ignorant and inexperienced, I needed correction and instruction; and I generally got both at these meetings.

He goes on to describe them:

---

[54] Wood, *History*, p. 297.
[55] Deacon, *A Comprehensive Account*, p. 121.
[56] 'On the Importance of Maintaining our Conferences', *GBRM* (1843), p. 46.
[57] Deacon, *A Comprehensive Account*, p. 122.
[58] Castle Donnington Church Book, 7 May 1815. At Castle Donnington Baptist Church.
[59] Deacon, *A Comprehensive Account*, p. 122.

We begin them in simplicity and sincerity of heart with a view to mutual benefit. We proposed to speak of anything which we heard or knew wrong in each other, as we were but two—to propose of difficulties—and say what could be done more or better for the advancement of religion. These were the three great things and with them we began our meetings.[60]

It will be seen that the type of 'conference' John Taylor had in Yorkshire was as much a spiritual discipline as a business meeting. His following comment reflects a change that took place in the nature of the conferences: 'Whether it be so at present or not, I do not so well know, for I have been, many years past, through infirmity prevented from a regular attendance at such meetings. I go to one now and then; and it appears to me that the original design is either not understood, or quite neglected. I am sorry to find it so. Lord help us.'[61] From this comment, it would seem that the original intention to provide mutual support and encouragement to the ministers and preachers of the Connexion was missing by 1820.

This may have been due to the growth of the Connexion. In 1803 the original Leicester Conference divided and the Nottingham Conference was formed. Ten years later they reunited and divided the area into four districts which they visited in turn. But continued growth in this part of the Connexion made meeting difficult for churches situated at the edge of the district. The resolution was the establishment of the Warwickshire Conference in 1816, discontinued in 1834 and re-organised in 1838. Although at its start in 1772 the Yorkshire Conference had confined attendance to ministers, later officers of the church were admitted, and ultimately ministers, officers and as many of the private members as chose to attend. The London Conference was formed in 1779 and was held twice a year. The Derbyshire Conference was formed in 1839 and the Cheshire and Lancashire Conference in 1840.

In addition to the personal questions recounted by John Taylor, the conferences addressed themselves to such questions as 'what more can be done to promote religion among us', or 'what steps can we take to promote the religion of Jesus'.[62] The increasing numbers must have hindered the extent to which personal participation was possible; the meetings became more formal with the sermons and business matters taking a more dominant role.

The nature of business discussed ranged from a minister seeking the advice of conference on prosecution of a thief, to advice on a settlement.[63] As to the question 'Is it right to Encourage unconverted Persons to sing in our Public assemblys?' the 1780 conference at Castle Donnington was undecided.[64] Support of the churches was

---

[60] Taylor, *Memoirs of John Taylor*, p. 36.
[61] Taylor, *Memoirs of John Taylor*, p. 36.
[62] 'Origin and Object of the Conferences', *GBM* (1865), p. 337.
[63] 'Minutes of the Monthly Conferences', *Transactions of the Baptist Historical Society* 5 (1916–17), p. 119; Bourne Church Book, 4 December 1834.
[64] 'Minutes of the Monthly Conference', *Transactions of the Baptist Historical Society* 5 (1916–17), p. 120.

enlisted for the building of a meeting house in Jamaica.[65] The summary judgements in the minutes of the early Leicestershire Conference are tempered by a desire to obtain a consensus of opinion among those present, often decided by a vote, but they still have the character of a dictate.

It was not always easy for preachers to transfer the connexional predilections of conferences to the local church situation. As one writer in 1798 observed, '...if there be such a thing as despotism among General Baptists, it is pretty generally transferred from the preachers to the people'. 'Despotism', he continues,

> consists in an undue exercise of power; and wherever power rests, it requires much wisdom and benevolence to keep it within due bounds, and to direct it in its various operations. For this reason as well as others, it seems best in ecclesiastical government to lodge the power in the hands of the people.[66]

It would appear that most General Baptists of the New Connexion would have sympathised with those sentiments.

At the local level, churches of the Connexion differed little from other Baptist churches. It was in relationships between the churches of the Connexion that the differences occurred. There lay within this structure of church meeting and conference a delicate balance of power between connexional aspirations and local autonomy — a structure that resulted in a tension that was present with the movement throughout its life.

In the early stages of its life, the organisational structure of the Connexion was regional rather than central. The rural nature of the Connexion gave local autonomy a high value. By 1822, fifty-two years after its inception, only five of the forty-four churches listed in the annual returns were in large towns or cities. By the middle of the nineteenth century articles appeared *On the importance of maintaining our Conferences* in 1843, and *The Origin and Object of Conferences* in 1865. While in the early stages of its life the regional 'Conference' was a centre of influence and identity, especially in areas where there was a concentration of churches, for others further away from these centres of influence, accessibility could be a problem; in 1845, the church at West Retford sought to 'try to establish a conference meeting in this part'.[67] Within the Connexion as a whole the growth of the organisation, better communications, and the emergence of the Baptist Union as a national force, diminished the power and influence of conference and the influence began to shift to the annual association and the Baptist Union.

---

[65] 'Minutes of the Monthly Conference', *Transactions of the Baptist Historical Society* 5 (1916–17), p. 124.

[66] *GBM* (1798), p. 361.

[67] West Retford and Gamston. 1843–1857, 10 February 1845. Nottingham Record Office. BP/20/2.

Annual Association or Assembly

The General Baptists had a strong tradition of associating, and for many years had held an annual assembly; the Particular Baptists, while having some large associations, had not put the same emphasis on central organisation. From the start, the assembly played an important role in the life of the Connexion providing a national forum for the movement. The annual assembly or association was instituted on the occasion of the withdrawal from the old General Baptist Assembly and constituted the formation of the New Connexion. After agreeing the 'Six Articles', one of the major concerns for this first assembly was, in Adam Taylor's words, 'that they should have full evidence, not only of the soundness of each other's faith but the genuineness of each other's piety'. It was agreed, that, at the next assembly, every minister 'do, give an account of his religious experience, that they may be satisfied concerning the reality of each other's conversion'.[68]

Thus continued membership of the assembly was on the basis of shared experience of personal conversion. Wood comments that much of the second meeting was occupied by ministers relating their experience.[69] Rules governing the association were worked out at a conference at Hugglescote in 1773. Attendance was limited to ministers or elders; if a church had neither, then they might nominate two brethren. Initially, subscription to the 'Six Articles' was required, but the General Baptist concern about creeds was reflected in the 1775 decision that 'subscription to a creed was not needful', and that 'the applicant for admission should give in his experience, and if the majority decided that he should be admitted a member, a declaration should be made to him of what the Connexion believed respecting the most fundamental doctrines; in order that it might be ascertained whether there was an agreement in religious sentiments'.[70] This rooted the membership of the Connexion in personal spiritual experience and in the early days of the movement it was individuals not churches that were admitted, making membership of the Connexion very different from that of Particular Baptist associations. The 1775 decision was an important change as it shifted the basis of association away from theology to experience. The growth of the movement forced a change to this spiritual fellowship. In 1777 the association meeting at Castle Donnington decided to admit churches; according to J.H. Wood this came about because of the growth of the churches thus: 'it was found necessary to establish some mode of admitting *them* into the Connexion'.[71] To this point it had been an association of individuals, but the decision now meant that it became a structure for churches, and an assembly of representatives. While applying churches were to submit their 'religious sentiments' for examination and approval, the emphasis on a spiritual fellowship of those who had experienced personal regeneration and renewal was diminished, although that element was still retained. At Nottingham in 1795, it was decided that only

---

[68] Taylor, *History*, II, p. 143.
[69] Wood, *History*, p. 179.
[70] Wood, *History*, pp. 179-80.
[71] Wood, *History*, p. 180.

representatives of churches could vote. The annual meeting was formally constituted as an assembly of delegates.[72]

The assembly was described as a 'kind of general conference of all the conferences of all the branches of the whole Connexion'.[73] The 1786 assembly of the Connexion made explicit the nature of its authority; an 'advertisement' was inserted on the inside first page of the minutes to the effect that,

> Whereas it has been intimated, and seems to be suspected by some persons, that the ministers and members of this association assume a dominion over churches, or individual ministers or members; we think it proper to inform them, and all others who may read our minutes, that we unanimously and decidedly reprobate every assumption of dominion over any church, or any individual, with whom we are connected. We consider every thing we say, to any case presented to our consideration as only a matter of judgement or advice, without any pretence to authority over the persons advised; and we leave them entirely at liberty to accede to, or deviate from the advice or judgement we give on any subject laid before us and if any should, after this free declaration, represent our conduct in a different manner, we consider such representation as very uncandid and unjust.[74]

It was a body from which advice could be sought, but it had no more authority than a conference. According to *A Comprehensive Account*, 'They do not esteem it a tribunal.'[75] The association dealt with 'cases relating to the whole Connexion, as well as any thing of a more private kind, if advice be sought, or, if it be thought for the good of the whole body. The Institutions of the Connexion were also regulated by the Association.'[76]

Such central government as there was was by consent. We have an example of this when Dan Taylor sought advice about a move from Wadsworth to Halifax, and his later move from Halifax to London. According to Adam Taylor, 'The removal of a Pastor from a church over which he had been ordained, unless in cases of apostacy or heresy, was very uncommon among the General Baptists.'[77] The Wadsworth church was reluctant to release Taylor and resisted the proposed move. The request of the Halifax church to Taylor for his ministry was put to the local conference, and thence, as the issue was still undecided, to the annual association. The question of the move aroused considerable discussion in the young movement. The assembly replied, 'We advise Birchcliffe to let brother T. go; we further advise Halifax to engage him.' Taylor sought to stay out of the argument. In his own words, 'I have been invariably passive in the matter from the beginning of the discussion of it; feeling, as I humbly hope thro' rich grace, a sincere desire to be anything or nothing

---

[72] E.A. Payne, *The Baptist Union: A Short History* (London: Carey Kingsgate Press, 1959), p. 30.
[73] Deacon, *A Comprehensive Account*, p. 123.
[74] Minutes General Baptist Assembly. Angus Library. 27 April. 1786.
[75] Deacon, *A Comprehensive Account*, p. 124.
[76] *A Brief Sketch of the Doctrine and Discipline*, p. 8.
[77] Taylor, *Memoirs of the Rev. Dan Taylor*, p. 113.

An Examination of the Organisational Structure 51

that my Lord and Saviour may be glorified, and his interest raised in the world.'[78] He expressed his views on the matter in a letter to his friend Thompson of Boston. Acknowledging that the move would be best for the General Baptist interest, he says, 'Circumstances between my people and those of Halifax are exceedingly perplexing. I know not how to act.'[79] Eventually a compromise was reached, both parties agreeing to leave the decision to 'providence'. Taylor would work for six months at Halifax, a supply being found for Wadsworth—the eventual outcome was his move to Halifax.

When two years later in 1785, the church meeting at Church Lane, Whitechapel, invited him to be their pastor, a precedent having already been set, it was felt that the greatest advantage would come from a move. At the assembly meeting in Boston that year, the question from the Donnington church, 'Has any Association a power to remove any minister from his people, without his people's consent?', was discussed. The response was, 'Answer No' with one 'yes'. The next question was, 'Suppose a minister be invited to leave his people, he consulteth the association; they approve of his remove, and suppose it will be for the better. He is convinced of it. Ought he in such a case to leave his people without their consent?' The answer was in the affirmative. The question was then put, 'does it appear on the whole likely to be for the Glory of God and the good of mankind that brother D. Taylor remove to London? Answer 17 yes Neuters 8.' It is interesting to note that Taylor's case did not settle the issue, or act as a precedent. In another request from the Longford church 'respecting the removal of brother Pollard', it was decided after discussion that 'he ought not to remove'. The voting was ten for and thirteen neuters.[80] As late as June 1800, the church at Melbourne in Leicestershire inquired of the association 'Whether it be right for any church standing in need of a minister to make application to a minister of another people in a private way without their knowledge who previously enjoy his labours?'[81]

To say, as Jackson does, that the 'General Association was the ruling assembly of the New Connexion'[82] is to overstate the case; the General Association or Assembly, unlike the Methodist Conference, could not compel compliance. 'The Association', said Adam Taylor, 'does not however pretend to any authority, to dictate to the churches, or impose its decisions on them. They offer the advice, as

---

[78] Dan Taylor, *The Consistent Christian or Truth, Peace, Holiness, Unanimity, Steadfastness and Zeal recommended to Professors of Christianity. The Substance of Five sermons by Dan Taylor to which is prefixed a brief account of the Authors removal from Wadsworth to Halifax* (Leeds, 1784), p. VII.

[79] Taylor, *Memoirs of the Rev. Dan Taylor*, p. 114.

[80] *Minutes of a General Baptist Association held at Boston, 27-28 April 1785*, pp. 9-10.

[81] Budge, 'Records of the most Material affairs', 15 June 1800.

[82] G. Jackson, 'The Evangelical work of Baptists in Leicestershire 1740–1820' (MA thesis, University of London, 1955), p. 273.

brethren, and leave them at full liberty to adopt or reject it as they judge best.'[83] He describes the role of the assembly or conference at the turn of the century thus:

> ...to maintain a mutual knowledge of the church, sympathy and friendship with them, a due care for their welfare and a readiness to assist them...free and friendly disquisition of theological subjects, and doctrinal and practical errors; and the giving of proper advice in any case in which a church or an individual requests it. For if any dispute or difficulty arise in any church and she applies to the conference for advice, the conference gives it to the utmost of its ability, disclaiming at the same time all authority and everything dictatorial.[84]

There were difficult cases that were unresolved even after appeal to the local conference and the annual association. This did not mean that little value was placed on the structure; the difficult cases, 'are but few in comparison of the many important cases which are investigated and treated so clearly as to completely satisfy contending parties of hesitating churches'.[85]

The association meeting at London in 1818 provides a typical example of an association agenda of this period. Firstly there were churches applying for membership of the Connexion. Their application usually included a statement of their theological position in relation to the Connexion. Thus the church at Seven Oaks, Kent, said, 'So far as we have been able to learn our sentiments on doctrinal points agree with those generally believed and preached by the New Connection (sic) of General Baptists.'[86] This was followed by cases from churches requiring financial aid. 'The building of a place of worship at Hose [in Leicestershire], was approved by the Association, and the case recommended to the attention of the churches.'[87] Then came requests from churches seeking help with ministry. Here suggestions were made as to men that churches might contact. When Church Lane, London, requested assistance, they received the following answer:

> We have seriously considered the request of the Friends in Church Lane, but cannot find a person whom we can cordially recommend to them in the capacity they desire. Feeling, however, the importance of the interest in London, and being anxious to support it by every means in our power, we have recommended a regular supply from Sister Churches, and earnestly request that the Churches concerned will agree to the following arrangement for the following year.[88]

There then followed a preaching plan listing men for the following year. This 'case' demonstrates the nature of the authority and influence the annual association had at this time. They could suggest and recommend, but not station a man at Church

---

[83] Adam Taylor, *GBR* 1 (1802), p. 20.
[84] Adam Taylor, *GBR* 1 (1802), pp. 22, 31, 34.
[85] Deacon, *A Comprehensive Account*, p. 124.
[86] *Minutes* (1818), p. 13.
[87] *Minutes* (1818), p. 13.
[88] *Minutes* (1818), p. 14.

Lane. Stoney Street in Nottingham was not so fortunate: 'The Association declined pointing out a Minister for Stoney Street, or answering the queries, till the next association.' This response may be due to the disagreements in the church at that time, which, as we shall see, the association took a hand in seeking to resolve.

Following the churches, came business from other connexional institutions, the academy, and the Itinerant Fund. Here money was apportioned to various situations, and advice given: 'The Ministers in Yorkshire were requested to afford to Nantwich all the help in their power the ensuing year, their expenses to be paid out of the Itinerant Fund.'[89] After dealing with two issues relating to trust deeds, the session closed by dealing with 'Miscellaneous Cases'. Here issues were addressed ranging from disagreements in churches as when 'Brethren Jarvis Miller, J. Bennett, and J. Newberry, were appointed to visit the friends in Stoney Street and endeavour to prevail upon them to come to amicable adjustment of their differences with their former friends', to concern over the rules of the association.[90] The early decades of the nineteenth century saw the multiplication of organisations in the Connexion, and the increasing length of agendas reflects this emerging denominational structure.

Institutional Development

Public Institutions

It was the emergence of these new priorities and goals in Nonconformist religious culture that affected the structure and growth of movements like the New Connexion. In the 1840 letter *Christian Exertion*, Pike identified the lack of money as a major problem facing the Connexion: 'there is too much backwardness to part with money for the sake of the Redeemer's cause; and when contributions are made, too much of a disposition to make them with a stinted not a liberal hand... Hence the want of means for carrying on with zeal and spirit our public institutions.'[91]

It was these 'public institutions' that constituted one of the emergent areas. In 1808, an Aged Ministers' Fund was established; its scope was a little wider than the title might suggest. It had three stated aims: to help 'aged and decaying ministers' who were unable to support themselves; to help churches that have ministers, 'but are incapable of making them, comfortable'; and to give help to small and poor churches who were unable to bear the whole cost of ministerial supply.[92] This endeavour was chiefly supported by the churches in Lincolnshire; it assisted men in churches and enabled some congregations to get ministerial aid. It became more widely known through appeals for funds in the *Repository*. In 1810 concern was expressed because opportunities to establish new causes were not being explored due to lack of finance. In an attempt to address this, the association in London that year proposed that a fund 'expressly devoted to meet the expences of attempts that might

---

[89] *Minutes* (1818), p. 15.
[90] *Minutes* (1818), p. 16.
[91] J.G. Pike, 'Christian Exertion', *Minutes* (1840), p. 39.
[92] *GBR* 5 (1808), p. 265.

be made to spread the gospel, or to revive it where it had decayed'.[93] The first use of this 'Itinerant Fund' was to finance a minister to visit several old General Baptist churches in Lincolnshire that were in difficulty. The Fund was limited in what it could do through lack of money; this is not surprising if Castle Donnington was in any way typical of churches in the Connexion.

> Collection for the Itinerant Fund. The ch not having collected for this fund for several years, and it being in an exhausted state at the Association B$^{rn\cdot}$ Bakewell and Bennett advanced £2 and B^r Oldershaw one pound. This was stated to the church and it was concluded to make a collection as soon as convenient and repay these B^{rn}.[94]

In 1821 the fund became 'The General Baptist Home Missionary Society' and was administered under the aegis of an association committee; the financial responsibility was devolved to districts and a committee appointed by each local conference. The object was to 'aid attempts to introduce and establish the gospel and the General Baptist Interest where they are not yet established; but that it afford occasional assistance towards sending ministers to visit decaying or disorganised Churches'.[95] Thirteen years later concern was expressed that work with small churches was robbing the society of its effectiveness. 'Whatever sympathy we may and ought to feel for those churches situated in villages, who are not able to support a regular ministry, yet it ought to be our great object to direct our labours and employ our resources in those places which are likely to be the most productive.'[96] It was acknowledged as a 'great pity' that they had not been able to establish a work in places like Sheffield, Leeds and Liverpool. 'There are thousands in these towns, who are living without God and without hope in the world. And there is little doubt but many would unite themselves with us in Christian fellowship, were our doctrines and discipline more generally known.'[97]

In 1810 the Derby General Baptist Religious Tract Society was formed. Its object was 'the gratuitous distribution of tracts'.[98] According to Adam Taylor, there was for many years an annual meeting of delegates from various Sunday schools. At some stage this merged with the Tract Society and became 'The Tract and Lord's Day School Society, and Juvenile Magazine'. In 1825, Joseph Winks, a publisher of tracts and Sunday school materials, who was also a powerful advocate for evangelistic activity, suggested applying the profits from the publications of this society to the home mission. Also contributing to denominational identity and acting as a channel of news and information within the movement were its

---

[93] Taylor, *History*, II, p. 458.
[94] Castle Donnington Church Book, 1 August 1819.
[95] *Minutes*, (1821), p. 21.
[96] Richard Ingham and Hugh Hunter 'Report on the Home Mission', *GBRM* (1835), p. 53.
[97] 'Report on the Home Mission', *GBRM* (1835), p. 54.
[98] Taylor, *History*, II, p. 465.

periodicals, *The General Baptist Magazine* 1798–1800, *The General Baptist Repository* 1802–21, *The General Baptist Repository, and Missionary Observer* 1822–53, which became the *General Baptist Magazine, Repository and Missionary Observer*, 1854-9, and subsequently, *The General Baptist Magazine and Missionary Observer*, 1860–63, and then in its final form *The General Baptist Magazine*. From 1822 the publications were managed and financially supported by the Connexion as they sometimes ran at a loss. The publications provided religious instruction, discussion of doctrinal issues and more general reading. The 'Missionary Observer' that was included gave news and information about the General Baptist Missionary Society.[99]

Another major contributor to denominational identity and consciousness was the formation of an academy for training ministers. Uniquely for Baptists the academy was an instrument of the Connexion and a denominational institution. Bryan Wilson argues that once the concept of training for leadership is acknowledged then 'a step to denominationalism has been taken'.[100] With the academy another structure was set in place that contributed to the growing denominational nature of the movement.

The development of denominational consciousness in terms of boundaries can be seen in a 'Case' brought to the 1802 association meeting in London. At this meeting Castle Donnington asked if the association could 'endeavour to form some rule, by which churches may be received into this Connexion, and when necessity requires it excluded from it'. The association did not feel a rigid boundary was possible: 'Ans. After due deliberation, the members of this association perceive such a diversity of circumstances in these cases, that they think no invariable rule can be laid down; but that it must be left in the same unrestricted state as in time past.'[101] This response reflects the openness and flexibility of the Connexion at this stage. Ease of entry and tolerance are two of Bryan Wilson's characteristics of a denomination.[102]

The above gives an indication of the extent to which the movement was developing an organisational structure and bureaucracy. The haphazard nature of the development reflects the energy and growth at this period. The proposals for re-organisation put before the association in 1835 attempted to correct this and limit the 'proliferation of Institutions'. Clause 17 said 'that no public institution shall hereafter be commenced in the Connexion without the previous knowledge, consent and approbation of an annual meeting'.[103]

---

[99] Rosemary Taylor, 'Early Baptist Periodicals 1790–1865', *Baptist Quarterly* 27.2 (April, 1977), pp. 55, 59.

[100] Wilson, *Patterns of Sectarianism*, p. 34.

[101] *Minutes* (1835), p. 30.

[102] Bryan Wilson (ed.), *Patterns of Sectarianism: Organisation and Ideology in Social and Religious Movements* (London: Heinemann, 1967), p. 25.

[103] *Minutes*, (1835), p. 30.

Missionary Society

The formation of the Missionary Society also played an important role in uniting the Connexion, providing a focus for its energy and activity, and it contributed in a significant way to the Connexion's denominational identity. Inspired by the example of the Particular Baptists who had founded the Baptist Missionary Society in 1792, in 1795 the conference at Leicester enquired of Samuel Pearce of Cannon Street, Birmingham, 'whether the General Baptist Churches would be allowed to send one Minister of their own Connexion on the same foundation, provided our churches in general contribute to the Fund'. At the following conference at Smalley on 26 May 1795 the matter was raised again: 'Ought we not to encourage our Churches to exert themselves in this business as soon as can be made convenient?' The question was raised about the wisdom of uniting with the Particular Baptists 'whose sentiments are so different to our own'. But as Pearce, who played a leading role in the infant society, did not reply, the matter was referred 'till a future Opportunity', and the opportunity of working together was lost.[104]

The success of the Particular Baptist venture brought pressure on the Connexion to form its own missionary society. J.G. Pike was the driving force behind this, the idea having at first met with resistance. The association meetings of 1802 and 1809 had felt that 'the present state of our Connexion' did not warrant it. Between 1814 and 1815 the idea of forming a New Connexion 'auxiliary' to the Baptist Missionary Society was mooted. This idea was rejected by Andrew Fuller who doubted whether the two denominations could unite.[105]

By 1816 attitudes had changed; the annual association meeting at Boston saw an 'almost unanimous vote passed recommending such a measure'. Pike was appointed secretary—a post he occupied until his death. In 1817, he wrote the association letter, 'Scriptural Motives for Exerting Ourselves Vigorously to Spread the Gospel Among the Heathen'. After giving a theological and scriptural basis for mission, Pike resorted to the theological identity of General Baptists in order to drive his appeal home: 'Shame upon us, if the pious Calvinist, who believes that, with respect to many, all effort is useless, should be all zeal and fervour; while our hearts remain contracted with selfishness, or chilled as with the icy hand of Spiritual death.' It was their 'Duty' as professed followers of 'The Lamb', as 'part of the church of Christ', to act in this matter.[106]

J.G. Pike's biography is full of references to the vigorous effort and extent of his missionary journeys promoting the cause of the work. His travelling and preaching contributed, in a significant way, to the emerging denominational identity, and had an integrative function, uniting the denomination around the cause. In 1822 he became joint editor of the *General Baptist Repository* providing the 'Missionary

---

[104] 'Minutes of the Monthly Conferences', *Transactions of the Baptist Historical Society* 5 (1916–17), pp. 115-126.

[105] Pike and Pike, *Memoir and Remains of J.G. Pike*, p. 12.

[106] *Minutes* (1817), pp. 27-29.

Intelligence'. He was also the author of the letter on *Christian Exertion* circulated in 1839. This was again a plea for involvement in mission.

Alongside the mission there was one other dominant structure and area of activity within the Connexion—that was the rise and development of Sunday school work. A commitment, such as the Sunday school, absorbed a vast amount of energy within the Connexion; the question of their effectiveness will be dealt with when we look at evangelism within the Connexion. Here we note that in terms of personnel, the Sunday school was the major organisation in the movement. With the Sunday school came a whole infrastructure of leaders' and teachers' meetings, of 'Unions', and events at a local and national level. The effect of this was to further erode the insularity of churches and help to develop that inter church co-operation which is characteristic of denominationalism.

Reorganisation

A Plan of Union

Adam Taylor noted that as the eighteenth century closed the structure of the organisation went through 'a considerable though silent change'.[107] Part of this silent change was the firming up of custom and tradition into established practice. There were problems with the leadership of the academy for training ministers, and the proliferation of organisations. These were a reflection of the emerging denominational structure which required greater denominational control. Concern over centralised control can be seen in the conversations that took place about 'Unions' and 'Connexions'. The desire for central control found a voice in an annual letter of 1820, 'Connexional Union and its duties', by William Pickering, and the letter of 1826, 'Unity of Connexional Exertion', by Adam Taylor, and in 1835, 'The formation of Christian Churches' by Richard Ingham.

The justification for denominational structures is to be found in the proposals for reorganisation that were brought to the 1835 assembly by Richard Ingham. While recognising that such formations were 'optional', and that, 'though the New Testament does not expressly enjoin the formation of such Unions, yet it seems to countenance their formation and existence'. Such unions, he argued, were valuable for pragmatic reasons.[108] In his recommendations, Ingham was seeking to hold together divergent tensions within the movement. On the one hand was the desire for independence and autonomy; on the other, the desire for Connexional authority which required a degree of surrender of independence to the denominational body. These tensions were reflected in the proposals for restructuring of 1835 which went to great lengths to preserve the autonomy of the local church:

> ...the Association shall not interfere with the private independence or internal government of any individual church, nor intermeddle in any affairs which do not

---

[107] Taylor, *History*, II, p. 328.
[108] *Minutes* (1835), p. 26.

affect the conditions of the Union and the character of the body; or, if interference in any case be expedient, it shall be only in the way of advice and recommendation. That the Association shall have the power to exercise a kind of friendly superintendence over the churches...and to give them advice, admonition, and exhortation, as the case may require.[109]

The phrases 'advice and recommendation' and 'a kind of friendly superintendence' seem to lack the power that would make effective connexional activity possible. There was considerable discussion about the proposed changes.[110] Article 7, which dealt with the power of the association to receive into the Connexion and the 'right to inspect, advise, admonish, exhort, and reprove, and also to suspend and exclude from the Connexion reprehensible, offending, and incorrigible churches', presented problems to some churches.[111] Such powers did not sit comfortably with strong independency. The first draft of the regulations met with considerable resistance from the churches, who, in Wood's words, had a 'jealous care' for their 'scriptural independence'.[112] 'As a church we have supported the various institutions of the Connexion and feel disposed still to do so; but we disapprove of any change in the name or any alteration in the constitution of the Connexion as settled in the 1770', said the Castle Donnington church in response to the proposals.[113] This response apart, there seems to have been a desire for a stronger denominational influence and identity. Francis Beardsall felt that 'the mistaken view of *independence* has been, and still continues to be, the chief cause of the want of success in the Home Mission' and that 'when the vital principle of union, with the love of Christ, is more generally diffused throughout our Connexion, we shall see the good pleasure of the Lord to prosper in our hands'.[114] He argued that it was lack of corporate activity that had contributed to the difficulty of getting men to take on the secretaryship of the Home Mission. 'Until the independency of churches is better understood, and a more cordial disposition to co-operate prevails, no man, I will venture to say, would keep office for many months.'[115] Joseph Jarrom, a senior minister in the Connexion and former tutor of the academy, said the following year, 'I fear the Connexion has suffered, and is suffering still, from what I hope to give no offence in calling, mere cavilling, in the indulgence of a morbid sensibility of independence.' He argued that, as in the case of every individual member of a church, each one of these churches must concede a portion of its independence.[116] But committed as it was to 'unanimity' in decision making, the revised constitution adopted in 1838 did little to

---

[109] *Minutes* (1835), pp. 28-29.
[110] Wood, *History*, p. 276.
[111] Richard Ingham, 'A Plan of Union', *GBRM* (1835), p. 289.
[112] Wood, *History*, p. 237; *GBRM* (1835), p. 450.
[113] Castle Donnington Church Book, 15 May 1836.
[114] F. Beardsall, 'Proposed Plan for the Management of the Home Mission', *GBRM* (1835), p. 93.
[115] *GBRM* (1835), p. 94.
[116] *GBRM* (1836), p. 56.

extend the powers of the association.[117] The growing institutionalisation of the movement is reflected in the comment in the proposals 'that the Association shall not be drained by Committees'.[118] The modified proposals were finally adopted in 1838. After this there was little major structural alteration to the Connexion until the union of 1891. Looking back, Thomas Cook saw the reorganisation of the Connexion in a negative way: 'After that period', he said, 'various changes came into operation which, I think, have retarded the progress of the General Baptist denomination...'[119]

As the Connexion moved towards the middle of the century, the prevailing attitude was one of optimism. This sense of optimism was reflected in *Christian Exertion*, J.G. Pike's 'Letter to the Churches' for 1840. He said of this period it was one 'in which our churches have been thus steadily increasing in numbers' and that 'the improvement in our places of worship has not been less considerable'.[120] It was an age of church building and improvement, 'many commodious meeting houses, some of them large and spacious have been erected. Nearly 80 have been built or purchased, and thirty more materially changed.'[121] This spirit of optimism, soon to be challenged, concealed tensions generated by the growth of the movement.

Connexional Authority

As we have noted there was in the Connexion a tension between connexional authority and local autonomy. We see a demonstration of this in the situation at Castle Donnington. In 1820 the church had divided over the minister's conduct. A small number left and set up another congregation. The church turned for help to the local conference, and three ministers were appointed to help resolve the issue. Connexional authority could not be imposed: 'Some letters were received from the minority signifying that they were not willing to submit the case to the arbitration of ministers but were willing to have their advice in the case.'[122] The church met with the ministers, William Felkin was in the chair, and the record in the church book gives an insight into the way he went about resolving the issue. 'He first enquired what was the object of the meeting, to which the Majority replied, it was to promote a union, the other assented. Mr Felkin then proposed to settle the business without investigation and enforced it by various arguments.'. A vote was then taken after which 'the meeting then adjourned and the noes were desired to stop with the minister for conversation. The neuters also stopped with them.' The content of that meeting is not recorded; we may assume that they experienced the full force of Felkin's 'advice and recommendation' and 'kind of friendly superintendence' (!) for

---

[117] *GBRM* (1835), p. 290.
[118] *GBRM* (1835), p. 290.
[119] Thomas Cook, *Preacher Pastor Mechanic: Memoir of the late Mr Samuel Deacon of Barton* (Leicester: W. Buck late Winkes, 1888), p. 193.
[120] J.G. Pike, 'Christian Exertion', letter, *GBRMO* (1840), p. 39.
[121] Pike, 'Christian Exertion', letter, *GBRMO* (1840), p. 39.
[122] Castle Donnington Church Book, 22 October 1820.

when the church met again in the afternoon we read that there were only six of the seceding group still standing out against reunion. Felkin drew the proceedings to a close with the adoption of the following proposition:

> Tht (sic) everything which has transpired respecting this unpleasant business be totally buried, and that no part of it be ever brought forward again on any occasion—And tht (sic) the two parts of the church shall immediately unite together; and that every thing respecting the Minister, the occasional preachers, the Church officers and all other things be considered as exactly in the same state as before the commencement of these unpleasant affairs and that in future it be the endeavour of the whole church to conduct all its affairs in the Spirit and according to the rules of holy Religion—And tht those six individuals who have signified their dissent from this mode of settlement should endeavour to aquiesce (sic) in this settlement & if they find they cannot do it that they peaceably leave the church.

> Signed W. Felkin
> T. Stevenson
> T. Orton.[123]

The Connexion had gone to Castle Donnington because they had been invited; they had no right of access. But the need was felt by some for greater authority to be vested in the Connexion.

The growing strength of these demands can be seen in the resolution passed in 1850 in which a church in Leicester was declared 'disorderly' for receiving members without any dismissal or recommendation from the Carley Street church.[124] The limited role of the association is seen again at Beeston in 1841, when the pastor resigned and, taking a number of members with him, formed a church.[125] The seceding group applied for admission to the Connexion; their 'case' was deferred to the following year and Jos. Goadby, A. Smith and J.G. Pike, were appointed to 'investigate the affair and endeavour to reconcile the parties'. The report of this group was something of a compromise: 'Beeston scarcely appears sufficiently populass (sic) to allow of continued prosperity for two churches of the same denomination: yet we cannot advise any attempts for a hasty reunion... We now cordially recommend that the second church be immediately received by the Association as one of the Churches of the Union.'[126] In effect they endorsed the situation; it demonstrates the extent to which the annual association lacked institutional teeth; all it could do was bark.

By 1866, the bark was becoming a bite—the denomination was taking the initiative. A committee was formed as the outcome of a case from Archdeacon Lane, Leicester, to deal with the 'premature and unwise formation of new churches'. In future 'dissentients before they secede' should bring their case to this committee for

---

[123] *Castle Donnington Church Book*, 31 October 1820.
[124] *Minutes* (1850), p. 32.
[125] *Minutes* (1841), pp. 7, 38.
[126] *Minutes* (1842), p. 27.

'mediation'. If the committee approved, then there would be 'no hesitation in receiving that church into the Connexion'. If they went ahead without the sanction of the committee they would not be recognised.[127] There were other changes. One writer, in a letter in the *General Baptist Magazine* in 1860, noted that churches no longer sought or requested the advice of the association or conference in the choice of a minister.[128] Churches in the Connexion were becoming more independent.

The annual association had originally been an organisation that supported the local conferences, providing a wider forum for issues raised by a fast expanding movement. It had provided support for ministry, planned the evangelistic strategy and helped to develop a literature for the movement. But organisations have a way of generating their own momentum and as the Connexion moved into the second half of the century it was faced with the need to cope not only with changing social structures and economic conditions but with the growth of its own institutional life—hence the need for mediation. Vastly improved travel and communications networks had emerged. As a result, there came an even greater denominational consciousness and tightening of boundaries as communication became easier. In 1865 a 'Board of Reference' for pastors and churches was set up which sought to make changes in pastorate easier.[129] Centrally organised, consisting of four senior ministers, it was a long way removed from the discussions in conference and the early associations about the stationing of ministers where the prime concern had been the evangelistic effectiveness of the movement.

Boundary Concerns

Baptism

The tensions generated by a growing denominationalism are reflected in two boundary disputes. The first concerned baptism. Baptism of believers entailed a view of the church as a bounded set, that is a closed community with a definite boundary, which is only crossed through baptism. Here the issue is not the theology of the act, so much as the function baptism plays in defining the boundaries of the church. Theoretically, baptism was a condition of membership and necessary before one could become a member of a New Connexion church. 'It is the indispensable duty of all who repent and believe the gospel, to be baptized by immersion in water, *in order to be initiated in a church state; and that no person ought to be received into the church without submission to that ordinance.*'[130] Baptism was seen by Dan Taylor as a door to active membership of a church:

> Baptism is an important duty, as it is enjoined by the Lord of Glory, and enforced by his own example, and the examples of all the primitive Christians, and by many other solemn considerations, yet is far from being the whole of duty. It is only as

---

[127] *Minutes* (1866), p. 36.
[128] 'Conditions of Connexional Union', *GBM* (1860), p. 148.
[129] *Minutes* (1865), p. 37.
[130] Taylor, *History*, II, pp. 141-42, italics added.

the porch in the house of God, where his family are all to be employed as capacities and circumstances admit, for the honour of his great name, and promotion of his interest.[131]

It was also, as we shall see, made a condition of taking the Lord's Supper. This understanding of baptism as a condition of membership was common to both Particular and General Baptist churches.

The boundaries of other churches were more open; membership of a Methodist class, and hence of a society, was open to anyone who 'desired to flee the wrath to come'. Thus from a Baptist perspective there were those in some churches who were not in a true 'church state'. This made for difficult relationships in the growing fraternity of the Evangelical Revival. The Connexion could not require compliance, although, as we have seen, it did ask for assent to the 'Six Articles' on admission. But there was a theological laxity, characteristic of denominations. One result of this was the emergence of an ongoing discussion about the nature of membership both within the Connexion and Particular Baptist churches. Should membership be 'open' to those who had not been baptised, or closed, reserved for believers only?

In the early part of the nineteenth century we see the beginnings of a dissolution of the close relationship between baptism and membership. The church at Archdeacon Lane opted for a individualistic approach to baptism, breaking the link between baptism and membership: 'Agreed that the Church thinks it thare (sic) duty to Baptise any Person that may be thought to be a real Christian though they may not enter into the church.'[132] In 1812, when one 'Creighton', a Methodist, requested baptism two brethren were 'requested to take an opportunity for conversing with him' and it was agreed to at the following church meeting.[133] This position was revised in 1827 when they decided 'that we shall not hereafter baptise any persons who do not intend to join our church or some other Baptist church'.[134] In the middle of the century, Matilda Seeds, making application for membership of the church at New Lenton, said, 'immersion is the proper mode of admission into the church'.[135]

A major change in the role of baptism came in the third quarter of the century, with a move away from baptism as a condition of membership, to a placing of it in the sphere of personal conviction. With baptisms held indoors and mid-week, even the act itself was privatised. Thomas Cook in 1877 complained that 'Baptisms and executions are now sometimes placed on a par—a few only being admitted as witnesses.'[136]

---

[131] Dan Taylor, *Our Saviour's Commission To His Ministers Explained and Improved: The Substance of a Sermon delivered at Canterbury and in Worship Street London. At the Administration of the Ordinance of Baptism* (Leeds, n.d.).

[132] Archdeacon Lane Minute Book No. 1, 25 December 1806. Leicester Record Office. N/B/179/101.

[133] Archdeacon Lane Minute Book No. 1, 15 November 1812.

[134] Archdeacon Lane Minute Book No. 1, 21 January 1827.

[135] Beeston Experience Books. Nottingham Record Office. BP/10/14/1-6

[136] Thomas Cook, 'Baptisms and Baptistries', *GBM* (1877), p. 100.

When Clifford opened his church at Westbourne Park, Paddington, baptism was not required for membership.[137] But, as in many other things, Clifford and his church were exceptions, and not all were ready for such changes. On 12 February 1879, the church at Friar Lane, Leicester, had placed before it the following recommendation from the deacons: that while baptism was a 'duty' there was no 'Scripture authority for making this rite a condition of membership' and that 'those who sincerely fail to see its obligation' should no longer find a 'bar to their reception into our Church fellowship'.[138] Even if the deacons were ready for open membership the church was not and after being referred back for two months the proposal was defeated. Ashby notes that it was another forty years before a comparable resolution was passed, and sixty before it became effective. The concern about baptism came to a head in the discussion which followed the publication of the circular letter of 1882. In this letter, 'The Conditions of Church Membership', the author, J.C. Jones, argued that *'separate local societies are but fractional parts* of the One Universal Church',[139] that membership of the 'Universal Church' was *'the voluntary and hearty surrender of a penitent and believing soul to the government of the risen and exalted Saviour'*, and that was all that was required. The teaching about baptism as the door of the church was, he said, a 'palpable and glaring error'.[140] For Jones, baptism was not a church ordinance, and the practice of proposing and visiting candidates had *'not the smallest scriptural authority'*.[141] Baptism, while a 'duty and privilege', was, he argued, an ordinance 'attended to as a personal duty independently of the recognition of the church'.[142] The letter by Jones indicates the way in which an individualistic view of the church was emerging. As may be imagined, Jones' apology for open fellowship was disputed. J. Fletcher took up the defence of Article 6: 'It means that neither we nor our fathers have interpreted the New Testament as we should. It means that Dan Taylor, and those who signed the sixth article above named, were utterly wrong in their view of Christ's teaching, and that Baptists generally have been wrong from the beginning until now.'[143]

Clifford stayed out of the debate until its conclusion. When he did get involved he adopted a pragmatic approach, pointing out that, to his best knowledge, there were only five churches in the Connexion that had adopted the practice; urging a care with language, he acknowledged that, while the issue was not one of numbers, it was worthwhile to know the 'facts'. He estimated five out of 189 churches, and 400 out of 25,000 members were involved in the practice of open membership.[144] He claimed that open fellowship churches were widespread among the Particulars: 'I judge, from

---

[137] Briggs, *English Baptists*, p. 53.
[138] Douglas Ashby, *Friar Lane: The Story of Three Hundred Years* (London: Carey Kingsgate Press. 1951), p. 76.
[139] *General Baptist Year Book* (1882), p. 3.
[140] *General Baptist Year Book* (1882), p. 5.
[141] *General Baptist Year Book* (1882), p. 9.
[142] *General Baptist Year Book* (1882), pp. 10-11.
[143] J. Fletcher, 'Conference on the Conditions of Membership', *GBM* (1883), p. 49.
[144] *GBM* (1883), p. 52.

my extended enquiries, more than two out of three of the leading churches of the Particular Baptist type are based on open fellowship... [T]hey are Baptist not because there is not an unimmersed person in the "fellowship", but because the teaching aim, and ideal, are framed to secure an intelligent and unconstrained recognition of the will of the Lord Jesus concerning baptism.'[145] He drew attention to the fact that a note was added to the *Year Book* in 1870 to the effect that not all the churches in the Connexion believed that baptism was a necessary condition of membership. That note had remained unchallenged until 1882. Interpretation and tradition were not, he suggested, the main question; he argued that the main point at issue was 'the relation of baptism to the church'.[146] After examining passages relating to baptism and the church in the New Testament, he said, 'But in no part of the Gospels, Acts, or Epistles, is it described as a condition of admission to the church. Uniformly and exclusively it is prescribed as a solemn transaction between the soul and the Saviour.'[147] For Clifford, baptism was 'a valuable public avowal of inward conviction in reference to Christ and His kingdom—a sign of subjection to Him... [I]t has no declared relation whatever to church fellowship.'[148] In reference to Peter and Cornelius, and Philip and the Ethiopian, Clifford said, '*Baptism, for both is a question of the soul and Christ; and not of the soul and the Church.*'[149] Given the extent to which Clifford placed baptism in the sphere of personal responsibility, it is little wonder that he espoused open fellowship: 'I dare not take part in an act of rejection from our Christian society of one soul that honestly and sincerely says to Christ, by the inspiration of the Father, and from a living conviction, "thou art the Christ, the Son of the living God".'[150] But, as John Briggs points out, there were inconsistencies in Clifford's position; while willing to leave baptism to individual conscience, his church constitution said that 'The obligation to be baptised springs out of the relation of the believer to the Church.'[151] There was, towards the end of the nineteenth century, a growing trend towards the removal of barriers, and a more open form of church membership.

Lord's Supper

Related to baptism was a second boundary question dealing with the nature of the church. In the debate surrounding the Lord's Supper, the issue was not the nature of the elements but the condition for admission to the table. Should the table be open to all or restricted to those in membership? It was decided at Castle Donnington that 'Friend Smith a friend of Ilkins[on] wishes to sit down with us at the lords supper. It is agreed he should today but not in future without a letter of Dismission from Ilkinson

---

[145] *GBM* (1883), p. 54.
[146] *GBM* (1883), p. 55.
[147] *GBM* (1883), p. 89.
[148] *GBM* (1883), p. 85.
[149] *GBM* (1883), pp. 86-87.
[150] *GBM* (1883), p. 92.
[151] Briggs, *English Baptists*, p. 53.

(sic) Church.'[152] The two year old church at Market Harborough received an application from 'a Miss Frances Green a member of the Independent church at Market Harboro' for permission to partake with us of the Lord's Supper, without being baptised'. After mentioning this to a visiting preacher, 'He advised us before adopting a practice not known in the G.B. churches to consult by letter two or three of the elder Ministers on the subject.' The church wrote to Pike of Derby, Goadby of Ashby and Thomas Stevenson of Leicestershire. On 25 October 1832 the church decided to admit members of 'Paedobaptist' churches on the following conditions: that application be made to and approved of by the church; that such application be confined to communion only, not membership. The concession did not apply to those 'who believe Baptism by immersion to be a positive Duty, but who continue to live in the neglect of such duty from any unworthy motive'. Applicants were 'expected to worship regularly with us, not only by forming a part of the congregation, but by becoming Subscribers to the Interest and contributing to our expenses according to their Ability &c &c'.[153] This verges on making a financial contribution a condition of sharing in the Lord's Supper! When, three days later, Thomas Stevenson 'came to preach and to administer the Ordinance of the Lord's Supper this day accompanied by Bro S. Hull of Leicester and although Miss Green was permitted to commune with us yet they both expressed their decided disapprobation of the step we had taken in our resolution of Oct. 25th. respecting opening the communion to unbaptised persons.'[154] Even communion with baptised members of other churches in the Connexion was frowned upon. The reorganisation proposals of 1835 deemed as irregular, 'allowing the members of sister churches that are near frequently to sit down with them at the table of the Lord, without the knowledge of the church to which they belong'.[155]

But towards the middle of the century things were changing; there was a growing practice of open communion. Although in some places it was bitterly contested (as at St Mary's Baptist Church, Norwich, where it was only settled by law[156]), the practice grew more widespread. In 1861 Spurgeon gave the trend the considerable weight of his influence; the trust deeds of the Metropolitan Tabernacle allowed a profession of faith to be the basis of admission to communion, even without baptism by immersion. The most common means of opening the table was for applicants to make application to the minister. So at Archdeacon Lane, one of the leading churches in the Connexion, decided on 21 March 1848 that while not changing the nature of the church it would 'continue to be wholly Baptist—composed only of persons who have been baptised on a profession of faith in Jesus Christ'; the church would, for the sake of 'unity' and 'love to all who love the the Ld Jesus Ct. in sincerity', open the communion table. This was on the

---

[152] Castle Donnington Church Book, 15 March 1812
[153] Market Harborough Church Book, 25 October 1832. Leicester Record Office. N/B/215/2.
[154] Market Harborough Church Book, 28 October 1832.
[155] Ingham, 'A Plan of Union', *GBRM* (1835), p. 291.
[156] See Payne, *Baptist Union*, pp. 87-88.

condition that after investigation the church was satisfied of their 'Xtn experience and obtaining what appears to them reasonable evidence of sincere piety and conscientiousness'.[157] In 1843, the church at Hugglescote gave its minister a free hand: 'Brother Orton is allowed to permit any person to take Ordinance with us of whose piety he is satisfied altho' such person is not a Baptist.'[158] Other churches decided differently: 'In reference to non members of the church communing with us it is Resolved. That no member of the church be allowed to invite any person being resident in the town for 3 Months to sit down to the ordinance of the Lord's supper without the concurrence of the officers of the Church.'[159] In 1883, 'after some discussion, it was resolved that a note be appended to article 6 intimating that the Association adopted open communion and that most of the churches have free communion and some of them practice open fellowship.'[160] By 1889, Archdeacon Lane's practice of open communion needed tidying up, and the church meeting resolved

> That a record be kept of those friends habitually communing with us at the Lord's Supper who are not baptised or in full fellowship with the Church and that they be supplied with Communion Cards, also that in future any who are professed Christians whether Members of other Churches or not who wish to share in the privileges of Communion at the Lord's Table be seen and reported to the church by the minister or Deacons and if suitable be accepted as communicants and be enrolled on the Church Register in a separate list provided for that purpose. This arrangement does not give the right to participate in the management of the Church Business as the deeds require such to be baptised Believers.[161]

In a church of 330 members this resulted in four names being placed on the list at the next meeting. It is also an indication that, although an issue hotly debated, it did not involve large numbers of people, and that, given safeguards such as those above, there was little threat to the fundamental nature of the church as was feared.

A New Connexion?

By 1840 all the major institutions of the Connexion were in place, and the committees and boards that followed were further expressions of denominational activity. In 1850 a Denominational Fund was established for the relief of 'those ministers who may be incapacitated by age or infirmity from statedly exercising the ministerial or pastoral office, and their widows'.[162] 1871 saw the formation of an

---

[157] Archdeacon Lane Church Book No. 3, 21 March 1848. Leicester Record Office. N/B/179/103.

[158] Minutes Hugglescote, 18 December 1843.

[159] Castle Donnington Church Book, 11 June 1860.

[160] *General Baptist Year Book* (1883), p. 30.

[161] Archdeacon Lane Church Nook No. 4, 9 January 1889. Leicester Record Office. N/B/179/106.

[162] 'Aged and Infirm Ministers Fund', *GBRM* (1850), p. 475.

'Arbitration Committee' for 'the friendly settlement of any point on which a difference may have arisen',[163] and in 1888 a 'Federation Board' to assist settlement in smaller churches. The latter sought to group small village churches who 'give up a portion of their independence for the purpose of securing a more efficient pastoral oversight'.[164] The Baptist Union had in 1887 set up a board of Introduction and Consultation which addressed procedures for the recognition of ministers for the Union's accredited list. John Briggs observes, 'The independency of the local church survived but with the assistance of national institutions: a new partnership was being forged between the local church exercising its freedom in calling a pastor and the Baptist Union offering recognition of that pastor's ministerial status and ever more often providing part of the salary, together with security for the Pastor in retirement.'[165]

The history of the New Connexion from its inception to the late 1830s and early 1840s reveals a process of denominational emergence. Key elements in the organisation of the Connexion were the conference and annual association, but its genius lay in its unity of spiritual experience, wedded to its congregational discipline. The individual elements were not new; the organisation of individual churches had much in common with Particular Baptists in terms of the authority of the scriptures, the role of the church meeting and the nature of the ministry. Even the Arminian theology of the Connexion was not such as to exclude Particular Baptists from its pulpits or from ministry among its constituents. The nature of their organisation reflected that of the Old General Baptists who had also held a regular annual assembly.

If anything, it was the local conference, essentially spiritual and evangelistic in nature, that was distinctive to the movement. It was the way in which this came together with the other elements that gave the organisation its distinguishing nature. But even the local conference was not a universal form within the Connexion. The structure seemed to work well for the Midland churches, and those who had their origin in the evangelistic work of Dan Taylor. It could be argued that churches that transferred into the Connexion brought with them other patterns of associating and that the spiritual fellowship and commitment to mission, enshrined in the early conferences, was not easily transferred. As the number of churches in the Connexion grew this aspect played a less significant role and had the effect of gradually diminishing the distinctiveness of the movement.

The very term 'Connexion' identified a particular way of relating together. This sense of mutual dependence and commitment to mission found its focus in the conference and assembly. As we have seen, the origin and purpose of the conference was the planning and organisation of the evangelistic work of the churches. It was, in nature, a mission structure. As the organisation grew from the sixteen churches of 1770 to the 220 churches and chapels of 1840, and the 275 churches, chapels and

---

[163] *Minutes* (1871), p. 13.
[164] George H. Bennett, 'The Federation of Churches', *GBM* (1888), p. 184.
[165] Briggs, *English Baptists*, p. 93.

preaching places of 1890, greater effort had to be put into the maintenance of the movement. The role of the conferences shifted from that of mission to maintenance. The concerns of conference shifted from organising preachers and the initiation of new work to a 'mutual knowledge of the churches, sympathy and fellowship with them, a due care for their welfare and a readiness to assist them'.[166] This is a fellowship function and is concerned with maintenance. The larger the organisation grew the greater the need for support functions of this kind.

Part of the problem was that the power base remained firmly in the local church. As was said of the oldest conference in Leicester, they disclaimed 'all authority and everything dictatorial'. There was an ambivalence concerning conference and to some extent the annual assembly. The movement was connexional in nature and yet the corporate decision-making bodies, conferences and assembly had little power. There was the expectation that conference and the assembly would give direction to the movement, but the central control and organisation needed for this never developed. As we have noted, power was lodged in the hands of the people. The concerns raised by the reorganisation of the movement in the late 1820s and early 1830s was symptomatic of this tension between a growing desire for central control on the one hand and local autonomy on the other. Greater central organisation might have been desired but the infrastructure necessary in terms of personnel was never developed. It is doubtful that the churches would have acceded to it had it existed. Throughout its life, the Connexion never had a full-time employee; it was run by committees of ministers and laymen, and was never able to develop fully its denominational aspirations. There is a sense in which the New Connexion of General Baptists never was a Connexion—their origins lay in Independency, they operated on Independent principles, and the power of the local congregation was never fully submitted to a connexional interest.

---

[166] Adam Taylor, *GBR* 1 (1802), p. 22.

CHAPTER 4

'The middle sphere of life': Aspects of the Social and Demographic Background to the New Connexion

Adapting to the Age

At the time of the formation of the New Connexion something of a siege mentality prevailed in Nonconformity. The old dissenting bodies felt strongly the political and social inferiority enforced on them by the Corporation and Test Acts of 1661 and 1673. The Corporation Act requiring members of municipal bodies to take an oath of allegiance and the Lord's Supper according to the rites of the Church of England, together with the Test Act directed at Catholics; effectively shut Dissenters out from public office. The legislation was directed at influence and wealth, thus its main impact was on the more prosperous urban churches; poorer and rural churches were not so affected by it. The Toleration Act of 1689 did little to relieve Dissenters of their civil disabilities; and there was constant activity on their part during the eighteenth century for its repeal. A.D. Gilbert makes the observation concerning Dissent:

> The picture was of an increasingly demoralised, introverted movement, which, having lost much of its original social and cultural impetus, was being prevented by its elitist self-conceptions from fashioning for itself a new social base among the lower classes.[1]

The General Baptists reflected the interests and concerns of Old Dissent. 'For it must be confessed', said John Deacon, 'that both the Particular and the General Baptists in those days had so much buckram about them as to be able to strut foremost in company with any set of non-descripts in England'.[2]

For Deacon it was this sense of social separation and distance that contributed to the emergence of the New Connexion as a separate body, while General Baptists might 'reform some of the leading doctrines of the Gospel' and be 'respectable' yet 'they were grown somewhat formal; and their formality seemed to set up a barrier in the way of those, who had not previously in habits of intimacy with them'.[3]

The constituency of the New Connexion was different from that of Gilbert's 'Old Dissent'; interestingly, Gilbert's more recent observation concerning the inwardness

---

[1] Gilbert, *Religion and Society*, p. 16.
[2] *GBM* (1798), p. 360. Buckram was a stiffening agent in clothing.
[3] *GBM* (1798), p.158.

of Old Dissent is confirmed by Deacon, who said: 'Dissenters then did not much accustom themselves to preaching in villages, nor go out of their way to seek "the lost sheep of the house of Israel". It cannot therefore be a matter of surprise that these people did not at once break through every obstacle, and join a Dissenting Body.'[4] This he contrasted with the preachers of the Barton group of churches who, though their preaching was unsophisticated and 'their situations and connections in life were among the lower class of society', yet found acceptance with their hearers. The essential element for him was their own experience, 'they entered into the spirit of religion for they felt its power'.[5] J.R. Godfrey says that the preachers of the New Connexion 'belonged to the common people, earning their bread as servants, labourers, and artisans'.[6] John Deacon, giving an account of the start of the Diseworth church, noted that

> whoever would receive them enjoyed their benediction; and whatever place they could obtain to answer their purpose, presently became sanctified by the Gospel of Christ. Here a weaver's shop was the first place thus honoured.[7]

The effectiveness of the new movement needs to be set against a broader background. McLeod points out that there is little agreement as to the nature of the relationship between social and religious change.[8] The Church of England was singularly unprepared to cope with the rise in new industries and the shift of population to the towns. The period between 1740 and 1830 Gilbert describes as 'an era of disaster' for the Church of England.[9] The effects of pluralism and absenteeism left large areas of the population, especially those in the more remote country areas, without pastoral care. One of the difficulties which faced the Anglican Church in the eighteenth century was this growth of population and migration to new industrial areas. It put too much pressure on an outdated administrative system based on existing parishes. Some of the newer industrial areas had several thousand people living within a single parish. Manchester, for example, with a population of at least 20,000 in 1750 had only one parish church. John Deacon, writing of this period which saw the emergence of the New Connexion, levels his criticism at the character of Anglicanism which 'alone laid the foundation for dissatisfaction and dissent'.[10] While there was a degree of hyperbole in Deacon's claims, A.D. Gilbert argues convincingly that 'There was an important inverse relationship, in short, between the decline of "Church" religiosity and the proliferation of "Chapel"

---

[4] *GBM* (1798), p.158.
[5] *GBM* (1798), p.326
[6] Cook, *Preacher Pastor Mechanic*, p. 206.
[7] *GBM* (1798), p. 358.
[8] H. McLeod, *Religion and the Working Class in Nineteenth Century Britain* (London: Macmillan, 1984), p. 2.
[9] Gilbert, *Religion and Society*, p. 27.
[10] *GBM* (1798) 158.

communities...'[11] To explain the failure of the Church of England in terms of character and location is not the whole answer. The problem was not larger numbers turning to Dissent but larger numbers absenting themselves from any place of worship; in some of the communities of the later eighteenth- and early nineteenth-centuries there had developed patterns of life in which the church had no or little part to play. It could be argued that in some of these communities the church had never had an influence.[12]

Though the preachers of the New Connexion and the New Dissent went to many people, there were some they did not reach. 'The weakness of the Established Churches left a religious vacuum which was only sometimes filled by Nonconformity or by militant secularism.'[13] John Taylor, speaking of the period just prior to the beginnings of the New Connexion's work in Yorkshire, hints at this religious vacuum; he says of the area north east of Halifax, 'Indeed there was little knowledge then of any of the denominations of dissenters; and few of the common people knew what a dissenter meant. I rather question if the name of Baptist had ever been heard in the valley of Shibden'.[14]

A.D. Gilbert suggests that by 1740 there were habits of neglect going back several generations and embedded in the structure of many local communities. For common people, superstition and magic were influential. A belief in witches, devils and magic was widespread and still held considerable influence. In 1807 William Parmone was publicly admonished by the church at Hugglescote for 'having consulted with persons commonly called conjurers, when he was in some difficulty respecting his house having been brok and some of his goods gone...'[15] Several members of the Melbourne church were upbraided for having 'given way to a deceitful woman who pretended to tell them things that was to come for which several gave her money'. Such action was deemed 'Diabolical and deserving of the severest censure of the Church and if not convinc'd of the Evil and reclaim'd to be excluded from it [the church]'.[16]

The constituency of the Connexion seems to have been different from that of Old Dissent. It was among the rural lower classes that the Connexion recruited, but although rural, it was not agricultural workers that formed the basis of its membership.

---

[11] Gilbert, *Religion and Society*, p. 94.
[12] McLeod, *Religion and the Working Class*.
[13] McLeod, *Religion and the Working Class*, pp. 17-18.
[14] Adam Taylor, *Memoirs of Rev. John Taylor*, p. 4.
[15] Minutes of Hugglescote General Baptist Church, Leicester Record Office. Nb/150/1-3, 14 February 1808.
[16] Budge, *Records Most Material*, 25 December 1783.

A Rural Movement?
Rural Nature

The New Connexion had emerged as a rural movement, and this it remained, with a few notable exceptions, throughout its life. As late as 1851, only nine of the 135 New Connexion churches were to be found in the towns that were, according to the 1851 Census, 'chief manufacturing districts'. Two of these churches were in Sheffield. When speaking of the New Connexion, it is important not to confuse rural with agricultural. As will be shown, a majority of the New Connexion churches were situated in the small manufacturing towns and villages of the Midlands. These towns and villages had an industrial base although sited in a rural situation. The term semi-rural could be used to describe them. The following table gives the number of New Connexion churches at the approximate time of their commencement in relation to the size of town or village. The figures below are for the counties of Nottinghamshire, Leicestershire and Derbyshire. The figures were taken as near as possible to the foundation of the churches.[17]

Distribution of New Connexion Churches in Relation to Village Size, 1832–1856

Size of Village	Number of New Connexion Churches
0-199	4
200-399	9
400-599	5
600-999	11
1,000-4,999	39
5,000-12,00	9
City suburbs	2
City	5

Table 1

Some of these villages were later absorbed into the fast expanding suburbs of Nottingham and Leicester. It will be seen from the above that the Connexion was strongest in the larger industrial villages.

The movement was an expression of industrial rural Dissent. Alan Everitt in *The Pattern of Rural Dissent* notes that 70% of the chapels were in country areas.[18] He sees a relationship between the patterns of land ownership and the presence of

---

[17] Information on the size of village had been taken from the 1832 and 1853 edition of William White's *History and Gazetteer and Directory of Nottinghamshire*, his *History and Gazetteer of Leicestershire* (1846) and *Gazetteer of Lincolnshire* (1856). Also Curtis' *Topographical History of the county of Leicestershire* (1831).

[18] Alan Everitt, *The Pattern of Rural Dissent: The Nineteenth Century* (Department of English Local History Occasional Papers, Second Series No. 4; Leicester: Leicester University Press, 1972), p. 19

Dissent. 'The greater the tendency to subdivision of land, the greater also was the tendency to dissent', says M.R. Watts.[19] The demographic characteristics of the New Connexion support this contention. In the counties of Leicestershire, Nottinghamshire, and Lincolnshire, we find in the eighty-one small towns and villages where New Connexion churches and their branches existed, the pattern of ownership is as follows:

Land Ownership Patterns

Land held by		
a single owner	18	(22.22%)
most held by single owner	3	(3.70%)
two owners	6	(7.40%)
several	33	(40.74%)
numerous	21	(25.92%)

Table 2

It will be seen from the above that the majority of New Connexion churches (66.66%) in these three counties were to be found in 'open villages' in which land was in the control of numerous owners. The lack of Dissent in villages has been attributed to establishment resistance. But not all large landowners were opposed to Nonconformity. In Nottinghamshire, five of the eleven New Connexion churches were in villages owned by the Duke of Portland.

One feature concerning the location of churches is that very few were the sole Nonconformist church in the village.[20] It was these industrial villages, rather than the new developing towns, that provided the major contribution in terms of constituency for the Connexion.

Framework Knitting

The dominant industry of the villages and towns in which New Connexion churches were formed was framework knitting. The number and location of stocking frames in 1844 were listed by Felkin in his *A History of the Machine-Wrought Hosiery and Lace Manufactures*.[21] Frames were present in 25% of the towns and villages in which there was a New Connexion interest. In Leicestershire, Derbyshire and Nottinghamshire (counties in which the New Connexion was strongest), knitting frames were present in thirty-two of the forty-three villages for which churches and branches were listed in the annual returns of the Connexion (74%). Of these thirty-two towns or villages, twenty-eight had more than 100 frames (65%) and fourteen, more than 200 (32%). Everitt considers that fifty frames constituted an industrial

---

[19] Watts, *The Dissenters*, II, p. 22.
[20] Everitt, *Rural Dissent*, p. 29.
[21] W.A. Felkin. *A History of the Machine-Wrought Hosiery and Lace Manufactures* (London: Longman Green, 1867), pp. 465-68.

village. Twenty-nine of the forty-three villages or towns in Leicestershire, Derbyshire and Nottinghamshire fall into this category. If we take away the three major centres of Leicester, Derby and Nottingham, over 60% of the New Connexion chapels in these counties were situated in towns or villages in which framework knitting was a dominant industry.

The extent to which this industry influenced one church, Hinckley, can be gauged from the returns in the 'Non Parochial Registers'.[22] The minister, James Taylor, included the occupation of fathers when he registered the birth of their children.

Table of Occupations at Hinckley

Barber	1	Gardener	1
Baker	1	Labourer	10
Brickmaker	2	Laceworker	2
Bricklayer	2	Miller	2
Bleacher	2	Painter and Glazier	1
Butcher	1	Painter	1
Clock and Watchmaker	1	Point or Needlemaker	1
Carpenter	1	Setter up	1
Cordwainer	1	Shoemaker	14
Framework Knitter	80	Wheelwright	2
Framesmith	5	Woodworker	1
Farmer	1		

Table 3

Of the 144 births registered between 1822 and 1837, the occupations are as above. Of the twenty-three occupations listed more than half are associated with framework knitting. In another Leicestershire village, Fleckney, ten of the fifteen attenders of the New Connexion church who registered a birth in 1837 were framework knitters. This was out of a total church membership of forty-three.[23]

Framework knitting was originally a domestic industry, 'essentially a cottage and family employment, occupying men and women and children in certain stages of the work'.[24] The Enclosure Acts generated a pool of labour on which the industry drew. By the beginning of the nineteenth century the simple domestic industry had given way to a more complex organisation in which the knitter increasingly lost degrees of control. The high cost of frames meant it was a capital based industry. The emergence of middlemen and the almost universal system of frame rents had a profound effect on the industry. According to Peter Head, 'once established, frame rent was too lucrative an institution to be voluntarily surrendered'.[25]

---

[22] Non Parochial Registers. 3187. Public Record Office, London.
[23] Non Parochial Registers. 1435. Public Record Office, London.
[24] Everitt, *Rural Dissent*, p. 34.
[25] Peter Head, 'Putting out in the Leicester Hosiery Industry in the Middle of the Nineteenth Century', *Transactions of the Leicestershire Archaeological and Historical*

There is no evidence that framework knitters were any more predisposed towards Dissent than any other occupation, but, given the extent of this industry in relation to the churches of the New Connexion, it enables us to see the kind of communities from which the church recruited, and the response of the Connexion to the pressures generated by the environment in which its members worked.

An idealised picture of the lot of the framework knitter at the time of the formation of the Connexion is given by Felkin in his *History*. He also gives an account of the decline in real wages that overtook framework knitters in the early part of the nineteenth century. In the 1760s a comfortable living could be secured by working ten hours a day and five days a week. By the 1830s, working fourteen hours a day and seven days a week 'scarcely sufficed for obtaining a bare maintenance'.[26] The organisation of the industry was the main cause of the poverty of the framework knitters, but their wages were also affected by changes in demand due to the disruption of the markets by wars and changing fashion. Knitters were also involved in several of the major upheavals during the nineteenth century, including Luddism and Chartism.

Economic Influences

Hinckley

Thomas Cooper, the Leicester chartist, gives a graphic account of the wretched condition of these workers who provided the major constituency for the Connexion. He went to report on a 'Chartist Meeting' for the *Leicester Mercury*.[27] Later he records the feeling of the men themselves:

> The real feeling of this class of men was fully expressed one day in the market-place when we were holding a meeting in the week. A poor religious stockinger said, 'Let us be patient a little longer, lads. Surely, God Almighty will help us soon.'

> 'Talk no more about thy Goddle Mighty! was the sneering rejoinder. There isn't one. If there was one, He wouldn't let us suffer as we do.'[28]

Felkin attributes the cause of low wages to the 'Parish apprentice system' which had, in earlier years, seen the 'construction of needless frames merely for rent, middle men making full charges for partial work, and payment of wages by truck'.[29] In 1811 the American market, on which the industry in the Midlands relied, closed. There were changes in fashion with the introduction of trousers and boots instead of

---

Society. XXXVII 1961–2 (Leicester: Leicestershire Archaeological and Historical Society, 1963), p. 54.

[26] Felkin, *History*, pp. 451-52.

[27] Thomas Cooper, *Life of Thomas Cooper written by Himself* (London, 1872), p.135.

[28] Cooper, *Life of Thomas Cooper written by Himself*, p. 173.

[29] Felkin, *History*, p. 461.

breeches. Bad harvests and high taxation following the Napoleonic wars led to high prices and there was considerable unemployment.

Hinckley was a centre of the industry and, as such, felt the full effects of the war and the fluctuation of trade cycles. Something of these effects are reflected in the annual 'State of the Church' reports, which churches submitted to the annual association, and entries in the church minute books. So we read '...the extreme depression of trade has produced in many an excess of care, which has devoured the vitals of religion and produced great coldness and indifference to the best of causes'.[30] In 1814, 'The cloud that has overshadowed us in the last year, has in a great measure been dissipated'.[31] Wages fell by 30%-40% in 1816-17 and there were large numbers unemployed. When 'Martha Warner & Wm Barwell's admission was postponed', a small group were appointed to converse with them 'on the subject of running into debt, & not keeping their word when they had promised payment, which has brought reproach upon their characters, and is likely to bring reproach on the sacred cause'.[32] Some found it too much and decided to emigrate:

> The committee then reported their conversation with *William Frith*. As to his attempting to go to America, his motives appeared to be good, tho' we think it was an imprudent step, & exposed him to censure from the world. It appears that his pecuniary difficulties had been, & still were, very great, owing to the great depression of trade.[33]

The 'State of the Church' report of 1818 reflects the difficulties: 'The pressure of the times and lowness of wages, operate unfavourably to religion'.[34] For Elizabeth Beeby the pressure of poverty resulted in her being charged with 'purloining coal'. When her case was brought before the church for discipline she denied the act, saying she was just taking sticks and the coal fell drawing attention to her. 'This is a perplexing case', says the minute book, 'as it is not easy to conceive how Mr M. could be mistaken; on the other hand it is difficult to believe the accused can be so wicked as to persist in solemnly denying what she must be conscious is true; having hitherto born an excellent character'. Expressing contrition at taking the sticks, she was found not guilty.[35] But life did not get any easier for the poverty-stricken members of the Hinckley church. The following year the church was 'greatly oppressed with poverty which operates unfavourably to vital religion'.[36] Poverty had a profound effect on the church. A repeated excuse for absence was 'not having

---

[30] *Reports* (1813), p. 7.
[31] *Reports* (1814), p. 9.
[32] Hinckley Church Book, 30 October 1817. Leicester Record Office.
[33] Hinckley Church Book, 28 January 1818.
[34] *Reports* (1818), p. 6.
[35] Hinckley Church Book, 28 October 1818.
[36] *Reports* (1819), p. 8.

clothes to appear decent in at Meeting', and 'extreme poverty and want of decent rayment'.[37]

Such was the effect of the depression that in September 1817 it was suggested that 'the church should break up or dissolve its connection, with the view of uniting again of such as were determined to fill up their places and perform their duties, as become Christians; and to employ their best exertions to promote the redeemers interests'.[38] Reconstituting the Hinckley church was treating the symptoms and not the cause; there was a period of relative stability until 1824 when again the report recorded 'we are discouraged by poverty and debt and the removal of friends to other places to obtain an honest living... Our town is at present in a state of confusion and distress occasioned by the lowness of wages'.[39] This was repeated the following year with the comment that 'all things considered, our congregation is as good as we can reasonably expect'.[40] By the end of 1825 depression had again set in. And for the Hinckley church the third bad year in a row followed, a 'year of uncommon temporal distress...' For some the solution was drastic: 'Three of our members and several of our hearers have recently emigrated to America'.[41] Things were no better in 1828: 'Our temporal affairs have been embarrassed. Many have left us and obtained better situations we believe, some in heaven and some on earth.'[42] The years 1829 to 1830 were also years of 'temporal distress' but, by 1832, things were beginning to look up: 'we have suffered formerly from low wages but no great stoppage has taken place in our trade...the prospect at Nuneaton continues encouraging, though the trade there has been nearly extinct for several months'.[43]

HINCKLEY MEMBERSHIP 1810–1840

When we look at the membership figures for the church over this period (see Fig. 1, below) we see the profound effect of such trade depressions on the membership. The church lost nearly 200 members in three years. Part of this loss may be accounted for by the formation of the Wolvey church in 1815 which accounted for a loss of eighty members, but it is still evident a heavy loss of members was followed by a long period of recovery (see Fig. 1).

They may have had work in 1832, but their troubles were not over, for in the October of that year the church book records that they 'agreed to unite with other denominations to hold a monthly prayer meeting on account of the pestilence'. This was most likely a reference to the cholera epidemic of that year, a situation no doubt aggravated by the poverty and malnutrition they had experienced.[44] The history of Hinckley is one of a town caught up in a declining industry; in that sense it is

---

[37] Hinckley Church Book, 30 July 1817 and 30 June 1818.
[38] Hinckley Church Book, 7 September 1817.
[39] *Reports* (1824), p. 9.
[40] *Reports* (1825), p. 12.
[41] *Reports* (1826), p. 11.
[42] *Reports* (1828), p.11.
[43] *Reports* (1832), p. 11
[44] Hinckley Church Book, 2 October 1832.

typical of many small towns and villages of the Connexion. Hinckley only differed in the extent and severity of its depression.[45] It is important as a reminder that churches do not exist in isolation from their environment.

Hinckley Membership 1810–1840

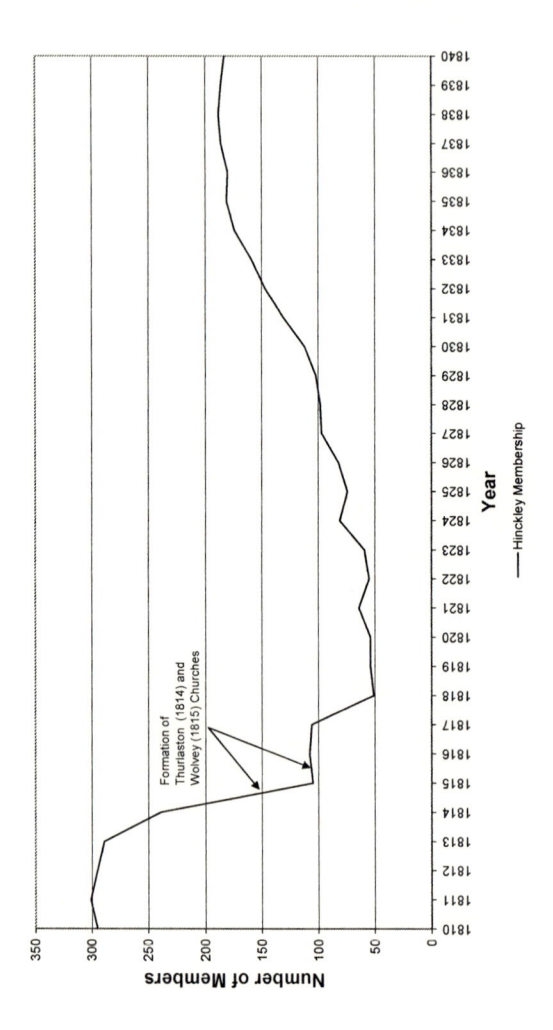

Figure 1

---

[45] Stephen A. Royle, '"The Spiritual Destitution is Excessive—the Poverty Overwhelming": Hinckley in the Mid-Nineteenth Century', *The Leicestershire Archaeological and Historical Society Transactions* 54 (1978–79), p. 53.

Wider Effects

While the effects of trade on the Hinckley church were dramatic, they were by no means unique. Many other churches in the New Connexion felt the 'pressure of the times'. John Stapleton, the minister of New Connexion church at Shepshead, just north of Leicester, gave evidence to the parliamentary commission that was set up to investigate the condition of the knitters in 1844–45. He reported on the condition of his village:

> I recollect towards the spring it was very serious; many young people seemed to be fast approaching to dissolution. I visited that winter, more especially, many families, and found that for weeks and months they never tasted a particle of animal food, nor cheese. The condition of the houses was most wretched; and I can perceive that ever since I came here, for soon after I came trade began to be worse in the winter season, it affects our congregation very much, because the poor people have not top coats, and many of the family have not clothes, so that they cannot turn out on the Sabbath-day in the depth of winter. Our attendance is exceeding thin on that account principally. I was called to a case about three months ago, I went to see a young female, a frame-work knitter; she was in a dying state when I went. In the first room there was no bedding, in the second room there were two bedsteads, and near that a bed of straw and hay. The furniture of the people is very bad, generally speaking, on account of the depression of the trade. [46]

He observed that 'great demoralization' was the result and that 'Generally speaking, they have got into that state of degradation, that when men come to a certain point, it leads then to despair.'[47] The obituary for a 'needlemaker', a trade related to framework knitting, of the Friar Lane church, Leicester, observed that 'his particular branch of trade suffered great reverses, so that to the end of his life he was comparatively a poor man'.[48] Although poor he was not prevented from being a deacon in the church for forty-two years.

It was not only framework knitters who suffered as a result of economic depression; there was also great distress in the northern cotton industry. The New Connexion pastor John Taylor, writing to his friend Burgess, of the situation in Yorkshire in January 1801, says,

> Since I wrote last five have died within a mile of Queenshead, four of whom are evidently dead through want, and one of them, is to be buried today, is starved to death in the plainest and strictest sense of the word. There is not one in a hundred who ever tastes bread made of oatmeal, or anything better than meal made from peas

---

[46] 'Evidence of Rev. J. Stapleton Parliamentary Inquiry into the condition of framework Knitters 1845', *The History and Development of the Hosiery Industry in Leicestershire* (Huntingdon: Priory Press, 1990), p. 89.

[47] 'Evidence of Rev. J. Stapleton Parliamentary Inquiry', p. 89.

[48] J.C. Pike, 'The Late Mr Samuel Wright of Leicester', *GBM* (1870), p. 50.

and beans. Mothers feed infants under a year old, with pottage made of wan meal. The distress is inexpressible.[49]

Later, commenting on the economic situation in and around Halifax in 1812, he observed,

> Poor people about us are extremely willing to work hard. Wages for Cottons are very low; not more than half a moderate rate. Poor people keep up their spirits generally above expectation. Many of our friends you know are among the poor, some among the poorest.[50]

In the middle of the century, such was the poverty in the North that an appeal fund was launched and in their meetings a number of churches discussed making a contribution.[51] One response to the depression of trade was, as we have already seen, the emigration of members; there are instances of this throughout the period. According to the Archdeacon Lane book as a result of the 'extreme depression of trade in Leicester several of our members have been compelled to leave the neighbourhood & others to emigrate; and we are grieved to state that some who once attended our place of worship are not kept away from the house of prayer by poverty and destitution'.[52] In 1848 the church at Kegworth reported that 'sixteen members have, with their families emigrated to the United States of America, being in all a loss to the Kegworth part of the church and congregation alone of nearly thirty persons. We feel this the more as they were amongst the most active and zealous in every department of Christian usefulness'.[53] The church lost a quarter of its membership. While a group or denomination may be 'working class' that did not mean that they were necessarily radical in politics, or that they espoused the cause of the poor. It was argued by the leaders of the Connexion that the framework knitters were not in the forefront of popular political agitation. In the general discontent in 1816, 'Their patience and self-restraint contrasted obviously with restless stirrings elsewhere'.[54] We see this quietist stance in the response of the Connexion to the difficulties of the age.

New Connexion Response to Conditions

In September 1819 Robert Hall formed the 'Framework Knitters Friendly and Relief Society of the Town and the County of Leicester'. The Society was non-political and took subscriptions from men in work and outside sympathisers. It was, in essence, a strike fund and not, as it would seem, charitable relief; lack of resources led to its

---

[49] Adam Taylor, *Memoirs of Rev. J. Taylor*, p. 74.
[50] Adam Taylor, *Memoirs of Rev. J. Taylor*, p.100
[51] Bourne Church Book, 3 December 1862.
[52] Archdeacon Lane Church Book, 24 January 1842.
[53] *Reports* (1848), p. 18.
[54] *Minutes* (1816), p.6.

collapse in 1824. Robert Hall was a Particular Baptist, so in what way did the Connexion respond to the situation? There is little evidence in the literature and minutes that the movement as a body adopted a radical stance, took up the cause of its brethren, or gave anything more than encouragement 'to labour...to acquire under the severest privations an entire submission to the will of God'.[55]

Bissill, writing in the Association Letter for 1815 said that 'we should ascribe our sufferings to our sins'.[56] We are not told how the members of the Hinckley church responded to that! Thomas Goadby's description of a day in May 1833, 'when the town was all astir with a demonstration, got up by some of the framework-knitters, to protest at one of the members voting against Halford's payment of wages Bill', which has the view of a detached observer rather than a sympathetic participator.[57]

Thomas Cooper, espousing the cause of the framework knitters, sought to enlist the support of Joseph Winks who was a printer and New Connexion pastor in Leicester: 'My old friend Winks believed in the justice of universal suffrage with myself, but as he belonged to the party of the old political leaders, and as they had decided to ask for the repeal of the Corn Laws, he kept aloof from the Chartists'.[58] Winks was, in fact, a vociferous member of the Leicester and Leicestershire Political Union. This group concerned themselves with the general political climate, 'the doings of the Corporation', Corn Law repeal, church rate tithes and education. Temple Patterson says that the leaders of this group, of which Winks was one, 'formed a kind of shadow town council'.[59] Winks' concerns seem to have been general political reform, especially of the Leicester Corporation, rather than the needs of one particular group, the framework knitters. He was very suspicious of radicalism. His advice to Cooper, who had been offered thirty shillings a week to run the Chartist newspaper in Leicester, was 'Have nothing to do with them, Tom', he said, 'you cannot depend on 'em; you'll not get the thirty shillings a week they have promised you'.[60] Robert Hall, the minister of the Harvey Lane Chapel, Leicester, was far more outspoken and active in his support for the framework knitters, publishing anonymously, *The Question at Issue between the Framework-Knitters and their Employers*.[61] This pamphlet supported the framework-knitters in their

---

[55] J. Bissill, 'Directions and Encouragements in Times of Temporal Distress', *Letter*, *GBR* (1815), p. 21.
[56] *GBR* (1815), p. 21
[57] Goadby and Goadby, *Not Saints But Men*, p. 144.
[58] Cooper, *Life of Thomas Cooper written by Himself*, p. 114.
[59] A. Temple Patterson, *Radical Leicester: A History of Leicester 1780–1850* (Leicester: University College, 1954), p. 188.
[60] Cooper, *Life of Thomas Cooper written by Himself*, p. 146.
[61] Temple Patterson, *Radical Leicester*, p. 132. See also Robert Hall, *An Appeal to the Public on the Subject of the Framwork-Knitters Fund* (Leicester: Thomas Combe, 3rd edn, 1820) and *A Reply to the Principal Objections Advanced by Cobbett and Others Against the Frame-work Knitters Friendly Society* (1821), Leicester Record Office pamphlet. Vol. 16.

associating together in order to better themselves. In it, Hall expressed a sense of powerlessness, being only able to offer 'a barren and impotent commiseration!'[62]

Governed as they were by the religious outlook of the age, the New Connexion did not view what was happening as a social evil and something to be challenged in the name of the gospel. Rather, when faced with a general sense of unrest and political agitation, they called for order. James Taylor, in the Association Letter for 1818, argued that in the best ordered state government was difficult, and appealed to the Connexion not to make the task of government more difficult 'by unreasonable speech and inconsistent behaviour in times of distress and ferment'. He continued:

> If any particular grievance should exist, of which there is a probability that it would be remedied by an application to our superiors, let us do this with that decorum which becomes our character, and, if it be not removed, let us bear it with patience and fortitude... So ought we to honour and support our governors, even though their proceedings may not altogether suit our inclinations or interests.[63]

Rather than involve themselves in politics they were urged to look within themselves: 'Is there no work for your thoughts and cares in the management of your own hearts? no rebellious lusts to subdue? no ignorance that requires study to remove it?' The list continues directing their attention to home and work in the church and concluding,

> Is there nothing you can do for the furtherance of the Gospel? Do not waste your time and thoughts about politics, but save your strength for this...some have been so affected, and their thoughts so occupied with their distresses, that they have lost their religion. Others have been so entangled in politics that they have made shipwreck of their faith.[64]

Such was the help offered to the members of the churches by the Connexion. The Chartist leader Finn was an exception to the generally passive acceptance of the situation. He was a framework knitter and lay pastor to what Temple Patterson calls a 'working-class congregation of General Baptists', the New Connexion church at Carley Street, Leicester. Finn was involved in unsuccessful attempts to form a union and establish a common wage; becoming involved in Chartism he exerted a moderating influence.[65] Although a Chartist, Finn, like Winks, favoured the repeal of the Corn Laws, and became chairman of the Leicester Working Men's Anti-Corn Law Association.[66] In our evaluation of the response of the Connexion we must be careful not to look for a contemporary response. Hall's 'barren and impotent

---

[62] Felkin, *History*, p. 442.

[63] James Taylor, 'Directions for Christian Conduct in Seasons of National Distress & Political Ferment', *Letter* (1818), p. 33.

[64] *GBR* (1818), pp. 33-34.

[65] Temple Patterson, *Radical Leicester*, pp. 300, 302.

[66] Temple Patterson, *Radical Leicester*, pp. 312, 313.

commiseration' was the response of the age, and we should not be too critical of the Connexion for failing to step outside that.

In addition to the economic troubles of the framework-knitters, the villages of the Midlands were experiencing the effects of the Enclosure Acts. One result of this was to reduce marginal cottagers and small holders to the status of wage labourers. As with the framework knitters, the agricultural workers thus affected experienced a loss of independence and a diminishing sense of personal worth.

Social Migration

The development or decline of a movement rarely, if ever, has a single or simple pattern of causes; development takes place through a complex pattern of interrelated elements. As the century progressed, it was felt by some that society was changing in ways that were unfavourable to the movement. These were changes that were brought about by the social aspirations of those within the church's sphere of influence. J.G. Pike thought that there were those who would have joined 'had our churches been formed on a system more accommodating to human prejudices, and had they allowed the genteeler [sic] part of society to unite with them without the self-denial of "going through the water to the fold"'.[67]

It may be that the aspirations were a reflection of Pike's own desires, rather than the leadership of the Connexion moving in the direction of the emerging middle class, 'the genteeler part of Society'. Pike, putting the case for higher stipends, speaks about the 'poorer friends' not understanding the 'extra calls and expenses' associated with the 'middle sphere of life' and that those who move in that sphere find 'a hundred a year altogether inadequate'.[68] In 1856 the church at Castle Donnington, with 258 members, offered their prospective minister '£80 per year & the Rent received for the large house which is now £8 per year'.[69]

Others felt that church members were being captured by social convention, that they were migrating away from their roots. On 14 July 1858, the *Freeman* carried an article entitled 'The Deserters'. This piece commented on the drift to the Church of England, and the reasons for it:

> It is undeniable that the sons and daughters of wealthy Dissenters, of those especially who have raised themselves pecuniarily in the world by their own exertions, quite often as not, to say the least, leave the worship of their fathers and their boyhood for that of the established church.[70]

While there were not many 'sons and daughters of wealthy Dissenters' in the Connexion, migration was a problem. Thomas Goadby, reflecting on changes that had taken place, in 1868 said,

---

[67] J.G. Pike, 'Christian Exertion', *Letter*, *GBRMO* (1840), p. 39.
[68] *GBRMO* (1840), p. 42.
[69] Castle Donnington Church Book, 18 February 1856.
[70] *Freeman*, 14 July 1858, p. 411.

we have aimed at gaining for ourselves the honours and accomplishments of modern life and securing for our churches a higher and more commanding position in the world...they have become too much the end of our ambition and not the means of our greater usefulness.[71]

Two years later William Underwood again drew attention to the problem of migration. He observed a move from the Connexion to the Particular Baptists rather than the Church of England:

...it is no uncommon thing for our members, when they rise in worldly position, or when their comfort is disturbed to retire from our connexion to that of the other section, which is considered to be more respectable or which has perchance a more able ministry or more attractive sanctuaries.[72]

The social migration of members was further compounded in larger cities by the growth of churches in the fast expanding suburbs. In Nottingham these churches were in working-class districts. Harrison comments that, unlike the Particular Baptist church at Friar Lane, which had many wealthy industrialists and 'provided Nottingham with its mayors for a third of the century and with a large proportion of the councillors for most of the century', there were few wealthy members in the Connexion.[73]

Part of the conflict for the New Connexion was that of identity; the aspiration of some to the 'genteeler' classes meant a loosening of its roots with those of the 'poorer sort'. Perhaps another reason lay, as we have suggested, in changes that were taking place in the demographic structure of the Connexion. Gilbert argues that, in the 1830s and 1840s, important social groups within the Evangelical Nonconformist constituency were not merely becoming less receptive to Nonconformist recruitment, 'they were becoming extinct'.[74] The framework knitters were such a group and we have previously noted the extent to which they were associated with the New Connexion. The middle of the century saw the beginning of the mechanisation of the framework knitting process thus beginning their gradual extinction.

The Connexion did not have a strong hold in the middle classes, and at the same time seemed to be losing its base in the working classes. The reasons for this are difficult to determine; maybe they felt that they had risen above the 'poorer sort'. The officers of the church at Archdeacon Lane, Leicester, 'after mature deliberation' said to the church that they did not

...think it advisable to recommend to the Church to have a separate service for the poorer Classes believing it would be detremental [sic] to those already established, at the same time we fear it would tend to deepen the prejudice prevalent amongst

---

[71] Thomas Goadby, 'Chairman's Address', *Minutes* (1868), pp. 63, 98.

[72] W. Underwood, 'Chairman's Address', *GBM* (1870), p. 276.

[73] F.M.W. Harrison, 'Approach of the New Connexion General Baptists to a Midland Industrial Town', *Baptist Quarterly* 33.1 (January, 1989), p. 17.

[74] Gilbert, *Religion and Society*, p. 146.

them hoping those friends who are deeply interested in their welfare will kindly invite them to attend any of the present services.[75]

The social divisions indicated here were most likely present in other churches as well. In the first half of the century, the members of the Connexion were more likely to be the recipients of help to the poor rather than the givers of it, but by the middle of the century things were changing. It was the Mansfield Road church, founded in 1849, that gave the lead to the Connexion in social work.[76] The church books of the period contain accounts of the formation of 'Dorcas Societies' which provided clothes for the poor and needy.[77]

The factors involved in a declining membership were many; the failure to recruit new members was a less complicated matter. Writing in 1868, John Clifford had a much more pertinent diagnosis: 'we have succeeded in becoming "genteel" and "highly respectable" but also very frigid and formal and lifeless; we should not marvel', said Clifford, 'that men will not enter our Ice House'. He perceived that,

> though it be a 'thing of beauty' splendid decorations do not drive out the cold and make it a comfortable house, if the atmosphere is frosty without being bracing, if the hand of brotherly love is clammy with the damps of death, if caste reigns only with less despotism within than without the church and the world's divisions obtrude with painful prominence in the circle of those redeemed by a common salvation and enjoying a common life in Christ, we must submit to the non-attendance of professed Christians at public worship as our well merited deserts.[78]

In saying this, he was addressing the decline of spiritual fervour and enthusiasm; the common cause of a previous generation had provided spiritual fellowship and warmth. The second generation did not hold so ardently to this cause; they seemed to be more formal in their relationships. They were becoming respectable. The problem was not just the decline of the framework knitter, nor the failure of mission, nor the growth of the institution, rather that of the nature of the church itself, its adoption of the values of middle-class Victorian society. This change was indicated by an entry in the Kegworth minute book for 1868, where money was donated for the building of a baptistry within the church. For a hundred years the Baptists at Kegworth had been sufficiently secure in their convictions to make their witness in the River Soar, but now they had come indoors.[79] At Castle Donnington so that the minister no longer got wet at baptisms, it was decided 'That a pair of waterproof boots be

---

[75] Archdeacon Lane Minute Book 4, 23 October 1861.
[76] Harrison, 'Approach of the New Connexion', p. 18.
[77] New Lenton Church Book, 21 January 1861. Nottingham Record Office NC/BP/10/5. Maltby Le Marsh Church Book 3. 1854–1874, 14 October 1867. Lincolnshire County Archives 16/Bapt/2.
[78] John Clifford, 'Non Attendance of Professed Christians at Public Worship', *GBM* (1868), p. 71.
[79] Kegworth Church Book (1868). Leicester Record Office N/B/159/1.

purchased by the Church for the occasion and for future Baptisms.'[80] The pressures of respectability encouraged the move from a public witness, an involvement in the world, to a private religious sub-culture. The experience of the New Connexion would seem to lend support to the suggestion by Richard Niebuhr that a movement accommodates itself to the prevailing cultural climate. In doing this, it tends to lose its original identity, 'it accepts a type of religious life more in conformity with its new economic interest and status'.[81]

The Anglican resurgence in the second half of the century generated another pressure on Free Church attendance. Writing in 1876, Clifford said that there were clergymen who sought 'to empty our chapels with the lever of parochial charities, forge fetters for human minds out of the beneficence of our forefathers, muffle the parental conscience with the garments of a clothing club and use the whip of the magistrate to lash an unwilling people to church'.[82] This had been the experience of the churches at Smalley and Rushall. At Smalley it was reported that 'During the past year we have suffered for the hostile influence of Puseyism, especially in our school at Smalley'. At Rushall things were even more difficult: 'We are at peace among ourselves, but greatly opposed by the clergyman of the parish, and his friends—many are afraid to attend the house of God, as one who was baptised has been turned out of his employment. Brethren, pray for us'.[83] Inducements were not new; in Shepshead the Roman Catholic priest had supplied children with clothing as an inducement to attend the Roman Catholic school.[84]

While some were 'driven' into church others went more willingly, as the *Freeman* had observed:

> continually we find individuals leaving Dissenting worship and attending that of the Established church. Very frequently it follows on removals to places where no old connections bind to former habits; and sometimes even from sheer religious illiteracy, combined generally with real, or obvious illiteracy on other subjects also. Many such persons never had any reason for attending a place of worship but its proximity, or the suggestion of friends, and the vague feeling of sincere desire to worship somehow.[85]

Clifford recognised that a process of redemption and lift was at work; he commented that 'the road to social position is through the churchyard, and it requires more conscience, more moral courage than some Dissenters can keep in the same house with increasing wealth and luxury, to restrain them from walking along that road'.[86]

---

[80] Castle Donnington Church Book 6, 17 November 1864.
[81] Richard H. Niebuhr, *The Social Sources of Denominationalism* (New York: Meridan, 1972), p. 89.
[82] John Clifford, *Religious Life in Rural Districts of England* (London: Yates & Alexander, 1876), p. 7.
[83] *Reports* (1843), p. 28, and (1846), p. 28.
[84] *History and Development of the Hosiery Industry in Leicestershire*, p. 89.
[85] *Freeman*, 14 July 1858, p. 411.
[86] Clifford, *Religious Life*, p. 16.

While some members of the Connexion chose to move up and out of the Connexion, the middle classes that were left were themselves a barrier to new recruitment. The crossing of class boundaries is a difficult process. Evidence from a variety of sources suggests that recruitment takes place more easily along the strata of society rather than across it.[87] While those strata were being laid down, as in the early decades of the century, recruitment took place at a number of levels. It would seem the General Baptists of the New Connexion had only a tenuous foothold in the lower middle classes, while the artisan base in the working classes was being eroded. In later Victorian society, as the class divisions hardened so recruitment vertically became much more difficult. In 1892 at Archdeacon Lane, Leicester, following a discussion about seat rents, it was observed by Mr Buckley that Sunday evenings were 'becoming more & more a working class congregation' and that the wealthy 'have & are one by one leaving the church and congregation'. He argued that 'the placing of tickets in seats creates and provides a monopoly & class interest against the interest & spiritual welfare of the masses contrary to the teaching of the free Gospel of our Lord'.[88] But the recommendations of the deacons prevailed and the rents and cards continued.

Speaking at the stone laying of Westbourne Park chapel in 1876, Clifford said, 'This generation, it is scarcely too much to say, has ceased to believe very heartily in the Christian Church'.[89] The words he uses are significant: it is not that people do not believe in the church any longer, but that they have 'ceased to believe very heartily'. The phrase sums up very accurately what was happening to Nonconformity as a whole and the General Baptists in particular. The Christian faith was now one of a number of commitments that a person might make. Legislation had meant shorter working hours and the opportunity of leisure pursuits. The church was having to compete for the attention of men and women. The nature of church life had changed from a basic community, an unquestioned 'given', to the provider of services, seeking to meet needs of individuals, and in this the church was in competition with other agencies. The Connexion, together with other churches, were living in a secular world in which the church was one voice among many that called for attention. For Clifford, the way forward for the church was to overcome this 'Painful inadequacy' and to go back to basics and confront the world with transformed lives: 'Christ Jesus built his church on men not on a book; on living and loving disciples enthusiastically attached to His Person... Personal discipleship to Christ, the evidence of faith in and loyalty to Him is the prime condition of church

---

[87] H. McLeod, *Class and Religion in the Late Victorian City* (London: Croom Helm, 1974), pp. 281-82. Donald McGavran, *Understanding Church Growth* (Grand Rapids, MI: Eerdmans, 1970), p. 198.

[88] Archdeacon Lane Minute 4, 5 October 1892.

[89] John Clifford, *A New Testament Church in its relation to the need and tendencies of the age: A Statement made in connection with the laying of the memorial stone Westbourne Park Chapel 10 July 1876* (London: Yates and Alexander, 1876), p. 5.

membership.'⁹⁰ Clifford's solution used one of the main dissolving agents of the old order, individualism. His appeal was for personal commitment.

Protest and Conflict

CHURCH RATES

The Connexion, in common with the rest of Nonconformity, found itself caught up in issues and disputes that were an expression of a growing self confidence. One of the factors affecting the development of religious groups are those influences operating at the national level, external to the church, such as broad economic or political value changes, which have been termed by Roozen and Carroll as 'National Contextual Factors'.⁹¹ One such influence was the church rates controversy which occupied the energies of the Connexion in the middle of the century. The Church of England had at the beginning of the century re-grouped around movements like the evangelical 'Clapham Sect' and the high church 'Hackney Phalanx'. This, together with the Oxford Tractarians, resulted in a far more aggressive stance on the part of the Church of England. The New Connexion found its energies were being absorbed in conflict, in attempts to establish and maintain what they felt was their rightful position in religious and national life. One expression of this conflict was the church rates controversy.

The church rate was a local levy on all ratepayers; the money raised was used for the repair and maintenance of Church of England buildings. Free Churchmen had to find the cost of erecting and maintaining their own places of worship; as a result, the rate was bitterly resented and it became a focus for discontent. There were occasions when political and religious feeling reached fever point. Between 1850 and 1868, when Gladstone's abolition bill received royal assent, there were some sixteen bills introduced into Parliament for the removal of church rates. At Castle Donnington a committee was formed 'respecting the best means to be employed for the entire and immediate abolition' of Church rates'.⁹² 'The petition to Parliament for abolishing Church Rates shall be laid in the vestry on Sunday next for signatures' was the decision of the church at New Lenton, Nottingham, one of many churches to respond in this way.⁹³

In the Midlands, an area of relative strength for the Anglicans, relationships with the Church of England were marked by competition, acrimony and some times considerable establishment harassment. In Leicester, the Particular Baptist, J.P. Mursell was closely associated with Edward Miall, who led the fight against the rate by refusing to pay. Their aim was not just the removal of the rate, but the

---

⁹⁰ Clifford, *A New Testament Church*, pp. 7-8.

⁹¹ D.A. Roozen and J.W. Carroll, 'Recent Trends in Church Membership and Participation: An Introduction', in Dean R. Hoge and David A. Roozen (eds) *Understanding Church Growth and Decline 1950–1978* (New York: The Pilgrim Press 2ⁿ edn, 1981), p. 39.

⁹² Castle Donnington Church Book 5, 22 January 1837.

⁹³ New Lenton Church Book, 29 February 1860.

disestablishment of the Church of England. St. Margaret's, the parish in which Miall lived, summoned him and twenty other non-payers. These protesters refused to appear before the magistrates' court in what they claimed was a spiritual matter. As a result some of their goods were seized and offered for sale by public auction, but according to Temple Patterson 'the demeanour of the attendant crowd was so menacing that no-one would venture a bid and they had to be disposed of privately'.[94] At another parish, St. Martin's, the same approach was adopted, and amongst a variety of items auctioned were eleven reams of paper belonging to the General Baptist and New Connexion pastor and printer J.F. Winks, a ferocious opponent of the rate.[95]

The initial involvement of the Connexion was fairly low key. In 1837 the annual association had been content to form a resolution to the government expressing thanks for the 'abolition of the vexatious and degrading impost'.[96] In Leicester, William Baines, a draper, was singled out as an example for non-payment of the rate, and sent to prison. The church at Archdeacon Lane held a special meeting at which a supportive address, presented by forty-nine male members of the church, was approved and sent to Baines in prison.[97] The following year, the association of 1841 urged members of the New Connexion on all 'suitable occasions to petition and protest' and to return to Parliament such members 'as shall compel the government...speedily to abolish these courts, and...relieve all dissenters from payment of those local exactions for the support of episcopal worship which are usually denominated church rates'.[98]

The *Baptist Reporter* (owned, edited and published by J.F. Winks) urged, in 1844, direct action: 'We advise all Baptists, as staunch opponents of such unjust impositions, to be found at their post in the parish vestry whenever a vote is proposed, and to secure, if possible, a report of the proceedings (for this is often of first importance) in the local newspapers'.[99] The General Baptist minister at Louth, J. Kiddal, attended the meeting when the rate was levied and objected, arguing that it required the majority of the meeting to render it legal, and moved that no rate be allowed. Should it be legally laid he would pay when asked, but would use all constitutional means to prevent this and to save the Dissenters from such an unjust impost. This amendment was seconded, and a debate followed, the outcome of which was a very large majority against the rate.[100] 'Confrontation', according to Gilbert, became an 'important theme' in Victorian religion.[101]

The first attempts at removal of the rate failed, and it was to take a campaign lasting some thirty years before the passing of the Compulsory Church Rates

---

[94] Temple Patterson, *Radical Leicester*, pp. 249-50.
[95] Temple Patterson, *Radical Leicester*, pp. 250-51.
[96] *Minutes* (1837), p. 19.
[97] Archdeacon Lane Church Book 3, 14 October 1840.
[98] *Minutes* (1841), pp. 34-38.
[99] *Baptist Reporter* (1845), p. 102.
[100] 'Church Rates at Louth', *GBRMO* (1854), pp. 279-80.
[101] Gilbert, *Religion and Society*, p. 142.

Abolition Act of 1868. It was Miall's contention that the failure of Nonconformists to rid themselves of the 'rate' was because they did not appreciate the necessity of campaigning against the establishment as such; to this end he worked for the disestablishment of the Church of England. In 1844 the Anti-State Church Association was formed. Its constitution stated 'That in matters of religion man is responsible to God alone; ...and that the application by law of the resources of the state to the maintenance of any form or forms of religious worship and instruction is contrary to reason, hostile to human liberty, and directly opposed to the word of God'.[102]

The New Connexion gave its support to this movement, churches in the depths of Lincolnshire sending representatives to London conferences and writing to members of Parliament.[103] Miall, editor of the *Nonconformist* and leader of the Anti-State Church Association, became a rallying point for the energies of Nonconformity in the struggle with the establishment. While there were examples of co-operation these were isolated, the general attitude in relation to the Church of England was one of conflict. Hugh Hunter, in the annual address to the Connexion in 1864, looked at the changes in the Church of England and said that

> while it professes to be the bulwark of Protestantism, it is rather by its demands, legally enforced from the inhabitants of Great Britain and Ireland, whether belonging to herself, to Rome, to conscientious dissent, or to infidelity, the bulwark of Popery in these Kingdoms being the great cause of national and legislative aid to those hugest and most pernicious errors by which Christianity, if not the world, has been disgraced and cursed.[104]

These were not the kind of words that would endear the Connexion to the Anglicans. The response of the Connexion to the call for action from Miall can be viewed as an example of a growing confidence and assertiveness. Along with other Nonconformists, the Connexion sought to change the existing social order. The demands of the Liberation Society were for recognition of the rights of Nonconformists within the existing social structure; the call for disestablishment was in part an expression of the growing confidence of Nonconformity. A side effect of these issues was that they absorbed the energies of the Connexion; the extent to which this affected their growth we will consider at a later stage.

---

[102] 'Constitution of the Anti-State Church Association, 1844' [extracts from a report in the *Eclectic Review* (1844), pp. 736-38], in David M. Thompson (ed.), *Nonconformity in the Nineteenth Century* (Birth of Modern Britain Series; London: Routledge & Kegan Paul, 1972), pp. 124-25.

[103] Maltby Le Marsh Church Book 2, 24 October 1853; Gosberton Church 2, 2 February, 1861. Lincolnshire County Archives 9/Bapt/1/3.

[104] Hugh Hunter, 'Annual Address', *Minutes* (1864), p. 7.

The Temperance Movement

Another expression of protest, common to all the churches, was the temperance movement; cutting across denominational and party lines it succeeded in effecting a profound change in religious attitudes to alcohol. The movement developed through a series of successive and overlapping phases which may be discerned in the involvement of the New Connexion. The first phase in the 1830s and 40s was a growing opposition to beer. Until this time, moderate drinking had not been an issue, many of the early conferences had met in inns. The widespread identification of Baptists with the temperance cause was relatively late. James Hopkinson of the New Connexion church at Stoney Street, Nottingham, tells how the Sunday school celebrated Queen Victoria's coronation by giving a dinner at which 'a quantity of Ale was likewise supplied to the children'. The result was 'they became very demonstrative and we could not keep them in order as part of them were intoxicated'.[105] At Friar Lane, Leicester, they supplied buns, fruit, ale, and beer as a Sunday school treat and counter attraction to 'race day' in 1826.[106] Temperance sermons were thought an 'obnoxious novelty' when Jabez Burns began a regular series in 1839.[107] When John Clifford went to Praed Street in 1858 and began to preach an annual abstinence sermon on behalf of the Abstinence Society he was openly denounced by officials of churches in Paddington.[108] Notwithstanding the reaction at Paddington the teetotal movement gained ground.

Its next phase was that of 'Gospel Temperance', the development of various national movements promoting abstinence. At this stage the movement centred around an individualist philosophy. By the 1850s the temperance movement was well established, with two main societies. The first grouping, the National Temperance League concerned itself with persuading people to give up drink and to sign the pledge, and was, according to Ian Sellers, 'akin in so many ways to religious revivalism'.[109] The second, the United Kingdom Alliance, was founded in 1853 and was concerned with implementing legislation. It was formed by Nathaniel Card, a Quaker, and the General Baptist Dr. Dawson Burns, a near neighbour of Clifford at Marylebone in London. Publishing his first temperance article at the age of twelve, Burns was, by seventeen, Assistant Secretary of the National Temperance Society, and a year later its Secretary. This he combined with editorship of the *Temperance Chronicle*. In 1850 he helped found the United Kingdom Alliance and was for twenty-five years its Metropolitan Superintendent. According to John Briggs he was 'A master of statistics', a 'formidable organizer of petitions and pressure-group politics'; Mrs Dawson Burns was equally active in women's temperance

---

[105] Briggs, *English Baptists*, p. 312.
[106] Friar Lane Teachers' Meeting Minutes (1826). Leicester Record Office 15D/66/35.
[107] G.W. McCree, 'The Late Dr. Jabez Burns', *GBM* (1876), p. 87.
[108] James Marchant, *Dr. John Clifford* (London: Cassell, 1924), p. 50.
[109] Ian Sellers, *Nineteenth-Century Nonconformity* (London: Edward Arnold, 1977), p. 41.

organizations.[110] This was a family affair, for the father, Jabez, made temperance the major part of his life's work. He was then called to the chair of the Baptist Union in 1850, he was the second New Connexion minister to hold this office. He was a frequent temperance lecturer and preacher both in this country and overseas. John Briggs says that he was 'A fluent editor and author, and the principal organizer of the world Temperance Convocation which met in London in 1846, and 1847, he was involved in ensuring that temperance appeared on the agenda of the Evangelical Alliance in orderly fashion'.[111] Dawson Burns was so involved in temperance issues that when he sought to lead a resistance to amalgamation with the Particular Baptists Clifford suggested that his temperance work meant that he was out of touch with true feeling about union in the churches.[112]

At a meeting in Leeds in 1847, the General Baptist Jabez Tunnicliff, together with a Mrs Carlile, the wife of an American Presbyterian and advocate of temperance work among children, formed the first temperance society for children. This later became the 'Band of Hope'. The movement grew rapidly and in 1855 a 'United Kingdom Band of Hope Union' was formed to draw the individual societies together. By the end of the century the union had some 26,000 bands with over three million registered members.[113]

Another early pioneer of temperance was Francis Beardsall, a General Baptist who had ministries in the East Midlands and went to Manchester in 1834. He was convinced that wine in the New Testament was unfermented, a subject on which he lectured. He campaigned against the use of alcohol in the communion service and manufactured non-fermented grape juice for communion purposes. He also produced the first temperance hymnbook. The acknowledgement at the turn of the century by 2,077 out of 2,900 Baptist churches that they used unfermented wine at communion gives some indication of his success.[114]

The United Kingdom Alliance is an example of the third phase of the movement which saw a move to bring about drink related legislation. Although, according to Ian Sellers, it was not terribly successful: 'What temperance enthusiasm it managed to generate in Westminster was effectively neutralized by the machinations of Gladstone and the indifference of the more politically astute Nonconformist politicians.'[115] The Alliance gave an opportunity for churches, not just individuals, to get involved. So, at the Ashby and Packington church meeting, 'The form of a Petition was read from "The British Association for the Promotion of Temperance" relative to the prohibition, at least, of the sale of intoxicating liquor on the Sabbath

---

[110] Briggs, *English Baptists*, p. 334.
[111] Briggs, *English Baptists*, p. 334.
[112] Briggs, *English Baptists*, p. 151.
[113] Kathleen Heasman, *Evangelicals in Action* (London: Geoffrey Bles, 1962), p. 136.
[114] Briggs, *English Baptists*, p. 331.
[115] Sellers, *Nineteenth-Century Nonconformity*, p. 41.

Aspects of the Social and Demographic Background 93

day. Agreed we will send a petition from each place Ashby and Packington, to each of the houses of Parliament.'[116]

The third phase in the 1860s and 70s saw the development of temperance organisations within denominations in addition to the national movements. The Baptist Total Abstinence Society was formed in 1874. John Clifford was one of the first two honorary secretaries. In his address *The Churches War with National Intemperance*, Clifford set out the agenda. He defined its objects as 'the formation of Temperance Societies' and the 'increase of total abstinence in and by the Baptist denomination by means of deputations, lectures, sermons, meetings, the circulation of literature'. According to Clifford,

> every church ought to be employing some of its power in this direction. A Temperance department with its meeting for adults, its Band of Hope for the young, its circulation of abstinence literature... Ought to stand side by side with the Sunday school and foreign mission work, and some of the energy inventiveness, zeal, prayer, and faith of the church should be put into it.[117]

The fastidious nature of some led to problems at what was meant to be an expression of love and unity, the Lord's Table. A minute of the Friar Lane church for 1869 reflects this:

> consulted with several of the Temperance friends who object to take the wine. They would be willing to sit together at the Ordinance and partake of the unfermented wine. By this means it was hoped that the difficulty arising from the conscientious scruples of some of the total abstainers would be met.

Twelve years later the unfermented wine offered as an alternative to satisfy the 'scruples' of some was adopted as the only wine to be used. As Douglas Ashby says, the 'scruples' of 1869 had become the norm of 1881.[118] Scruples posed problems for the Archdeacon Lane church during a rebuilding project. Thinking of meeting in the Temperance Hall for worship, the question of communion arose, and a deputation was sent 'to wait upon the Chairman of the Directors of the Temperance Hall company to ascertain whether the same would be acceptable without infringing upon the rules of the Temperance Cause...'[119] In some places temperance engendered more than administrative difficulties; there was real division over the issue. In 1846 the Connexion church at Manchester reported that there was 'a division over the temperance question' the result of which was 'many of our members were allowed to withdraw'. The statistical returns indicate forty-one excluded and thirty-seven

---

[116] Ashby and Packington Church Book, 10 April 1848. Leicester Record Office N/9/1.

[117] John Clifford, 'The Churches War with National Intemperance: A paper read at the conference of the British Total Abstinence Association held at Newcastle' (8 October London, 1874), pp. 1, 13.

[118] Ashby, *Friar Lane*, pp. 70 and 77.

[119] Archdeacon Lane Minute Book 4, 26 May 1864.

withdrawn. The previous year the church had reported 160 members.[120] At Tydd St.Giles they were 'not in pleasant circumstances...as there is great vexatious agitation upon the wine question. Many refuse to sit down with us at the table of the Lord, and have done so for two or three years past. We fear the perplexing agitation will terminate in the loss of several members.'[121] The difficulties over fermented wine at Maltby Le Marsh were resolved by brother Newman who 'kindly consented to provide that wine they would prefer, and that the fermented wine be used by the remaining parties of the Church'.[122] Clifford quotes a letter from a church officer which reflects the movement's divisive nature: 'We have seen so many churches split up, and the cause of Christ so materially injured by the intemperance of abstainers, that we should hesitate long before inviting as a pastor a partisan of the teetotal movement'.[123] The above supports Gilbert's contention that the movement created division within rather than between denominations.[124]

The final stage of the movement was marked by the development of counter attractions to the public house. The wife of Thomas Cook established a Temperance Hotel in Leicester, and in London Clifford built a pub which sought to provide all the social advantages of the public house, yet with out drink.[125] 'Clifford's Inn' was intended to be a 'place of rest and refreshment'.[126] When Thomas Cook organised his first railway excursion in 1841, from Market Harborough to Leicester, it was to attend a temperance meeting. What was emerging with the temperance movement was the counter culture of the 'chapel' with the ubiquitous urn for 'tea meetings'; 'a large gathering of our friends, first upon the shore at Mablethorpe:—then to tea at Maltby'; tea was accompanied by speakers.[127] Organisations emerged for children and adults which offered educational and leisure opportunities, a church community very different from its eighteenth-century forbears.

John Kent argues that a complex movement, such as temperance, can only be understood 'if one assumes that actual abstention from alcohol was never the end, but only the means, of the great campaign'.[128] The appeal of the movement worked at a number of levels for evangelicalism; it was 'like a kind of cement' impervious to higher criticism; for the religious middle class it represented a 'repudiation of the social values of those whom they were expected to regard as their social superiors, as well as their contempt for the values of the working classes'.[129] It was a statement of

---

[120] *Reports* (1845), p. 5. (1846), p. 23.

[121] *Reports* (1846), p. 31.

[122] Maltby Le Marsh Church Book 3, 14 January 1867.

[123] John Clifford, *Thou Shalt not Hide Thyself. An Argument and an appeal for the Cure of Britain's Intemperance* (London: W. Tweedie, 1877), p. 11.

[124] Gilbert, *Religion and Society*, p. 165.

[125] Briggs, *English Baptists*, p. 333.

[126] Marchant, *Dr. John Clifford*, p. 71.

[127] Maltby Le Marsh Church Book 3, 7 August 1851.

[128] John Kent, *Holding the Fort: Studies in Victorian Revivalism* (London: Epworth Press, 1978), p. 88.

[129] Kent, *Holding the Fort*, p. 88.

independence; the blue ribbon became an expression of dissent, but in this case it was dissent from culture, either proletariat or middle class.

Kathleen Heasman draws attention to the confusion which arose between 'total abstinence' and 'salvation'. In the later stages of the gospel temperance movement, 'conversion' was not regarded as authentic unless accompanied by a signing of the pledge.[130] Patricia Kruppa argues that Spurgeon was a somewhat reluctant convert.[131] Spurgeon was concerned that the movement, by concentrating on external issues, would neglect the central issue of humanity's sinful nature: 'Nothing less than to see men new creatures in Christ must satisfy us, and many will utterly slay drunkenness, and hang a bit of blue ribbon over its grave, and yet all the while remain utterly bad at heart'.[132] Spurgeon's concern here was that the movement represented a shift from belief to ethics as the measurement of Christianity.

The significance of the abstinence movement for the Connexion, as for Nonconformity in general, has been variously assessed. It has been seen as a marker for the secularisation of the church, a withdrawal into a chapel community in the face of an increasingly alien world. It also provided an opportunity for churches to have an agreed agenda without quibbling over questions of doctrine, and as such became a 'solvent of the individualism of Protestant Dissent'.[133] Thus, in addressing these issues the Connexion was drawn into closer relationships with the Particular Baptists against a common enemy.

Protest, characteristic of the period, over issues like church rates and drink, as well as providing a common agenda, was also an expression of the growing confidence of Dissent. The emergence of the Evangelical Alliance in 1846 is an indicator of a growing consensus within Nonconformity. The denominational structures were developing, but the New Connexion being small in size found itself struggling. So it was that, in the face of falling membership and changes within the social structures of society, there was a growing recognition of their common heritage with the Particular Baptists, a heritage that now drew them together rather than held them apart.

---

[130] Heasman, *Evangelicals in Action*, p. 129.
[131] Kruppa, *A Preacher's Progress*, p. 223.
[132] Kruppa, *A Preacher's Progress*, p. 223.
[133] Sellers, *Nineteenth-Century Nonconformity*, p. 42.

CHAPTER 5

The Progress of the Gospel: An Examination of the Development and Evangelistic Strategy of the New Connexion

The development and growth of the Connexion may be considered to have four overlapping stages: a period of initial growth from 1770 to 1815; which was followed by a period of consolidation 1815 to 1840; then stagnation from 1840–1870; and the beginnings of decline from 1870 onwards. These stages correspond loosely to the 'progressive', 'marginal', 'recessive' and 'residual' typology of movements identifed by Currie, Gilbert and Horsley.[1] The first of these phases, that of initial growth, is characterised by rapid and free recruitment from both within and without the church constituencies. The major source of this growth in the years following the formation of the Connexion in 1770 was itinerancy and church planting.

Initial Growth 1770–1815
Itinerancy and Church Planting

The graph below gives the rate of growth as a percentage per annum. The figures here and below are taken from the annual returns made by each church to the Connexion. Every year they were required to provide information on the number of members, the number baptized, the number received from other churches, numbers dismissed to other churches in the Connexion and the numbers excluded, withdrawn, or dead. The figures for each year are in the published minutes of the Connexion. A database for the period 1800–1891, has been compiled, comprising some eleven thousand records. While inaccurate reporting is present in a small number of churches, generally the records provide a reliable indicator of what was happening in the Connexion as a whole.[2] Figures supporting the graphs will be found in the Appendices.

---

[1] Currie, Gilbert, Horsley, *Churches and Churchgoers*, p. 8.
[2] Figures are based on the numbers entered in the annual returns of the Connexion From 1800 on figures for the population aged 15 and over are taken from Gilbert, Currie and Horsley, *Churches and Churchgoers*, p. 65. The annual percentage growth is calculated as follows (Y = Year) Y2–Y1 * Y1 x 100 = % of annual growth.

Development and Evangelistic Strategy 97

From 1815 onwards the percentage growth of the population is given, which enables a comparison to be made between the growth of the Connexion and the population. From this it will be seen that until 1845 the Connexion maintained a rate of growth greater than that of the population. After that date, while there are occasions when it is greater, for the most part the growth of the Connexion does not keep pace with the increase in population.

Simple numerical tables do not reveal the dynamics of growth in the same way as an annual percentage growth rate, but for purposes of comparison they are included in Appendix 5 where they are given in total and by county.

Annual Percentage Growth, 1770–1815

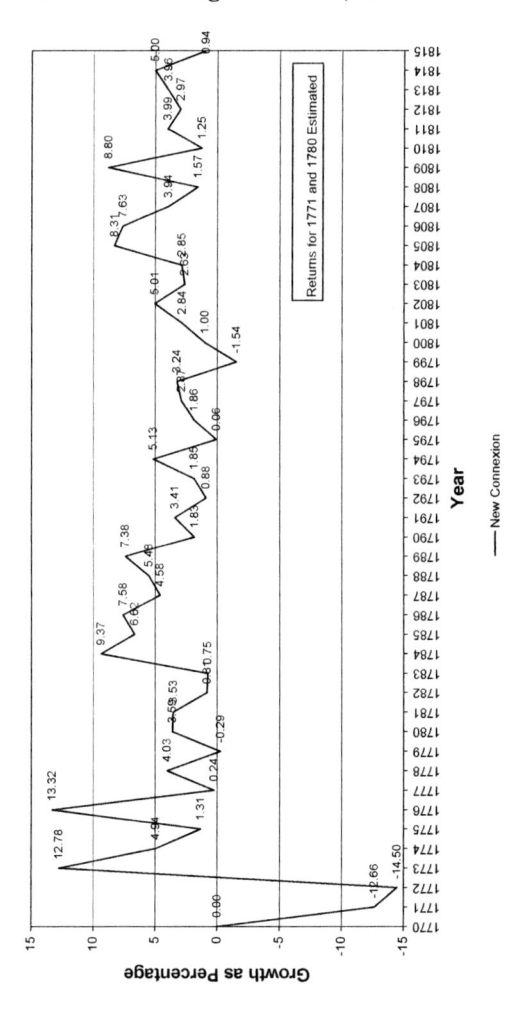

Figure 2

Characteristic of this initial period are alternating peaks of large growth followed by quieter spells: the cycle appears approximately every ten years. It will also be noticed that after the initial burst of growth the peaks become noticeably less high (see Fig. 1 above). The period following 1800, while not peaking as high as the early days of the movement, was nevertheless one of continuously high growth rates. Sustained recruitment like this was never again achieved by the Connexion. What were the factors that contributed to the pattern of development?

The Barton preachers had adopted the practice of preaching in homes, a strategy similar to that of Methodism.[3] Wesley's dictum to his preachers had been 'your only duty is to save souls'; this was followed by the strategy 'go not to those who need you but to those who need you most'.[4] We find a similar sense of mission in the Connexion. Adam Taylor says of the early preachers, 'They had one great object, which they constantly kept in view:—this was to instruct ignorant sinners in the great plan of salvation, and to persuade them to embrace it. To this they directed all their efforts'.[5] The early days of the movement were essentially pragmatic in approach; in this the Connexion was similar to Methodism. Wherever a group of hearers could be gathered there a 'Preaching centre' would be established. The annual association of 1778 'strongly advised the churches to encourage their ministers to preach as often as they could, in the villages around their respective stations'.[6] The Toleration Act (1689) had allowed Dissenters freedom of worship if they registered their meeting places. At Bourne in Lincolnshire it was recorded in the minutes, 'we have had preaching for more than a year in John Markings House in Morton, he is not a member but has got his house registered'. It was also noted, 'This is a dark village unto which we go to preach once a fortnight Lord's Day evening'.[7] It was these preaching stations that were the basis of growth for the New Connexion. The strategy adopted was similar to the practice of itinerancy amongst Particular Baptists and Independents which, as with Methodism, made use of lay preachers.[8] The importance of lay preaching to Dan Taylor can be gauged by his starting a weekly class at his first pastorate at Birchcliffe for men who wished to learn how to preach.[9] The strategy was simple; there would be open air preaching during the summer months, followed by the renting of a room in winter. Frequently the house was the home of a New Connexion member as with John Bairstow of Queenshead, who was a convert of Taylor's. His room in Queenshead was fitted out for worship. Dan Taylor preached once a month, and his brother John began a ministry there that was to last the rest of his life. A building was erected in 1773, and a church was formed

---

[3] Deacon, 'History of General Baptists', *GBM* (1798), p. 182.

[4] John Wesley, *The Works of John Wesley A.M.* (1856), VIII, p. 298.

[5] Taylor, *History*, II, p. 62.

[6] Taylor, *History*, II, p. 218.

[7] Gilbert, *Religion and Society*, 34-35; Bourne Minute Book (1799).

[8] Deryck Lovegrove, 'Particular Baptist Itinerant Preachers during the Late Eighteenth and Early Nineteenth Centuries', *Baptist Quarterly* 28.3 (July, 1979), p. 127.

[9] C.E. Shipley (ed.), *The Baptists of Yorkshire: Being the Centenary Memorial Volume of the Yorkshire Baptist Association* (London: Kingsgate Press, 1912), p 106.

by the dismission of seventeen members of the Birchcliffe fellowship. John Taylor became its pastor. From the Birchcliffe church preaching was established at Shore, Halifax and Burnley, these eventually becoming independent churches.[10] When Joseph Goadby, Sr, started the work at Packington in Leicestershire he adopted a similar approach; a room was hired and licensed preaching begun. After two years, in 1801, the Packington church decided 'to purchase a cottage in Mill Lane, Ashby, for a meeting house' and Joseph Goadby 'went over to Barton to collect for it'. The cottage was altered to suit the needs of the congregation and opened for worship two months later.[11] Taylor adopted the same strategy following his move to London. At Mile End 'he hired a house near his own residence...and fitted it up for public worship'. Taylor did this with a view to enabling his students to exercise their 'ministerial abilities' and also with 'the hopes of extending the cause of the Redeemer'.[12] A work could be started by a New Connexion member moving into an area where there was no Connexion cause and establishing a base for preaching; as with the church at Hucknall, which was started by the Simpson family who moved from Kirkby-Woodhouse.[13] It was not, however, left to individual initiative alone. When the Alford branch of the Maltby Le Marsh church in Lincolnshire 'determined to purchase the meeting house at Alford in which we have worshipped nearly three years', the minutes of the Maltby church said that the establishing of preaching and the hire of a meeting-house was 'the act of the Church'.[14] In 1814, the church at Retford, Nottingham, with a membership of seventy-three, maintained regular preaching at five different places.[15]

Such causes did not view themselves as distinct churches, but as branch works of a mother church. In the initial stages of the development of the Midland group, it was viewed as one church with different congregations: 'it is proper to observe that though Melbourne is twelve or fourteen miles distant from Barton, yet the people there and in all other places where any joined the Church were considered as belonging to Barton, and attended there to receive the Lord's supper once a month'.[16] The responsibility for the work was connexional. Such preaching stations would be supplied with preachers from the main cause and other churches in the area.[17] The Derby cause was initially supported by the work of N. and T. Pickering, ministers

---

[10] Shipley (ed.), *The Baptists of Yorkshire*, p. 106; Taylor, *Memoirs*, p. 102.

[11] Goadby and Goadby, *Not Saints but Men*, pp. 48-49.

[12] Taylor, *Memoirs*, 218.

[13] Stuart Arnold, *Built upon the Foundation: Being the History of the General Baptist Church at Hucknall Nottinghamshire, 1849-1949* (Nottingham: Notts. Newspapers, 1948), p. 8.

[14] Maltby Le Marsh Church Book 2, 2 September 1831. Lincolnshire Archives 16/Bapt/3.

[15] Taylor, *History*, II, p. 363.

[16] J.D. [John Deacon of Friar Lane, Leicester], 'A History of the General Baptist Churches', *GBM* (1798), p. 229.

[17] J.D. [John Deacon], 'A History of the General Baptist Churches', *GBM* (1798), p. 229.

from the Castle Donnington church. Following the recommendation of conference at Smalley in July 1791, the cause was taken up by the Melbourne church, in the persons of F. Smith and J. Smedley. J. Goddard, from the Ilkeston church, attended once a month, being freed for this by the ministers of the church at Kirkby-Woodhouse who supplied his place.[18] Churches were not always as supportive of such initiatives as one might expect. When, in 1803, William and Mary Fowkes from Ilkeston established preaching in a licensed house at Beeston, Nottingham, they met with success, both there and at Chilwell, Nottingham. They 'made application to the Church at Ilkiston [sic] to be dismissed to form a new church', but Ilkeston did not approve and discouraged them. Undaunted, as some of the attenders were in membership at the Lenton church, Nottingham, the Beeston group applied to them for dismissal and the formation into a new church, which was 'cordially approved'. Subsequently the Chilwell group made a further application for dismission which was granted in March 1804.[19]

The direction of the evangelistic thrust of the movement was governed by both conference and local initiative. The conference, composed of leaders of the various causes, would determine where the preachers should go, but it was the local churches who took the initiative in establishing a preaching station. Support would continue until the new group was large enough to support a ministry in its own right. At this point there would be an amicable separation.

Such a strategy had its problems. John Taylor comments on the hiring of a room at Halifax in the spring of 1815 and of his serving at the various outposts: 'It has been thought by many, and I believe it is true, that the cause at Queenshead suffered an injury, by my being engaged so much elsewhere. For two years, I was only one Lord's day more than half my time at home.'[20] Concern for the organisational structure also impeded the growth of the work. Considering the effectiveness of Dan Taylor's itinerant and church planting ministry in Yorkshire, the wisdom of sanctioning his move to London may be questioned. The author of *The Baptists of Yorkshire* felt this. He commented on Dan Taylor's move to London, that it 'caused a general decline in the prosperity of the Connexion in Yorkshire'.[21] The returns would seem to indicate that contention. In 1786 there were four churches with 235 members; by 1800, following Taylor's move, although there were six churches, the membership had fallen to less than 200.

---

[18] S. Taylor Hall, Records of the First General Baptist Church in Derby. MSS 1942. 1. East Midland Baptist Association Archive.

[19] Nether Street Beeston Book No. 1. Nottingham Record Office BP/29/4.

[20] John Taylor, *Memoirs*, p. 37.

[21] W.E. Blomfield, 'The Baptist Churches of Yorkshire in the 17th and 18th Centuries' in Shipley (ed.), *Baptists of Yorkshire*, p. 108.

Itinerancy

A great part of this evangelistic activity was in the hands of preachers who went into the surrounding countryside. These preaching excursions were undertaken by pastors, who viewed it as part of their ministry, by ministers or lay-preachers who had some other occupation, and by students of the Academy, although the contribution of the latter was very limited, especially when it was situated in London. Lay preachers made a significant contribution to the work. One example was Joseph Donisthorpe, a blacksmith and clockmaker, who, having an experience of coming to faith and forgiveness, did not keep it to himself. 'One evening, when a considerable number of his neighbours were assembled in his kitchen, occupying all the seats, so he himself had to sit upon the table; after he had heard and answered several questions, and given required explanations, he began to describe man's lost condition' and found himself preaching. Through his skill as a craftsman, Donisthorpe was able to continue 'first as an evangelist, and afterwards as a pastor, to preach the gospel free of charge'.[22] Deryck Lovegrove says that 'lay involvement itself requires careful definition, for a range of semi-ministerial functions including exhortation, the reading of published sermons, the leadership of prayer meetings and gatherings for edifying conversation together with preaching in the full sense of the word were in many cases subsumed under the single heading of "lay itinerancy"'.[23] A characteristic of itinerancy was that a 'considerable degree of flexibility and movement existed between the different forms of commitment to itinerancy'.[24] Julia Stewart Werner makes the comment that whether or not Primitive Methodism took root in a given locality was largely contingent on the evangelist's finding a haven for preaching.[25]

Of the seventy churches listed in 1817, twenty were formed by a process of church planting from a previously established work in the Midland group. In the Northern group five were formed in this way. Two churches in Yorkshire were new churches, one formed independently (Stayleybridge), the other by the joint exertions of the Yorkshire ministers. Six churches were formed by the joint efforts of several churches. The remainder were mostly General Baptist churches already in existence prior to the formation of the Connexion, or they were churches formed as a result of migration on the part of General Baptists to urban areas. The following diagrammatic table (Fig. 2) sets out the way in which the Barton group of churches grew through the process of itinerancy and congregational planting. The five main centres are underlined.

---

[22] *Barton Memorials*, pp. 102, 105. See also F.M.W. Harrison, 'The Approach of the New Connexion General Baptists to a Midland Industrial Town', *Baptist Quarterly* 33.1 (1989), p. 16.

[23] Lovegrove, 'Particular Baptist Itinerant Preachers', p. 134.

[24] Lovegrove, 'Particular Baptist Itinerant Preachers', p.135

[25] Julia Stewart Werner, *The Primitive Methodist Connexion* (n.pl.: The University of Wisconsin Press, 1984), p. 99.

Development of the Barton Group of Churches

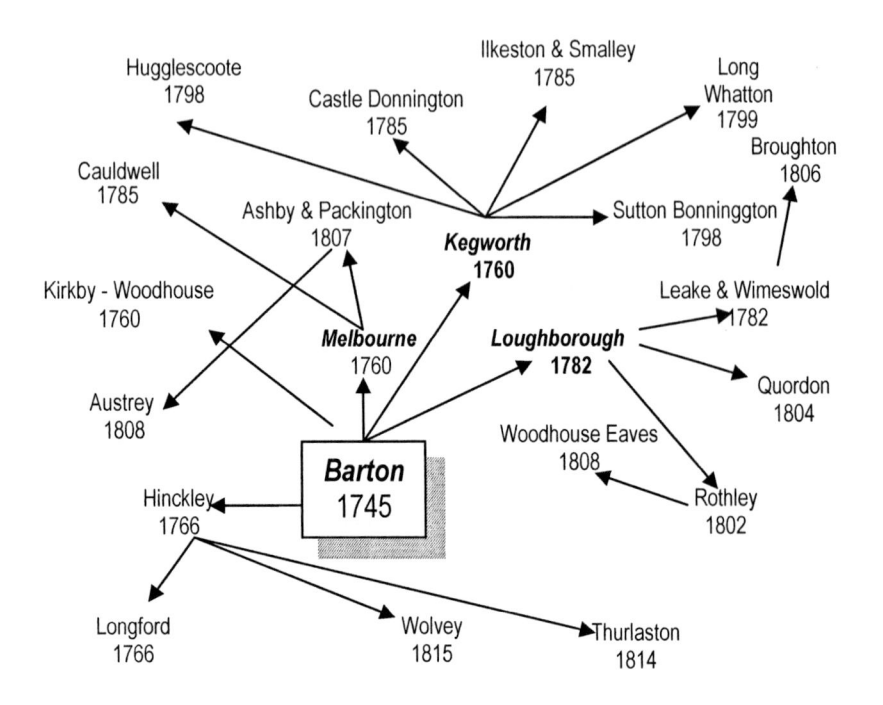

```
Hugglescoote          Ilkeston & Smalley      Long
1798                  1785                    Whatton
         Castle Donnington                    1799
         1785                                          Broughton
Cauldwell                                              1806
1785     Ashby & Packington      Sutton Bonninggton
         1807        Kegworth    1798
                     1760
Kirkby - Woodhouse                        Leake & Wimeswold
1760                                      1782
         Melbourne    Loughborough
         1760         1782
Austrey                                   Quordon
1808                                      1804
                     Woodhouse Eaves
                     1808
         Barton
Hinckley 1745                    Rothley
1766                             1802

Longford             Wolvey      Thurlaston
1766                 1815        1814
```

Figure 3

By 1802 the strategy had been tried and proved.[26] In a 'Letter to the Churches' that year, Dan Taylor urged them to look at what had proved effective, on the principle that 'all other things being equal, it generally pleases God by the same means, or by means nearly similar to revive or to advance his own work'.[27] The rate of church planting was just under one a year; from 1770–1815 forty-two new churches were planted.

---

[26] This was not the only evangelistic strategy amongst Baptists. See Deryck W Lovegrove, *Established Church, Sectarian People: Itinerancy and the Transformation o, English Dissent, 1780–1830* (Cambridge: Cambridge University Press, 1988). Also G.F Nuttall, 'The Rise of Independency in Lincolnshire', *The Journal of the United Reformec Church History Society* 4.1 (1987), pp. 35-50.

[27] Dan Taylor, 'Reports of the Churches', *Letter* (1802), p. 22.

Development and Evangelistic Strategy

The Role of Church Members

The work of conversion was the responsibility of the whole church, not that of the minister alone. Taylor could encourage the churches in this, for in the thirty years he had been at the head of the movement he had seen it grow from some 1,635 members in 1770 to 3,715 in 1802. For the church in which 'conversion work goes on slowly' he suggests that one possible cause is 'in part in yourselves'. Archdeacon Lane church meeting in Leicester 'agreed to reconsider the propriety of appointing persons to see and have conversation with any persons they may see seriously disposed and regular in their attendance on Divine Worship'.[28] The establishment of preaching centres or 'stations' was not sufficient by itself, effective outreach required the active cooperation of church members. Taylor asks the churches,

> Do you constantly endeavour to co-operate with us in your private advices and instructions, given to your children; or other relatives and acquaintance? Do your lives adorn your profession? ... Do you by your conduct 'hold forth the word of life?' ... Do you let the world see, beloved brethren, by your spirit and general conversation, that Jesus Christ 'gave himself up for us, that he might redeem us from all iniquity, and purify to himself a peculiar people jealous of good works'.[29]

It was lifestyle and personal conversation about the gospel, by the members of Connexion churches, that was the key to the effectiveness of outreach. The London Conference at Chesham on 9 March 1809 suggested the work could be encouraged by, amongst other things, 'social prayer and Christian conference'.[30]

In addressing the personal responsibility of each member for the work of evangelism amongst friends and family, Taylor drew attention to a sphere of activity that was potentially most fruitful. In their examination of church growth, Currie, Gilbert and Horsley say, 'In general, those persons who are church members or significantly disposed towards church membership, will be related to each other by familial or other ties'. They argue that:

> A church's membership is itself a human community, and it recruits new members from the children of existing members and from the families that make up the 'constituency' of persons significantly disposed toward membership through the operation of some psychological or sociological factor.[31]

The church at Hugglescote recognised that this personal contact ought to continue after conversion. An entry in the church book for August 1815 says, 'members newly admitted are too frequently neglected and that it would be better that friends

---

[28] Archdeacon Lane Church Book No. 1 (12 October 1807).
[29] Taylor, *Letter* (1802), p. 24.
[30] *GBR* 2 (1812), p. 264.
[31] Currie, Gilbert, Horsley, *Churches and Churchgoers*, p. 6.

should converse with them and enquire the state of their minds and endeavour to assist them'.[32]

In 1813 the churches of the Connexion received a letter exhorting them to a 'Public Spirit in the Promotion of Religion'. 'Public Spirit' was defined as that disposition of mind which 'inclines a person to give up a portion of his own happiness for that of his fellow creature'.[33] Thomas Stevenson, Sr, of Loughborough, who wrote the letter and was later to become tutor to the Education Society, sensed that 'the zeal and public spirit, which distinguished our worthy Brethren the fathers of the cause, has of late years suffered a very serious decline'.[34] Churches, it was felt, were lax in their evangelistic duty, they were inward looking, confining 'their views and their efforts to that society, with which they are particularly connected'. Stevenson felt that the problem was a lack of proper ministerial training. He argued that an institution was needed and that its lack 'must without a miracle tend most essentially to obstruct the progress of the cause'.[35] He seems to have overlooked the fact that the fathers of the cause were without the benefit of such an 'institution'.

In Stevenson's appeal there is a fundamental shift from the responsibility of all to engage in the work of evangelism to the support of an institution that would do the work. While Stevenson's desire for a respectable ministry may reflect some of the social aspirations of the movement, it is also a move from lay to ministerial responsibility. Such a move is an indicator of a shift away from 'sectarian' orientation towards a 'church' orientation.[36]

As the initial phase of development drew to a close the institutionalisation of mission and evangelism was reflected in the formation of the Itinerant Fund in 1810; this became the Home Mission in 1821. The Itinerant Fund was a means of organizing itinerant work within the Connexion, but it shifted the emphasis to the ministry rather than the laity. The 1810 association, meeting in London, considered the cases of several 'decayed' churches in Lincolnshire. It was decided to send a minister to work among them for a few weeks, and a fund was established to defray the expenses. The following year the subject came up again and it was resolved 'that a fund be raised for promoting the cause of religion and the General Baptist interest'. The management, and distribution of the fund was vested in the annual association.[37] This Itinerant Fund was used to initiate work in new areas and to support churches in difficulty. In 1821 it became the General Baptist Home Missionary Society. In the same year, Particular Baptists in London established the similarly named Baptist

---

[32] Hugglescote Church Book, 20 August, 1815. Leicester Record Office. NB/150/2.

[33] Thomas Stevenson, 'Public Spirit in the Promotion of Religion', *Letter* (1813), p. 16.

[34] Stevenson, 'Public Spirit in the Promotion of Religion', p. 17.

[35] Stevenson, 'Public Spirit in the Promotion of Religion', p. 18.

[36] Loren Craig Shull, 'The General Baptist Process: From Sect to Denomination' (Southern Baptist Theological Seminary, DPhil thesis, 1985), pp. 57, 135.

[37] Wood, *History*, pp. 311-12.

Home Missionary Society.[38] The aim of the Home Mission was 'The Introduction of the Gospel and the General Baptist Interest into places where they are not already established', and sending suitable ministers to visit 'decaying or disorganised churches'.[39]

The 'Letter to the Churches' for 1821, entitled 'Home Mission', called for 'every united and strenuous support on the part of the church for this organisation'.[40] Frederick Deacon, the author of the letter, was aware of the financial demands on churches: 'Nor would we have you be alarmed with the idea that the society we now advocate and support will injure the Foreign Mission. We would not have her considered as the rival, but as the *lovely sister* of that invaluable institution.'[41] But the Home Mission lacked the glamour of its overseas sister, and it never attracted the kind of financial support that would have made it a really effective agent of mission. In 1821, the Society was decentralised and the financial responsibility given to the different districts of the Connexion; reports from these districts were still to be presented at the annual association. A Village Mission was formed and a village missionary or Bible reader employed. A further reorganisation took place in 1828, which reaffirmed the role of conference and the expenditure of locally raised funds without the intervention of a general committee. By decentralising the work opportunity for strategic investment of funds lost out to local concerns. In 1829, Thomas Stevenson, speaking at the Midland district of the Home Mission at Nottingham, sought to recover some of the old spirit, he said, 'we must in this matter, turn missionaries, and preach to the people as if we were for the first time preaching to heathens.'[42] When in 1828 Thomas Cook served as a village missionary, James Taylor of Hinckley, a leading minister in the Connexion, questioned his authorisation to make financial calls on churches.[43] Reflecting at a later date on this era of the Connexion's life, Cook observed, in rosy retrospect, 'that no home mission work of the present day bears any comparison with that carried out by these devoted men. And it is to be regretted that some system of itinerancy is not adopted with a view to the revival and sustentation of the interest which was excited from the year 1770 down to 1830'.[44]

---

[38] Watts, *The Dissenters*, II, p. 136.
[39] Frederick Deacon, 'Home Mission', *Letter* (1821), p. 23. The letter is signed F. Deacon, but attributed to J. Deacon in a list of the published Letters to the Churches in the *Minutes* of 1876. Frederick Deacon was the son of John Deacon of the Friar Lane Church, Leicester, and led a secession from Friar Lane to form the Dover Street Church, Leicester in 1822. See Ashby, *Friar Lane*, pp. 43, 51.
[40] Frederick Deacon, 'Home Mission', p. 24.
[41] Frederick Deacon, 'Home Mission', p. 25.
[42] Wood, *History*, pp. 312-13.
[43] Cook, *Preacher Pastor Mechanic*, p. 193.
[44] Cook, *Preacher Pastor Mechanic*, p. 193.

Marginal Growth 1816–1840

Marginal Phase

The period of progressive development was followed by a slow-down in recruitment and the beginnings of an inward-looking approach to growth. This may be termed the marginal phase and loosely covers the period 1815 to 1840. It was the last period in which continued growth was a feature of the movement, as Figure 3 shows.

The growth rates at the beginning of the century were never again achieved by the Connexion; and while the growth rate of the period after 1839 levels out, it does so at a lower level. A growth rate around 2% was needed to keep pace with natural loss through deaths, transfers and exclusions (see Fig. 3 below). The period following the Napoleonic wars was one of great social and economic dislocation. This provided an opportunity for growth for some church groupings. The Primitive Methodists, drawing on a group socially similar to the New Connexion, took advantage of a climate favourable to revivalism. Their move into Leicestershire in the summer of 1817 provided a 'rich harvest of converts'.[45] For the New Connexion the harvest was good, but not as good as it had been a decade earlier. The period between 1805 and 1809 saw the highest annual percentage growth rate in the life of the Connexion. As can be seen in Figure 3, between 1815 and 1840 the annual percentage growth rate levelled out at around 5%, which was almost half that of the previous period.

Thomas Stevenson called the Connexion to adopt a strategy for the new centres of urban population, but his appeal for an educated ministry also represents an inward turn towards a church orientation. Stevenson, writing the Association Letter for 1813 'Public Spirit in the Promotion of Religion', rightly perceived the areas of greatest need to be in the new centres of urban population: 'our principal attention and most vigorous efforts should be directed to the large towns'.[46] He points to the fact that other denominations saw the obvious need and had responded to a far greater degree than the General Baptists. The returns from the churches for that year, 1813, confirm his observation. They indicate the New Connexion was mainly confined to small towns and villages. Of the 62 churches listed less only eight were in large centres of population. There was one each in Birmingham, Derby, Halifax, two in Leicester and three in London. Such evangelistic strategy as the Connexion had, was based around the establishment of preaching centres, familial and community relationships being the basis for the gathering of such congregations. This, while suited to small towns and villages, was not as effective in the impersonality of the new urban centres. But the Connexion did not seem able to develop a strategy that would enable them to move into the cities. It was this failure to move into these new towns and industrial areas at an early stage, that was to contribute as much as anything to the stagnation of the Connexion.

---

[45] Werner, *Primitive Methodist Connexion*, p. 91.
[46] *Letter* (1813), p. 18.

Development and Evangelistic Strategy

Annual Percentage Growth, 1816–1840

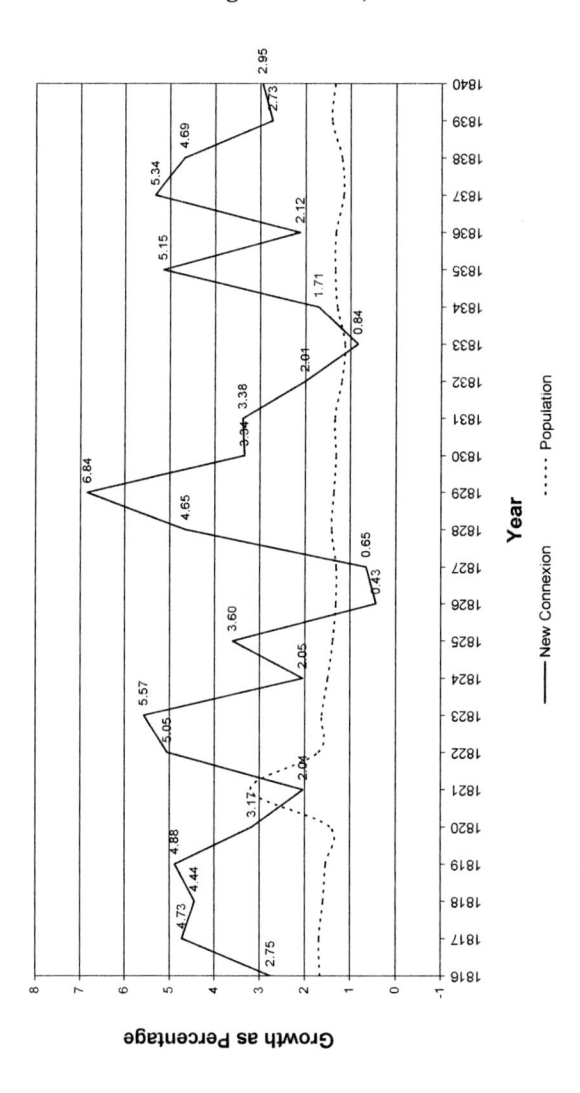

Figure 4

Evangelistic Strategy

We see another indicator of this inward turn on the part of the Connexion in the development of a full-time ministry. A major difference between the New Connexion and the Primitive Methodists was where they stood on the matter of evangelism.

Jackson argues that the New Connexion was becoming increasingly rigid and that there was an emerging professional class of ministers who 'impeded the spontaneous extension of preaching to new centres'. He says that 'In earlier times, a preacher would gladly have left his home to carry the message to dark corners, without counting the cost either in money or personal suffering; under the changing conditions, carping questions of authorisation and finance hindered initiative'.[47] One reason for this may be the age of the movement, while Primitive Methodism still had the vitality of a new movement, the Connexion was forty-five years old, its first generation of leaders was passing away and leadership was moving into the second generation. Niebuhr has drawn attention to the problem of inertia that confronts a movement in the second generation.[48] Another factor lies in a view of the church that confines the responsibility for initiatives in evangelism to the 'ministry'. This limits the growth of a movement to the evangelistic concern of its professional ministry.

Primitive Methodism had a structure that enabled a quick response to receptive areas.[49] The Connexion, drawing on its independent background, had a more static form of settled pastoral ministry that inhibited flexibility. It looked to the 'ministry' for initiatives in evangelism. The author of a *Brief Sketch of the Doctrine and Discipline of the GENERAL BAPTIST Churches* in 1824 noted that, 'It may be proper to add that, recently, most of the Ministers of this denomination have been much engaged in Preaching the Gospel in the open Air'.[50] The dependence on ministers meant that the Connexion was not able to move into receptive areas as rapidly as the Methodists. It was this, together with an inability effectually to mobilise its converts that hindered the rapid expansion of the Connexion.

The lack of concern for growth in the New Connexion was commented on by the sisters Bertha and Lilian Goadby, granddaughters of Joseph Goadby, Sr (1774–1841) and joint authors of *Not Saints but Men*. In this family history they noted that the 'work of church extension did not play as important a part during Joseph Goadby the younger's pastorate at Leicestershire as it did during his father's life at Ashby'.[51] As we have seen, leadership played an important part in the evangelistic thrust of the movement.

---

[47] G. Jackson 'The Evangelical Work of Baptists in Leicestershire 1740–1820' (University of London, MA thesis, 1955), p. 276.

[48] Niebuhr, *The Social Sources of Denominationalism*, p. 54.

[49] K.D.M. Snell, *Church and Chapel in the North Midlands: Religious Observance in the Nineteenth Century* (Department of English Local History Occasional Papers, 4th Series, No. 3; Leicester: Leicester University Press. 1991), p. 21.

[50] *Doctrine and Discipline,* p. 8, emphasis original.

[51] Goadby and Goadby, *Not Saints but Men,* p. 108.

Sunday School and Evangelism

Currie, Gilbert and Horsley argue that one of the indicators of the marginal stage of growth is a growing dependence on 'autogenous', or internal, growth.[52] The churches had viewed Sunday schools as an evangelistic agency from their beginnings.[53] As early as 1801, the Connexion had begun to look inward to the Sunday school which was described as the 'hope of the next generation'.[54] We see this turning to the internal constituency reflected in the concerns of the Connexion over the Sunday school. Towards the middle of the century it was viewed as a major source of recruitment by the movement. In 1833, the Stoney Street church in Nottingham reported that 'not a few who have joined us received their first serious impressions in a Sabbath School'.[55] The Lincolnshire and Cambridgeshire General Baptist Sunday School Union asked teachers to discuss the question, 'Can any plan be adopted to promote the early conversion of our children?', and urged the monthly visitation of parents.[56]

A 'resource' to 'replenish the church', was the way William Underwood described the Sunday school. 'We turn', he said, 'to the children educated there, with the same anxiety and expectation as one felt by the florist when he surveys the rising plants in his nursery... The numbers contained in those training institutions encourage our hopes of the church's increase'.[57] We find horticultural imagery again in 1868 where the Sunday school was said by a correspondent to the *General Baptist Magazine* of 1868 to be a 'nursery in which the saplings are nurtured and trained that they may become pillars in the Church of God'. Was this hope justified? This correspondent thought so, that year his church had baptised twelve from the Sunday school, nine of whom were from outside the church and were 'members of irreligious families, and had no religious home training'.[58] The Nottingham General Baptist Preachers Union which sent men to the church at Daybrook, Nottingham, recorded in the minutes of their monthly meeting,

> The work of conversion began about 2 months since amongst the Senior Scholars of our school & we rejoice to state that in addition to our present number of candidates we have many more whose heart the [Lord] hath touched & we hope ere long will be decided followers of Jesus. The young men's class continues steadily to

---

[52] Currie, Gilbert and Horsley, *Churches and Churchgoers*, p. 8.
[53] Deryck Lovegrove, 'Idealism and Association in Early Nineteenth Century Dissent', in W.J. Sheils and Diana Wood (eds), *Voluntary Religion* (Oxford: Basil Blackwell, 1986), p. 310.
[54] Dan Taylor, 'Concurrence of people with their ministers', *Letter* (1801), p. 19.
[55] *Minutes* (1833), p. 13.
[56] Lincolnshire and Cambridgeshire General Baptist Sunday School Union Minute Book, 29 July 1858. Lincolnshire County Archives. 17/Bapt/3.
[57] Quoted by Underwood, 'Sunday Schools', *Letter* (1850), p. 44.
[58] *GBM* (1868), p. 207.

improve, we may say 5 young men have recently given their hearts to God and are walking in the way of heaven.[59]

The encouraging report was repeated the following month. It should be noted, however, that these conversions took place at a time of general growth within the Connexion.

Comparison of Church Growth vs Sunday School, 1845–1890

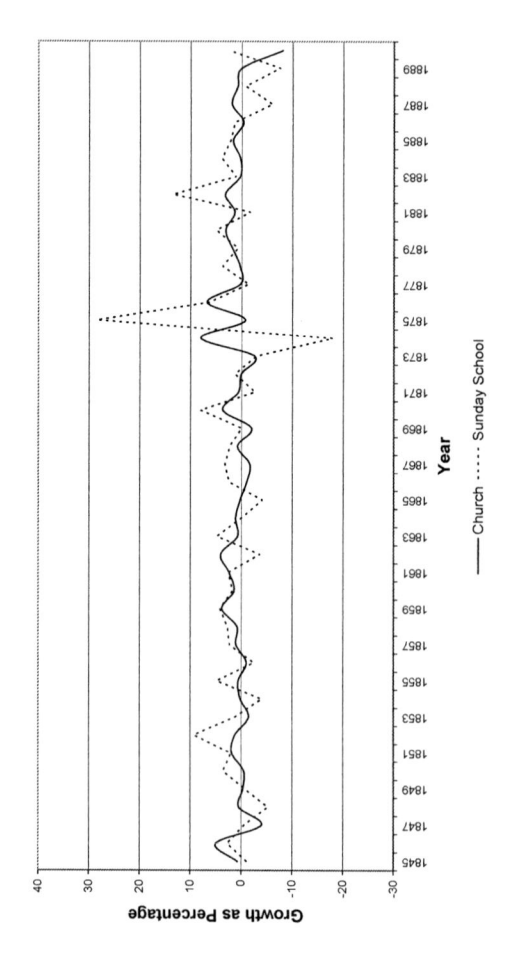

Figure 5

---

[59] Minute Book of the General Baptist Preachers Union, 3 September 1849–6 June 1870, 28 May 1860. Nottingham Record Office BP/12/4.

When we compare the growth of the Sunday school with the increase in membership, we see that there is no evidence to suggest that Sunday school growth led to church growth. If anything, the Sunday school follows the church in its pattern of growth (see Fig. 4 above).

This growing dependence on the recruiting potential of the Sunday school marks a significant change of attitude. At the beginning of the century the Sunday school had been an important but auxiliary agency in terms of evangelism. The churches had not relied on recruiting from this group that had already been subject to the influence of the church, rather they had gone outside to the 'world'. The change in thinking that looked at the Sunday school as a 'nursery' for the church implies that some interim stage, some form of pre-evangelism, was necessary before gospel preaching would be effective. It is an attitude that reflects the way in which the Connexion was becoming removed from the constituency from which it wished to recruit, to the extent that pre-evangelism in the Sunday school was felt necessary. Here was a group that was already exposed to Christian culture, and should therefore be more receptive to the gospel.

However, there was recognition on the part of some that this was not the case, that the Sunday school was not always effective in terms of recruitment. Underwood cites a minister in Manchester who felt that 'As a whole our Sabbath Schools have proved a failure'.[60] This was supported by John Clifford who said, 'Doubtless "the masses" have to a prodigious extent been in our Sunday schools, and through our bungling in part it is that they are now outside our churches and aliens from our institutions'.[61]

Underwood hints at, but does not admit to, the evangelistic failure of Sunday schools. It seems to have been a failure to keep the older children and see them make the transition into full membership of the church. This is reflected in his suggestion for 'Adult Bible Classes' by which means those who come 'could be retained to a riper age'. He is also aware that 'the Conversion of Senior scholars before they pass from beneath the care of their teachers, is extremely important'.[62] The writer in the *Baptist Reporter* was far more outspoken in his condemnation, and attributed the failure to teachers who 'instruct more "in the letter" than in "the spirit" of the Bible'.[63] In 1870, Clifford said that the goal of the Sunday school was not the teaching of reading and writing, rather 'We shall have to lead the children into a loving and trusting regard for Christ Jesus, to a felt sympathy with His spirit'.[64] Fred Thompson, in an article 'Chapel and School—The Missing Link', urged teachers to involve themselves with the children outside the 'three hours on Sunday'. Failure here, he argued, meant that 'Sunday schools instead of being made what they

---

[60] Underwood, *Letter* (1850), p. 44; *GBRM* (1832), pp. 95-96. See also *Baptist Reporter* (1864), p.433

[61] John Clifford, 'What becomes of our old Scholars?', *GBM* (1877), p. 21.

[62] Underwood, *Letter* (1850), p. 47.

[63] *Baptist Reporter* (1864), p. 433.

[64] John Clifford, 'Sunday schools of the Future', *GBM* (1870), p. 226.

might be made...are, comparatively speaking, huge failures. Two or three per cent. per annum gained to the church!'[65] In 1873 concern was again expressed about the relationship between the child and the church in an article 'The conversion of the young and their reception into the church'.[66]

In 1876, W. Jones of Bradford was asking 'What do we labour for? is it that the children may learn to read? No'. Neither did he feel it was to catechise them; his goal was conversion, 'if that child have not "Christ within, the hope of glory", I have failed in my mission...my aim is to secure the conversion of that child to lead it to Christ'.[67] Clifford described the 'prodigious disproportion between the quantity of teaching work done, all over the land, and all the year round, in our Sabbath Schools, and the carefully ascertained results in additions to the membership of our churches, is to say the least, a ghastly revelation!'[68] Citing the records of the Metropolitan Sunday School Union, he estimated that for the decades 1870–1890 the average number of scholars who became members of churches was, in London, twelve in a thousand, or 1.2% per year, in the country it was fourteen per thousand, or 1.4 percent per year. He comments, 'To use a hackneyed and well-worn figure which describes the Sunday school as the nursery of the church, we may well ask, Where is the gardener that would be content with so small a number of saplings transplanted out of his training ground into the productive orchards of the world?'[69]

Although there was a relatively small return on the investment in the Sunday school the large numbers involved made it seem worthwhile, and a little return in an age of generally declining numbers was most welcome. The above gives some indication of the change of agenda from education to conversion.

Part of the difficulty of recruiting from the Sunday school may not have been conversion as such, but the difficulty of integrating the poor, who constituted the majority of the Sunday school, into middle-class churches.[70] John Clifford observed, 'Hitherto we have only gained one class. We must have all... The wealthy and the well taught shun the Sunday school as though it retained the pauper objects and features that gave it birth'.[71] Ian Sellers says 'the offspring of respectable church members were often discouraged from attending the institutions themselves, had perforce to accompany their parents to the adult services, grew bored, and fell away in adulthood'.[72]

Philip Cliff argues of the early days of the Sunday school, that one should not look for instant results but that a 'passage of say, ten years, between a child's

---

[65] Fred Thompson, 'Chapel and School—The Missing Link', *GBM* (1871), p. 300.

[66] J.P. Tetley, 'The Conversion of the Young and their Reception into the Church', *GBM* (1873),p.8.

[67] W. Jones, 'How may Sunday school teachers most effectually secure the conversion of their Scholars?', *GBM* (1876), p. 330.

[68] John Clifford, 'The passage from School to Church', *GBM* (1880), p. 244.

[69] Clifford, 'The passage from School to Church', *GBM* (1880), p. 244.

[70] McLeod, *Religion and the Working Class*, p. 23.

[71] Clifford, 'Sunday schools of the Future', *GBM* (1870), p. 228.

[72] Sellers, *Nineteenth-Century Nonconformity*, p. 37.

leaving the Sunday school and his becoming a church member'; then he says, 'one can begin to see some reason for the rapid growth in church membership'.[73] While this may be true for the early part of the century, Gilbert estimates only 3% per year between 1818 and 1900.[74] One might have expected the growth of the Connexion to follow this, but as we have seen the evidence from the returns shows that the Connexion rarely achieved this rate of growth in the second half of the century.

One indirect effect of Sunday schools in relation to evangelism was the amount of people they absorbed in staffing. 'Sunday school work is taking the primacy in our modes of Christian work, and is winning the best hearts and heads of the church', said Clifford in the *General Baptist Magazine* of 1882.[75] The work of the Sunday school was often at the expense of other areas of evangelism; the itinerant lay preacher confronting his fellows with the claims of the gospel had become the Sunday school teacher most often working with children, and having little influence on their parents. The lower middle classes involved with church life were experiencing the opportunity for leisure; this new resource of manpower was directed into support of the institutional structure. For those who taught in it, the Sunday school brought prestige and position, a sense of worth and value. The Sunday school offered to the church member the opportunity for advancement through the ever-growing infrastructure of teacher's meetings and Sunday school unions. The Sunday school became the domain of the layman, to the extent that it was often independent of the church, as at Friar Lane, Leicester, when, in 1807, the school became a self-governing body, the teachers forming a committee for its management.[76] Schools could even become a rival institution. One contributor to the *General Baptist Magazine* described the relationship as being 'somewhat loose and unsatisfactory'.[77] Another correspondent responded to the criticism that the 'Sabbath School' was in danger of 'usurping the place of the church' and that it was 'practically...a rival' robbing the church of their presence.[78] An article in the *Baptist Reporter* spoke of 'dissatisfaction' on the part of church officers; rather than a 'nursery for the church' Sunday schools were 'a separate establishment, under different management—a sort of independent body resenting any interference by the church or its officers...a little republic, making its own laws electing its own officers and governing itself'.[79] The practice of Sunday schools holding their own services was, in the view of Underwood, a leading minister in the Connexion, 'open to serious objection'. But, twenty years later, John Clifford was to endorse the practice of separate services for

---

[73] Philip Cliff, *The Rise and the Development of the Sunday School Movement in England 1780–1980* (Redhill: National Christian Education Council, 1986), p. 124.

[74] Currie Gilbert and Horsley, *Churches and Churchgoers*, p. 88.

[75] John Clifford, 'The General Baptist Church in 1882', *GBM* (1882), p. 366.

[76] Ashby, *Friar Lane*, p. 41.

[77] Joseph Cotton, 'The Relation of the Church to the Sunday school', *GBM* (1865), p. 362.

[78] 'Church and the Sunday school', *GBM* (1868), p. 207.

[79] 'The Precise Relation that the Sunday school should sustain to the Church', *Baptist Reporter* (1864), pp. 431-34.

children in his advocacy of the development of a 'Children's Church'.[80] Reading the church minute books one becomes aware of a frequent undercurrent of tension between the Sunday school and the church. In December 1837, at Archdeacon Lane, Leicester, this tension came into the open and the church sought to bring the Sunday school under its control.[81]

But their action did not resolve the problem, for four years later there was a dispute about writing on the Sabbath.[82] The following month the minister, T. Stevenson, made some general comments about the school and sought to explain the resolution respecting writing on the Sabbath, and there was

> a long discussion or rather warm remarks on the subject, shewing that the matter in question was not really the writing on the Sabbath day, but a strife for power, and supremacy in the Government of the School.[83]

The dispute resulted in the resignation of twenty-three teachers, and the decisions of the previous meeting were upheld, the minute concludes, 'Thus the decision of the church is again proved that must & will have its legitimate right to rule & manage the School'.[84] At the following church meeting on 17 May 1841 a number applied to withdraw from fellowship. It was decided that they be 'allowed to withdraw believing that the spirit & cause they have adopted in attempting to injure the character of our pastor & cause a division in the church, they are unworthy of a place in the Church & we could not commune with them'.[85] The energies expended in power struggles between Sunday school and church meant that there was less energy available for the evangelistic mission of the church. But this was hidden from the church by the apparent effectiveness of the Sunday school movement. Even with all its troubles Archdeacon Lane could report for 1859, 'we have much cause to rejoice in the power and Influence of the Love and Grace of God by which 45 have been added to our Church; 40 of these are from the families & School connected to our Place of Worship'.[86]

Following Forster's Education Act of 1870, in which the state assumed responsibility for education, there was improved provision for day Schools. These new schools eschewed any credal basis or denominational distinctive, and it was left to local schools to decide whether or not any religious instruction should be given.[87]

The concern about conversion indicates that the churches were aware that they had a limited period of time in which to recruit the children. In addition to the failure to win in significant numbers those brought into the ambit of the church through the

---

[80] John Clifford, 'Sunday schools of the Future', *GBM* (1870), p. 225.
[81] Archdeacon Lane Minute Book No. 3 (11 December 1837).
[82] Archdeacon Lane Minute Book No. 3 (15 February 1841).
[83] Archdeacon Lane Minute Book No. 3 (15 March 1841)
[84] Archdeacon Lane Minute Book No. 3 (15 March 1841)
[85] Archdeacon Lane Minute Book No. 3 (17 May 1841).
[86] 'States of the Churches', *Minutes* (1859), p. 20.
[87] Cliff, *Sunday School Movement*, p. 162.

Sunday school, there had been a failure to recruit from within its own ranks. 'Where are some of the children and children's children of the prominent laymen of former years? why are they not with us...where are the sons of our ministers? where the young preachers of promise and hope of whom we expected much in the last ten or twenty years?', asked Thomas Goadby as chairman of the Connexion in 1868.[88] Clifford was also concerned about the failure to recruit their own children, 'The offspring of the most pious parents do not give the evidence we desire that they are taught of the Lord'.[89] These questions identified the problem facing all conversionist movements, that of the second generation. The second generation, says Niebuhr, 'holds its convictions as a heritage' as opposed to the first generation who came by their convictions 'painfully and held them at a bitter cost'.[90] The hopes for a revival of the Connexion's fortunes through the Sunday school were not fulfilled, the preoccupation with children's work was to continue to the detriment of other areas of mission.

One Man Ministry

For the Barton preachers and Dan Taylor, every member of the church had a contribution to make in the proclamation of the gospel. In his history of the Connexion, Adam Taylor says, 'The most striking feature in the character of these professors, both private members and ministers, was an earnestness in their religious pursuits', and, he continues, 'Nothing afforded them more pleasure, than to be made an instrument of awakening a sinner to flee from the wrath to come'.[91] This was not the case by the 1850s, 60s and 70s; during that time, there was a tendency towards centralisation, to placing things in the hands of the professional ministry. 'Is it right for the pastor of a Christian church to refuse to encourage occasional preachers through a spirit of monopoly?', complained one letter writer to the *General Baptist Magazine* in 1866.[92] When the Connexion was formed the pastor had been the leader of a group of people who themselves had been involved in ministry, but over a period of time the work of ministry seems to have devolved to the pastor. In 1868 John Clifford, seeking to understand why the Connexion was not recruiting, asked the question, 'Why do the working classes stand aloft from our places of worship?' In answering that question he lay the fault at the decline of lay involvement which included parental responsibility, and to the 'all-engrossing character of business pursuits'. But his main target was 'the professional spirit'. He drew attention to

---

[88] Thomas Goadby, 'Chairman's Address', *Minutes* (1868), p. 4.
[89] John Clifford, 'Sunday schools of the Future', *GBM* (1870), p. 226.
[90] Niebuhr, *The Social Sources of Denominationalism*, p. 54. For a fuller discussion see J. Milton Yinger, *Religion, Society and the Individual: An Introduction to the Sociology of Religion* (New York: Macmillan, 11th edn, 1968), p. 147; and B.R. Wilson (ed.), *Patterns of Sectarianism: Organisation and Ideology in Social and Religious Movements* (London: Heinmann, 1967), p. 38.
[91] Taylor, *History*, II, pp. 57-58.
[92] *GBM* (1866), p. 93.

what he considered a significant change in the nature of the ministry. This change he saw in the area of dominance of the 'one man system', 'which is not the system we inherited and the professional spirit which is not the spirit of the first Baptists'.[93] He argued that their increasing professionalism was at the expense of 'the call and right of every Christian to a sphere of usefulness in the Lord's Body'. For him a fundamental change had taken place in the nature of the church:

> I cannot reject the impression that we have fallen into the snare of the Free Churches of our day, viz that of nourishing the 'professional sentiment' in regard to the ministry. With all our might we must war against the tendency to centralisation of spiritual functions.[94]

Again, in 1875 we read, 'The success of the church as a converting institution is made to depend on the minister mainly, and five or six officials together with a few Sabbath school teachers.'[95] W. Marsh, writing in September 1876, said that the minister was expected to do 'nearly the whole religious work of the community, and be the prime mover in every branch of Christian activity'.[96] This article, 'People outside the church and how to reach them', was an appeal for lay ministry and personal evangelism on the part of church members, for, Marsh argued, 'the greater number of members let their gifts lie unused'.[97] Clifford said that there was need to 'accord a brotherly welcome to men who have not passed through the curriculum of a scholastic education if they can prove themselves prophets trained of the Lord'.[98] Clifford sought to redress the situation. His appeal was to 'make the church a congregation of ministers, a body of witnesses for the Lord'.[99]

The evangelistic campaigns of Moody and Sankey provided some opportunity for involvement, as they were characteristically lay campaigns. By 1887, there were complaints about this type of united mission, such as that by 'A Layman' (W. Richardson) in the *General Baptist Magazine*:

> The parade of gownsmen is too imposing and military—like processions and august orations strike me as being as unreasonable... How few of the unwashed are caught by such displays! On sober reflection I thought the same showy fashionable air was

---

[93] John Clifford, 'Non attendance of professed Christians at public worship', *Letter* (1868), pp. 68,70.
[94] Clifford, 'Non attendance of professed Christians at public worship', p. 71.
[95] John Clifford, 'How the revival Works', *GBM* (1875), p. 24.
[96] W. March, 'People outside the church and how to reach them', *GBM* (1876), p. 325.
[97] March, 'People outside the church and how to reach them', p. 326.
[98] Clifford, 'Non attendance of professed Christians', p. 70.
[99] John Clifford, *Religious Life in the Rural Districts of England* [paper read at the Baptist Union at Birmingham 2-5 October 1876] (London: Yates and Alexander, 1876) p. 1.

present at Mr Moody's meeting—church-goers, chapel-goers, in silks and satins, resembling a concert audience, abounded.[100]

While there were isolated instances of missionary congregations, generally speaking the evangelistic work of the churches was much more structured and dependent on the initiatives of ministers, conference and associations.

Stagnation 1840-1870

Deceptive Growth

The third or recessive stage of growth is characterised by declining recruitment and a downward trend in membership. As Queen Victoria came to the throne, the New Connexion, together with other Nonconformists, were experiencing a period of growth. There had been a 43% increase in membership of the Connexion since the beginning of the decade. There had been a steady increase in numbers at home, and the mission work overseas was beginning to show fruit. It was a period of chapel building and enlarging.[101] In 1835, of the ninety-two churches which submitted reports to the association, fourteen were involved in enlargements or alterations to their chapels. Stoney Street, Nottingham, may have been large, but it was not untypical of the Connexion in the late 1830s and 40s: 'During the year our congregations have been such as to induce us to commence the enlargement of our chapel...at present we have ten places in the suburbs of Nottingham where we regularly preach the gospel'.[102]

As the New Connexion moved into the fourth decade of the nineteenth century the movement appeared to be in a healthy condition. In fact, the growth was deceptive. The Connexion was losing ground against the growth in population. From 1820 onwards, with a few exceptions, the general rate of growth declined. The large increase in 1852 was offset by a corresponding decline the following year. 1845 marked the end of the period of consistent growth as the graph below indicates (see Figure 5).

William Underwood expressed his concern about the growth of the denomination in 1856, and made the observation that, 'to remain stationary as to members requires a large annual accession of new members'.[103] His observation was sound, as the following table showing the percentage density of the Connexion to the population indicates (see Table 6 below).

---

[100] *GBM* (1887), p. 458.
[101] Cook, *Preacher Pastor Mechanic*, p. 193.
[102] *Minutes* (1834), p. 13.
[103] William Underwood, 'Our Denomination: Its state and what is needful to its progress', *GBM* (1856), p. 51.

118   *The Tribe of Dan*

Annual Percentage Growth Rate, 1841–1870

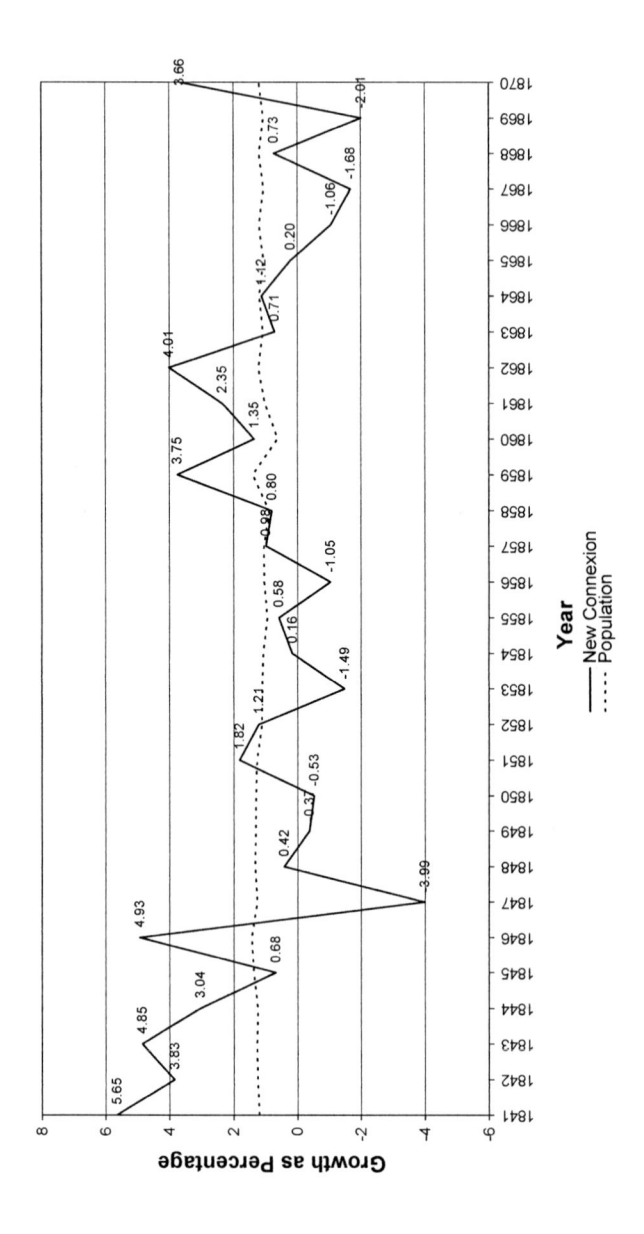

Figure 6

New Connexion Membership as Density of Population

1800	.0499335
1805	.0577712
1810	.0694879
1815	.0762014
1820	.0854197
1825	.0931895
1830	.1052942
1835	.1116564
1840	.1249273
1845	.1399919
1850	.131403
1855	.1272688
1860	.1282967
1865	.1246654
1870	.1240719
1875	.12250737
1880	.1297272
1885	.1301148
1890	.1148697

Table 4

The down turn in growth becomes even more evident when we look at the figures in graph form (Fig. 8 below).

The problem was that the Connexion was not recruiting sufficient numbers to make significant positive gains. If we take 2% as being a base for what Peter Wagner describes as biological growth, that is the recruitment through existing filial relationships, we get a more accurate reflection of the conversion from the community external to the church.[104]

While there were apparent signs of prosperity, such as chapel building, there seemed little cause for concern. In 1840 J.G. Pike discerned that the Connexion was not growing as rapidly as some other denominations. Looking to the report of the London Baptist Association, which had grown by 'an average addition of upwards of 25 for each church', he observed that when this was compared with the New Connexion it was 'greatly beyond the increase that our churches then had, or probably ever did enjoy'. He sensed that all was not as well as it appeared, that despite the evident signs of prosperity 'other Christians are greatly outstripping us in the race of holy effort and pious benevolence' and that 'whatever in past years may have been the efforts of our churches to spread the Redeemer's cause, they are not

---

[104] Peter Wagner, 'Guidelines for Making Basic Church Growth Calculations', in *Reporting Church Growth* (n.pl.: Fuller Evangelistic Association, 1977). 5.

now equal to those of several other denominations'.[105] Ian Sellers speaks of Baptists experiencing a 'golden decade' in the 1860s.[106] But it was to be an Indian summer before the onset of winter. The period 1840–1870 marked a crucial stage in the life of the Connexion. It marked the beginning of a period of gradual decline that with few exceptions went unchecked.

Population Density of the New Connexion, 1800–1890

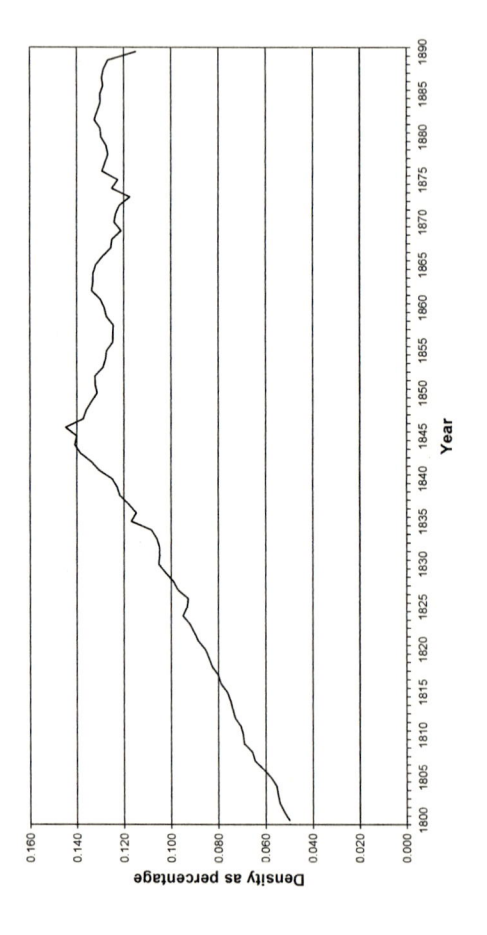

Figure 7

---

[105] J.G. Pike, 'Christian exertion', *Letter* (1840), p. 39.
[106] Sellers, *Nineteenth-Century Nonconformity*, p. 32.

The publication of the 1851 Mann Census in 1854 confirmed the concerns that had been aired, and provoked a spell of self-analysis. In the Census returns some churches failed sufficiently to identify themselves as New Connexion General Baptists, and are thus listed under 'Baptists Unspecified' and General Baptists. The report on the Census in the *General Baptist Magazine* drew attention to this distortion, but it was Horace Mann's calculation that 60% of England's population were absent from a place of worship that appalled.[107] Callum G. Brown convincingly argues that this non-attendance was not something new, rather that industrialisation brought it into the open, by breaking up the old ties between land and church.[108]

In September 1859 a special series of meetings were held to discuss the question, 'Can any means be devised for improving and extending our denomination?'[109] The consultation at Leicester heard four papers. The first was a statistical analysis of the Connexion's progress by T. Yates of Wirksworth,[110] which recognised that the growth of the Connexion was not keeping pace with either the population or other nonconforming communities. In the second paper, Jabez Burns looked at the 'Hindrances'.[111] While there had been some growth in towns more effort was needed, especially in the light of 'the stationary or retrograde condition of our churches in the smaller towns and villages of the Connexion'. He saw the greatest problem as 'the formation of small and necessarily feeble churches, which have not been able to sustain an efficient ministry, and have lacked almost, if not entirely pastoral oversight and healthy discipline'. The result was that they lacked the 'esteem and confidence' of those outside the church. It was these churches that were going to be lost to the Connexion unless something was done. He argued for something like the Methodist circuit and a revival of the old style of connexional ministry of churches like Barton and Castle Donnington.[112] These comments would seem to imply that the itinerancy characteristic of the early part of the century had died out. J.F. Winks in his paper also made an appeal for the revival of itineracy, but he suggested two men supported by the Home Mission be 'wholly given to the work'.[113] This appeal was, to some extent, fulfilled the following year, when Thomas Cooper, the 'Chartist', was appointed as a part time evangelist.[114] Joint evangelistic work with the Particular Baptists became a possibility with the formation of the Midland Union. Concentrating on the counties of Derbyshire, Leicestershire and Nottinghamshire, James Manning was appointed to work alternate months with the

---

[107] 'The Census of 1851, on Religious Worship', *GBM* (1854), p. 123.
[108] Callum G. Brown, 'Did Urbanization Secularize Britain?', *Urban History Year Book* (1988), p. 2.
[109] 'Report of proceedings at the Special Meeting Held at Friar Lane Chapel, Liecester, on Wednesday Sept. 28, 1859, for the Extension of the General Baptist Connexion', *GBM* (1859), p. 441.
[110] *GBM* (1859), p. 442.
[111] *GBM* (1859), p. 445
[112] *GBM* (1859), p. 446.
[113] *GBM* (1859), p. 452.
[114] *Minutes* (1860), p. 36.

two sections of the denomination.[115] But again this was an approach to evangelism that was dependent on funding and a 'professional', or full-time ministry. The last paper of the 1859 conference, by W. Marshall of Loughborough, was an appeal to use local preachers, and for their proper training, equipping and sanction. The problem identified was that of the quality of lay preachers. The result of poor or bad preaching was 'the congregation is annoyed...children laugh...and one respectable family after another leave the place'.[116] The Yorkshire Conference of 1860 considered 'The means of extending the Connexion especially in the Yorkshire district'. The writer thought that it was the 'serious deficiency' in ministers that hindered growth. This lack of ministers in the rural churches was, he said, due to the 'exceeding small and inadequate' salaries of rural churches.[117] This again reflects a view of evangelism as dependent on full-time ministry and its funding. It may also reflect a better-educated and more aware laity. The very structure and nature of Nonconformity means it is self-limiting; the lower social limit for the Connexion, as with other Nonconformists, was governed by the financial independence of chapels. The need to be self-supporting, and thus to finance ministry, precluded an appeal to people with very low incomes. The relationship between ministry and evangelism meant that for many small churches in the New Connexion, working on the threshold of viability, the inability to fund ministry impeded their evangelistic thrust. For the New Connexion, with its large number of small chapels, which were only just on the threshold of financial viability, full-time ministry was a luxury they could not afford.[118]

John Clifford, early in his ministry at Praed Street, London, mooted a different concept of evangelism. He argued that what was needed was an every member ministry; 'power', he said, has been given by the Lord 'to teach and preach in the name of Jesus to every believer in Christ'; home and work place are to be viewed as an opportunity for 'self-sacrifice and holy effort'. Here Clifford introduces personal evangelism, a theme to which he was to return many times. For Clifford, love for Christ issues in an obligatory love for fellow men and women which in turn demands 'effort' in evangelism. This effort consists of 'direct conversation on the subject of the soul's salvation'. Clifford put his hearers on the offensive in evangelism. If an opportunity to talk about the faith did not readily present itself then they were to 'immediately seek one'.[119] Clifford gave a practical opportunity for this 'direct conversation' in his ministry at Praed Street, where people seeking 'guidance on matters relating to the Christian life' were requested to stay for a 'CONVERSATIONAL MEETING' at the conclusion of the service. About a dozen

---

[115] W.R. Stevenson, 'Our Midland Union Evangelist', *GBM* (1877), p. 315.

[116] W. Marshall, 'Lay Agency, With Special Reference to the Further Efficiency of our Local Preachers', *GBM* (1859), p. 458.

[117] 'The means of extending the Connexion especially in the Yorkshire district', *GBM* (1860), p. 49.

[118] John D. Gay, *The Geography of Religion in England* (London: Duckworth, 1971) p. 107.

[119] John Clifford, 'The Christian's Work', *GBM* (1859), p. 465.

'skilled as religious advisers' were on hand, after the pastor had spoken, 'encouraging a frank statement of difficulties', then 'the conversationalists go to their work'.[120] Clifford estimates that in the course of five or six years some 300 people became members of the church through this method, and that, in 1881, it had recently been re-introduced with similar effectiveness. By this method Clifford effectively devolved the evangelistic ministry into the body of the church.

He addressed the issue again in 1877 in 'Individualism in Christian Work', where he gives further expression to the importance of personal evangelism. 'Divine as the work of preaching to people undoubtedly is, it fails of its supreme purpose if it is not followed by individualism in Christian work'.[121] A new element here is the practical concern that should accompany the spoken word: 'A few grains of personal, practical, brother-helping love, are worth tons of the most elegant and sanctified "talk"'.[122] It was this practical concern that was to characterise Clifford's ministry and teaching about evangelism.

With regard to this concept of personal evangelism Clifford was almost alone. When C. Clarke considered 'The present state of the General Baptist Denomination', he attributed the causes of decrease to 'lack of earnest Home Missionary spirit', 'the scale of ministerial remuneration' and having 'to contend against an increasing amount of worldliness'. These, together with people not feeling the necessity to be baptized and join with a church, were, he suggested, the major contributors to the decline.[123] In the course of his address he calls for 'individual work by church members' saying that, it was 'unjust' and 'useless' to expect the minister to do every thing. This, while an appeal for ministry on the part of the church members, is not as explicit in its evangelistic content as it was with Clifford.

Clifford, as secretary to the annual association, reflecting on the returns for 1870 and preceding years, expressed his concern about the lack of growth of the Connexion. He laid part of the blame at the feet of the foreign mission in Orissa: 'Has not the all absorbing attention demanded by the affairs of the Foreign Missionary Society in certain years caused to some extent the decrease of the denomination at home?'[124] It certainly affected the church at Archdeacon Lane, where the formation of a 'missionary association' had, according to the minutes, 'taken precedence of the home debt,' and it was felt 'needful to attend immediately to our own collection & and arrange for that without delay'[125] T. Gill of Allerton had, in 1868, made a similar observation in relation to the Yorkshire churches who, he said,

---

[120] John Clifford, 'Leaves from Our Church Books', *GBM* (1881), p. 143.
[121] John Clifford, 'Individualism in Christian Work', *GBM* (1877), p. 409.
[122] *GBM* (1877), p. 411.
[123] C. Clarke, 'The present state of the General Baptist Denomination', *GBM* (1868), pp. 99-101.
[124] *Minutes* (1870), p. 56.
[125] Archdeacon Lane Church Book No. 2, 25 May 1828.

had been criticised for their 'Lack of liberality towards foreign Missions'. But it was, he said, these churches that had seen 140% growth in the last thirty years.[126]

Clifford felt the mission had absorbed the energy of the denomination. It certainly absorbed its financial resources. In 1862, the first year for which financial returns are given in the annual statistics, the overseas mission received nine times as much as the home mission.[127] It was not the financial effort alone. Thomas Goadby notes that there was a relationship between periods when emphasis was put on mission work and decline at home. 1824 to 1826 saw a move into the West Indies, 1825 saw a decline in numbers, 1845 the mission to China, followed two years later by a decline. 1864 and 1865 saw the movement seeking to relieve a large debt incurred by the mission, and this was 'followed by years of serious decline'.[128] In assessing Goadby's argument, it should be noted that the Wesleyan Methodist Church also experienced decline in those years, in fact these were periods of general decline in Nonconformity.[129] Goadby's observation that 'there is a point up to which the spread of the Gospel amongst the heathen is increase of power, beyond, it is weakness and difficulty', is valid if the work overseas is resourced at the expense of the work at home. This perception was hidden from the majority of the Connexion by the apparent vitality of the work at home, and the almost totem value that was given to the Orrisa mission.

Demographic Changes

It was this period that saw the attention of the Connexion focus on the growing urban population. There was a continuing tension between the demands of the towns and the need of a predominantly rural movement. The power base of the Connexion was in small industrial towns and the industrial villages of the Midlands and South Yorkshire, and there was a tendency for it to be influenced by rural concerns. But the population drift was from the countryside to the new urban areas, which were expanding not only by migration but by the fertility of the town populations themselves.[130] 'We are pained to observe in how many of the large towns we have no existence', said one writer in response to the publication of the 1851 Census. The appeal 'What new town have we taken up...?' of 1861 expressed the same concern which was again voiced in 1865.[131] But the Connexion failed to move into these areas. Clifford said, 'we have devoted a larger attention to Rural than to Urban

---

[126] T. Gill, 'Why are we, as a denomination not making greater progress?', *GBM* (1868), p. 169.

[127] *Minutes* (1862), pp. 11-15.

[128] Thomas Goadby, 'The Christian Ministry of the Future', *Letter* (187), p. 56.

[129] Currie, Gilbert, Horsley, *Churches and Churchgoers*, p. 41.

[130] W.H.B. Court. *A Concise Economic History of Britain From 1750 to Recent Times* (Cambridge: Cambridge University Press, 1964), p. 232.

[131] 'The Census of 1851', *GBM* (1854), p. 126; B. Wood, 'Home Missionary Effort Will Pay', *GBM* (1861), p.324; 'Are we to extend as a Denomination', *GBM* (1865), p 50.

manufacturing population and at a recent date were stronger in the latter parts of the country'. He put his finger on the problem facing the Connexion:

> Letter after letter has come to hand assuring me that the struggle for existence is becoming more and more keen, because men and women are becoming more and more scarce. Science is improving man out of the agricultural village, and substituting machines which do his work better and in less time...[132]

It was not only science that was affecting the villages; as a result of greater capital and changes in tenure there was an outward migration of owners and the more prosperous residents into the countryside around the villages emphasising a separation of class by a separation of dwelling.[133] This was the case in the Fenlands of South Lincolnshire where enclosure and drainage brought division of land and new settlement patterns as people left the old village centres to move to the newly drained lands. This, according to R.W. Ambler, had the effect of 'accentuating a process of dispersal'.[134] These changes were accompanied by a move from settled to migratory patterns of agricultural work. 'The best brains, the eagerest ambition, and the forcefullest characters are all drafted into the towns... The towns for the past twenty years have been emasculating the villages—draining them of their best men and women; and for the last ten years in ever increasing ratio', said H. Godkin in 1886.[135] He suggested that the depressed state of church life in the villages was compounded by the multiplicity of chapels, thus making each of them 'a weak cause'. He argued for a union of Free Churches, but it would depend on being willing to 'cultivate agreements' rather than 'nourish our differences'.[136] He acknowledged that other attempts to deal with the work in villages by grouping were not a success. 'The villages do not like such grouping, it spoils their independence...it imports the controlling hand and the not always acceptable advice of a board of outsiders'.[137] Godkin argued for the grouping of village churches under the leadership and in the circuit of town churches 'without the despotism of Methodism on the one hand, or the weakness of independency on the other'. At the end of the letter he acknowledges that this proposal is a 'forlorn hope'. 'Forlorn in that so much has been said, and advised, and grumbled and suggested, and yet the one object we all desire has not been realized—the healthy activity of religious truth in the villages'.[138]

---

[132] Clifford, *Religious Life in the Rural Districts*, p. 6.

[133] G.H. Dury, 'The East Midlands and the Peak', in W.G. East and G.H. Dury (eds), *Regions of the British Isles* (London: Thomas Nelson and Sons, 1963), p. 134.

[134] R.W. Ambler, 'Ranters to Chapel Builders: Primitive Methodism in the South Lincolnshire Fenland c. 1820–1875', in W.J. Sheils and Diana Wood (eds), *Voluntary Religion* (Studies in Church History; Oxford: Basil Blackwell, 1986), p. 320.

[135] H. Godkin, 'The Ministry of Religious Truth in the Villages of England', *Letter* (1886), p. 1.

[136] Godkin, 'The Ministry of Religious Truth in the Villages of England', p. 2.

[137] Godkin, 'The Ministry of Religious Truth in the Villages of England', p. 3.

[138] Godkin, 'The Ministry of Religious Truth in the Villages of England', pp. 3, 8.

The following table charts the development of the Connexion by size of church in two counties. In Lincolnshire churches were long established and mainly rural. In Yorkshire a large number of churches were in developing towns.

Comparison of Churches in Yorkshire and Lincolnshire

Year	Yorkshire Churches	0-49	50-99	100-199	200+	Lincolnshire Churches	0-49	50-99	100-199	200+
1866	18	2	1	10	5	18	4	7	3	4
1867	19	2	4	8	5	16	5	4	3	4
1868	20	2	6	9	8	16	6	4	2	4
1869	20	2	5	8	5	17	6	5	2	4
1870	20	2	5	8	5	17	6	4	3	4
1871	20	2	5	8	5	17	6	4	4	3
1872	20 1 N/R	1	6	5	6	18 1 N/R	6	4	4	3
1873	21 2 N/R	2	5	7	5	18 3 N/R	5	4	4	2
1874	21	2	8	7	6	19 1 N/R	7	4	4	3
1875	24 2 N/R	1	6	8	7	18 2 N/R	5	5	3	3
1876	24	2	6	9	7	18	7	4	4	3
1877	24	1	7	9	7	18	7	4	4	3
1878	24	2	5	10	7	18	7	5	2	4
1879	24	2	5	10	7	18	7	4	3	4
1880	23	2	5	9	7	20	10	4	2	4
1881	22	1	5	9	7	19	8	4	3	4
1882	22	1	4	10	7	20	9	5	2	4
1883	22	1	4	10	7	20	8	5	3	4
1884	22	1	5	10	6	20	7	6	3	4
1885	22	1	6	10	6	20	18	2	5	3
1886	22	1	4	10	6	20	10	1	6	3
1887	22	1	5	8	8	20	11	0	6	3
1888	21	1	5	7	8	20	11	1	5	3
1889	21	1	5	5	10	20	11	1	5	3
1890	20 1 N/R	0	4	6	9	20 2 N/R	11	2	2	3

N/R = No return for that year. Figures taken from the annual returns of the churches.

Table 5

The most obvious difference lies in the number of churches under fifty members with Lincolnshire having three times that of Yorkshire. But it is in the band of 100-200 members that the most significant difference occurs. It was this group that showed the greatest growth, both in Yorkshire and Lincolnshire. churches above 200 also grew significantly. There seems to have been a self-limiting dynamic at work in the smaller churches as they tended to remain static.

It is worth noting that the growth was in membership of established churches not the development of new causes, as the number of churches remained much the same throughout the period. In the period 1866–90 the average membership per church in Lincolnshire fell from 102 to seventy-four, in Yorkshire it grew from 165 to 185.

The heartland of the Connexion in the East Midlands was also undergoing changes in the distribution of population. By 1851 the area had seen a general increase in numbers especially in the exposed coalfaces of the middle Trent valley and the Derbyshire coalfields. According to Dury, in the period 1851–1901 'rural parts mostly suffered a distinct loss of population during these fifty years'.[139] There was an out migration from rural Leicestershire and Lincolnshire and in the latter, according to J.V. Beckett, the 'migratory trickle became a flood during the flight from the land in the agricultural depression of the final two decades of the century'.[140] The church book at Bourne talks, in 1887, about the 'depressed condition of the whole district' which it gives as a reason for not undertaking a new work.[141] The percentage of population constituting the rural class of density was less in 1901 than in 1851, or indeed than in 1801.[142] The Connexion, locked into buildings and settled congregations, found adaption to the changes difficult. F.W. Goadby felt that 'the sooner we get to the city and learn our true relative position the better for us and the village too'.[143]

To what extent was the challenge to make a strategic effort to the towns and manufacturing areas taken up? Of sixty-two new churches formed between 1850 and 1890, twenty-five were in what may be considered an urban environment. At the ninety-ninth annual association the chairman, Thomas Goadby, took the Connexion to task over its lack of growth: 'It is impossible I think to account for this deficiency upon any other hypothesis than the decline of evangelistic zeal in our churches'. So central was this evangelistic concern to his concept of the church that he said, 'when the power of reclaiming the lost dies out of the church it ceases to be the church'. He laid the failure at the door of the ministry.[144]

By the late 1860s and early 1870s there was a growing awareness that something was wrong and that the Connexion was not recruiting. There were a number of questioning sermons, addresses and letters. Thomas Barass, in July 1866, asked, 'Why is there so little visible success?'[145] In 1867, W.R. Stevenson of Nottingham,

---

[139] Dury, *The East Midlands*, p. 203; Margery Tranter, David A. Barton and Paul S. Ell (eds), *The Derbyshire Returns to the 1851 Religious Census* (Chesterfield: Derbyshire Record Society, 1995), pp. XII-XX.

[140] J.V. Beckett, 'The East Midlands from A.D. 1000', in Barry Cunliffe and David Hey (eds), *A Regional History of England* (London: Longman, 1988), p. 191.

[141] Bourne Church Book, 21April 1887.

[142] Dury, *The East Midlands and the Peak*, p. 203.

[143] F.W. Goadby, 'On Being Swamped', *GBM* (1867), p. 340.

[144] T. Goadby, 'Chairmans Address', *Minutes* (1868), pp. 46, 53, 55.

[145] Thomas Barass, *GBM* (1866), p. 300.

commenting on the failure to recruit, looked back over the previous fifteen years and observed, 'we have done little more than fill up the breaches made in our ranks by death and removals'.[146]

In 1868, Thomas Goadby, speaking as President, observed, 'About 150 churches and 100 ministers working ten years and the clear gain only 48.' He linked the lack of growth to the death of the first generation. 'It is remarkable that the period of the beginning of our decline saw the last days of the fathers of this body'. Looking to their concern for evangelism he asked the question, 'Have we not failed in some measure to tread in the footsteps of their hallowed trail?'[147] The review, in 1880, of *The Churches of Nottinghamshire* was an analysis of the provision for worship in the county by Goodeve Mabbs.[148] This book confirmed John Clifford's concern and caused him to reflect. In the book, Mabbs compared the number of sittings provided with those required. According to Clifford this showed a far greater oversupply in the rural areas compared with that of the towns. He commented, 'Broadly that points the direction for future evangelical enterprise as plainly as possible'. Following a detailed analysis of the parishes he said,

> These deficiencies show in what direction our churches should expend their evangelizing zeal; and at the same time constitute a distinct summons to aggressive activity. Nottinghamshire General Baptists have much more to do in Arnold, Snenton, Lenton, Radford, Carlton, in Saint Mary's Nottingham and in Worksop. Let our churches, pastors, and local preachers study these needs.[149]

But as we have seen the authority structures within the Connexion made such action difficult if not impossible. When the returns of the Connexion are examined, it was the formation of new churches in urban areas that provided the growth: notably in Yorkshire, Leicester and London. When it came to recruiting, location seemed to be more important than the age or size of a church.[150]

By the 1890s the development of the major urban centres of the Connexion was complete. Although opening some sixteen churches in the last decade of its life, these were spread throughout the country. With perhaps the exception of London, which saw six churches added and Leicester with three, the Connexion had failed to establish itself in any significant way in the new and expanding urban areas. There was no breakthrough, the Connexion had missed the season of opportunity presented by urban development.

---

[146] W.R. Stevenson, 'Presidents Address', *Minutes* (1867), p. 4.

[147] T. Goadby, 'Chairman's Address', *Minutes* (1868), p. 52

[148] Goodeve Mabbs, *The Churches in Nottinghamshire* (London and Derby Benrose/Nottingham: J. Durn, 1880).

[149] John Clifford, 'Church Worship in Nottinghamshire', *GBM* (1880), p. 103.

[150] See Appendix 7 for tables showing number of baptisms per 1,000 members by age and size of church.

Development and Evangelistic Strategy

Beginnings of Decline 1871–1891

Revivalism

The final stage of development in the Connexion sees the beginnings of decline and may be termed the 'residual' stage. In this phase the external constituency of a church or group virtually ceases to exist (as was the case with the framework knitters), and recruitment becomes increasingly difficult, both internally and externally.[151]

In the period 1870–1890 there are only four times when the annual percentage growth of the Connexion goes above 2% (see Figure 7 below). The most significant two occasions coincide with the visit of Moody and Sankey in 1874 and 1876.

When the membership statistics of the Connexion are examined for the period 1840–1890 some interesting features emerge: while there are short term cycles of between five and ten years there are also larger peaks in 1849, 1859–60, 1874–76 and 1881–83, which coincide with the periods of revival.

The concerns of 'revivalism' bring into sharp focus the inability to recruit. Prior to 1820 religious revivals were unstructured, spontaneous and seen as an outpouring of God's Spirit. W.R. Ward maintains that at this stage it was a rural phenomenon, and that

> the brakes rarely come off more suddenly than they did for rural immigrants to the great northern towns in the first two decades of the nineteenth century. Sudden release from old social pressures and the personal disorientation to which this often led, exposed them to a religious excitement of a very high voltage, aptly known as 'wildfire'.[152]

Clowes, Bourne and Dow, with their 'Camp Meetings' introduced a more structured approach to revivalism amongst the Primitive Methodists. As J.G. Pike looked at the strategy of the Connexion, he argued that they had not used popular methods to appeal to the masses:

> we have not sought proselytes by approximation to the fashionable system in the land of our pilgrimage, nor endeavoured to swell our numbers by opening our doors to welcome, with eager haste, crowds that never were converted, but that felt a transient desire to flee the wrath to come.[153]

---

[151] Currie, Gilbert, Horsley, *Churches and Churchgoers*, p. 9.
[152] Ward, *Religion and Society*, p. 79.
[153] J.G. Pike, 'Christian Exertion', *Letter* (1840), p. 39.

Annual Percentage Growth, 1871-1890

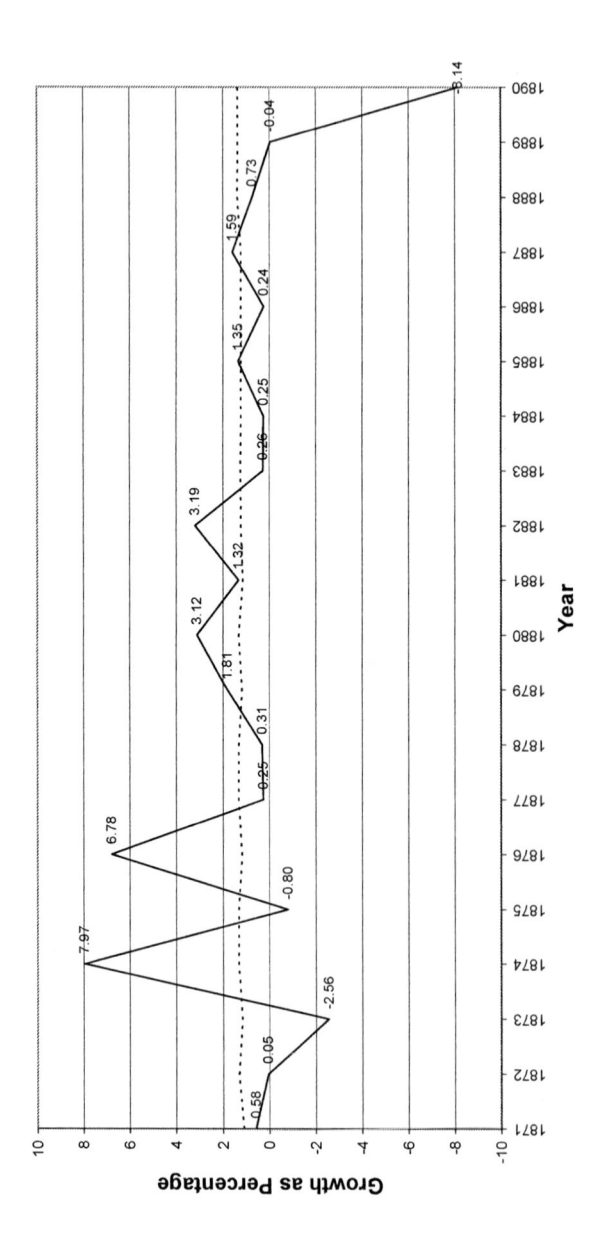

Figure 8

His reflection on the revivalism and the holiness movement which had so contributed to the growth of Primitive Methodism in the Midlands area suggested the New Connexion had avoided such methods. Writing in 1847, the historian of the Connexion, J.H. Wood, took a different view from Pike. He says of the Connexion, 'among other means adopted for promoting the prosperity of the body, was that of holding frequent religious services, the principal features of which were special prayer-meetings and direct and pointed addresses to different classes of characters. Such services were held in many parts of the Connexion; in some instances the results were of a very pleasing nature'.[154]

The extent to which revival played a part in the life of a church was very often determined by the attitude of the minister. Styling himself 'evangelist', a correspondent in the *Baptist Reporter* says of the attitude of ministers towards revivalism, 'Some treat the matter with indifference others with contempt. I regard this as a sad calamity...especially as many of these are persons of influence...'[155] Wood's contention that revival services were held in many parts of the Connexion is supported by evidence from church minute books, which from the 1840s onward contain resolutions concerning special times of prayer and meetings for revival. In July 1842, the congregation of Leake and Wimeswold thought it 'highly desirable that something be done to promote a revival of religion and that the friends make it a matter of prayer'. 'Lamenting' their 'spiritual apathy' they arranged special meetings in September 1846 in order to seek 'forgiveness' and 'revival'.[156] Retford and Gamston held revival meetings in 1844; Nether Street, Beeston, in 1845 sought 'steps to cause a revival of religion', and in the October of the following year held a week of special services.[157] On 3 May 1859 it was proposed 'that we have a camp meeting'—language more usually associated with Primitive Methodists than General Baptists.[158] The General Baptist Preachers Union minute book speaks about revival at Woodhouse in May 1858, and revival in the Sunday school at Daybrook, Nottingham, although this seems to have been spontaneous rather than structured. In 1864 the church at Hyson Green, Nottingham, decided that 'stimulated by the success of our Brethren at Prospect Place, we are about to commence some revival services'.[159]

Following the stirrings in Scotland and the North of England in 1859 prayer for revival again comes onto the agenda of churches in the Connexion. The 1859

---

[154] Wood, *History*, p. 237.

[155] *Baptist Reporter* (1844), p. 276.

[156] Leake and Wimeswold Church Book, 31 July 1842, 20 September 1846. Nottingham Record Office BP/37/2..

[157] Retford and Gamston Church Book, 19 September 1844. Nottinghamshire Record Office BP/20/2. Nether Street Beeston Church Book, 28 December 1845, 29 October 1846. Nottinghamshire Record Office BP/29/5.

[158] Nether Street Beeston Church Book, 3 May 1859. Nottinghamshire Record Office BP/29/5.

[159] Minute Book of the General Baptist Preachers Union, 31 May 1858, 28 May 1860, 16 May 1864. Nottingham Record Office RO/BP/12/4.

Revival was viewed by some with concern. While earlier revivals 'broke out' some felt this one was 'manufactured'. This may indicate the growing professionalism, and structured approach together with the application of transatlantic techniques of revivalism.[160] Another criticism was that they were 'local excitements', arising from a 'temporary local stimulus, which when it has passed away leaves the church in a state of exhaustion'.[161] The concern was that these events produced a 'dim ill-defined sense of guilt and disharmony with God'. The unnamed writer felt that what was needed was a much more thorough conviction of sin, 'a consciousness of personal rebellion against Him, and personal insult offered to Him in the rejection of His mercy and the crucifixion of His Son'.[162]

George Coltman of Fleckney was concerned about the superficial nature of revivalism. He argued that the religious excitement of revival was mistaken for real conversion:

> A good deal of the sensation that goes by that name is nothing more than the excitement of animal feelings...there are many who sing, and sing loudly too, in excited assemblies 'Happy day, when Jesus washed my sins away' and ' I do believe, I will believe that Jesus died for me' &, whose subsequent conduct prove they know nothing experimentally about the new birth; and while I hail with delight a revival of 'pure religion' I do not expect much from the excitement of the present day.[163]

Mark Johnson argues that the influx of converts from revivals initiated a process of theological erosion on two levels. First, theology was modified in the direction of a popular evangelism designed to attract. This was not so much of a problem for the Connexion as those of a Calvinist background. Secondly, those who came in did not experience the careful and elaborate discipline of a former generation.[164] Coltman picked up on the latter. He looked to the failure of some churches which were 'not sufficiently careful in the reception of candidates for baptism', and leaving new Christians after baptism 'without the loving sympathy and watchful care and guidance of the church'. The concern expressed by Coltman and others was that churches had espoused this approach to evangelism.[165]

In 1863, the Evangelical Alliance gave their approval, calling the churches to prayer for revival, a call to which the Connexion church at New Lenton, Nottingham, responded.[166] Four months later, ignoring the wisdom of the writer of the article 'Religious Revival', who said that 'a true revival of religion cannot be manufactured mechanically', they planned a week of special revival services for the

---

[160] Kent, *Holding the Fort*, p. 87.
[161] 'Religious Revival', *GBM* (1859), p. 162.
[162] *GBM* (1859), p. 164.
[163] George Coltman, *GBM* (1867), pp. 310, 366.
[164] Mark D. Johnson, *The Dissolution of Dissent, 1850–1918* (New York: Garland Publishing, 1987), p. 10.
[165] George Coltman, 'Decrease of the Denomination', *GBM* (1867), p. 310 'Denominational Decrease and Union with Particular Baptists', *GBM* (1867), p. 366.
[166] New Lenton Church Book, 27 October 1863. Leicester Record Office. BP/10/5.

Development and Evangelistic Strategy 133

end of February 1864.[167] These included public 'experience meetings'. The success of the meetings led to their being extended a further three weeks. On 1 April 1864 a memorandum was entered into the minutes expressing gratitude to God for the blessing received. The services had been held every night except Friday for three weeks. Other local ministers had been called in to assist Mr Burrows, the minister. At the close of each service there was a prayer meeting, and 'the penitents were directed to repair to the Vestry, when several interesting cases were treated, and hopefully noted as subjects of adopting grace'. This practice reflects a pattern very similar to that of Dwight L. Moody, the American evangelist who made use of an 'enquiry room', although predating his visit by some ten years.[168] The 'public Experiencing meeting' was found to be 'a very blessed season', and it was said that 'every service has been crowned with singular results'.[169] The following table sets out the number of applications for membership received in the subsequent three months.

New Lenton Membership Additions, 1864

Date	Restored to fellowship	Baptism and membership
April 3	6	38
April 20	1	23
April 27	4	9
May 9		11
May 11		8
May 29	1	11
May 30		5

Table 6

As was common in the Connexion, when making application for membership and baptism, candidates were required to give their testimony or experience. Forty-six of these testimonies remain. Although labelled 'Beeston Experience Books' they relate to the revival meetings at New Lenton. There were twice as many women as men, thirty-two to fourteen. The age ranges were from fifteen to fifty; fifteen were between fifteen and twenty, and twenty between twenty-one and thirty, six between thirty-one and forty, and four over forty. Only one gives no age of conversion. All but four mention the Sunday school, and some were teachers, like Mary Smith, aged thirty-four, who had been in the Sunday school twenty years. This again confirms the role the Sunday school played in terms of recruitment. Most of the testimonies refer to a period of searching prior to conversion. William Tilson said he was 'oscillating to and from for nine years'. He was an exception, for many it was

---

[167] 'Religious Revival', *GBM* (1859), p. 164.
[168] Kent. *Holding the Fort*, p. 204.
[169] New Lenton Church Book, 1 April 1864.

months and for most it was a period of weeks.[170] For many the services provided an opportunity to make a definite act of commitment: 'I feel that I got my ticket right through for Heaven', said Henry Woodly, aged nineteen. The influences that brought people to that point varied greatly, from the death of a mother, husband or friend (Lucy Good, Harriet Riddels and John Biffin) to witnessing a baptism (Jane Megg and Doris Shepherd), conversation with a friend (George Gunn), or the impact of the services 'which greatly affected me', said Elizabeth Osborn.[171] For some the experience of forgiveness did not come in the meeting, William Hirchin says, 'I was invited by Mr Shauson to stop after the prayer meeting for the Inquirers class, & though very reluctant to stop I was very glad afterwards. Obtained peace at home about 3 weeks since, while engaging in prayer'.[172] With the majority a relationship of some kind may be traced to the church, either through family or friends or the church structures. Methodist backgrounds feature frequently in the testimonies. In the church memorandum the meetings were described as a time of 'spiritual harvest', but it was a harvest field that was within the hedge provided by the church infrastructure, especially the Sunday school; few converts were from fields outside the church.

While there had been a tentative approach to the 1859 Revival, Moody and Sankey received a much warmer welcome. The 1874 Revival in Scotland and stirrings in the North of England provided the background to their visit. Their arrival in 1875 was warmly greeted by Clifford, his hopes of the northern revival were that 'the fire may spread among our churches', and in the *General Baptist Magazine* of 1874 he reproduced revival testimonies.[173] In an article, 'How the Revival Works', Clifford cites with approval the lay involvement, the way it brought the different denominations together in the work of mission, and the emphasis on personal evangelism in the enquiry rooms.[174] The same issue of the *General Baptist Magazine* also carried reports of the meetings at Birmingham, and articles on Moody's preaching. There was also another article by Clifford, 'Lessons for the Churches from the Revival', which made much the same points as the previous one. By 1888, T.R. Stevenson was espousing revivals; for him revivals 'begin with the church. Let this be most carefully noted', he said, 'all who long for them should bear it in mind'.[175] The target of these campaigns was mainly the internal constituency of the church.[176]

As we now know, the hopes of growth engendered by the Revival were not to be fulfilled. The statistics of the Connexion show there were only a very few years between 1870 and 1891 in which they achieved an overall growth rate. While the

---

[170] Beeston Experience Books. Nottingham Record Office B/P/10/14/3.
[171] Beeston Experience Books. Nottingham Record Office B/P/10/14/4
[172] Beeston Experience Books. Nottingham Record Office B/P/10/14/3
[173] John Clifford, 'Incidents and and Features of the Present Revival', *GBM* (187), pp 148-49.
[174] Clifford, 'How the revival works', *GBM* (1874), pp. 24-25.
[175] T.R. Stevenson, 'Revivals. A Paper read at the Midland Conference Castle Donnington', *GBM* (1888) 122.
[176] Sellers, *Nineteenth-Century Nonconformity*, p. 33.

revivals of 1859 and 1875 produce an increase in membership, it was not sustained. It may be that the appeal of the revivals lay in the Arminian theology with which the Connexion would have been sympathetic. Gilbert argues that the impact of the revivals lies in a conjunction of religious excitement and political activism, and that the 1859–60 Revival 'coincided with the most intense phase of popular agitation during the prolonged campaign against church rates' and that 'it affected an unusual, and temporary, bridging of the gap between the Victorian Churches and their external constituencies'.[177] This being the case, revivalism is another indicator of the withdrawal of the churches, who were now only spasmodically at one with their constituencies. To some extent the use of revival indicates that the church was experiencing difficulties in recruiting even from within its own community and was turning to these agencies for help.

The Leakage Issue

The concerns about numbers and lack of growth in the period following 1870 came into the open over the issue of 'Leakage'. Concern was expressed about the difference in numbers between those people who were received into membership by various means and the number of members. The two should have been the same, but this was not the case. The Connexion became very concerned in the late 1870s and 80s about this 'Leakage'.

In order to understand what was happening it is necessary to consider the ways in which new members were added to New Connexion churches. There were two basic means. The first was conversion growth; this required giving an account of conversion experience to the church, and would subsequently be accompanied by baptism. There was no automatic transfer of children into membership. They, too, had to go through the same process of profession; the baptism of children as believers, while not unknown, was not at all common. The second method of entry was through transfer of membership. Persons previously baptized in a New Connexion church could transfer their membership to another fellowship. As baptism was a condition of membership for the greater part of our period, the majority of churches adopted a practice of 'closed membership', that is, only baptized believers were received into membership. From the very early days there had been a compromise in relation to Particular Baptists, who on removal had applied to join a General Baptist church. Their reception into membership was the decision of the local church, the greater majority being happy to receive such applications. Persons whose membership had lapsed, for whatever reason, could be restored at the discretion of the church meeting. Because baptism and membership are directly related to conversion, the records of the Connexion reflect the appeal of conversionist theology.

'Leakage'—decrease in membership numbers—arose because of the failure of migrant members to re-register as members on their removal from one district to

---

[177] Gilbert, *Religion and Society*, pp. 194-95.

another. It was also caused by the loss of members through the erasure column. Names were erased for a number of reasons: church discipline, death, but the major reason was non-attendance. Leakage was also the indicator of another wider problem, that of the failure to keep members. In 1845, one Methodist had observed of Baptists, 'they are good marksmen but they do not bag the game'.[178] As George Coltman looked at the annual returns for the New Connexion in 1867, he felt that while they may be harvesting, they were dropping or spoiling as much if not more than they gathered. He drew attention to an overall decrease of the denomination.[179]

The issue of 'leakage', first aired by Coltman, was again brought to the association by the secretary John Clifford, who in 1869 drew attention to the fact that three-quarters of the additions through baptism were offset by loss through erasure. This large loss he explained as due to the churches being 'vigilant and severe in the revision of church lists'.[180] This revision was done through the erasure of names, the numbers being reflected in the erasure column of the annual returns.

The issue came to a head with the discussion of the membership crisis of 1883. W. March in the association letter for that year, 'The Erasure Column in our Year Book', drew attention to the increasing loss of members through erasure. For whatever reason, a large number of people did not value membership sufficiently enough to attend; and others, who moved, did not make joining another New Connexion church in their new place of residence a priority. This latter group may have been hampered by the relatively small number of New Connexion churches outside the Midlands, although it needs to be noted that a previous generation had formed churches according to their convictions. But at this stage in the life of the movement those convictions do not seem to have been sufficiently different or strong to warrant such action. But, as W. March had pointed out in the circular letter for 1883, while one could explain the decline of 1869 in terms of a tidying up of the membership rolls, how would one explain the following year, 1870, which was no better? In that year there were 1,201 baptisms, and 754 in the erasure column, which prompted Clifford to say, 'the increase is not so large as might have been expected', and he again blamed the purifying of returns.[181] But the trend continued. In 1879, the 1,067 erasures almost equalled the 1,147 baptisms. In that year, E.C. Pike said, 'that for the last three years we find the erasures to amount to considerably more than two-thirds, not far from three fourths of the number of Baptisms. This surely points to a looseness in our church life which is at once a reproach and a sore evil'.[182]

Looking at the totals for the years 1870 to 1883, March concludes that the 'erasures are reaching serious proportions both in separate churches and in the entire denomination. The mischief is not confined to village, town or city communities; it has become chronic, and is a growing rather than a decreasing evil'.[183] He cites the

---

[178] Quoted in R.S. Lee, 'Baptists in Lancashire', p. 70.
[179] Coltman, *GBM* (1867), p. 309.
[180] Clifford, 'Concerning the Statistics of the Churches', *GBM* (1869), p. 151.
[181] *Minutes* (1870), p. 51.
[182] W. March, 'The Erasure Column in our year Book', *Letter* (1883), p. 2.
[183] *Minutes* (1883), pp 4-5.

Development and Evangelistic Strategy 137

association secretaries who attribute the 'leakage' to: absenteeism on the part of professing Christians from the house of God; removal to fresh places of abode without in some cases joining any other church; want of appreciation for Christian fellowship; looseness in our church life; drifting away from Christian duties and privileges; sensational and spurious revivalism.[184]

In the early days of the Connexion church discipline had sought to restore non-attenders. It was an increasing practice to deal with non-attendance by erasure rather than discipline. The observation of A.D. Gilbert concerning secularisation and the mid-Victorian 'crisis of faith', that 'membership retention has not been a major problem', would have to be questioned so far as the New Connexion is concerned.[185] March saw the leakage of members as 'like a great sieve, through which 734 members are lost annually; it is like a wide breach in a goodly building, which, if not restored, will imperil the whole fabric'.[186]

W.R. Stevenson, speaking at the Midland Conference in May 1883, attributed part of the problem to 'not paying sufficient attention to the teaching and training of converts after their union with the church, in order that instead of losing their interest in spiritual things they may be led to cleave to the Lord with purpose of heart'.[187] In his analysis of 'Our lapsed Members' he gives what he considers to be the most common reasons for erasure and exclusion. These were: strong drink; sexual relationships before marriage, especially of young people; failure in business; Christian women 'chiefly in the humbler walks of life' marrying non-Christian husbands; and failure to join another church following a move. It was felt in relation to the last reason that steps needed to be taken, 'otherwise, in these days of movement on the part of the English population, we shall as a Connexion suffer great leakage in our membership from this cause'.[188] The final two reasons were a loss of interest in spiritual things, and disaffected relationships through misunderstanding or church quarrels. John Clifford argued that:

> these large erasures are chiefly in the *town* churches, and are generally found associated with a change of pastorate. The fact is, denominationalism, though not dead is 'sleeping;' and in our busy towns few persons, I fear, elect their religious home on the grounds of identity with the church in its view of baptism, or creed on the 'Atonement.' It is the preacher who fills the vision, moral and social affinities sway the choice not doctrine.[189]

The problem of erasures was not peculiar to the New Connexion alone. Joseph Fletcher, speaking to the London Baptist Association, described the erasures as '"vinegar to the teeth, and smoke to the eyes" of our Association Secretaries from

---

[184] *Letter* (1883), p. 6.
[185] Gilbert, *Religion and Society*, pp. 179, 184.
[186] *Letter* (1883), p. 5.
[187] W.R. Stevenson, 'Our Lapsed Members', *GBM* (1883), p. 241.
[188] Stevenson, 'Our Lapsed Members', p. 245.
[189] John Clifford, 'General Baptists in 1883', *GBM* (1883), p. 363.

one end of the land to the other'. The 'melancholy fact' was, he said, 'that *on an average our churches erase more than half the number they baptise*'.[190] The discussion of the erasure column is interesting because it reflects the value that was given to faith and its visible expression in membership of a church. It represents those who have at some time 'believed' sufficiently to want to join a church, who then at a later date let their membership slip. Leakage is, therefore, an indicator of the value or utility of membership; and, as such, reflects not just the failure to re-register, but the declining attraction of the church.[191] Clifford's observation that denominationalism was 'sleeping', and that religious preference was determined by social rather than theological choices indicates the declining value of denominations in the face of personal choice. According to Currie, Gilbert and Horsley the value of church membership is related to social prestige and power.[192] In this connection, the General Baptists suffered on two fronts. They were experiencing the general secular drift of society, but, in addition to that, it would seem generally that the Connexion lacked social appeal. On the one hand it was not clearly identified with the working class, and, on the other, had low social value for the aspiring middle class. It was argued that 'leakage' represented not a loss, but a transfer to other churches: 'And is it not a fact that hundreds, if not thousands who have been trained in our families, taught in our Sunday schools, and blest under our ministry, are constantly being enrolled in other churches?'[193] This shift to other churches is a factor to be remembered when considering the causes for decline and the source of the leakage, and, if true, further emphasises the declining attraction and utility of the Connexion.

Institutional Church

Attempts were made by churches to compete with a growing number of secular attractions. Movements such as the PSA (Pleasant Sunday Afternoon service), the 'Brotherhood' movement and a number of youth organisations emerged. Clifford raised the question as to how far the Christian faith had penetrated the daily lives of ordinary men and women. He asserted that although the church should be involved in alleviating the needs of the poor, and challenging the world of business and industry, its crucial role was the interior life of man.[194] He saw the work of the church as 'saving men, perfecting human character, and helping the progress of the world'.[195] For Clifford, the church had a central and critical role to play in this process of transformation; it was his conviction that 'the one principal work of the church of

---

[190] Joseph Fletcher, 'Church Leakage its causes and cure', *GBM* (1890), p. 211.
[191] Curry, Gilbert and Horsley, *Churches and Churchgoers*, p. 63.
[192] Curry, Gilbert and Horsley, *Churches and Churchgoers*, p. 63.
[193] W. Orton, 'Needs and Prospects', *GBM* (1883), p. 258.
[194] Clifford, 'Jesus Christ and Modern Social Life', *GBM* (1872), p. 19.
[195] Clifford, *A New Testament church in its relation to the need and tendencies of the age* (London: Yates & Alexander, 1876), p. 7.

the loving Saviour is to feed a real and true love amongst members'.[196] Perceptive as he was, Clifford was still a man of his age, and his accommodation to the age was reflected in the way in which the church was to express that ideal. David Thompson notes that from the very beginning of Clifford's ministry at Praed Street, 'he envisaged the church as having a public ministry'.[197] He quotes Clifford's first church report:

> We exist as a church and congregation, not only for our spiritual improvement, but also and specially for saving the souls and bodies in the neighbourhood in which we are located. We have a private object, the consolation and help of each other in the endeavours after spiritual manhood. We have a public object, in the decrease of the evils of society, and the increase of individual and social good by the dissemination of the Gospel of Christ.[198]

Clifford further defined his concept of the church at the dedication of Westbourne Park in 1877, when he said that the 'churches that do not serve man in his deepest and most abiding needs are only fit to be trodden underfoot of men'.[199] For Clifford, the church had to be actively involved in the world:

> The Gospel is the power of God unto Salvation: but it is not the Gospel as a book, as so many reams of paper and pints of printers ink; it is not the gospel as a message merely, uttered in the street and left in the cold, unsupported by a body of warm glowing life... The Gospel is God's power to save men as it lives and breathes in men.[200]

What was needed if the gospel was to live and breathe was Christian 'Manhood' not a 'puling sentimentalism', rather,

> a brave and courageous spirit; doing a good days work and enjoying it; striking evil at the heart and scotching it, standing with an open face towards all light as coming from the God of light, and in a frank and man-respecting manner making known the message of God, and seeking to persuade men to accept it.[201]

This Christian manhood is a world embracing, not a world rejecting faith. For Clifford the only effective solution to reaching the masses 'will be found in putting

---

[196] Clifford, *A New Testament church in its relation to the need and tendencies of the age*, p. 13.
[197] David Thompson, 'John Clifford's Social Gospel', *Baptist Quarterly* 31.5 (January, 1986), p. 202.
[198] Thompson, 'Social Gospel', pp. 202-203.
[199] John Clifford, *The Church of Christ its Work character and message* [An Address delivered at the dedication of Westborne Park Chapel Sept 3rd.] (London: Malborough, 1877), p. 5.
[200] Clifford, *Church of Christ*, pp. 5-6.
[201] Clifford, *Church of Christ*, p. 12.

societies of Christian men and women in the midst of the people and steadily and earnestly directing their energies to the amelioration of their condition'.[202]

In Clifford we meet a well-articulated expression of the 'social gospel'. He sought to put this into effect in his church at Westbourne Park. When Clifford first went to Praed Street in 1857, prior to its rebuilding at Westbourne Park, the membership stood at 171; by 1890 it stood at 1,406. His effectiveness in fulfilling his desire may be judged from the account that J.H. Rushbrooke, who later became the architect of the Baptist World Alliance, gave of his visit to Westbourne Park as a sixteen year old:

> It was a new kind of preaching to me and it arrested me at once. Moreover, I noticed that the congregation was of unusual composition. More than half were young men, and the searching and manly directness of the preacher appealed to them. Dr. Clifford inspired men with the belief that life is a noble vocation.[203]

D.W. Bebbington says of Clifford, 'There was an intellectual tone to his church at Westbourne Park almost unique among London Baptists'.[204]

Clifford had started the 'Institute' in 1885. The church report for 1888 gave its objects as the 'establishment and carrying on of such agencies as shall afford legitimate recreation and contribute to the social and intellectual well-being of our members'.[205] This featured a Sunday afternoon gathering for fellowship and cooperative study of the scriptures, Christian Endeavour, Sunday evening socials, a permanent building society, benefit society, cricket club, gymnasium, rambling club, cycling club, and temperance society.[206] In addition to this there was an educational 'Institute', which included literary and scientific lectures, the teaching of languages and practical concerns such as building construction and dress making. There was also a training class for lay preachers, mission work in the poorer parts of London and a whole range of philanthropic concerns. When appealing for funds in 1887 Clifford said,' it is the duty of the church to do all it can to fill the leisure with cheerful and refreshing engagements and to aid in the fight against the numerous seductions of our city'.[207] 'Cultural domination over the neighbourhood' is the way Ian Sellers describes these 'institutional churches'.[208] Clifford's church was unique among churches in the New Connexion in the extent and range of facilities offered. The majority of churches in the Connexion, in common with the rest of Nonconformity, offered far less ambitious programmes, if they could offer them at all. Sellers identifies a number of dangers associated with this approach. First, there was the 'bricks and mortar trap' and the associated problem of finance, development

---

[202] Clifford, *Church of Christ*, p. 15.
[203] Marchant, *Dr. John Clifford*, p. 61.
[204] Bebbington, *Nonconformist Conscience*, p. 145.
[205] Marchant, *Dr. John Clifford*, p. 63.
[206] Marchant, *Dr. John Clifford*, p. 65.
[207] John Clifford, 'A Fancy Fair in Arcadia', *GBM* (1887), p. 459.
[208] Sellers, *Nineteenth-Century Nonconformity*, p. 49.

of para-church structures where the primary loyalty was to the organisation and to the chapel 'only insofar as their branch happened to meet on a particular set of premises'. With some groups there was a demand for special forms of worship to be provided. Sellers argues that this shattered 'the church idea into fragments' and turned 'mission hall and subagencies from being feeders to the mother church into ends in themselves'. The 'institutional' approach brought with it the problem of nominal association rather than membership and finally the relegation of the church to a subculture.[209] Hugh McLeod argues that the 'movement to make the churches centres for recreation of the local population was one aspect of the decline of Evangelicalism and the advance of a Liberalism that defined the Christian task in more secular terms'. While there may have been an advance of liberalism in Clifford, it was coupled with a thoroughgoing demand for conversion.[210]

Attempts were made on the part of churches to make worship more attractive. Worship changed from being a corporate expression of a personal relationship with God to something that approached entertainment. Participation was no longer the overflow of a full heart, it was something that had to be structured. As early as 1857 Mansfield Road, Nottingham, delegates enquired at the assembly 'as to the desirableness of using scripture liturgies'. The response of the assembly, while not endorsing the idea, did leave the door open: 'while we cannot recommend the adoption of any liturgical form of prayer, we do recommend that every encouragement be given to earnest responses by the congregation'. In the larger churches we find white gowns for baptisms, scriptural liturgies, chanting, and singing of the *Gloria Patri*. The *Freeman* complained of the growing practice of reading discourses, and expressed regret at the reading of prayers in some quarters.[211] But such changes while they may have added to 'respectability' did not stem the decline.[212] In 1867, the minutes complained, 'what coldness, what flatness too often pervades our public services!' and that, while the churches were orderly and 'respectable', 'formality too often characterises our meetings for prayer'.[213] Stevenson, having asked the question 'is there not something that we lack?', supplied his own answer, 'it seems to me that one thing we need as a denomination, is a greater amount of Holy Christian Enthusiasm'.[214] This stands in marked contrast to the early days when vitality and enthusiasm had been characteristic of the movement, as evidenced in the adoption of the then novel practice of hymn singing. For the church at Gosberton in Lincolnshire the provision of entertainment formed their evangelistic strategy. According to a newspaper cutting, the minister, W.F. Dart, provided a series of five concerts, assisted in four others, gave two humorous lectures at the chapel, and conducted two services of song. Together with other

---

[209] Sellers, *Nineteenth-Century Nonconformity*, pp. 49-50.
[210] McLeod, *Class and Religion*, p. 114.
[211] *Freeman* 25 February, 1857, p. 83.
[212] Archdeacon Lane Book 4, 20 April 1864.
[213] *Minutes* (1867), p. 6.
[214] *Minutes* (1867), p. 5.

entertainments there were, according to the local paper, 'sixteen pleasant winter evenings'. According to the report Dart said,

> It was no use telling people to shun vicious amusements unless the church provided something better. This is what he had been trying to do. He was glad that the Gosberton people knew how to behave themselves. He had been very much gratified with the kind attention they had given him in his efforts to provide them with healthy amusement and although for the present there would be no more concerts, he hoped that in the days of the coming summer they would remember the lesson which had been taught this winter, viz, not to forget the forsaking of themselves together. Nothing would give him greater pleasure than to know all their places of worship were filled with attentive congregations.[215]

The changes in the nature of worship reflected a trend in all the churches. Robert Currie, commenting on worship in Methodist churches, says, 'Worship meant decorous behaviour in chapel, trained choirs, respectable and edifying sermons. It had relatively little to do with Christianity'.[216] T.W. Matthews warned, 'but woe to us, if in a faultless exterior, we should lose the inward life of communion with the Father and with his Son Jesus Christ'; 'we cannot hope', he continued, 'to rival the world churches in the gorgeousness of their ritual', and so the New Connexion should 'equal them or exceed them in the simplicity of our faith, the fervour of our piety, and the consecration of our heart to God'. For him, the 'use of a liturgy, however unexceptionable in itself, will rather tend to deadness and self deception, than to the maintenance and reanimation of spiritual worship'.[217]

At the start of the last decade of the century the movement was failing to recruit on two fronts. It was failing to convert from society at large, and it was also failing to win and hold those from within its own ranks. Thus Currie has commented, 'The denominations are labourers sent to the harvest. In the early nineteenth century they worked fast, dropping or spoiling a lot of the crop, but gathering a very great deal. Even after 1890, the harvest is still, at least occasionally, ripe. But the labourers' muscles are feebler and their reflexes slower. They lose and spoil less. But they gather far less'.[218]

By 1870 the Connexion was no longer growing. The concern brought about by the decline expressed itself in a tendency to look to one's nearest allies rather than take an initiative in reaching out to new groups and new areas. The dominant concerns of the next decades were decline, and union with the Particular Baptists.

---

[215] Lincolnshire County Archives, 9/Bapt/1/4.
[216] Currie, *Methodism Divided*, p. 130.
[217] T.W. Matthews, 'Chairman's Address', *Minutes* (1865), p. 6.
[218] Currie, *Methodism Divided*, p. 97.

CHAPTER 6

'Labour, poverty, dependence and anxiety': Ministry in the New Connexion

Dan Taylor

The Nature of Dan Taylor's Authority

The New Connexion did not adopt the General Baptist practice of appointing messengers. So, although Taylor's role was in many ways similar, when churches consulted him it was as a brother and a friend, albeit one who exercised considerable influence. When, at an association meeting in 1781, the church at Longford asked a question about believers marrying non-believers, they requested Mr Taylor to write an answer to them.[1] When in 1782, the church in Kegworth were getting the worst of a public disputation with their minister Mr Wootan, Dan Taylor was sent for and a meeting arranged: '... Mr T. obtained as great credit from the modesty, gentleness and good temper with which he conducted it, as by the force and pertinency of his arguments'.[2] It was these visits and his personality that were the basis of his authority. The value of his journeys should not be underestimated. In days of poor communication he was a valued source of information. When considering a move to London, Taylor pointed out that his connections with the country churches would probably oblige him to make frequent visits to them. When he moved, the church agreed that 'Mr. T. should be left to his full liberty respecting his journeys, being well persuaded that he will not be absent more sabbaths than he can well avoid'.[3] Reading through the *Memoirs* one cannot fail to be impressed by his energy for such expeditions. On one not untypical occasion, in the space of weeks, he 'preached twenty times, attended two Conferences and travelled at least three hundred miles'.[4] To isolated churches, ministers and conferences, Dan Taylor *was* the New Connexion. His travels gave him a perspective which few others shared. He was able to represent the mind of the organisation as a whole to an isolated conference, church or minister. It was natural that they should turn to him when seeking counsel or advice.

Jackson, in his discussion of Baptist evangelical work in Leicestershire, draws a comparison between Taylor and Wesley: 'Dan Taylor exercised an authority in the New Connexion, loosely comparable with that of Wesley among the Methodists'.

---

[1] Taylor, *Memoirs of the Rev. Dan Taylor*, p. 109.
[2] Taylor, *History*, II, p. 155; *Memoirs of the Rev. Dan Taylor*, pp. 111-12.
[3] Taylor, *Memoirs of the Rev. Dan Taylor*, p. 170.
[4] Taylor, *Memoirs of the Rev. Dan Taylor*, p. 188.

But while Taylor exercised his authority as a 'wise father', Wesley was 'apt to descend on communities like a wolf on the fold'. Jackson sees the contrast lying in the different characters of the two leaders.[5] While Jackson looks to Taylor's strength of character, he is not comparing like with like. The two men came from completely different social backgrounds. Wesley was the son of a clergyman educated at Oxford; Taylor was the son of a Yorkshire miner who taught himself to read and write. Taylor was denied the advantages of Wesley in terms of education and class. He was a man who drew himself out of the working class by his industry and doggedness of character. It was this strength of character that was Taylor's greatest asset. It may be that part of his attraction was the way in which he reflected and was an example of the contemporary aspirations in terms of self-help and improvement. Niebuhr has suggested that 'where the lower strata of society find themselves religiously expatriated by a faith which neither meets their psychological needs nor sets forward an appealing ethical ideal...the right leader finds little difficulty in launching a new movement'.[6] The Connexion's deference to Taylor may indicate that it recognised in him someone well able to articulate their convictions and needs. The problem with such leadership is the vacuum left on the death of the leader.

Order or Orders

Pastors and Ministers

The understanding of ministry within the Connexion had its roots in Independency and was one that had much in common with both the Particular and Old General Baptists. While Dan Taylor exercised leadership at a national level, in the local churches the leadership was in the hands of pastors, elders, ministers and deacons. The nomenclature describing local ministry is a little vague, as some terms are interchangeable. In the Connexion the term 'minister' was used to describe a recognised preacher, though he need not necessarily be ordained or have charge of a church. A 'pastor' was usually an ordained minister having the care of a congregation or congregations. Some confusion enters here as 'minister' became the preferred description of 'pastors' in the nineteenth century.

There were a number of ways into ministry in the Connexion. In the early life of the movement a 'call' from God was sufficient basis for a man to start preaching. This inward call would be recognised by the church of which he was a member. An example is Melbourne: 'Br Thos Mee did at this time open his mind to the church respecting his inclinations to appear in a public Capacity'. The church agreed for him to 'Exercise upon tryal [sic] in preaching, or keeping other meetings as might appear proper, for two or three months, in order to their being better inabled [sic] to form a Judgement of his gifts and qualifications for so Arduous a work'.[7] The

---

[5] George Jackson, 'Evangelical Work of the Baptists in Leicestershire 1740–1820' (University of London, MA thesis, 1955), p. 287.

[6] Niebuhr, *The Social Sources of Denominationalism*, pp. 31-32.

[7] Budge, 'Records Most Material', 25 December 1776 at Melbourne.

comment on John Derry, who became minister of the Barton church in 1824, was that 'He had no college training but knew human nature, the world, and the Bible'. He was minister of the church for twenty-four years. It was under his ministry that the church grew to its greatest number.[8]

We gain an insight into Taylor's understanding of church and ministry from an address that he delivered to young ministers at Coningsby in 1766:

> The question is then, what is implied in the Lord's making him a ruler over his household? I answer I suppose 1st. That the Lord in His providence prepare for him a family who are willing to obey him, under Christ, and submit to his authority in what he urges and inculcates upon them from the word of God. ... having given themselves up to the Lord to be devoted to Him they are now desirous to give themselves up to this person as their minister and ruler.
>
> 2nd. That these persons thus inclin'd and determined in their mind, do regularly and unanimously choose and actually call him to take this charge over them.[9]

Here we see the importance of the local church or congregation; for Taylor, a pastor is only a pastor in relation to a church, which office he holds by virtue of a call from the church. The concept of a 'call' was common to Particular Baptists and Independents as well as General Baptists, and central to their understanding of ministry. The 'call' was twofold: there was the call of God to the individual, and then there was the call of a church. The *General Baptist Repository* lists the marks of a call: the man must 'be converted', a 'humble pious Christian', have 'abilities for the ministry', a 'preaching desire', an 'inclination to be engaged in the ministry', a 'sense of the importance of the work and his fitness for it', able to be used for the 'encouragement of Christian brethren', and, finally, someone who has been 'made useful in his labours'.[10] In the early days of the movement permission to 'call' was often sought from the prospective minister's church. At Castle Donnington in 1775 we have an example of a church releasing a member following such a call:

> The case of Bro' Badderley relative to a Request from the Brethren of Barton in the Beans for him to act as a minister among them at some times with a view for him to be a Stated minister among them if approved of. It is agreed that he shall go and preach among [them?] for the present and the latter part of their request left for further consideration.[11]

Ministers also sought the wisdom of the wider fellowship, as when J. Peggs received an invitation to the church at Bourne: 'Mr Peggs being connected with the Midland Conference and wishing to obtain the advice of his friends laid the case

---

[8] Cook, *Preacher Pastor and Mechanic*, p. 213.

[9] Dan Taylor, *The Faithful and Wise Steward: An address to Young Ministers and Others at Coningsby in Lincolnshire* (Leeds, 1776), p. 11.

[10] *GBR* Vol. 3 No. 16 (1808), pp. 157-60.

[11] Castle Donnington Church Book 1, 12 April 1775. Also Ashby, *Friar Lane*, p. 33.

before that body met at Loughborough who advised him to accept the invitation'.[12] Churches as well as ministers sought advice, as when the church at Austrey asked the Leicestershire Conference concerning a prospective minister, 'does this conference recommend us to invite him?'[13]

But by 1849 there was less of a willing compliance. When the church at Hugglescote requested the church at Ashby and Packington that 'Brother Yates might be liberated 2 Sabbaths to supply on probation', the church at Ashby refused. But the desire of the meeting at Ashby did not deter Thomas Yates; he later accepted the call to Hugglescote.[14] At Bourne, although asked to reconsider, the minister J.H. Wood ultimately accepted an invitation to the pastorate at Sutterton, Lincolnshire.[15]

Exactly what rights were conferred on a minister in a call are unclear. When J.B. Pike of Bourne came under pressure to leave the church in 1863, he claimed that 'the pulpit and all appertaining to it' was his 'freehold for life' and that 'no power in this realm could dispossess him'. He agreed to resign on condition that he received an 'adequate pecuniary consideration'. The church vigorously resisted this claim, but in order to avoid 'strife' settled for a sum equivalent to two years' wages.[16] Pike's position seems to reflect a concept of freehold nearer to Anglicanism than to Independency. James Greenwood, who succeeded J.B. Pike at Bourne after a year's probation, received a call to the church for five years in 1865. In his letter of acceptance he sets out his understanding of the relation between church and minister: 'In my opinion a minister of the Gospel belongs to the Church of Christ at large and ought to be so employed, as that the results of his labours may be most to the advantage of that church, when all its interests are taken into account'.[17] Greenwood, with his wider concept of ministry, did not feel bound to the five-year call that the church had issued, he left after six months. While the church might determine periods of service, decisions about spheres of ministry were becoming a personal decision of the minister, rather than corporate decisions arrived at for the good of the Connexion.

While a minister's authority to rule came from God, a call invested the man with the authority to 'rule'. For Dan Taylor the sphere of a minister's authority was related to the 'word of God'. Again, to quote Taylor, 'No minister has any right to impose any work upon the people he has the charge of but what is taught in the word of God'.[18] Taylor urged an active assumption of this authority.

> It is not enough that he lay these things before them, and coldly tell them the Lord hath enjoined these or the other duties, but he must (as the very term ruler implies)

---

[12] Bourne Church Book, 4 December 1834.
[13] *GBR* Vol. 3 No. 13 (1808), p. 32.
[14] Ashby and Packington, 9 April 1849. Leicester Record Office NB/9/1.
[15] Bourne Church Book, November 1855.
[16] Bourne Church Book, October 1863.
[17] Bourne Church Book, 18 December 1865.
[18] Taylor, *Faithful and Wise Steward*, p. 13.

insist upon it, that they may be performed; and if they are not, we are under an obligation to proceed toward and against the offender...[19]

While a minister in a New Connexion church might be a leader and a ruler, he was such by consent of the congregation. The Connexion's roots were firmly embedded in the congregational theology of Baptists and the Independents.

Elders and Helps

There was no separated order of ministry in the Connexion. In 1608 John Smyth, pastor of the first General Baptist Church, held that, 'the Presbyery of the Church is vniforme [sic] & that the triformed Presbyterie [sic] consisting of three kinds of Elders viz. Pastors, Teachers, Rulers is none of Gods Ordinance but mans devise'. He was explicit on the point that 'all the Elders of the Church are Pastors: & that lay Elders (so called) are Antichristian'.[20] The Connexion followed in this tradition. Together with the 'pastor' or 'minister' were 'elders'; these officers helped in the spiritual oversight of the fellowship. The function of an elder was complementary to that of a pastor, and elders often exercised a teaching function. So we read that the church meeting at Castle Donnington 'Agreed to chuse [sic] by ballot an teaching ruling Elder or pastor this day 2 months'.[21] A letter in the *General Baptist Magazine* of 1798 asked, 'is it consistent with scripture, for a person to have the office of an Elder who is incapable of teaching in public, even though otherwise well qualified?'[22] As with the Old General Baptists, elders were selected by a general majority and ordained by other elders. The Old General Baptists did not permit an elder to officiate in another church unless specially invited. There is a single mention of a woman as elder, Mrs Dixon, in the Barton church, although this may have been due to the Moravian influence of William Kendrick or because the origin of the Barton group was unconnected with the General Baptist tradition.[23] The practice of eldership was irregular within the New Connexion and there was, as the nineteenth century progressed, a tendency for the deacons and diaconate to absorb the functions of elders. Taylor notes the lack of consistency in practice with respect to elders:

> In imitation of the primitive churches in this particular, there are many Christian societies, in modern times that make it a constant rule to have a plurality of Elders to preside amongst them. This is the case with many churches in the General

---

[19] Taylor, *Faithful and Wise Steward*, p. 15
[20] John Smyth, 'Differences of the Churches of the Separation, 1608', in McBeth (ed.), *Sourcebook for Baptist Heritage*, p. 15.
[21] Castle Donnington Church Book, 27 August 1815.
[22] *GBM* (1798), p. 34.
[23] Taylor, *History*, II, p. 16. Edwin Welch, 'The Origins of the New Connexion of General Baptists in Leicestershire', *Transactions of the Leicestershire Archaeological and Historical Society* 69 (1995), p. 62.

Baptist Connexion, but in this particular the whole Connexion is far from being uniform. Many of their churches have only one Elder.[24]

This statement was followed by an appeal for the churches to model themselves 'after the first Christians', which was the justification for the ministry. The Connexion thought that in their appeal to the New Testament they had strong grounds for the establishment of an eldership as a part of the 'primitive' practice.

This appeal to the New Testament is reflected in the office of 'helps', which existed in a number of churches. These, according to Samuel Deacon, were 'not perhaps officers, but such as were capable of doing good; and therefore were employed as helps or assistants'. 'But', he continues, 'as their qualifications and work are not particularly pointed out, little can be said with certainty about them'.[25] We have in the Hugglescote church book the following account of selection: 'The Elders or helps wish to decline their office. Agreed for Bro. Tho. Savil to continue on again. Appointed B. Newbold to engage in the helps office with B. Tho. Savil'.[26] The function of this group was to visit the sick and help in the exercise of discipline. At Castle Donnington the 'church officers' and 'helps', together with the 'Collectors' (those responsible for collecting the pew rents), formed a committee to investigate a financial 'deficiency' in the accounts.[27]

Deacons

The third type of office was that of deacon. For both General and Particular Baptists 'every church has power given them from Christ for their better well being to choose to themselves meet persons into the office of Pastors, Teachers, Elders, Deacons'.[28] As with elders, deacons in the New Connexion were elected and ordained. We read that the Hinckley church, 'Desired J.H. Small to officiate in the deacons office till next Xtmas [sic] on trial, with a view to the ordination of deacons at that, if the way open'.[29] There are accounts of the ordination of deacons as at Queenshead, Yorkshire, on 13 October 1813.[30] John Jarman outlined their responsibilities in an address *The Duties of the office of Deacon on the occasion of appointment of Deacons to the Church at Castle-Gate Nottingham*.[31] For Jarman, a deacon was 'expressly chosen to serve tables', that is 'To minister to the wants of the poor of the church'. Part of

---

[24] *GBR* Vol. 2 (1805), p. 214.
[25] Samuel Deacon, 'On Church Order and Discipline', *Letter* (1833), p. 25.
[26] Hugglescote Church Book, 20 January 1805.
[27] Castle Donnington Church Book, 24 April 1831.
[28] 'Article 36 First London Confession 1644', in McBeth (ed.), *Sourcebook for Baptist Heritage*, p. 50.
[29] Hinckley Baptist Church Minutes, 28 July 1829.
[30] *GBR* No. 23 Vol. 5 (1813), p. 274.
[31] J. Jarman, *The Duties of the Office of Deacons: A Discourse delivered at the Ordination of Deacons in the Church Assembling in Castle-Gate Nottingham* (Sutton Nottingham, 1828), p. 5.

this duty he saw as ensuring that 'a suitable provision be made for the temporal support of your pastor'.[32] They were also to provide for the Lord's Table, and to 'attend to those things which relate to the worship of God in general'.[33] But Jarman did not confine the work of deacons to practical matters alone: 'I conclude the office involves some duties of a higher character than merely *serving tables*. Some of the same things are required in deacons as in pastors'. While this did not include administering the Lord's Supper, he did expect them to encourage and instruct inquirers, to counsel and 'caution and reprove'. This last is to be done in order that the personal element in discipline may be removed, '*that the ministry* [that is the pastor] *may not be blamed*'.[34] Jarman's comments show the beginnings of a fusion of the role of deacon and elder, a synthesis that took place in many churches of the Connexion during the nineteenth century. It is tempting to see a connection between this and the growth of full-time ministry. For Samuel Deacon, 'care of the church's temporal concerns', 'its treasure', and 'those things which are necessary for the comfort and support of the Minister', were the major areas of responsibility.[35] Having taken on the role of deacon, it was not always easy to lay it down, as Bro. Beer at Castle Donnington discovered in 1777:

> The case of Bro & Sister Beer was considered respecting his giving up the Office of a Deacon it appeared very unlawful by what was said relative thereto it doth appear that the chief reason for his so doing was to please his wife. They were then called by the church to attend the next Church Meeting to be held at Kegworth.[36]

While election for life was not questioned in the early life of the Connexion, by 1861 it was questioned: 'it seem unreasonable almost monstrous to appoint any person for the term of his natural life', said a correspondent to the *General Baptist Magazine*. The writer said that while it was 'pretty easy' to get rid of a minister, that was not the case with a deacon: 'on our usual system not even old age, remote residence, hypochondriasis [sic], lameness, deafness, or other infirmity of body mind or temper, relieves the church from the incubus; and the work which should be done by every church is done without the guidance of proper officers, or it is not done at all'.[37] The article was an appeal for limited terms of office for deacons. A 'Live Deacon', writing in the *General Baptist Magazine* in 1877, described the work of deacons varying with the church. In some the work was that of assisting the pastor, visiting the 'sick and erring', and there was also responsibility for the management of business and finance, the cleaning of the chapel and the 'order and decorum of public worship'. In other churches the work was limited to the business council, finance and worship, while elders were responsible for visiting the sick, assisting in

---

[32] Jarman, *The Duties of the Office of Deacons*, p. 6.
[33] Jarman, *The Duties of the Office of Deacons*, p. 7.
[34] Jarman, *The Duties of the Office of Deacons*, p. 9, italics original.
[35] Samuel Deacon, 'Church Order and Discipline', *Letter* (1833), p. 25.
[36] Castle Donnington Church Book, 11 December 1777.
[37] 'Rotary Deacons', *GBM* (1861), p. 224.

preaching and teaching, and the pastoral care of the church. As to a common pattern, he said, 'No all-sufficing rule can be framed'.[38] The two comments above reflect the growing importance and influence of deacons in the latter stages of the life of the Connexion. As the churches developed a greater emphasis on organisation so the role of deacons came to the fore.

Ordination

Approval for Ministry

Ordination was originally seen as a formal setting apart for leadership or ministry in the church, it was a significant event for both General and Particular Baptists, and was often accompanied by fasting and prayer.[39] The *Baptist Reporter* of 1848 described it as a 'setting apart to the pastoral office'.[40] A call to a church did not necessarily require ordination, as with the case of William Brand of Castle Donnington who, in 1817, sought ordination after 'election to the pastoral office'.[41] Ordination was not confined to ministers and pastors, but was also used in relation to elders and deacons. At Melbourne in Derbyshire in 1779 it was concluded, 'that Br. Norton & Br. T. Farmer should be ordained to the office of deacons'.[42] Practice in the Connexion drew on its General Baptist origins in which the emphasis was on church 'order'; ordination did not convey a special status. 'Although every believer is a member of the Body of Christ', says an early Baptist confession,

> yet is not everyone therefore a teacher, elder, or deacon, but only such as are orderly appointed to such offices. The vocation or election of the said officer is performed by the church with fasting and prayer to God.[43]

The New Connexion drew on this tradition. While the Connexion recognised a difference between ministry in the church as a whole and that of a separated order, the difference was not one of status but function which consisted of due authorisation. The church book from Castle Donnington charts the manner in which such men were appointed and authorised:

> 2. The Case of Bro' Ben Wooton whether he shall become Publickley [sic] called and Act as a Minister it is agreed that he shall so act.

> 3. The Case of Bro' Crofts considered relating to his Acting as a Minister amongst us. It is agreed that he shall so act occasionly til the next quarterly Church Meeting.

---

[38] 'Diaconal Duties', *GBM* (1877), p. 387.
[39] 'The Meaning and Practice of Ordination among Baptists', McBeth (ed.) *Sourcebook for Baptist Heritage*, p. 378.
[40] *The Baptist Reporter* (1848), p. 106.
[41] Castle Donnington Church Book 3, 17 May 1817.
[42] Budge, 'Records Most Material', 7 April 1779.
[43] McGlothlin, *Baptist Confessions* (London: Baptist Historical Society), pp. 60-61.

4. The Case of Bro' Badderly Considered whether he shall be encouraged to Act as a Minister at any time. It is agreed that he shall so Act Occasionly at present.

5. A letter from Bro' Gothard was read wherin he signifieth his desire to exercise his Ministerial Gifts that he supposes himself to be Possessed of It is agreed that he may read a portion of the Scripture and speak from it if the brethren desire Him.[44]

Six months later we read, 'It is thought best that Bro' Badderly do not preach any more at present'.[45] Here we see the active part the church meeting played in the process of assessing ability for ministry. Although approval from the church was all that was needed, it was not easily given: 'The Case of Bro' Badderly relating to his standing on occasion as preacher as agreed to last Church Meeting but it was agreed that Bro' Tarrat, Bro' Pickering and Bakewell shall have some further talk with him about his so Acting'.[46] With some men it was decided that a period of trial would be the best way to assess their ability. As the movement expanded there was a continual demand for ministry: 'Dos [sic] the friends know of any Friends that appear to have some qualification to speak a little in publick [sic]', was the appeal in the Donnington church book in 1813.[47]

A similar process of being chosen from among the congregation was employed in the appointment of a pastor. This practice continued well into the nineteenth century. While churches were free to appoint ministers from the congregation, not all were in a position to do so. There existed both a formal and an informal means of introduction between churches and pastors. The formal route was for the church to apply to the conference. The informal route was by recommendation:

A Petitionary Letter read from Maltby in Lincolnshire requesting our assistance in the finding & providing for them A Gospel Minister. But no other help appeared at present for them, than that A young Man in Br. Taylors Ch, had at our last Yorkshire Association been ask'd to go down and stay with them for a few Months the ensuing winter to make tryal [sic], But was not certain whether he wou'd chuse [sic] to go Or that some of the Ministers in the present Connection pay them a visit once a Quarter.[48]

In 1865 a 'Board of Reference for Pastors and Churches' was set up; it sought to facilitate the moving of ministers from one church to another and to 'secure the supply of vacant pastorates with suitable men'. It was composed of ministers elected by the annual association.[49] The fact that it was composed of ministers is another indication of the growing ascendancy of ministerial leadership over lay leadership. In

---

[44] Castle Donnington Church Book, 6 November 1777.
[45] Castle Donnington Church Book, 23 April 1777, Kegworth
[46] Castle Donnington Church Book, 24 June 1776.
[47] Castle Donnington Church Book, 1 May 1813.
[48] Budge, 'Records Most Material', 29 June 1779. That he was to stay and 'make tryal' indicates that what is in mind here is a settled ministry and not just a pulpit supply.
[49] 'Cases From Conferences', *Minutes* (1865), p. 37.

1881 a scheme for ministerial settlement was proposed to the association. The Yorkshire ministers, while approving, expressed a desire for representation from the local conferences.[50] As we have already seen, the local 'conference' and 'annual association' had a voice in the decision where ministers were stationed.

Authority Conferred

The question was raised in 1815, 'Is the method of persons taking upon them the office of Pastors without being ordained to that office, sanctioned by primitive precedent, or the New Testament?' The answer was 'No'. Further it was stated, 'the Association earnestly and affectionately request that Churches and ministers who have followed this practice, would seriously consider it and act more scripturaly in future'.[51] The earnest and affectionate request is an expression of the desire for organisation and control on the part the Connexion. In this they were expressing a common conviction in the Connexion that recognition and authorisation of ministry is wider than the local church, and that proper order was needed. To some extent what a man could do in church was determined by 'ordination'. In answer to a query 'What works may a minister perform before ordination?', the editors of the *General Baptist Repository* state an unordained minister may 'preach', 'pray in public', 'visit Christian friends', and 'exert his talents in thousands of ways for the edification of the Church, and the conversion of sinners'.[52] However, the issue of lay administration presented a major problem.

The conference at Barton on 27 July 1773, in answer to the query 'Is a person in the office of ruling Elder, and ordained to that office, qualified by virtue of his office to administer the Lord's Supper, if the church to which he belongs call him to it?' decided by a majority 'that he is not qualified'. The church at Castle Donnington was responsible for the supply of ministry for themselves and the other congregations that were linked with them, so in 1811 we read, 'Request from Kegworth for Minister to administer the Ordinance to them agreed'.[53] Although churches differed in their practice, generally ordination of a minister or pastor seems to have conferred a particular responsibility, that of administering the Lord's Supper. This responsibility was not viewed as a difference in status, it was a functional difference, that of good order in the church. The position of elders in relation to administration of the Supper is unclear; some churches permitted it, others did not. In 1810, the association made it clear that they believed the ordination to the office of deacon did not qualify a person to administer the Lord's Supper.[54] At the Leicester Conference of 28 December 1813, it was concluded 'that it was improper for unordained ministers to

---

[50] Minutes of the Lancashire and Yorkshire Conference, 8 June 1881.
[51] *Minutes* (1815), p. 15.
[52] 'Answers To Queries', *GBR* (1836), p. 100.
[53] Castle Donnington Church Book, 1 September 1811.
[54] Michael Walker, 'Presidency of the Lord's Table among Nineteenth Century English Baptists', *Baptist Quarterly* 32.5 (January, 1988), p. 217.

administer the Lord's Supper.'[55] But editors of the *Repository* were unwilling to confine administration to those ordained, although it would seem that was where their desire lay:

> It is not asserted that there is any express and particular law, forbidding the practice; but that the general rule of conforming as closely as possible to the order observed in the primitive churches would lead to the employment of ordained ministers at the supper...and Some have maintained that in no circumstances whatever ought an unordained person to administer the ordinance; but we question whether we could go so far.[56]

The guiding principle in their response seems to be adherence to the 'order observed in the primitive churches'. Such a situation is not viewed as wrong, but an 'irregularity which churches ought to prevent when they are able.' This ambiguity, which had been present for some time, did not prevent William Brand, the minister at Castle Donnington, from having scruples:

> A letter was read from the minister signifying to the C^h that he felt it his duty to decline the administration of the Lord's supper & otherwise acting as the Pastor of the C^h seeing he had never been set apart to that office as the primitive pastors were.[57]

In discussing the implications of his forthcoming ordination, he sets out his position with respect to the Lord's Supper. The letter is quoted fairly extensively as it gives an insight into the understanding of authorisation of leadership in the local church:

> Let it be observed then That I have been accustomed to consider the administration of the Lord's Supper to belong to the Elders of the Ch especially such Elders as are Pastors. Now when I had been here one year the Ch concluded that I should be the minister for an unlimited time. Consequently I was not then the Pastor nor in a state of probation for the office when I declined the administration of the Lord's Supper, and therefore in my view I had no scriptural right to administer it; and *on this ground I declined.*

> But the late vote of the Ch chusing [sic] me to be ordained to the Pastoral office, I must be free to say, has, in my view placed me in a situation entirely different and given me a scriptural right to administer the Lord's Supper and also to perform all other duties of the office to which I have been chosen and *on this ground* I do now *consistently* administer the ordinance.

---

[55] *GBR* 30.5 (1813), p. 275.
[56] 'Answers To Queries', *GBR* (1836), p. 100.
[57] Castle Donnington Church Book, August 1815.

You recollect however I did not attempt to do this till the Ch had agreed to desire it; and no doubt the friends in general thought I could do it *consistently* or they would not have wished it.

It is well known that neighbouring Ministers had long been reluctant to come; and when they understood the Ch had left it with me either to procure them to administer the ordinance or to do it myself their reluctance seemed no way removed, for they were free to assure me I *must now do it myself*.[58]

One feature in the above was the practice of calling in 'neighbouring Ministers' in order to administer the Supper when there was no ordained person present in the church.

Laying on of Hands

At the time of the reorganisation of the Connexion in 1835, the issue of ordination again came to the fore under the guise of a discussion on the nature and place of the 'Imposition of Hands' as a distinct but related subject in the ordination of church officers. This practice had been common with the General Baptists for all members at reception into church membership. But its requirement for all was rejected by the Connexion, and was one of the issues over which reunion negotiations failed in 1784.[59] The discussion in the pages of the *General Baptist Repository* and the *Baptist Reporter* centred around the significance of the act and what, if anything, was communicated to the recipient. Was the Spirit communicated by this act or not? The discussion reflects the differing understanding of the nature of ordination. One party felt that it was a divine institution, 'a means or sign conferring official authority; or, in other words, ordination is the means which the Saviour has instituted for the regular appointment unto office in his church'; and laying hands on the person so appointed is 'a prescribed, appropriate, accompanying rite.'[60] In the *Baptist Reporter* ordination was described as 'that which is used to designate a practice'.[61] The other position held that

> the practice of laying on of hands in ordination is not divinely authorized; that our lord did not attend to it, nor have we any intimation that he instituted it; that it is not always spoken of in connection with ordination; and therefore, we have no reason to conclude that it was a constant and essential part of the ordination service.[62]

---

[58] Castle Donnington Church Book, 17 May 1817.
[59] Whitley, *Minutes of the General Assembly*, II, p. 182.
[60] 'On Imposition of Hands', *GBR* (1835), p. 14.
[61] *Baptist Reporter* (1848), p. 107.
[62] 'On Imposition of Hands', *GBR* (1835), pp. 296-97. See also *Baptist Reporter* (1848), p. 68.

The contributors to the discussion were divided over what was happening in ordination. One party argued that 'hands were not imposed...for the purpose of conferring spiritual gifts', and said that when hands were laid on by the 'presbytery' in 1 Timothy 4.14 and 2 Timothy 1.6 they 'were not laid on in reference to any such bestowment, but simply in respect to his being set apart to the ministry'.[63] The other party was of the opinion that 'hands were imposed exclusively as a means or sign of conferring the Holy Spirit, in His miraculous operations' and that 'the design and intention of this ceremony was to communicate miraculous gifts'.[64] It was argued that while laying on of hands was for the bestowal of gifts, those gifts were 'peculiar to the apostolic age', and that it had little or nothing to do with the ordination service as then practised: 'that our Lord did not intend it, nor have we any intimation that he instituted it'. Further, the writer contends that the practice 'furnishes an argument against our consistency' and sees the practice having its authority in Rome.[65]

The question of ordination revolves around the nature of church authority. As John Briggs says, 'the argument was that the verb "ordain" in Scripture merely meant to appoint and that no ceremony was necessary for the labourer to start upon his labours; ordination ceremonies suggested a church authority present in those ordaining which was foreign to Baptist understandings of the Church'.[66] For the Connexion, with its emphasis on connexional life, the ordination service provided an opportunity to give practical demonstration to this concept by the presence of a number of ministers in the service. John Taylor, the brother of Dan, gave an account of the week prior to his ordination in the late summer of 1773:

> On the Lord's day evening I had to preach at Birchcliffe, before the ministers who had come to ordain me, as none had heard me except my brother Dan. On the Monday evening preached at a house in Halifax. On Tuesday Mr Thompson asked me what questions he thought proper; and heard my confession of faith. On Wednesday we came to Queenshead and the chapel was opened. On Thursday I was Ordained. A long time of Solomn [sic] worship was occupied: introductory discourse, reading the scriptures and prayer, questions to me and the church, confession of Faith, prayer with laying on of hands, a long heavy charge, [By his brother] which, Mr Thompson said contained six hundred particulars. In the afternoon we had a short service, when Mr Tarratt preached.[67]

By 1831 things were a little more simplified, although the same basic structure remains. So when George Picknance was 'solemnly set apart to the pastoral office over the General Baptist Church Seven Oaks, Kent' on 28 March 1831, there were four other General Baptist ministers present. The service opened with singing and prayer. This was followed by questions to the minister and his statement of faith.

---

[63] *GBR* (1835), p. 13.
[64] *GBR* (1835), p. 295.
[65] *GBR* (1835), p. 297.
[66] Briggs, *English Baptists*, p. 87.
[67] Taylor, *Memoir John Taylor*, p. 31.

Then followed the ordination prayer with the laying on of hands and an address. In the afternoon there was another service of singing and a further address. The induction of James Greenwood at Bourne in 1865 gives us an insight into the nature of the relationship between pastor and people. In that service the people were asked if they were 'intending to pray and work with him', if 'in a spirit of Christian love' they would be willing to 'bear with such deficiencies as a young & inexperienced though good and earnest man may display', and would they 'treat his counsels & admonitions with respect and endeavour to esteem him very highly in love for his work's sake?' The response of the church was,

> if our esteemed brother has not enjoyed that long experience which more aged ministers possess, yet believing him to be earnest & sincere and faithful to his divine master and to us, we trust we shall listen to his counsels with respect, esteem and love him for his works sake, and always endeavour to hold up his hands in carrying on the great work of ministry to which he is called.[68]

The church members gave their assent to this statement by standing. Two features of these statements should be noted. First, it is the office, not the man that commands respect; honour was given for 'his work's sake'. Second, the work of ministry needs congregational support, members will 'always endeavour to hold up his hands'. There is a recognition that ministry cannot be exercised without the active cooperation of the congregation.

In 1852, John Wallis argued that it was the local church alone that could determine ordination, and that only duly appointed men could administer the Lord's Supper. However, he thought that the local church did not have to appoint a pastor, it could authorise someone from among its own members to preside.[69] One development which took place was that the emphasis on the church within the Connexion, which it had inherited from Independency, was slowly giving way to the individualism inherent in the theology of the Evangelical Revival. Michael Walker argues that the 'underlying concern' of Baptist churches until the end of the eighteenth century was 'that of church order', and that the understanding of ministry was related to that.[70] In 1856, William Underwood, arguing for a trained and recognised ministry, said that many churches in the Connexion were too small to 'support even single men in the sole exercises of the ministry'.[71] The expectations of churches in terms of ministry had changed. 'The age is too enlightened to tolerate men as teachers who have never learned, and the churches know better than to expect that to be imparted which was never acquired'. He concluded that people 'must be deluded or demented who suppose, or at least act on the supposition, that it [the ministry] can be honourably followed by men of the lowest qualifications'.[72] Such

---

[68] Bourne Church Book, 3 April 1865.
[69] Walker, 'Presidency of the Lords Table', p. 219.
[70] Walker, 'Presidency of the Lords Table', p. 221.
[71] William Underwood, 'Our Denomination', *GBR* (1856), p. 51.
[72] Underwood, 'Our Denomination'.

stipulations further hindered the flexibility of churches to cope with a changing situation, or to make use of the gifted layman whose ministry had been so vital in the establishing of the movement. The layman was giving way to the full-time, trained minister.

What is the significance of concerns about ordination and the formal recognition of ministry? Within the Connexion, there seem to be a number of conflicting pressures at work. First, the Evangelical Revival had given the layman a new and much more significant role in church life. This had the effect of taking some of the elitism out of ministry. It is possible to argue that concerns about ordination reflected a desire to give back status to ministers; and at a time when Nonconformity was seeking respectability the aspirations of congregations and the respectability of ministers were related. However, over and against this, the teachings and practices of the Oxford Movement aroused fears of 'espousing orders'.[73] Along with this deacons came to be regarded as 'laymen' as distinct from ordained ministers.[74]

The middle of the century had seen a number of ministers emerge who were impatient with forms and ceremonies, men like John Clifford who placed an emphasis on the inner nature of spirituality, and laid little stress on outward forms. There was a decline in the practice of laying on of hands in the Connexion and other parts of Nonconformity, and the word 'ordination' dropped out of use. By 1885 ordination and commissioning services had given way to welcome meetings.[75] What was lost in this was the old understanding of ministry for good church 'order'. These developments with regard to ministry seemed to be moving in different directions: on the one hand, a renewed concern for ordination as a reaction to the Evangelical Revival; and, on the other, a down-grading of ministry as a result of the Anglo-Catholic movement. This apparent contradiction reflects something of the ambiguity that surrounded the nature and position of ministry within the Connexion. That there was some uncertainty about a minister's position in relation to the church is reflected in the question put to the church meeting in 1873 by J.A. Jones, the pastor at Gosberton, Lincolnshire, who was about to retire. He asked if the meeting considered him as 'belonging to the church apart from his pastorate'. The church thought that he was still a member.[76]

Academy

Changes in leadership were coupled with another important indicator of denominational emergence, the move from part-time to a trained, full-time ministry. It is an area that reflects a shift in values within the Connexion and is another indication of a developing denominationalism.

---

[73] Walker, 'Presidency of the Lords Table', p. 209.
[74] Walker, 'Presidency of the Lords Table', p. 209.
[75] 'The Meaning and Practice of Ordination among Baptists', in McBeth, *Sourcebook for Baptist Heritage*, p. 377.
[76] Gosberton Church Book 2, 11 December 1873.

For men entering the ministry in the early days of the Connexion there was little, if any, formal training. For the first quarter of a century, the Connexion seems to have been satisfied with its leadership by lay preachers and part-time pastors. Dan Taylor while at Birchcliffe started a weekly class for a small number who wished to learn how to preach. His first students were Richard Folds, Jeremy Ingham and his brother John Taylor. For some the effectiveness of the organisation was related to the quality of its ministry. It was felt that an educated or trained ministry was needed. This was voiced in the *General Baptist Repository* of 1811 where we read, 'it is with much concern that many others besides myself view the apathy which prevails in the minds of professors in general, among the General Baptists, as it respects the education of young men for the ministry'.[77] Churches had been pastored by men with little or no formal education or theological training. As the power of the Evangelical Revival began to wane, so perceived needs within the Connexion began to change. It was felt that the lay preacher or minister was no longer adequate to the situation; what was required was a properly trained ministry. Where this desire came from is difficult to determine. Yinger suggests that, as the leadership of movements become more established, they look for ways to assume continuity of power. Wilson, on the other hand, says that this kind of move comes about as 'the result of the wider social process of the secular society'.[78] Adam Taylor attributed the call for some form of ministerial training to the fact that the churches 'increased in number and respectability'.[79] It needs to be borne in mind that the General Baptists had a concern for ministerial training going back several generations, the London General Baptists having proposed a college in 1702. This early concern was revived in 1793, and the first student taken into training in 1796.[80] The emergence of the Academy needs to be seen against this background. The Academy began in 1797 when, at the instigation of Robert Smith of Nottingham, a committee was formed in order to oversee training for ministers. The idea for a training institution came before the association in Boston in 1798, where it met with approval. The sum of £175 was raised through subscriptions following an appeal at the 1797 association, with further promises of £16 per annum. In 1798, Dan Taylor was asked to provide personal tuition for a small number of students.[81] It was an appropriate choice, since from his days in Yorkshire Taylor had been concerned for a well-equipped ministry. In the year before his appointment he had written, 'I am so distressed at times on account of the state of the ministry among General Baptists, that I am almost ready in my own apprehension to lie down and die'. He saw the solution in terms of

---

[77] *GBR* (1811), p. 22.

[78] J. Milton Yinger, *Religion Society and the Individual: An Introduction to the Sociology of Religion* (New York: Macmillan, 11th edn, 1968), p. 147; Bryan R. Wilson *Religion in Secular Society: A Sociological Comment* (London: E.A. Watts 1966), p 136.

[79] Taylor, *History*, II, p. 330.

[80] H. Forman, 'Baptist Provision for Ministerial Education in the 18th Century' *Baptist Quarterly* 27.8 (October, 1978), p. 363.

[81] Taylor, *Memoirs of the Rev. Dan Taylor*, p. 218.

training for the ministry, but felt reluctant to 'push this', because he did not want to be seen to be seeking a position or advancement for himself. It was for him 'the only thing I wish to see before I die'.[82] His wish was granted, for during the next thirteen years he took young men into his home at Mile End, London, and provided them with personal instruction.

The men who came had little or no formal education; there was a broad-based basic instruction which consisted of English, the Bible, history, geography, and moral philosophy. The charge of £50 per annum covered tuition and board and lodging.[83] By the time he resigned in 1811, nineteen students had received instruction, and the Academy was placed in the hands of a committee. A student's account of the academy under Taylor is given by Joseph Goadby, Sr, who in 1798 spent six months with Taylor. According to Goadby, students started work at six in the morning and after breakfast were lectured by Taylor on 'the work of the ministry', 'Biblical Geography' and the 'Art of Sermon Making'. They studied Hebrew, Greek and English grammar and logic. Despite their studies they still had time for a walk every day, to listen to debates in the House of Commons and visit the British Museum.[84] In addition to studies they supplied the pulpit at Taylor's church as, according to Adam Taylor, Dan Taylor was only 'one Lord's day in every six or eight weeks with his people'.[85]

The increasing age of Dan Taylor, dissatisfaction with the committee, and the location of the Academy in London, far from the centres of strength in the movement, generated discontent and paved the way for a re-organisation in 1813. The governors resigned and handed over the management of the institution to the annual association—further evidence of the growing denominational structure. A committee was appointed, and Taylor's 'Six Articles' were reaffirmed as its distinctive theological basis.[86]

The reason for the Academy moving to Wisbech in 1813 is not clear. Certainly dissatisfaction with London was a component, but why Wisbech? It was just as remote from the centres of the Connexion as London. The most likely factor was that Joseph Jarrom, who ministered there, was available as tutor. He presided over the Academy from 1813 to 1837, during which time thirty-six men were prepared for the ministry. They included Richard Ingham and the Goadby brothers, Joseph and John, men who were to play an important part in the life of the movement. In addition, there were James Pegg and William Brampton who were the first missionaries of the movement. One of Jarrom's students was John Wilders, who entered the Academy in 1837. Born on 22 December 1807, he worked on the stocking frame from boyhood until he entered the Academy in 1836. Although lacking a formal education he was, according to Wood, 'a striking example

---

[82] Taylor, *Memoirs of the Rev. Dan Taylor*, p. 216.

[83] F.M. Harrison, 'The Nottinghamshire Baptists: Mission, Worship, Training', *Baptist Quarterly* 25.7 (July, 1974), p. 324.

[84] Goadby and Goadby, *Not Saints But Men*, pp. 32-35.

[85] Taylor, *Memoirs of the Rev. Dan Taylor*, p. 217.

[86] *Minutes* (1813), p. 13.

of...endeavours at self improvement'.[87] He developed an interest in languages when fourteen years old, first learning Latin, then French and Greek. This was followed by Hebrew, German, Italian and Syriac. He also had an interest in botany, mathematics and English literature. He spent a year in the Academy, then six months at Hinckley, from where he received a call to the General Baptist church at Smalley in Derbyshire, remaining until his death in 1847. Wilders is an example of the aspirations of Dissent in terms of education. This desire the Academy could only meet in a limited way.

The year 1814 saw an appeal to the association to 'use all proper means to discover ministerial talents' and 'not to suffer them by inattention and neglect to continue in their present uneducated, unimproved state'.[88] By 1825 criticisms concerning the Academy were being voiced; it was felt that its location could be nearer the Midlands. There was also criticism of Jarrom who was felt to be too staid and formal. According to Harrison, 'Churches wanted a more lively, evangelistic ministry'.[89]

The needs perceived by some of the churches differed from that of the committee responsible for the Academy. In 1825, the *General Baptist Repository* carried a prospectus for an 'Educational Society', formed in the November of that year by delegates of the churches at Barton, Ibstock and Austrey. The churches of the Midlands were, at the time of this announcement, in the middle of an economic depression and the growth of the movement was at its lowest point for ten years. Small village churches found it difficult enough to finance any ministry, let alone a full-time pastor. Feeling in the churches was, at least according to the Nether Street church in Beeston, Nottingham, that 'such an establishment would be better in this part of the Connexion'.[90] It was a view that prevailed. Thomas Stevenson of Baxter Gate, Loughborough, was appointed tutor with the assistance of his son, the Rev. John Stevenson, MA. The men would continue in work, but the society would equip village preachers who would 'Preach with their tongues, walk with their feet and work with their hands'.[91] The Educational Society was an attempt to meet the needs of the poor smaller churches (which constituted the majority of the Connexion), unable to afford full-time pastors, through the development of a self-financing, semi-professional ministry. It was also a reassertion of the value of laymen. But hopes for this venture were not fulfilled. The 'Institution' to all intents and purposes became another 'Academy'.[92]

The continuing illness of Jarrom in 1836 and 1837, and his subsequent resignation on health grounds, again prompted discussion about the nature and location of the Wisbech Academy. In 1838, the association appointed a committee to consider the future. They recommended 'that it is highly desirable in the opinion of

---

[87] Wood, *History*, p. 269.
[88] *Minutes* (1814), p. 12.
[89] Harrison, 'The Nottinghamshire Baptists', p. 324.
[90] Nether Street Beeston Book 1, 14 March 1824.
[91] Harrison, 'Baptists of Nottinghamshire', p. 305.
[92] Harrison, 'Baptists of Nottinghamshire', p. 484.

this Association that the energies of the Connexion be concentrated in the support of one Academical institution'.[93] The outcome was the union of the Academy and the Educational Society at Loughborough under Thomas Stevenson. The commitment of the Connexion was reaffirmed in 1838 when, under the major reorganisation of the Connexion, the churches were 'earnestly requested to make an annual collection for...the instruction of young men for the ministry'.[94] The concerns about equipping preachers are reflected in the 1840 report on Henry Rose: 'Mr Rose, not discovering a great aptitude in classical studies, and yet possessing a pleasing degree of zeal and pulpit talent has been permitted to supply the church at Whittlesea for several months...and it is pleasing to add, that the Divine blessing appears evidently to rest upon him'.[95]

The Academy had a nomadic existence, seemingly changing location with its tutor.[96] After a brief period in London under John Stevenson, the association decided in 1843 after considerable discussion 'That the location of the Academy shall be in the Midlands'. Stevenson being unwilling to move, Joseph Wallis was appointed tutor and relieved of pastoral responsibilities in order to teach full-time at Leicester. John Clifford says of this period, 'I regard the time I spent at the Midland Baptist College in Leicester as two of the most interesting years of my long life. I look back to them with the deepest thankfulness, and count them among the most formative of my experience'.[97] There was again controversy about location in 1856, when there was a move by S.C. Sarjant to separate the theological from the secular education, and move the institution to London where they could take advantage of the new university. A suggestion was put forward by E.C. Pike that the Academy should share premises with the Particular Baptist Stepney College, which was in the process of moving to a new site at Regent's Park. Each college would retain its own identity, but the Connexion would share tutors and premises and pay the Regent's Park College for the board and class fees of each student. Dr. Angus, the principal, thought that 'out of a four year course, all our differences might be taught in one month'.[98] It was not to be; the parochialism of the Midland churches was too strong and the Academy remained in Leicester. A review of the denomination in 1856 described the Academy as 'incompletely officered...defective in its working apparatus...and so often involved in financial difficulties'.[99] The death of Wallis in 1857 provoked another discussion and the College moved to Sherwood Rise, Nottingham, with William Underwood as tutor. In 1861, the Connexion raised the money for purpose-built buildings at Chilwell, Nottingham. It remained there until the founding of Nottingham University, where 'in order that the Baptist students might there study classics and science' the College was moved to premises in

---

[93] *Minutes* (1838), p. 24.
[94] *Minutes* (1838), p. 21.
[95] *Minutes* (1840), p. 32.
[96] W.J. Avery, 'The Late Midland College', *Baptist Quarterly* 1 (1922–23), p. 220.
[97] James Marchant, *Dr. John Clifford* (London: Cassell, 1924), p. 21.
[98] J.C. Pike, 'The Academy', *GBR* (1856), p. 460.
[99] 'Our Denomination', *GBM* (1856), p. 52.

Nottingham, where it remained until the demise of the Connexion. Following the death of Thomas Goadby, who served the college from 1873–1889, difficulty was found in appointing a tutor and a 'syndicate' of local ministers became responsible. At this time the period of study was lengthened from four years to five. In 1891 Thomas Witton Davies became principal; the following year the life of the Connexion came to an end with the union of the two Baptist bodies.

The College continued with diminishing numbers until it closed in 1920. According to John Clifford, the College's distinctive nature was that it was 'the College of a denomination'. Avery argues that it was the demise of the New Connexion in which the concerns of the College were vested, that was the major contributor to its end, 'the Connexional spirit was lacking'.[100] Kenneth Brown has a different explanation. He says that by the end of Victoria's reign, 'The expansion of alternative employment opportunities meant that the ministry no longer represented the major vehicle of social advancement for ambitious young nonconformists'.[101] While that may be so, there is still force in Clifford's argument. The Academy had been an expression of the life of the Connexion, and had contributed to maintaining its distinctiveness as a denomination. The Connexion had as a body supported the College for many years. With the Union of 1891, the reason for its independent existence came to an end; this, together with the removal of the financial obligation, meant that there was little to sustain the Academy, and falling numbers finally contributed to its closure.

Concerns of Ministry

Income

'If you give yourself up to the work of the ministry, you must submit to a life of labour, poverty, dependence and anxiety; and insure a heavy portion of toil and indigence to your children'. So said a writer in the *General Baptist Repository* of 1810. Ministerial aid was, he said, rather a 'bestowal of charity' than an 'equitable recompense for service performed', and it was 'more frequently proportioned to the whim and prejudice of the giver than to the wants of the receiver'. He observed that 'Till this subject is better understood and more conscientiously attended to, it is vain to expect that men of ability and spirit will engage in the ministry'.[102] Kenneth Brown says that major concerns of most Baptist ministers were 'income and amenable working relationships'.[103] There were a few large churches where a good stipend was available, but for the majority of churches in the Connexion the financial basis was very insecure.

---

[100] W.J. Avery 'The Late Midand College', p. 330.

[101] Kenneth D. Brown, *A Social History of the Nonconformist Ministry in England and Wales 1800–1930* (Oxford: Clarendon, 1988), p. 223.

[102] *GBR* 17.3 (1810), p. 213.

[103] Kenneth D. Brown, 'The Baptist Ministry of Victorian England and Wales: A Social Profile', *Baptist Quarterly* 32.3 (July, 1987), p. 115.

Dan Taylor, writing about 1773 to his friend William Thompson at Boston, said of his ministry in Yorkshire,

> I have fourteen boarders come to hand, with a pretty numerous family beside, and some time to take up with Mr Ingham, my young assistant, and my son: and the hay harvest having been just at the same time, and above twenty day scholars, sometimes nearly thirty, with everything to provide for my boarders, and much concern for two pretty large and widely extended churches, besides the new interest raising at Halifax, must, you will grant, have considerably thronged me.[104]

It was common in the Nonconformist ministry for men to support themselves in this way. In 1785, the association heard a case from Sutton Coldfield: 'Whereas the church at Sutton Coldfield think they cannot advance above £20 pounds a year towards brother Austins support, and he does not think it appears likely he can do with less than £50 a year, they solicit the assistance and advice of the churches in the Connexion. Answer, we advise brother Austin to turn his thoughts to some way of business, unanimously with only 7 neuters.'[105] Joseph Goadby faced a similar situation when he went to his first church at Ashby-de-la-Zouch in July 1799. The congregation were meeting in a barn and could only pay him £20 a year, half of this was provided by the church at Melbourne.[106] In order to support his wife and family he worked at his trade of staymaking.[107] J.G. Pike, the force behind the missionary society of the Connexion, started his ministry at Derby in 1809 with £50 a year. The church's letter of invitation said the reason for the smallness of the stipend was due to 'our general low circumstances and a want of ability to perform more honourable conditions'.[108] Thirteen years later, the church having grown from fifty to 114, and with a small income from a school, he was still financially straitened.[109]

When depressions of trade came, ministers as well as churches were affected. There was a special church meeting called at Castle Donnington to consider the situation of its minister:

> The worsted spinning business in which Mr Brand was engaged having in a considerable degree declined—which caused a deficiency in his income—he found it necessary for the support and comfort of his family to engage in manual labour six days a week and twelve hours each day—This appeared to several friends inconsistent with his character and duty as a minister—would hinder his progress in

---

[104] Taylor, *Memoirs of the Rev. Dan Taylor*, p. 92.

[105] *Minutes* (1785), p. 10.

[106] 'Our brethren at Packington are endeavouring to procure brother Goadby of Bosworth to settle among them and request to know whether we will give them some assistance in providing (a) bread for him. Agreed to give our Packington friends for one year the the sum of Ten pounds to be paid at 4 times the first time to be midsummer next if Brother Goadby settles among them'. Budge, 'Records most material', 14 April 1799.

[107] Goadby and Goadby, *Not Saints but Men*, p. 43.

[108] Pike and Pike, *Memoir and Remains of J.G. Pike*, p. 61.

[109] Pike and Pike, *Memoir and Remains of J.G. Pike*, p. 93.

knowledge and usefulness and also be injurious to the interests of the church the neighbourhood and the Connection.[110]

While the church did not like him working, there is no record of any increase of salary. Brown says of Baptists that 'men slipped in and out of the pastorate as economic circumstances dictated'.[111] This is true of the Connexion whose geographical base in the East Midlands was predominantly composed of rural and artisan workers. In 1806, T. Stevenson, who ran a school and was minister of the church at Archdeacon Lane, Leicester, came to a 'painful persuasion' of the church's inability to continue his support, even if it could be found. He said that 'he could have no comfort in receiving it from some persons who could not but with great difficulty support themselves'.[112]

The church at Retford and Gamston in Nottinghamshire adopted a novel approach to fund-raising. They agreed to give the minister, J.J. Dalton, the sum of £80 per annum, an increase of £10, on condition that he lend the church the sum of £250 for five years interest free, which was to go towards the building of the proposed new chapel.[113] Two years later the same church took advantage of the Baptist Union Augmentation Fund. The church book records the decision: 'That £10 be paid by the church in order that we may receive the sum of £20 in return to increase our minister's salary'.[114] In some of the village churches of Lincolnshire funding the ministry was a continual problem. At Bourne in 1850 we read in the church book, 'the subject of Mr Deacon's resignation was resumed & after long consideration in which the pecuniary difficulty of retaining his services was principally dwelt upon it was agreed that he be requested to stay'.[115] When in 1880 James Ellis resigned, following difficulties at Gosberton, Lincolnshire, he said that 'he had been advised to at once remove his connection with people who did not appear to understand the communal duties of professing Christians'. The church was indebted to him of a sum of £60: 'he had lost his money but the church had lost its honour'. Ellis had experienced problems almost as soon as he arrived. He was, he said, 'the third pastor who had been so used and by the same person the fact will be noteworthy to those who follow me'.[116] His advice was not heeded for the church minutes record 'Mr Darts resignation of the pastorate at the close of his fourth year Sept 30th. was tendered, and accepted on account of financial inability to retain him'.[117] While men worked under such difficulties and constraints it is little wonder that the Connexion did not develop the national leadership that was needed. While there was an emerging denominational bureaucracy, the Connexion did not have the financial resources that

---

[110] Castle Donnington Church Book, 26 February 1815.
[111] Brown, 'Baptist Ministry of Victorian England', p. 115.
[112] Archdeacon Lane Minute Book No 1, 18 August 1810.
[113] Retford and Gamston Book 2, 22 May 1871.
[114] Retford and Gamston Book 2, 29 January. 1873.
[115] Bourne Church Book, 2 May 1850.
[116] Gosberton Church Book, 12 May 1880.
[117] Gosberton Church Book, 10 July 1893.

would enable able it to release men from the pastoral ministry in order to get a broad view of the movement, and to give it that central control and coherence that was needed.

Personal Relationships

One of the major areas of concern in ministry was conflict in the church. This conflict with congregations came about for a variety of reasons. Mr Wooton left the church at Kegworth after a doctrinal dispute in 1781. But more often it was of a personal nature. When in 1818 the minister William Felkin was accused of 'having quite lost his character', the minute writer at Kegworth observed: 'The baseness and cruelty of some in this affair who w^d fair pass for great Saints, w^d make a heathen blush'.[118] In 1859, the church had a further conflict with their pastor, John Taylor, as a result of which he resigned.[119] At Castle Donnington a personal dispute developed into a church split. The minister, William Brand, was accused in a church meeting of striking a lad that worked with him in his worsted business. William Brand 'defended himself against the slander' that was, according to the minute writer, brought by 'enemies of the cause'.[120] Brand left the church to decide the issue. The outcome was as follows:

> At the close it appeared that 31 persons then present thought that, though he might preach elsewhere, he should cease preaching at Donnington for 2 months. Four thought he should be excluded. And 36 thought he should go on as usual obtaining however under present circumstances as many exchanges as he well can. 'Behold how great a matter a little fire kindleth'!! The Lord pardon the indiscretion of his unworthy servant and heal the wounds which have thus been given to the cause of truth and love.[121]

The words of the writer were to be prophetic as the discussion was to drag on for over a year. The following month the church postponed the Lord's Supper 'till the business respecting the minister is settled'. William Brand was also requested to attend a meeting to hear charges that were to be brought against him. Although no charges were levelled, a committee was formed which, according to the minute writer, 'seem to have for its object the dismission of the minister from his office'.[122] The church began to divide over the issue.

At the following church meeting, while there were some things in which the minister 'acknowledged himself blameable', certain members wanted the church to censure him. The 'elders seemed unwilling to put this motion'.[123] The disagreement

---

[118] Kegworth Church Book, 13 September 1818.
[119] Kegworth Church Book, 9 January 1859.
[120] Castle Donnington Church Book, 1 December 1919.
[121] Castle Donnington Church Book, 1 December 1919.
[122] Castle Donnington Church Book, 13 February 1820.
[123] Castle Donnington Church Book, 19 March 1820.

rumbled on; another vote was proposed in April. The minute writer records of that church meeting, 'Many friends still objected to it as not being justified by the circumstances', but it was agreed by the church to bring the issue forward again after the afternoon service. At that meeting William Brand, 'much affected', put his position. The church passed a resolution that the issue 'should not again be brought into the church meeting', in effect saying that the offence did not justify his dismissal.[124]

But the church was still divided between those who supported Brand and those who wanted to see him go. In May the decision of the previous month was rescinded.[125] By now the issue had moved from censure to whether or not he should continue in office. Joseph Oldershaw, who was behind the move to get rid of Brand, withdrew from the church. A fortnight later, 'the sense of the Church having been taken', it was decided by 122 to 26 that he should remain, 39 abstaining.[126] Following this decision the church divided; the minute book charts the attempts at reconciliation that took place over the next few months, the outcome of which was that William Brand was asked to limit his preaching to once a fortnight only. In September the 'minority' withdrew and set up a separate interest in Donnington.[127] The issue was finally resolved in October, when ministers from the association were called in to talk to both parties. The result was a reconciliation with all but six.[128] It comes as little surprise to read that in January the following year William Brand gave notice of his resignation as from March.[129] In May that year a reconciliation took place with the recalcitrant members, but at the cost of the ministry.[130]

Although there was a notional degree of connexional authority, as churches in the 'independent' subject to the will of members in decisions of the church meetings, there was in practice little or no subjection to higher authority. This applied both to self-willed ministers, deacons, and congregations who wielded the power of the purse. Even when the authority of the association was invoked, it was by application to them. The Connexion does not seem to have intervened on the basis of its own authority.

Lay Ministry

Ministry in the Connexion presents a bewildering pattern. In addition to 'stated' pastors or ministers, there were also a variety of lay preachers, some settled, others itinerant, yet others working with mission agencies or other groupings. Thomas Cook of travel fame is an example of an itinerant minister. In 1828, aged twenty, he was appointed an agent for the Connexion's Home Mission Society. After being

---

[124] Castle Donnington Church Book, 9 April 1820.
[125] Castle Donnington Church Book, 7 May 1820.
[126] Castle Donnington Church Book, 21 May 1820.
[127] Castle Donnington Church Book, 24 Sepember 1820.
[128] Castle Donnington Church Book, 31 October 1820.
[129] Castle Donnington Church Book, 14 January 1821.
[130] Castle Donnington Church Book, 6 May 1821.

'solemnly set apart for the work' he began a four-year period of itinerancy in the counties of Rutland, Northamptonshire and parts of Lincolnshire. In 1829 he made a tour of the Midland counties, visiting most of the churches of the Connexion. John Briggs estimates he travelled 2,700 miles in the course of this tour.[131] His work involved preaching and the sale or distribution of tracts, books and Bibles. The work brought him into contact with a large number of churches in the Connexion and gave him an affection for the denomination which never left him. The work came to an end when 'the zeal of the churches became less ardent and the funds were not sufficiently large to warrant the continuance of a paid agent'.[132]

Thomas Cook was prepared for this work by first becoming a lay preacher. This was a major opportunity for service in the Connexion. The movement had, from its inception, depended on men who were willing to engage in this type of ministry.

The Stoney Street church, Nottingham, was one of the larger churches in the Connexion. Some time between 1815 and 1823, a Stoney Street Preachers Plan was established. This organisation was variously referred to as the 'Stoney Street Preachers', 'The Stoney Street Itinerant Society' and the 'Itinerant Meeting'. Following a division in the church in 1849, a 'General Baptist Preachers Union' was formed, the result of which was two organisations, the dominant one being the 'Preachers Union'.[133] The members of both groups served the churches around Nottingham. The obituary in 1870 for one of the founder members of both organisations, John Ploughwright, says he was 'an emphatic "Itinerant" having preached fifty five years, walked 80,000 miles, and preached 5,000 sermons'.[134] According to Harrison, the preachers were men of 'humble circumstances'. For example, John Ploughwright was a toll keeper. When E. Stevenson died in 1874 his widow was given £2.5.0, the result of a collection among the preachers. The minutes of the Nottinghamshire Baptist preachers record that they were so poor that 'it was said that there was not a candle in the house and Bro Stevenson died in the dark'.[135]

We see a reflection of the social composition of preachers in 'Lay Agency', an address by W. Marshall, himself a lay preacher, to the 1859 Leicester Conference on the 'Extension of the General Baptist Connexion'. By the term 'Lay Agency' he identified Sunday school teachers, distributors of tracts, 'the agents of our Dorcas and benevolent societies, the visitors of the sick and dying; in fact, all church members who do not sustain the pastoral office are, or ought to be, included in our list of lay agents'.[136] But the main subject of his address was the lay preachers. He appealed for men 'who through natural talents, educational advantages, and social position, are best qualified for the office...' Rather than the 'manufacturer', the 'solicitor', the

---

[131] Briggs, *English Baptists*, p. 333. Also Cook, Preacher Pastor Mechanic, p. 190.
[132] J.R. Godfrey, *Historic Memorials of Barton & Melbourne General Baptist Churches* (London: Elliot Stock, 1891), pp. 171-72.
[133] Harrison, 'Nottinghamshire Baptists', p. 319.
[134] *GBM* (1870), p. 250.
[135] In Harrison, 'Nottinghamshire Baptists', p. 320.
[136] 'Lay Agency', *GBM* (1859), p. 455.

'grocer', and the 'draper', men 'occupying a respectable social position', he noted that the local preachers were composed of the 'shoemaker', the 'stocking maker', the 'warehouse-man' and the 'porter'. This comment gives us an indication of the type of men who were involved as local preachers. The problem Marshall identified was the need to 'improve our class of men': 'Send your comparatively illiterate men, who have had no educational advantages, who are pressed down by poverty, and who have scarcely a moment's time for preparation, and the effect will soon be apparent upon a congregation'. He then goes on to make the telling observation: 'Depend upon it, my friends, it is no use trying to ignore the fact, other things being equal, a man's social position will have an influence'.[137] He concluded the address by drawing attention to the changes that had taken place in the cultural and educational standards of the churches served by local preachers: 'our congregations, we must remember, read, and occupy a very different position as regards their intelligence to what they did some fifty years ago'.[138]

The Nottingham General Baptist Preachers Union tried to exert some process of selection and training with respect to preachers. A minute of 1852 states, 'In consequence of the report received respecting Brother Hodges the meeting was of the opinion that he might be more useful some other way than in preaching'. They also required that their preachers be 'accredited' members and preachers of a Baptist church.[139] A preaching plan was published and novices were required to go out with more experienced men while their abilities were evaluated. The Methodist circuit plan would seem to be the pattern imitated. But the Nottingham lay preachers, in common with other preachers in the Connexion, never occupied the place in the denominational structure of their Methodist counterparts. It was felt by one writer in the *General Baptist Magazine* of 1866 that some ministers refused to encourage an 'occasional preacher' through a 'spirit of Monopoly'.[140] This letter provoked a discussion in the letter columns of the magazine. 'Spectator', a layman and writer of the original letter, contended that what was needed was 'some authority...that would bring lay agency into order and under some control'. He argued that ministers would then see lay preachers as a 'co-working agency'. The problem was that such a proposal would require a further centralisation of power: 'we should require various centres of authority that should take under complete control the entire field of lay agency'.[141] That lay preachers were needed was not questioned; just over half the pulpits in the Connexion did not have a stated minister in 1866. The issue was that of recognition, regulation and quality. As one contributor to the debate commented, 'is not their existence, as part of the agency of the body, practically ignored?'[142]

Preachers' unions were helpful, but they did not have a formal place in the structure of the Connexion. Speaking at a local preachers' conference in

---

[137] *GBM* (1859), p. 456.
[138] *GBM* (1859), p. 460.
[139] Minute Book of the General Baptist Preachers Union, 7 June 1852, 7 March 1853.
[140] 'Lay Preachers', *GBM* (1866), p. 93.
[141] *GBM* (1866), p. 214.
[142] *GBM* (1866), p. 254.

Leicestershire in 1877, W. Richardson again addressed the role of the local preacher in connexional structures. He identified three possible approaches: first, that of 'Colportage' based on the method employed by the Metropolitan Tabernacle; secondly 'Evangelistic' [it was suggested that the executive of the Preachers' Association be part of the Home Mission Committee]; thirdly the Derby plan of regular visitation of the churches.[143]

The discussion concerning the role of lay preaching in the second half of the nineteenth century is an indication that the Connexion was unclear about the role of its lay preachers. It was a discussion that went beyond the Connexion. In 1857, the *Freeman* carried an article on lay preaching in which it was advocated as a means of evangelisation in places like Manchester and Liverpool. Speaking for Baptists generally it said, 'we have not as a body recognised the importance of this form of work as we ought to have done'.[144] The writer argued that

> the most obvious and most grave evil of all is, that there is no organisation of the scattered efforts, and that the church takes no care who goes to preach, or who does not. Hence all village lay preaching is in the hands of anybody who likes to undertake it; and many mischiefs come about not the least of which is the contempt often thrown on the whole thing, because unfit men have by the criminal negligence of a church undertaken the work.[145]

The solution was, in the writer's view, greater control: 'the church should hold on and exercise the power of calling to, or restraining from this and every other form of diffusing the gospel'.[146] By 1882 a number of preachers' associations had emerged. In the largest of the conferences, the Midland Conference, there were three, at Nottingham, Derby and Leicester respectively.[147] In London, John Clifford presided over the General Baptist Gospel Mission and Preachers' Institute. The thirty students had lectures on 'Biblical Interpretation' from Clifford; other ministers lectured on 'Preaching' and 'English Composition'. There was critical reading of prescribed theological texts and a sermon class.[148]

The value of lay preachers was not questioned, but there were problems which affected their usefulness: first, there was no formal structure for 'recognition'; and, secondly, there were concerns about the authority of ordained ministers being undermined. At its inception, the New Connexion had been an expression of the felt needs and aspirations of the social group from which it was formed. Its leaders had arisen from among its own ranks and had echoed the aspirations of the group. But by the 1830s and 40s, a change had taken place; the educational background of the

---

[143] W. Richardson. 'The Local Preacher and His Work', *GBM* (1877), p. 260.
[144] *Freeman*, 19 August 1857, p. 487.
[145] *Freeman*, 19 August 1857, p. 487
[146] *Freeman*, 19 August 1857, p. 487
[147] George Payne, 'Village Churches, Local Preachers, and the Denomination', *GBM* (1882), p. 258.
[148] 'General Baptist Preachers Institute', *GBM* (1882), p. 427.

shoemaker, stocking maker, warehouse man and porter, were felt to be deficient. There appears to have emerged a strand of leadership that reflected a different class and set of attitudes from the members. The leaders and their constituency no longer spoke with one voice. Marshall appealed to the Connexion to 'send your parties who are in more favourable circumstances, or send a mixture of the two, and you may then manage to keep alive your cause, and increase your churches'.[149] It was John Clifford who appealed to the Connexion to 'accord a brotherly welcome to men who have not passed though the curriculum of a scholastic education if they can prove themselves prophets trained of the Lord'.[150]

In his address *The Work of Church Leaders*, delivered to the London Baptist Association in 1879, Clifford defined as leaders 'pastors, deacons or elders, superintendents of schools, secretaries or managers of different departments of Christian activity'. He said that leadership in the church meant taking the initiative; 'our first and main duty is to *lead*', and for him leadership was exercised through quality of character rather than status. He said, 'A life derived immediately from the Lord Jesus Christ, enriched from day to day by fellowship with His spirit, saturated with His grace,—this is the initial and supreme qualification for the leadership of souls'. Such a passion, he argued, should 'compel us to that courageous adaption of denominational machinery which fits it for its special work in each hour'.[151] However, Clifford's adaptation was the development of the 'institutional church' with its multiple agencies and activities. The involvement of the 'lay agency' was institutionalised in the General Baptist Institute, and in running the church programme. The independent gospel preaching and church planting of the early days of the movement had disappeared. Although conceived of as a missionary agency, the development of Westbourne Park into an 'institutional church' pointed the Connexion to a very different model of church life from that of the fathers of the movement. Having said that, Clifford acknowledged the pulpit contribution of men from all walks of life, and the church at Westbourne Park was given the opportunity to hear them.[152]

Dan Taylor and John Clifford

In the history of the Connexion there were two significant personalties in terms of leadership: at the beginning, Dan Taylor, and, at the end of the life of the Connexion, John Clifford. Both men played an important role, the one assisting in its birth, the other in laying the Connexion to rest. But it was more than years that separated these men; they lived in two very different worlds. In the world in which Taylor preached the existence of God was unquestioned. For Taylor and the early

---

[149] 'Lay Agency', *GBM* (1859), p. 456.

[150] John Clifford, 'Non-Attendance of Professed Christians at Public Worship', *Letter* (1868), p. 71. See also 'Chairman's Address', *Minutes* (1868), p. 71.

[151] John Clifford, *The Work of Christian Leaders* (London: Marlborough, 1879), p 14.

[152] W.S. Stroud, 'John Clifford', *Baptist Quarterly* 6 (1932–33), p. 308.

preachers of the New Connexion the issue was the nature of a people's relationship to God; the word proclaimed was one that was heard and responded to by ordinary men and women. For Clifford things were very different; society no longer shared the same assumptions about religion, and such religious assumptions as existed were now challenged by scepticism and disbelief. This left in its wake doubt and uncertainty.

In the early days Dan Taylor had been looked to for all manner of guidance. With his death in November 1816, leadership passed to the annual association and conferences. It is interesting to compare the New Connexion with Methodism. Wesley sought to fill the vacuum his death would leave by investing power within Methodism in the Conference. The effect of this was the 'consolidation of a new bureaucracy of ministers'.[153] It was one of these ministers, Jabez Bunting, who came to exercise an influence and control over Methodism that had only been equalled by Wesley himself. It was a leadership exercised through the organisation and control of the ministry.

The New Connexion had no Jabez Bunting. When Dan Taylor died there was no one to fill his place. As we have seen, while he was alive, he gave direction to the movement; but there was no 'Elisha' upon whom the leadership cloak might fall. There were men of ability like John Bissill, Joseph Jarrom, John Gregory Pike, Richard Ingham, and Hugh Hunter, but none of them had the quality of dynamic leadership that had been Taylor's. Consequently, the Connexion lacked the direction and organisation that such leadership generates. Apart from J.G. Pike, with his missionary interest, no one emerged with a larger vision, with a concern for the movement as a whole. What central bureaucracy the New Connexion had was run by men who held pastoral office and were responsible for local churches, men who in many cases held some other occupation as well, and were thus unable to give their full attention to the affairs of the Connexion. J.G. Pike's church complained to the 1825 Leicester Association about the frequent absences of their minister and of the church suffering as a result.[154] Pecuniary difficulties, a local church leadership that jealously guarded the prerogatives of the church in relation to the activities of ministers, impeded the centralised development of the Connexion. An egalitarian theology that was highly suspicious of an ecclesiastical infrastructure did not encourage central leadership and meant that there was little incentive for men to develop a national consciousness on behalf of the movement.

It was not until the 1860s and the appearance of John Clifford that the Connexion found another leader of the stature of Dan Taylor. He gave to the movement that quality of leadership that had a broad vision. He was a man in tune with the age, and on becoming editor of the *General Baptist Magazine* in 1870, a post he occupied for fourteen years, he was given a voice in the denomination. Clifford's contribution to the Connexion was significant. He understood the difficulties of leading Baptist

---

[153] E.P. Thompson, *The Making of the English Working Class* (London: Penguin, 1963), p. 351.
[154] Pike and Pike, *Memoir and Remains of J.G. Pike,* p. 175.

churches. He said of the government of Baptist churches, 'It is really the best we know of, and it is abominable'; what was needed was 'intelligent and patient leading'.[155] He was also aware of the divisive nature of church conflicts.[156] For Clifford the business of the Connexion was mission; for him the 'mainspring' of all activity was the 'love of souls, inspired and fed by the love of Christ'.[157]

This consideration of leadership within the New Connexion leads to the conclusion that the shift to full-time ministry within the Connexion was a significant factor in attenuating evangelism. At the foundation of the Connexion, differences between the laymen and ministers were minimal. As we have seen, men were able to slip in and out of full-time ministry with little difficulty. Training and preparation for both groups was much the same. Ordination, when practised, had been for good 'order' and had required no special provision apart from a 'call' from a church. This situation had been encouraged by the dynamic of the Revival in terms of growth, with an emphasis on expansion rather than on maintenance.

The pressures of chapel life, and seemingly automatic growth, led ministers towards a greater concern for maintenance rather than mission. Ministerial concerns over finance and 'respectability' are indicators of the beginning of an ever-widening gulf between ministers and laymen. This differentiation between ministers and laymen is another indicator of denominationalism in the Connexion.

The development of the Academy, and the kind of training given there, reflect the concern of churches for a better-informed and cultured ministry, for men able to run the emerging organisations. This, in turn, meant that the men thus attracted, were more concerned about the standard of preaching and conducting 'decorous worship services' than they were about mission and evangelism. The emergence of the Loughborough 'Educational Society' reflects the concerns of some about these changes. In the early days of the movement laymen had taken a significant role in leadership; as the effects of the Revival waned and the denominational structure developed, the emphasis in ministry shifted even further from laymen to the 'ministry'. The full-time minister became the model and basis of what became known as the 'One man system'. This gradually began to dominate and the role of the layman diminished.[158] In the one-man system the minister did everything. One result of this change was to shift the responsibility for initiatives in evangelism to the 'ministry'. This meant that the growth of the movement was affected by ministerial attitudes to evangelism.

At one time the major opportunity for service had been preaching; the development of Sunday schools and similar organisations changed all this. Evangelistic preaching had now to compete with other forms of service at the same time. The employment of lay preachers became more formal. Lay preaching became an indoor ministry to the converted, and to small and struggling causes; a ministry of encouragement more than evangelism.

---

[155] Clifford, *The Work of Christian Leaders*, p. 5.
[156] Clifford, *The Work of Christian Leaders*, p. 6.
[157] Clifford, *The Work of Christian Leaders*, p. 12.
[158] See above 'The Progress of the Gospel' and 'One Man Ministry'.

Recognising, as he did, the importance of evangelism and mission to the life of the Connexion, it fell to Clifford, whose ministry was at the end of the movement's life, to be one of the main architects of the final act of retrenchment, union with the Particular Baptists.

CHAPTER 7

'Union not absorption': The Development of Discussions with Particular Baptists which led to Union in 1891

Early Relationships

The amalgamation of the New Connexion with the Baptist Union in 1891 marked the end of its existence as a separate organisation. Such a possibility could not have been considered in 1770 when the demarcation lines between Particular and General Baptists were clearly and firmly drawn on a theological basis. The Particular Baptists held, for the most part, to a rigid Calvinism and stressed the independency and autonomy of the local church. The New Connexion reflected the General Baptist tradition in which there was a structural commitment, to the wider church as a corporate body, what John Briggs calls a 'partial presbyterianism'.[1] The period following 1770 saw a major theological readjustment of high-Calvinism in Particular Baptist churches.[2] The Evangelical Revival also influenced the understanding of the nature of the church on the part of both groups of Baptists. Distinctions between the two bodies, while very real at a doctrinal level, were not great, for as Baptists they held much in common in terms of history and church government.

We start by seeking to identify these distinctions. The New Connexion was part of the General Baptist tradition, which had from its inception a strong corporate identity. Their position in relation to assemblies or councils had been set out in *An Orthodox Creed, or a Protestant Confession of Faith* of 1678:

> General councils, or assemblies, consisting of Bishops, Elders and Brethren, of the several churches of Christ, and being legally convened, and met together out of all the churches, and the churches appearing there by their representatives, make but one church, and have lawful right, and suffrage in this general meeting, or assembly, to act in the name of Christ; ...the decisive voice in such general

---

[1] Briggs, *English Baptists*, p. 105. See also G.F. Nuttall, 'Assembly and Association in Dissent, 1687–1831', in G. Cumming and D. Baker (eds), *Councils and Assemblies* (Studies in Church History, 7; Oxford: Basil Blackwell, 1971).

[2] For a fuller discussion see also Geoffrey F. Nuttall, 'Calvinism in Free Church History', *Baptist Quarterly* 22.8 (October, 1968), pp. 418-19.

assemblies is the major part, and such general assemblies have lawful power to hear, and determine, as also to excommunicate.[3]

On the basis of the phrase 'make but one church', Geoffery Reynolds argues for the connexional nature of General Baptists, saying they were 'not independents in the commonly accepted use of the term'.[4]

It was the practice of the General Baptists to hold a 'General Assembly' in London. It was from this body that those who formed the New Connexion seceded. When the Connexion was formed in 1770 it established a regular meeting in London; the Connexion holding its own assembly alongside that of the General Baptists. The Connexion maintained fraternal links with the older body through Dan Taylor who attended the General Baptist Assembly and played an active part until 1803. Gilbert Boyce, the 'Messenger' of the old assembly, tried to effect a reconciliation between the two groups of General Baptists, but these efforts came to a close when Boyce, Mr. Joseph Proud from Wisbech and Mr. Clark of Lincolnshire, attended the Connexion association meeting at Boston in 1785. Appealing to Acts and Hebrews, they required laying on of hands and abstention from eating blood as a condition of reunion.[5] This was unacceptable to the Connexion and rejected.[6] For a number of years some members of the Connexion attended both the General Baptist Assembly and their own.

In 1795, the Connexion decided that its own assembly should be constituted as a meeting of 'delegates', and that in order to vote, one needed to be a 'representative' of a church (both words are used interchangeably).[7] Prior to that, the Connexion had admitted individual ministers whose churches had been unwilling to join. The personal membership was possible because the basis of relationship within the Connexion was in a common spiritual experience rather than a credal statement. With this decision the assembly became the corporate voice for the Connexion.

The Particular Baptists, on the other hand, had a much looser structure. There was a greater emphasis on independency. However, the Abingdon Association of Particular Baptist Churches concluded 'that particular churches of Christ ought to hold a firm communion each with other'; the *Second London Confession* of 1677 determined that the 'messengers' of 'churches holding communion together' are 'not entrusted with any Church-power properly so called', and that such a group could not 'impose their determination on the Churches, or Officers'.[8] There is an important difference between 'communion' or fellowship, and 'Church power' or authority, the

---

[3] Payne, *Baptist Union*, p. 30.

[4] Geoffrey G. Reynolds, *First Among Equals: A Study of the Basis of Association and Oversight among Baptist Churches* (Bath: Berkshire, Southern, and Oxfordshire and East Gloucestershire Baptist Associations, 1993), p. 94.

[5] Wood, *History*, p. 188.

[6] Whitley discusses the nature of the relationship in *Minutes of the General Baptist Association*, 27-28 April 1785, p. 188

[7] Taylor, *History*, II, pp. 213, 324, 328.

[8] Reynolds, *First among Equals*, pp. 56-57.

latter being explicitly rejected. The influence of this confession was modified by the adoption of the 1689 *Second London Confession* which became determinative. It was the confessional basis of churches, associations and the Baptist Union until 1832.

Points of Convergence

While these differences of practice and theology were substantial, there was a mutual recognition of each other's position. This mutual recognition is a feature of denominations. A denomination, in Martin's words, recognises 'that while there are doubtless many keys to many mansions it is at least in possession of one of them, and that any one who thinks that he has the sole means to open the heavenly door is plainly mistaken'.[9] After the first decade of its life the Connexion began to move away from 'sectarian' values; there was a recognition that there were 'sheep in other folds'.

The view was expressed that 'Church fellowship, though a most sacred duty and an invaluable privilege, is a voluntary personal act, and can be controuled [sic] by no human power'.[10] The tenor of this view is that church membership is an individual and personal choice, but in practice this was not the case as decisions about membership lay with the church meeting.

The Evangelical Revival influenced both General Baptists of the New Connexion and Particular Baptists, bringing together those whose heart was for evangelism. The main agent of the convergence between the two bodies was Andrew Fuller. The publication of his book *A Gospel Worthy of All Acceptation*, allowing as it did for invitations to faith, broke the rigid grip of the high-Calvinism of John Gill and John Brine. As a result one of the major sources of division between the two elements of Baptist life was removed and the way opened up for cooperation. We see the weakening of theological conviction on both sides. So when the church at Cauldwell started a work at Burton on Trent the ministry was 'generally supplied by Brother Moss formally of the Particular Baptist denomination, who has joined us'.[11] At Portsea, Hampshire, 'some, Particular Baptist Ministers kept the church together' while it was without a minister.[12]

Another point of convergence was in the concern for overseas mission. Motivated by the example of the Baptist Missionary Society, the General Baptists sought at first to participate in the work. In 1812, J.G. Pike made overtures to Andrew Fuller, who was secretary to the Baptist Missionary Society, but while there had been a degree of convergence, they were not yet sufficiently close for co-operation in the venture, and General Baptist participation was rejected. However J.G. Pike, with the help of the New Connexion church at Derby, undertook the support of a native

---

[9] D.A. Martin, 'The Denomination', *The British Journal of Sociology* 13 (1962), p 5.
[10] 'On Dismissing Members to Other Churches', *GBR* (1831), p. 452.
[11] *Minutes* (1814), p. 7.
[12] *Minutes* (1821), p. 15.

preacher at Serampore. A letter from Fuller to Pike alludes to this coming together. After mentioning the doctrinal differences between the two bodies, he says,

> If you think proper to support a native preacher, I have this to say in favour of it, that I dare say he will never have heard of the General and Particular Baptists, but merely of Jesus as the only name given under heaven by which sinners can be saved, and that all are welcome to mercy in that name, I said that I should like this. The reason is, I hope it would tend to draw the friends of Christ nearer together, and to a better understanding of each other's views and feelings.[13]

Following Fuller's rejection of Pike's overtures, the Connexion went on to form its own society in 1816. William Ward of the Baptist Missionary Society helped with the training of the first Connexion missionaries, W. Brampton and J. Peggs from the church at Sutterton, Lincolnshire. It was the Serampore leadership who directed Brampton and Peggs to Orissa, which became the mission base.[14] The development of cooperation in overseas mission acted as harbinger of closer ties at home.

Union of Particular Baptists 1812 and 1832

The development of a Union among the Particular Baptists provided a forum for cooperative action between the two groups. The Particular Baptists had always had a decentralised ecclesiology. Although annual associations had been part of their structure from an early stage they were based on credal assent to propositional truth, and geographical affinity. After 1696, when London Baptists declined to meet, there was no national forum.

The development of a Union within the Particular Baptists came about in two stages. In June 1812, some sixty Particular Baptist ministers met in the Carter Lane Church in London; the outcome of this meeting was the formation of a Union which held its first Assembly in 1813. The aims of this Union were the stimulation of fellowship, the support of missions, equipping men for the ministry, and the establishment of certain funds. To some extent this first attempt at union was a product of its time, a period that was rich in voluntary and religious societies, a connection which Joseph Ivimey made in his article 'Union essential to Prosperity'.[15] The major architect of this first Union was John Howard Hinton, who had been advocating such a confederacy for some time. In his address to the consultative committee called to form the Union, he set out the nature and function of such bodies. He defined a Union in the following terms, 'Churches who mutually and cordially agree in all the leading truths of Divine revelation'. And union had to be 'durable and profitable' if it was to be built on. Hinton did not view the proposed Union as exclusive, it was for those who were willing to share in prayer, property,

---

[13] Pike and Pike, *Memoir and Remains of J.G. Pike*, p. 86.
[14] Briggs, *English Baptists*, p. 101.
[15] Joseph Ivimey, 'Union Essential to Prosperity', *Baptist Magazine* 3 (1811), pp. 234-37. Although unsigned this is attributed to Ivimey by Payne, *Baptist Union*, p. 18.

new works, support of ministry, new buildings and work oversees. The invitation was extended to other Christian societies

> who, though they do not work in the same denomination with ourselves, and are also distinguished from each other by various professional shades, yet cordially receive and zealously disseminate those leading doctrines of our holy faith which have ever been 'the power of God unto Salvation'.[16]

There were evident limitations to this Union. It did not have the full support of all Particular Baptists; being attended, according to Payne, by little more than a seventh of the ministers.[17] One Particular Baptist expressed the fragmented nature of his denomination in the following way: 'we are a rope of sand, without cement, and consequently without strength'.[18] The Union lacked the authority of the New Connexion Assembly, and the disconnected nature of Particular Baptists meant that the infant organisation did not find widespread acceptance. S.M. Stone suggests that economic conditions, heavy taxation due to the Napoleonic war and the severe depression that followed it, were contributing factors to the failure of the endeavour.[19] W.T. Whitley is fairly dismissive of this first Union, citing outdated methods, limited aims, only a day's meeting for worship and conference, a lack of practical aims, and absence of vital leadership, as reasons for its failure.[20] Ian Sellers describes it as a 'social occasion for London ministers'.[21] Difficulties with the Union and a general air of reform led to an extensive re-modelling in 1832.

Briggs argues that 'Fullerism' had 'created the potential for the unification of a divided denomination'.[22] He quotes a plea in the *New Baptist Miscellany* of December 1830 for a closer relationship between the two bodies which encouraged General Baptists to participate in associations and their committees. There was also a plea for better communication and a rejection of 'party spirit'.[23] The *General Baptist Repository* of 1831, while welcoming local cooperation, was not so sure that to 'merge all distinction' was necessarily a good thing, and questioned the Particular Baptist lack of denominational identity and organization: 'the difference in sentiment in the two bodies, is such that in the present state of things, this circumstance alone, must necessarily prevent their becoming one denomination'. But having expressed reservation about formal union, it encouraged fraternal relationships.[24]

In the re-organisation attempted in 1831, the older theological formula and doctrinal tests were omitted, and the new constitution spoke only of the 'Sentiments

---

[16] McBeth, *Sourcebook for Baptist Heritage*, p. 188.
[17] Payne, *Baptist Union*, p. 26.
[18] Cited by Stone, 'A Survey of Baptist Expansion', p. 105.
[19] Stone, 'A Survey of Baptist Expansion', p. 113.
[20] Whitley, *History*, p. 205.
[21] Sellers, *Nineteenth Century Nonconformity*, p. 4.
[22] Briggs, *English Baptists*, p. 99.
[23] Briggs, *English Baptists*, p. 104.
[24] 'On the Proposed Union Between Particular and General Baptists', *GBR* (1831), pp 95-96.

The Discussions with Particular Baptists 179

usually denominated evangelical'.[25] This phrase, argues Roger Hayden, 'was well understood by a generation which faced the impact of Anglo-Catholic development'.[26] The thrust of the new structure, which was approved the following year, was to unite the resources of both Particular and General in a common denominational concern for evangelism. The new wording made it much easier for the churches of the Connexion to participate in the Union. The basis of participation by the Connexion was that of individual churches. Clifford was to argue this point forcefully in 1874 when confessional representation was being urged; he said that they had enrolled 'In no sense as General Baptists, or as a General Baptist Association', but as '*Baptist* Churches'.[27] The new Union extended a welcome to the Connexion; the 1834 report of the Baptist Union spoke of 'our valued brethren the General Baptists; who though they differ from us in some minor matters, are one with us in our common Head'.[28] These proposals met with a ready response, when, in 1835, the New Connexion resolved 'after considerable conversation' that 'as an Association, we cordially approve of the Union', and four men were appointed 'to be our Representatives at the next annual meeting of the Union'.[29]

The closer relationships sought in the 1832 Union did not only operate at the level of association life. The Castle Donnington church, meeting at Sawley on 14 May 1837, resolved that: 'the letter from the Baptist Union...be considered at the next meeting. And the minutes of their Annual meeting to be publicly read on a previous Friday evening'.[30] In 1841, the Rev. John Howard Hinton wrote to J.G. Pike asking him to accept the post of chairman at the next annual session of the Union:

> The principal object is, that our chairman should be one whose tenure of the office may at once demonstrate and foster the union we desire to cultivate. Most sincere gratification would it afford us all to see you in it, especially as representing the body of General Baptists, who have from the first been a constituent part of the Union...[31]

Hinton, in making his appeal to Pike, tends to overstate the General Baptist commitment. Pike accepted. In 1850, another General Baptist, Jabez Burns, was chairman. Both these men had extensive ministries outside the Connexion; Pike's related to overseas mission and Burns with the temperance movement, and this may have contributed to their invitation. While the influence of the Union had grown under Hinton's time as secretary the attendance dipped following the decision in 1845

---

[25] Payne, *Baptist Union*, p. 61.
[26] Roger Hayden, 'Baptists Covenants and Confessions', in Paul S. Fiddes *et al.*, *Bound to Love* (London: The Baptist Union, 1985), p. 29.
[27] John Clifford, 'The Baptist Union: Baptists Generally; and General Baptists in Particular', *GBM* (1874), p. 450.
[28] Stone, 'A Survey of Baptist Expansion', p. 125.
[29] *Minutes* 1835), p. 24.
[30] Castle Donnington Church Book, 14 May 1837.
[31] Pike and Pike, *Memoir and Remains of J.G. Pike*, p. 247.

to hold the meetings away from London. The 200 who had met in 1840 had dropped to sixty by 1848 when the Union again met in London.[32] In 1844 new associations joined and there was by the end of the decade considerable increase both in numbers and prestige. In 1843 the secretaries of the Baptist Union, William Harris Murch, Edward Steane and Hinton, sought to encourage greater participation of the Connexion in the Union, 'with which some of them, perhaps are scarcely acquainted'. The appeal in the correspondence columns of the *General Baptist Repository* closed by encouraging the attendance of the churches at the next session.[33] In 1855, G.A. Syme, speaking at the General Baptist Assembly at Mansfield Road, Nottingham, urged a joint assembly. This was realised in 1857 when, at the Baptist Union meetings in Nottingham, there was a session at the Derby Road church to which the churches of the Connexion were especially invited. The Connexion were encouraged to attend this meeting, but it was considered 'premature to take any further steps at the present Association'.[34] Such actions introduced a period when the possibility of closer relationships and talk about amalgamation was extensively aired.

Mid-century Conversations

By the 1850s there was a growing recognition of the value of the Union on the part of both groups; and an awareness that something more than cooperation between the two bodies was needed. At the 1857 meeting, William Underwood of the Connexion church at Chesham moved a resolution voicing 'sincere gratification' to the Union and expressed the hope that 'there may be added an enlarged exercise of fraternal affection and co-operation'; the resolution was carried.[35] The possibility of organic union was discussed. In July of the following year, the *Freeman* carried an article which sought to allay concern about the 'doctrinal sentiments' of the General Baptists in the south and west of the country. It assured its readers, 'We know them to be thoroughly evangelical and soundly orthodox'.[36] Hinton, aged seventy-two, addressed the Union in 1863. In his message he reflected on the state of the denomination, having contributed in a major way to the convergence of the two bodies, he recognised that there was much yet to be done. 'Denominational union among Baptists', he said, 'has been slow in manifestation and difficult of cultivation'. He drew attention to the divisions. There were not only the two major groups, General and Particular, but there were also a number of divisions within the Particular Baptists. There was 'High and Moderate Calvinism', which was further divided over communion. He concluded, 'We have then six parties'.[37] Payne argues

---

[32] *Baptist Reporter* (1864), p. 195.
[33] 'The Baptist Union', *GBR* (1843), p. 78.
[34] 'Cases from Churches', *Minutes* (1857), pp. 29, 310.
[35] *Freeman*, 19 August 1857, p 393.
[36] *Freeman*, 7 July 1858, p. 395.
[37] Cited by Payne, *Baptist Union*, pp. 85-86.

that Hinton's reticence was due to a fear that moves towards union with the New Connexion would expose and aggravate the divisions amongst Particular Baptists.[38]

But others were not so pessimistic as Hinton. James Phillip Mursell of Leicester, on taking the chair of the Baptist Union in 1864, set out what he felt should be its objectives, the second of which was 'the supersession, on practicable, sound and safe principles of the distinction between General and Particular Baptists'.[39]

A mid-century analysis of the developing relationship between General and Particular Baptists was well expressed in a contribution to the *General Baptist Magazine* in 1861, entitled 'Union of the Baptist Bodies', by William Underwood, Principal of the General Baptist College. His paper clarifies the nature of the differences, and the extent of the difficulties with union from the General Baptist perspective. He wanted to know in what way they would come closer together. He asked for specifics not 'vague generalities'. Looking at the differences, he thought the names General and Particular were not 'definite or accurate as distinguishing epithets', and 'might be dropped without detriment'. Theological differences were real; while the 'greater proportion' of Particular Baptists were only '*Semi-Calvinistic*', Calvinism,' moderate or unmitigated—semi or entire', was still 'the prevailing faith of Particular Baptists'. But he said of the General Baptists, 'while we may not be strict Arminians, we are *Anti-Calvinists*'. Underwood recognised that while the doctrinal basis 'had been different from the beginning', changes had taken place. He recognised that 'the strain of our preaching, and the tenor of our practice may have been brought into nearer accordance owing to the growing prevalence, among our brethren, of the Hintonian opinion, that redemption, while it is particular, "has in addition a universal aspect"'.[40] This was a reference to John Howard Hinton's book *Moderate Calvinism re-examined*, which presented, according to an anonymous General Baptist reviewer, 'the word without the Spirit, the offer of salvation without the will to save'.[41] The crucial issue for Underwood was, 'will they renounce their Calvinism? or, shall we embrace it?' He asked what kind of union would it be 'which should comprehend many thousands of independent thinkers and out-speaking talkers who hold such opposite beliefs?' Other difficulties lay with the nature of the Baptist Union which 'has no federal authority' over its various institutions. 'With whom could our Association negotiate?', the Union having no corporate voice or authority, 'to whom could we surrender, or with whom we could stipulate?'[42] The *Freeman* had made the same point in 1855: 'we have no tribunal, no seat of authority, to which we can appeal. There is no body, it may be said, by which the question of union could be entertained'.[43] Further difficulties lay in the nature of the management of the General Baptists' College and Missionary Society, both of which were governed by the association. Another area of concern for

---

[38] Cited by Payne, *Baptist Union*, p. 87.
[39] Cited by Payne, *Baptist Union*, p. 98.
[40] W. Underwood, 'Union of the Baptist Bodies', *GBM* (1861), p. 182.
[41] Hinton's 'Moderate Calvinism Re-Examined', *GBM* (1861), p. 204.
[42] Underwood, 'Union of the Baptist Bodies', p. 183.
[43] *Freeman*, 7 February 1855, p. 395.

Underwood was the annual meetings of the Particular Baptists in London. Not only did distance present an obstacle, but the meetings themselves were 'not the meetings of *Churches* represented by delegates. They are meetings of *Societies* supported by the churches'. This contrasted with the annual meeting of the Connexion which had a degree of decision-making authority within the Connexion, and where 'everything that is projected and proposed is discussed and decided by the "messengers of the churches"'. In using the term 'messengers' Underwood is not referring to the Old General Baptist office of messenger, for the Connexion had never adopted or appointed 'messengers'; the term is used as a description of church representatives. He says, 'As an aggregation of ministers, of representatives of churches, and of church members, our annual association is quite unique'.[44] In identifying theses areas to be addressed Underwood pinpointed the key issues that were constantly to recur in discussions about union. He concluded by pointing out that so far the union issue was 'all talk', there had been 'no joint action toward the attainment of these ends'. While there had been anonymous correspondence in the *Freeman*, apparently from the Particular Baptists, there had been no formal approaches, and Underwood concluded, 'we have no clear proof of a desire, on the part of the other denomination, for a closer union, or nearer approach'.[45]

J.B. Pike writing the association 'Letter' in 1862 expressed concern that, as yet, no practical steps towards union had been taken. 'We cannot advance further than we have done', he said. What was needed was a 'reciprocity of sentiment' on the part of the Particular Baptists.[46] Two years later we read that the General Baptist Association 'rejoices to hear that it was proposed to hold an autumnal meeting of the Baptist Union at Birmingham during this present year, and recommends the churches of this Association to send delegates to that Meeting'.[47] While there was a limited degree of theological convergence, the late 1850s and 1860s saw a practical convergence at the level of the local church.

Crossing the Boundaries

Practical and Theological Convergence

The Connexion, though cautious, was supportive of these moves, and the question concerning 'a closer union among the different sections of Evangelical Baptists' was put to the 1857 meeting of the Connexion. The response of the assembly was, 'Resolved: that we approve of union as far as practicable with all other evangelical Baptist bodies...'[48] Churches of the Connexion were encouraged to attend the forthcoming autumnal session of the Baptist Union in Nottingham. General and Particular Baptists at that meeting acknowledged in a resolution, 'The vital unity

---

[44] Underwood, 'Union of the Baptist Bodies', pp. 181-85.
[45] Underwood, 'Union of the Baptist Bodies', p. 185.
[46] J.B. Pike, 'Union of Particular and General Baptists', *Letter* (1862), p 45.
[47] *Minutes* (1864), p. 36.
[48] 'Cases from Churches', *Minutes* (1857), p. 29.

which prevails among them, through their common regard to "one Lord, one faith, one baptism"'.[49] Harrison says that one result of this meeting was that 'within a few years practically every Nottingham Baptist Church, General or Particular, had joined the Union'.[50] A practical convergence between the two bodies had been taking place for some time. In 1844, when Mrs Cooke moved from Castle Donnington, she been advised to 'ask for a formal dismission and to unite with the nearest Baptist Church'.[51] When John Glover moved from Hugglescote to Birmingham in 1848 and had requested a dismission, the church at Hugglescote required 'B^r Smith to write a friendly note to Mr Rowe the Particular Baptist minister at Birmingham respecting our friend Glover'.[52] In 1858, the *Freeman* observed, 'Already our members are freely dismissed from one community to the other; in many instances our ministers have passed over the separating boundary without any questioning of their consistency or any stain upon their orthodoxy'.[53] The evidence from the church books would support the above and at least part of the claim of Jabez Burns, who in 1866 observed that often when people moved to a new district they 'find no difficulty in uniting with the other part of the Baptist body, and seldom find any substantial difference in the doctrinal teaching which they hear'. He saw behind this practical convergence a theological consensus, commenting,

> Indeed this aspect of the subject is totally different to what it was half a century ago. Now high Calvinistic preaching is limited to a comparatively small number of churches: and the great majority of Baptist churches have the Atoning sacrifice of Jesus as fully, freely, and universally presented as among ourselves. Indeed the distinguished ministers of the other department of Baptists occupy, as a rule, the same general position in doctrinal preaching with our own brethren, so that the gulf no longer exists in preventing them from coming to us, or our going to them.[54]

The extent of the cross over among ministers may be gauged from the 1875 *Baptist Handbook* which printed names of colleges where ministers had trained. Out of the 115 General Baptist ministers listed, forty-nine had been trained in the Academy or General Baptist College, twenty-four at Particular Baptist colleges; others had studied at Scottish universities, one or two at Congregational colleges and many had received no formal college training at all.[55] By 1889, just less than half (seventy-three of 151) of the ministers in the Connexion had been trained in the General Baptist College.[56] The rigid demarcation lines of a former generation were by this process eroded, the distinctions between the two groups of Baptists were becoming less important to churches seeking men. Ministers crossed between the

---

[49] Underwood, *History of the English Baptists*, p. 214.
[50] Harrison, *It All Began Here*, p. 45.
[51] Castle Donnington Church Book, Church meeting at Sawley, 1 January 1844.
[52] Hugglescoote Church Book, 20 March.1848.
[53] *Freeman*, 7 July 1858, p. 395.
[54] Jabez Burns, 'On the Support of Connexional Institutions', *Letter* (1866), p. 42.
[55] Harrison, *It All Began Here*, p. 45.
[56] *Minutes* (1889), pp. 63-64, 69.

two groups with increasing frequency.[57] The practical convergence at the institutional level reflected the growing erosion of differences amongst members of churches. In 1865, T.W. Matthews as president of the Connexion could say,

> The inquiry seems now-a-days to be, not how widely do we differ, but how nearly do we agree? The desire frequently expressed in our associations for a closer union with the larger section of the Baptists seems, by a process as silent yet as sure as chemical affinity to be gradually fulfilling itself.[58]

The strength of the commitment to union on the part of the Connexion was reflected in the decisions about the proposed building fund for the Connexion. There were attempts to link it at first with a similar fund for the Particular Baptists, but there were

> considerable legal difficulties in the way of a change of constitution... At the same time, they [the building committee] are most anxious to avoid anything in the regulations that may be adopted that would in the least degree tend to fetter or hinder united action on the part of the whole Baptist body at any future time.[59]

This commitment on the part of the building committee was endorsed by the rest of the association. It was resolved to form a Chapel Building Fund and 'that it be exclusively a loan fund for Baptists without distinction'.[60] The association had decided to back its conversations in a practical way. But, as John Clifford pointed out, the churches were somewhat behind the association: '£3.1.6^d per annum is the measure of the esteem in which the General Baptists held that august and useful institution', he said, reflecting on the financial contribution of churches to the Union. He urged greater support, saying, 'It is I believe the only machinery by which an amalgamation of the two bodies of Baptists can be effected'.[61]

The strength of the convergence is further evidenced by the formation of a Midland Baptist Union in 1870. An advertisement for this claimed it was 'intended to embrace more particularly the Baptist Churches of both sections of the denomination in the three counties of Nottingham, Derbyshire, and Leicestershire'.[62] Harrison notes that the attempt was short-lived because the structure was imposed on the churches and was in addition to the General and Particular Baptist associations.[63]

---

[57] See Harrison, 'Baptists of Nottinghamshire,' p. 327, for examples.
[58] *Minutes* (1865), p. 5.
[59] *Minutes* (1865), p. 34.
[60] *Minutes,* (1865), p. 35.
[61] John Clifford, *GBM* (1865), p. 57.
[62] *GBM* (1870), p. 341.
[63] Harrison, 'Baptists of Nottinghamshire', p. 329.

Cautious Voices

Amid the enthusiasm there was the occasional cautious voice. George Coltman felt that 'though the Calvinistic element in the Particular Baptist body is much weaker than it was fifty years ago, it is still far too strong for the majority of General Baptists to accept'. The Connexion was 'viewed with suspicion' by Particular Baptists who considered them 'theologically very nearly allied to Socinians'. He thought that even if formal union between the two bodies were to be effected, 'real union would still remain a thing to be desired'.[64] Thomas Goadby as President in 1868 voiced the concern of some: 'It is, I believe', he said, 'the desire of our churches to preserve their autonomy as a Connexion'. He foresaw in the haste to join with the Particulars the loss of Connexional character. His plea was for 'Union not absorption, brotherly love, not denominational integration; catholicity of spirit, not dissolution of the body, these are our truest maxims and our wisest watchword'.[65] In February 1868, C. Clarke of Ashby-de-la-Zouch, speaking at the Midland Conference at Loughborough and reflecting on the lack of growth within the Connexion, suggested that the cause might be in part due to the fact that their work as a separate group was nearly finished: 'we do not increase as a *distinct* denomination because *as such* a great part of our work has been done. We have lived, worked, and triumphed. There is no need now that we should be distinct from the other section of the Baptist body'.[66]

The early discussions took place against the background of cooperative action fostered by the formation of the Evangelical Alliance, working together in the areas of education and temperance, and a flurry of interdenominational activity surrounding the 1859 Revival. In 1860, the association chairman, Richard Kenny, spoke of the encouragement that had come from 'being permitted to engage in fervent and united devotional exercises in company with brethren and sisters belonging to other sections of the church universal'.[67] The minute writer at Maltby in Lincolnshire noted, on the opening of the new chapel in Westgate in 1862, that 'amongst the tea makers were ladies from every nonconformist church the town' and that 'the desirability of closer union and more fraternal feeling and action were topics ably handled by the various speakers'.[68]

Obstacles

In the middle years of the century, the need often expressed by the Connexion was that of parity with the Particular Baptists rather than an expression of their own distinctives:

---

[64] George Coltman, 'Denominational Decrease and Union with Particular Baptists', *GBM* (1867), p. 366.
[65] Thomas Goadby, 'President's Address' *Minutes* (1868), p. 49.
[66] C. Clarke, 'The present state of the Baptist denomination', *GBM* (1868), p. 101.
[67] R. Kenny, 'Chairmans Address', *GBM* (1860), p. 282.
[68] Maltby Le Marsh Church Book 4, 29 October 1863.

Too frequently has it happened that we have been looked upon as aliens and strangers: and if we have presumed to claim any near ecclesiastical kinship with the other religious leaders of the age, our relationship to them has been somewhat reluctantly acknowledged.[69]

Frederick W. Goadby, writing in the *General Baptist Magazine* of 1867, said the most common objection that he had come across was that of 'being swamped'. He said, 'We shall, by mingling with our Particular Baptist friends, meet many who have had greater educational advantages than some of us and also many others who are better known in the world than are the majority of the General Baptists'.[70] But, Goadby argued, 'Zeal for Christ's Kingdom should not be measured by the extent of personal influence or reputation'. He felt that the Connexion should be 'contented to be lost, to have no name among men if thereby we can advance the knowledge of His name'.[71] For Goadby, parity would involve a loss of identity. James Salisbury of Hugglescote, speaking as chairman of the association in 1869, questioned 'whether Class distinctions are not often too strenuously maintained, and whether assumptions of social pre-eminence have not proved serious checks to co-operation causes of needless isolation and just grounds for complaint on the part of those who are less favoured than others of their brethren, either in worldly position or education', although he did recognise that the 'envying and jealousies' of the poor did not help the situation.[72] If, as Wilson says, a movement needs to maintain dissimilarity to persist, then the New Connexion was on the way to losing its identity as a separate movement, as it was looking for points of correspondence rather than asserting its own identity.[73] Loss of identity concerned the young John Clifford: 'if we rightly understood what we have and hold as General Baptists, and knew the theological sentiments still aroused on the other side, we should not breathe another word about "absorption" for the next twenty years at least'.[74] When appointments were made within the Union on the basis of representation of theological beliefs within the union this prompted from Clifford the outburst, 'why can't a man leave his close or open communion, his broad or limited atonement theories at the door when he enters a union where all meet as *Baptists*?'.[75] But moves towards closer relationships received a further check in 1873 when Clifford's prophetic words were about to be fulfilled.

In 1873 the editor of the *Baptist Union Handbook*, in an unguarded moment, wrote that the General Baptists of the New Connexion had 'seceded from the larger body more than a century ago'. The following year, *The Baptist* suggested that there were Calvinists in the New Connexion. This aroused Clifford who was not prepared

---

[69] W. Underwood, 'Chairman's Address', *Minutes* (1870), p. 6.
[70] F.W. Goadby, 'On Being Swamped', *GBM* (1867), p. 340.
[71] 'On Being Swamped', p. 340
[72] J. Salisbury, 'Chairman's Address', *GBM* (1869), p. 12.
[73] Wilson, *Patterns of Sectarianism*, p. 41.
[74] Clifford, 'Secretaries Report', *General Baptist Year Book* (1870), p. 56.
[75] John Clifford, 'The Congregational and Baptist Unions', *GBM* (1872), p. 335-6.

to accept Calvinism on any terms as a condition of union. Writing in *The General Baptist Magazine* he asserted that the Connexion was committed to its distinctive beliefs. He said, 'we were never further from Calvinism than we are today'. Men trained at the Connexion's college at Chilwell were not taught, he said, 'a theology which makes the sovereignty of power rather than of love the cardinal and all determining feature of the Divine nature which is contrary to the Spirit of Christ and to the teaching of the New Testament'. He emphasised his point by adding, 'much as we would sacrifice for the doctrine of believer's baptism we would go much further in the same direction for the proclamation of an utterly unrestricted atonement'. He finished, 'speaking for ourselves as General Baptists, we do not doubt that we are doing more work for Christ and men, in the state in which we now are, than by any change that has yet been suggested'.[76]

To what extent the disagreement had any effect on the coming together of the two bodies is difficult to ascertain. Practically it marked the end of the current discussions; it was to be sixteen years before the issue of amalgamation was formally raised, and twenty years before the final steps to union were taken. The prevailing optimism of the previous two decades was soon checked. Further steps towards union were resisted by some General Baptist churches in Lancashire and conversations were 'delayed till northern scruples could be allayed'.[77]

The Baptist Union continued to develop as a denominational agency: as when Augmentation and Annuity funds were created in the 1870s for the support of ministry. The General Baptist church at Retford took advantage of this in order 'to increase our minister's salary'.[78] In 1873, it was agreed that the Union become 'The Baptist Union of Great Britain and Ireland'. Charles Stovel carried out a revision of the basis of the Baptist Union. A new constitution was drawn up which emphasised central organisation. It was his motion that saw the removal of the older phrase 'the sentiments usually denominated evangelical' which had been the basis of fellowship. In its place was put a new 'Declaration of Principle' which emphasised independency and baptism: 'In this Union it is fully recognised that every separate church has liberty to interpret and administer the laws of Christ, and that the immersion of believers is the only Christian baptism'.[79] The lack of any doctrinal expression was to be a problem. The reason given for this was that all Baptist churches were evangelical, though Spurgeon saw this as a drift away from evangelical principles.[80] The removal of anything that approached a credal definition as a basis of fellowship had two effects. First, it got over the issue of 'strict' or 'open communion', and, secondly, it opened the door to closer relationships with the New Connexion; but the earlier opportunity had now passed. John Briggs sets the discussion between the two

---

[76] Clifford, 'The Baptist Union: Baptists Generally; and General Baptists in Particular', p. 455.
[77] Cited in Underwood, *History of English Baptists*, p. 215.
[78] Retford and Gamston Book 2, 29 January 1873.
[79] Payne, *Baptist Union*, p. 109.
[80] Clifford, 'The Baptist Union: Baptists Generally; and General Baptists in Particular', pp. 453-54; Kruppa, *A Preachers Progress*, p. 414.

groups in a wider context. There was in 1877 some discussion about a merger between all congregational Christians, but while various proposals were aired the suggestion came to nothing.[81] This period also saw some branches of Methodism discussing possible union.[82]

No Debates!

The increasing number of General Baptists serving on the council and committees of the Baptist Union enabled their position to be more effectively represented. The main contributor to the improvement was John Clifford, who was by now a force to be reckoned with in the denomination as a whole. In a short article, 'General Baptists in the Twentieth Century', written at the beginning of 1885, Clifford saw a merger of the two bodies as a possibility by that date. He even countenanced the idea of union with the Independents 'to whom we are so closely akin'. The possibility of this happening was that the

> Calvinism our fathers fought against is no longer able to walk uprightly, if indeed to walk at all; and certainly Paedo-baptism, is driven for ever from the pages of the New Testament; and so therefore the ritual and theological conditions which wrought so mightily in giving us our organic shape cease to operate. Denominationalism is everywhere in a state of flux.

But by 1885 ancient General Baptist suspicion about creeds had again raised its head. Clifford felt that a debate of the theological issues would not help moves towards union, for, as Underwood had pointed out in 1861, the two systems were irreconcilable. 'No debates, as in 1861 and 1862', said Clifford 'or we shall, as then, have years of dissipated energy and marred work.'[83]

The avoidance of theological controversy is seen in the 'Articles of Incorporation' which the Connexion drew up in 1885. It was felt necessary to explain the absence of articles of religion:

> In the original draft there were ample doctrinal statements. But when the committee sat on the scheme at Leicester all these were reduced to one comprehensive sentence. It was that one object of the association should be 'the propagation of religious teaching in consonance with that upheld by the New Connexion of General Baptists in their various churches.'

> But when that came to be considered, the general, indeed the almost unanimous feeling of the Committee seemed to be, that it would not be wise to fetter either

---

[81] Briggs, *English Baptists*, p. 120.
[82] Currie, *Methodism Divided*, p. 319.
[83] John Clifford, 'General Baptists in the Twentieth Century', *GBM* (1885), p. 5.

ourselves of our prosperity by declaring that we believe anything. In these days Articles of Religion must look after themselves.[84]

The secretary of the Hyson Green church, Nottingham, in his 1878 report, expressed the same distrust of creeds: 'that we meet as General Baptists, that cannot save us, for we must ever recollect that creeds are not the truth, but only the verbal shadow'.[85]

The Down Grade Controversy

Concern about a credal basis of relationship came to the fore in the 'Down Grade' controversy of 1887. In this debate Spurgeon challenged the orthodoxy of some members of the Union and called for a credal confession. The issue was provoked by publication of two articles in the March edition of *The Sword and Trowel*, Spurgeon's magazine. Spurgeon said that the question at issue was not Calvinism versus Arminianism, but between the gospel and modern thought.[86] He took the discussion as an opportunity for a public statement of his own position. When the Baptist Union met in Sheffield that year the issue was not discussed. This offended Spurgeon. Subsequent reporting of the issue further inflamed the situation, and on Friday the 28 October Spurgeon wrote to Samuel Booth, Secretary of the Baptist Union, withdrawing from it. In the November issue of the *The Sword and Trowel* Spurgeon set out his reasons for leaving and further implicated the Union: 'we are unable to call these things "Christian Unions", they begin to look like confederacies in Evil'.[87] Spurgeon's desire had been for the Union to adopt a doctrinal statement of which he could approve. The unsubstantiated charges against its members irked the Union, and at a council meeting on the 18 January 1888, they accepted Spurgeon's resignation, none objecting.

It is surprising that so few churches followed Spurgeon out of the Union; apart from a few close followers, there was no great exodus of men or churches. McBeth explains this: 'In some ways Spurgeon was larger than the denomination; he could well do without the Union, but most of the other pastors could not, many were financially dependent on the union'.[88] The significance of this event was the surprising strength of the Union, which had by this time remarkable effectiveness as a basis for fellowship.

It was Clifford's lot to be president of the Union in 1888; his presidential address 'The Great Forty Years; The Primitive Christian Faith, its real substance and best defence', was a rationale for the decisions which the council would take later in the day, the substance of which was that the Union would not determine a standard of belief as a basis for fellowship. Whether due to Clifford's influence or not, the

---

[84] 'The General Baptists as by Law Established', *GBM* (1885), p. 169.
[85] Hyson Green Church Book (1878), p. 44.
[86] John Clifford, 'Editorial Notes', *GBM* (1887), p. 187.
[87] *GBM* (1887), p. 142.
[88] McBeth, *Baptist Heritage*, p. 304.

declaratory statement that the Union produced looked to experience rather than to doctrine, for it said that the Union was composed of those ministers and churches who not only 'believe the facts and doctrines of the Gospel' but 'have undergone the spiritual change expressed or implied in them'.[89] As has been discussed elsewhere, the essential nature of the Connexion lay in its reference point being spiritual experience and not credal assent. This is a position which the Union seems to have adopted. The declaration also set out six facts or doctrines: 'commonly believed by the churches of the Union'.[90] These were: the divine inspiration and authority of the Holy Scriptures; the fallen and sinful state of man; the person and work of Jesus Christ; justification by faith; the work of the Holy Spirit; and the resurrection and the judgement at the Last Day. These were intended to express the orthodoxy of the Union and are a general statement of belief: assent to them was not required as a basis of membership within the Union. In this they differed from the 'Six Articles', drawn up by the Connexion, which sought to define differences, and had initially required assent.

Spurgeon's hoped-for return did not happen and his position was not without support, even in the Connexion. Writing just prior to the amalgamation, Thomas Cook viewed the changes that had taken place in the Connexion somewhat negatively, and wanted to retain the Six Articles as a basis of faith.[91] It could be argued that one effect of the controversy was to take the theological heat out of the moves towards union. While they were not the same issues as those surrounding the amalgamation, the desire for harmonious relationships was strong following the Down Grade controversy. It was the willingness to function without a credal basis that enabled the moves towards union to continue. Like the Connexion's predecessors, the General Baptists of the eighteenth century, the choice was for denominational unity at the expense of doctrinal agreement, the difference being that this time it was unity between Generals and Particulars; it was not just limited to General Baptists. Spurgeon's concerns were about real and serious doctrinal differences among Baptists, yet for the sake of union these were ignored. While by far the greater majority of the New Connexion were theologically orthodox, they still maintained relationships with the older body of General Baptists, whose theological history was much more suspect. As late as 1890, two delegates from the Old General Baptists were present at the annual assembly.[92]

Amalgamation

It was at the May Meeting in 1886 that Charles Williams, the President of the Baptist Union, in the context of an address on rural evangelism, made a strong plea for 'a complete amalgamation of the two sections of the Baptist body'.[93] Clifford

---

[89] Payne, *Baptist Union*, p. 140.
[90] Payne, *Baptist Union*, p. 140.
[91] Cook, *Memoir of Samuel Deacon*, p. 199.
[92] *General Baptist Year Book* (1890), p. 21.
[93] Briggs, *English Baptists*, p. 138.

responded to this by writing an open letter to the *Christian World, Freeman* and *Baptist* in which he set out the history of cooperative action between the two bodies. He assured the president of the Baptist Union that the Connexion would be 'glad to assist him to signalize his year of office by initiating a movement for completing the Union of two Christian bodies separated since their origin at the beginning of the seventeenth century'.[94] W.H. Tetley, addressing the Connexion as chairman, said in 1888 that he did not understand what kept them apart: 'in fact it is an enigma what does hinder. No satisfactory answer to that question is forthcoming'.[95] Tetley was overstating his case, for the differences had not gone away! And, as R.J. Fletcher showed in his address as chairman the following year, they were much the same as when set out by Underwood in 1861.[96] What was different was the willingness on both sides to set them aside in order to come together. In 1888, Dr. John Haslam formally raised the question of amalgamation in the autumn meeting of the Baptist Union in Huddersfield. Although there were voices of caution the moves towards union went ahead. 'This conference is of the opinion that a fusion of the two denominations is desirable and heartily approve of the action of the Rev. J. Haslam in asking the Council of the Baptist Union to arrange for a meeting of exploration of both sides to discuss preliminary arrangement' was the unanimous resolution of the Lancashire and Yorkshire Conference meeting on 16 January 1889.[97] The outcome of the Huddersfield meeting was a report *Amalgamation of the General and Particular Baptists*, which was brought before the assembly in Birmingham 1889.[98]

The Connexion discussed the question of amalgamation at its Walsall Assembly the same year. It was at this meeting that the first formal steps in bringing the two bodies together were taken and when Rev. Watson Dyson moved the resolution, 'That the Association apply for affiliation with the Baptist Union'; it was carried unanimously.[99] Two other resolutions were also moved. The first was, 'This Association expresses a hearty desire for complete and thoroughgoing union—union not of fragments of one body, but of all and the whole, and, as far as may be with the whole of the Particular Baptists'. The second motion called on the Baptist Union to 'take steps to promote an amalgamation of the kind named, this Association is fully prepared to give effect to any practical proposal that may be made to it'. The first was passed fifty-one to twelve in favour, the second carried unanimously.[100] The Connexion was not going to be broken up piece by piece.

The General Baptist Association met next in Nottingham in August 1890 and at that meeting there was an air of expectation and excitement. Samuel Booth, in his

---

[94] John Clifford, 'The Queen's Jubilee and the Union of Particular and General Baptists', *GBM* (1887), p. 103.
[95] *General Baptist Year Book* (1888), p. 15.
[96] *General Baptist Year Book* (1889), p. 4.
[97] Minute Book Lancashire and Yorkshire Conference, 16 January 1889.
[98] *Year Book & Minutes of the General Baptist Association of the New Connexion* (1889), p. 25.
[99] *General Baptist Year Book* (1889), p. 25.
[100] *General Baptist Year Book Minutes* (1889), p. 25.

role as secretary, was present representing the Baptist Union. Booth had toured the country in his work for the Union, and was well known to the Connexion.[101] Opponents of the union were there ready to state their case. The proposals for amalgamation which had been submitted to and approved at the Baptist Union meeting in Birmingham the previous October were brought to the association for approval. The substance of these was that a new association should be formed for the churches of Nottingham, Derby, Leicester and Lincoln, that the General Baptist West Midland Conference and the Particular Baptist Midland Association should become one association. The remainder of the General Baptist churches were advised to join with the nearest appropriate county association.[102] Proposals for the Missionary Society were that 'the two Baptist Missionary Societies should be completely united'. Then, with an eye to the coming centenary celebrations of the older Society, 'that the proposed union should be completed by June, 1891'. This was in order that a united work might be celebrated, as, said the preamble to the recommendation, 'Carey belongs to us all'.[103]

Following the recommendations there was an open debate, in which the arguments for and against were rehearsed. R.C. Jones of Spalding remarked that 'they could not have fusion without heat, and certainly the temperature seemed to be rising'.[104] Following the assembly considerable discussion of the issues took place in the *General Baptist Magazine*.

Opposition

The leading opponents to Union were Dr. Dawson Burns, the temperance advocate, J.R. Godfrey of Melbourne, and the ageing Thomas Cook. Burns conducted a campaign against the merger through the letters column of the *General Baptist Magazine*. He contended that what was proposed was not an amalgamation of two kindred bodies, but what was required of General Baptists was 'that our Conferences should dissolve their Connexional connection, and be lost as General Baptists among the other Baptist County Associations of the country'. He argued, 'This is not our amalgamation with another denomination; it is our extinction as a denomination'. He called it an act of 'Connexional Suicide, which, in the name of amalgamation we are invited to perpetrate'.[105] The eighty-year old Thomas Cook expressed his feelings at the end of his book *Preacher Pastor and Mechanic: a Memoir of Samuel Deacon of Barton*. In 'A personal retrospect' he again lamented the failure to reaffirm the 'Six Articles' or use them as a basis of faith. Such an action, he thought, 'would almost seem to be preliminary to the more general repudiation of everything in the shape of articles of belief'. He said that, 'the churches of the New Connexion from 1770 to

---

[101] Minute Book of the Lancashire and Yorkshire Conference, 12 September 1883.
[102] *Minutes* (1890), p. 23.
[103] *Minutes* (1890), pp. 23-24.
[104] *Minutes* (1890), p. 32.
[105] Dawson Burns, 'The Proposed Extinction of the General Baptist Connexion. A Protest and an Appeal', *GBM* (1890), pp. 326-7.

1830 would have resisted such divisions, for General Baptists of that period were men who held distinctive principles, and adhered to them with steadfastness'.[106]

For some the Connexion's Orissa Mission was regarded as a kind of glue that held the churches together; lose the mission and the Connexion was lost. J.R. Godfrey, a passionate supporter of the Orissa Mission, had argued in 1888 that 'We G.B's should have to surrender all real management and control, we could not expect nor could we ask for more than a small number on the committee'. He saw the mission as central to the life of the Connexion: 'The foreign Mission is the supreme force binding our churches together, as shown by the contributions given for its support... It is the keystone of the denominational arch; take it away and we shall soon cease to be'.[107]

The arguments against union fall into three groups. First, there were theological difficulties. It was maintained that even a modified Calvinism was still Calvinism and was theologically irreconcilable with the 'unlimited atonement' belief of the General Baptists. If these distinctions were to be ignored was this not the beginning of the erosion of all distinctions? 'If the fusion is to lead to the levelling of all doctrinal distinctions as to General Redemption, why should it not level all distinctions as to Baptism the less important question?'[108] Linked to this was the issue of fellowship. The Connexion had been formed around, and had at its heart, an evangelical experience of conversion, which had given a particular character to its fellowship. Where would they find in the Union that spiritual fellowship that they had in the Connexion?

The second area of concern was structural and organisational. What kind of organisation would the Union have? The connexional structure and nature of General Baptist organisation meant that the various agencies of the denomination, the college, the Home Mission Building Fund, etc., were under the control of the Connexion; they were organisationally a much more coherent body than the Particular Baptists whose denominational concerns were run by various independent management committees or societies. Concerns in this area applied especially to the Orissa Mission. Union would mean handing over their denominational institutions to independent managers.

Thirdly, and closely associated with the previous concern, it was asked with whom were they negotiating? Had they not been part of the Union from its inception? If that was the case, who or what was representing the Particular Baptists? There was also concern about the extent to which the churches had been consulted.

Responding, Clifford, who was the main agent and architect of the union on the General Baptist side, said that the concerns about the end of fellowship were unfounded. He optimistically saw the General Baptist college becoming the focus of fellowship. He did not see the fusion as preventing fellowship. The issues of theology and consultation Clifford dealt with together. He argued that the churches

---

[106] Cook, *Preacher Pastor Mechanic*, pp. 199-200.

[107] J.R. Godfrey, 'The Union of the two Baptist Missionary Societies', *GBM* (1888), p. 454.

[108] Dawson Burns, 'Fidelity to the General Baptist Connexion', *GBM* (1890), p. 407.

were ahead of the denominational body in the choosing of ministers: 'The theological and spiritual trend of the churches is more accurately revealed by these acts than by anything else...the churches have decided in favour of fusion, and have only been waiting for the opportunity to effect it'.[109] This response reflects Clifford's pragmatic approach to theology which is dealt with below. Clifford challenged Burns' assessment of the situation. He contended that his preoccupation with the temperance movement meant that he was not in touch with the true feeling in the churches. Had he been more frequently and intimately associated with the denomination, 'He would have seen that the churches have decided the question, and that it only remained for their leaders to give effect to that decision at the right moment'.[110] For Clifford, the approach to union was essentially pragmatic and neither history nor theology was involved: *'The fact is, this fusion is to be effected without respect to historical theological statements and present doctrinal opinion on either side.'*[111] Clifford knew that discussion of such issues would wreck any chance of the two bodies coming together. The reason he was able to lay aside these considerations, and the strength of his commitment to the process, is found in his final argument, 'God wills it'. This prompted Burns to respond that such an arguments 'appear to preclude all protest and bar all appeal'. And, he remonstrated, how had Clifford 'ascertained that God wills the General Baptist Association to be so fused with other Baptist Associations? ... I have not received any such revelation'. It was not, argued Burns, a union of two denominations but 'a fusion of separate churches and pastors'.[112]

There can be little question that Clifford's forceful advocacy of the amalgamation was the major contribution to its successful outcome, but it was only because he was willing to set aside the traditional ecclesiastical disciplines of history and theology. The source and strength of his commitment to the union of the two bodies is found in his final argument, 'God wills it'. How did Clifford arrive at this position? As a young man he had read, and been strongly influenced, by the Swiss writer Alexandre Vinet. This, together with Emerson and later Carlyle, was formative in shaping his thinking.[113] From these Romantic writers, he derived the concept of divine immanence, seeing the presence and activity of God in the events and circumstances of daily life. After his training at the Midland College, Clifford studied at the University of London and gained degrees in arts, science, and law. In doing this he was exposed to, and shared some of the then current scientific thinking about the progressive nature of existence. Clifford made use of these ideas and theories for his own purposes. This meant that for him the Kingdom of God was to be established in this world. These scientific and philosophical concepts were combined with a strong pragmatism. An illuminating comment is made by one of his deacons, W.S. Stroud, who said of Clifford, 'in the technical sense of the word

---

[109] John Clifford, 'The Fusion of Baptists', *GBM* (1890), p. 366.
[110] John Clifford, 'The Fusion of Baptists', p. 367.
[111] John Clifford, 'The Fusion of Baptists', p. 368, italics his.
[112] Burns, 'Fidelity to the General Baptist Connexion', *GBM* (1890), pp. 405-407.
[113] Watts, 'John Clifford', pp. 26, 41, 114-15.

he was not a theologian... In the specialized meaning of the word there is little theology in his sermons'.[114] Clifford expressed his theology in a practical way, in that his preaching and writing called for practical commitment to the purposes of God in this world. Clifford was a pragmatist and this combined with his sense of the immanence of God, endowed events with a special significance. So he prefaces 'God wills it' with 'The new time has brought this new duty'. He saw in the events that were taking place in the denomination the working out of the purposes of God, and that a practical commitment to them was needed if the Kingdom of God was to be established in this world. It was in this sense that 'God wills it'. Clifford's approach reflects the contemporary idealism which influenced many churchmen, notably Charles Gore and the *Lux Mundi* group in the Church of England. The inherent weakness in this position was that of tying the Christian faith to a particular way of viewing human experience and circumstances. For Romanticism in general, and Clifford was a romantic, nature 'red in tooth and claw' became an insoluble problem, it was unable to do justice to the doctrine of sin and evil.[115]

In order to accomplish the union of the 'institutions', the Baptist Union Corporation was formed in 1890. This was in part a preparation for union and in part a result of the growing financial obligations of the Union. It allowed for the fusion of the missionary societies and the various building funds.

The contents of what was known as the 'Walsall Resolution' was communicated to the churches. For the church at Castle Donnington, preoccupied with building new Sunday school rooms, the event went by almost unnoticed, receiving only three lines in the minute book: 'at a thinly attended meeting duly called for the consideration of the subject it was resolved, "That we approve of the fusion of the two bodies" there was no opposition'.[116] Things were discussed a little more fully at Hyson Green, Nottingham:

A lengthy discussion followed the Pastor's remarks, the general tenor of which was favourable to union. However a fear was shown by some of being expected to subscribe to a Calvinistic creed and ultimately the resolution was amended as follows 'that should the condition agreed to in the Walsall resolution respecting the union of the General and Particular Baptists be complied with and no demand to subscribe to a Calvinistic creed be made, the addition of this church will be heartily accorded'.[117]

The April and March church meetings at Bourne discussed the amalgamation and approved provided 'that the interests of our Denominational Institutions do not suffer' and that there was 'proportional representation'.[118] After having

---

[114] W.S. Stroud, 'John Clifford', *Baptist Quarterly* 6 (1932–33), p. 307.
[115] For further discussion see B.M.G. Reardon, *Religious Thought in the Victorian Age London* (London: Longman, 1980), pp. 430-31.
[116] Castle Donnington Church Book, 30 April 1891.
[117] Hyson Green Church Book, p. 345.
[118] Bourne Church Book, 23 March and 21 April. 1891.

communicated with their churches the General Baptist Conference met. The Eastern Conference, at Boston in April 1891, reported that all but two were for the union. The larger Midland Conference met in May at Barton. Of the eighty-one churches circulated, only forty-two had replied, thirty-eight were in favour and four against.

On the 25 June 1891 the final assembly of the General Baptist Association took place in Burnley. Clifford put to the assembly the 'invitation offered'. Burns launched a last ditch resistance, proposing an amendment opposing it. The debate lasted four hours but, on voting, the amendment was lost. The resolution in favour of amalgamation with the Baptist Union was carried by 155 votes to thirty-nine. In his history of *The Baptist Union*, Ernest Payne remarks that 'With remarkable ease and amity, the older distinctions passed from the mind of the denomination as a whole'.[119] Perhaps Payne's commitment to the ecumenical movement allowed him to view the removal of distinctions in such a positive light. For the General Baptists of Yorkshire it had not been an easy decision to join an association that had a Calvinistic statement of belief, and the voting was very close: '13 to join Yorks. Assn. 10 opposed. 3 undecided'.[120]

The resolution was in fact absorption; the old distinctions did not pass away, the theological differences were transferred to the new Union. What happened was that, in terms of organisation, the Particular Baptist structures prevailed. It was only in the East Midlands, with the formation of the new East Midland Baptist Association, that something approaching a union took place: the rest of the Connexion was absorbed and the distinctive connexional emphasis of the General Baptists was lost. The theological position of the merged body was not articulated, the differences being glossed over for the sake of unity. This theological ambiguity was on occasions to resurface and be a source of problems down to the present day, as with the Christological dispute of the early 1970s in which Michael Taylor questioned the divinity of Christ.[121]

The last assembly of the Midland Conference was held on the 29 September 1891 at Long Eaton. With the close of that meeting the New Connexion ceased to exist. The 'tribe of Dan' passed into history.

Reasons for Union

We have traced out the history of the Connexion and are left with the question why, after 121 years, did the Connexion allow itself to be absorbed, and lose its separate identity? The history of the Connexion spanned one of the greatest periods of growth in the history of the church in England, yet the early evangelistic emphasis had palled. The independence and protest of Dan Taylor became the desire for 'fusion' of John Clifford. We move now to consider four possible explanations for the demise of the Connexion.

---

[119] Payne, *Baptist Union*, p. 147.
[120] Minute Book of the Lancashire and Yorkshire Conference, 20 January 1892.
[121] See McBeth, *Baptist Heritage*, p. 517 for fuller details.

The Secularisation Argument

The first argument says that moves to reunions are the result of the pressure on the churches from an increasingly secular society. According to this view the conflicts that kept churches apart assume a much less important role as churches under pressure look for allies. Larry Skinner defines secularism as 'an attitude of indifference to religious institutions and practices or even to religious questions as such'.[122] To what extent did secularisation contribute to the coming together of the two Baptist bodies? Had the Connexion turned its attention from the supernatural and next life and become more preoccupied with, and similar to, the surrounding society? Had it become weakened and lost the vitality of its youth?

At the end of our period many members of the Connexion had experienced rising standards of living, and were involved in the development of societies and activities outside the church. They also came into contact with the wider abandonment of belief in God as an explanation of the reality they experienced, and the secular drift of a society that sought to explain life without the benefit of a religious interpretation. R.S. Lee argues that a shift had taken place amongst Baptists, and that the early pietism and mysticism characteristic of the Evangelical Revival had given way to more pragmatic and practical concerns in which the importance of faith was in its effect on conduct and environment.[123] There can be little doubt that these factors contributed to a lowering of commitment and involvement, and reduced the vitality of life in the churches. The most noticeable product of secularisation, so far as churches are concerned, is simply disbelief in the supernatural. Robert Currie points out that in this climate of lower involvement, inter- and intra-organizational conflict also decreased, rival doctrines and systems were not so important.[124] Munson argues that it was not just a passive response to society at large, but a positive adoption of secular values: 'the Nonconformists had come to identify the Christian Religion with the values and secular goals of their times, the most important of which was an acceptance of the immutability of progress "through change" '.[125] At the end of his study of reunion in the Methodist Church, Robert Currie contends that 'close examination of the process of reunion shows that in advanced societies ecumenicalism is the product of an ageing religion'.[126] This, together with the argument of Bryan Wilson that re-union and ecumenicism are a reflection of a church's weakness in the face of an increasing secularised society, comprise what we might call the 'secularisation argument' which is one way of accounting for the demise of organisations like the Connexion. The Wilson thesis argues, first, that churches come together as a result of the weakness of religion in an increasingly

---

[122] Larry Skinner, 'The Meaning of Secularisation', *International Yearbook for the Sociology of Religion* 3 (1967), p. 51

[123] Lee, 'Baptists in Yorkshire', pp. 42-43.

[124] R. Currie, *Methodism Divided: A Study in the Sociology of Ecumenicalism* (London: Faber and Faber, 1968), p. 313.

[125] James Munson, *The Nonconformists: In Search of a Lost Culture* (London: SPCK, 1991), p. 117.

[126] Currie, *Methodism Divided*, p. 316.

secularised society; secondly, that this process is predominantly a clerical concern; finally, that amalgamations are seen as involving a compromise of principle or theology and are therefore a further sign of weakness.[127]

How valid is this assessment of the 1891 amalgamation of General and Particular Baptists? The discussions took place against the background of a concern about the increasing wave of secularism that was sweeping over the churches. This, together with the concern over 'erasure', which represented a failure of the Connexion to hold its membership, as much as a failure to convert, about which there was also concern, gives weight to the argument. To what extent was it a clerical concern? After the false start of the 1860s, the moves that led to union from 1889 onwards were originated by Avery and Clifford from the General Baptists, and Booth representing the Particular Baptists. It was from a fairly small core group that the main energy and drive for the project came. Of the fifteen members of the joint committee that was formed to deal with the negotiations, only one was not a minister, Mr Foulkes Griffiths, who was the General Baptist Association solicitor. With only a few exceptions, those who contributed to the debate through the various denominational journals were ministers.

David Thompson argues that one of the problems in accepting the Wilson-Currie thesis is that it is dependent on a sociological understanding of the emergence of the denominations of Nonconformity. While historians recognise that the division that gave rise to the nineteenth-century denominations involved more than theology, the issue is complicated and the exact role theology plays is difficult to determine. Thompson argues that Wilson's approach does not take theology sufficiently into account. Wilson's understanding of religious vitality as the presence of division and social tension has inherent problems. 'To assume that division is a sign of religious vigour is bound to lead to the conclusion that union is a sign of weakness: the argument therefore becomes deductive rather than inductive and its force as an historical (and, one might have thought, as a sociological) analysis disappears'.[128] 'All this', he says, 'is not to deny the force of Wilson's observation on the social changes which have weakened English nonconformity; but it is to deny that the development of ecumenical attitudes can be explained in sociological terms alone, without reference to accompanying theological developments'.[129] While acknowledging the profound impact of secularism on the Connexion and Particular Baptists it needs to be seen in the context of the theological developments that took place among Baptists during this period. It would be difficult to explain the loss of influence of religious values and institutions without reference to doctrine. This leads us to our next consideration, the theological argument.

---

[127] David M. Thompson, 'Theological and Sociological Approaches to the Motivation of the Ecumenical Movement', in D. Baker (ed.), *Religious Motivation. Biographical and Sociological Problems for the Church Historian* (Studies in Church History, XV; Oxford: Basil Blackwell 1978), p. 468.

[128] Thompson, 'Theological and Sociological Approaches', p. 475.

[129] Thompson, 'Theological and Sociological Approaches', p. 472.

The Theological Convergence Argument

While it is understandable that a sociologist like Wilson should play down the role of doctrine, John Kent argues that doctrines play a more significant role in the early stages of a movement than they do two or three generations later when membership has more hereditary characteristics, and the original doctrinal concerns are not held so strongly: 'the members are no longer pressed to maintain their separate identity over against other religious bodies, but aspire instead to assert the movement's status as a respectable Protestant evangelical denomination'.[130] This theological argument looks to the removal of differences, the growing theological consensus, and the development of a common theological agenda, as the explanations for reunion. It is argued that it was this erosion of former differences and the freedom from credal and confessional documents that made union possible.[131]

It is an argument favoured by the older generation of denominational historians. So John Bateman, in his biography of John Clifford, writes of the two Baptist bodies, 'Gradually their differences paled before increasing charity, and possibilities of discussing union became evident'.[132] A.C. Underwood, in his history of the Baptist denomination published in 1947, says that 'The breakdown of Calvinism among the Particular Baptists was an indispensable prerequisite to the fusion of 1891', and that 'the General Baptists came to feel that their testimony to the truth that Christ "tasted death for every man" had been so universally accepted by all associated with the Baptist Union that their existence as a separate denomination was no longer necessary',[133] and we have already noted Ernest Payne's observation on 'ease and amity' with which 'the older distinctions passed from the mind of the denomination as a whole'.[134]

There are two main elements to the theological argument. First modifications to high-Calvinism following the publication of Andrew Fuller's book *A Gospel worthy of all Acceptation* in 1785. We have previously explored the subsequent theological convergence due to the position he espoused. Perhaps it should be noted that the changes were within Calvinism; as the General Baptists were at pains to point out, the move was towards their position.

Given the changes mentioned above, and bearing in mind that for the most part Baptists were consistent in their support of traditional beliefs, both bodies of Baptists had by 1891 abandoned credal definitions of faith as a basis for fellowship. The Down Grade controversy brought into the open concern about emerging theological trends and the prudence of adopting a non-credalist position. This

---

[130] Kent, *Holding the Fort*, p. 303.

[131] E.A. Payne, 'The Development of Nonconformist Theological Education in the Nineteenth Century, with Special Reference to Regent's Park College', in E.A. Payne (ed.), *Studies in History and Religion* (London: Lutterworth Press, 1942), p. 248, discussed by Briggs, *English Baptists*, p. 171.

[132] Charles T. Bateman, *John Clifford: Free Church Leader and Preacher* (London: National Council of the Evangelical Free Churches, 1904), p. 142.

[133] Underwood, *History of the English Baptists*, pp. 202, 216.

[134] Payne, *Baptist Union*, p. 146 (see above p. 196).

position was well expressed in 1888 by H.R. Murray, in 'Our creed; or the Baptist rule of faith':

> as a body we should rejoice in our freedom; for it is peculiar to us as a denomination that we have no human creed or confession of faith to which we are compelled to subscribe upon pain of penalty or expulsion. We are under the dominion, in matters of faith and doctrine, of no Synod, Conference, or Board. The only court of appeal we recognise is the Bible; the only creed we know, the words of Christ and His apostles.[135]

Again this lack of a confessional documents is seen as a reference point for reunion by Payne.[136] Doctrinal non-credalism was also present among Particular Baptists Hugh Stowell Brown and Charles Williams, who asserted the right of each man to his own interpretation of scripture. Williams rejected Spurgeon's plea for a creed during the down grade debate because it would have been a denial of the theological freedom for which they stood.[137] Lee argues that in Lancashire the churches' commitment to evangelism resulted in

> an essentially empirical religion, governed in all its aspects by the need to win converts. This preoccupation drew the separated factions of the denomination into one body, it produced a toleration of differences in an attempt to remove obstacles to co-operation in proselytism, it swept aside the distracting problems of contemporary scholarship, secular or religious, and insisted on a total submission to the bible and its Gospel.[138]

There can be no doubt that this non-credalist approach overcame one of the major barriers to reunion. One of the problems with the argument is that it tends to play down the very real theological divisions within the denominations. Not all General Baptists were happy about the situation. Thomas Goadby, writing in 1882, expressed his concern about a non-credalist approach:

> The growing disposition of our time to depreciate and disregard the obligations of denominationalism is, it is to be feared, far less due to growing charity and brotherly-kindness than to an increasing indifference to the truths our fathers fought and suffered to establish and perpetuate, and a general lowering of the tone of moral and religious conviction.[139]

---

[135] H.R. Murray, 'Our Creed or the Baptist Rule of Faith', *GBM* (March 1888), pp. 81-85, cited by Briggs, *English Baptists*, p. 173.

[136] Payne, 'The Development of Nonconformist Theological Education', p. 248, in Briggs, *English Baptists*, p. 171.

[137] Lee, 'Baptists in Lancashire', p. 48.

[138] Lee, 'Baptists in Lancashire', p. 67.

[139] Thomas Goadby, 'The Principles of our Denominational Cohesion', *GBM* (1882), p. 7.

Little mention is made of these concerns by the older historians, or the fact that Clifford, who was an avowed non-credalist, explicitly rejected discussion of theological issues in the reunion debates.

In the desire to emphasise 'unity' other theological factors which contributed to reunion are often ignored. Both bodies of Baptists and Congregationalists were facing the limitations of 'Independency' as a principle of organisation.[140] John Briggs draws attention to the demise of the concept of the church as a covenant community. For Old Dissent the church was the gathered local body of true believers covenanting in a common life under God, 'to walk together in all the ordinances of Christ, in a mutual consent, covenant, or agreement'.[141] But, argues Ian Sellers, the concept of the church as a fellowship of believers taken out of the world and under the discipline of the church meeting, gave way to a stressing of their democratic character, and by stressing their historic contribution to secular democracy the churches would put themselves in harmony with the times.[142] According to W.R. Ward, as the understanding of the church moved from the gathering of the saints out of a corrupt church to the conversion of sinners out of the world, 'the harder it was to maintain the full independence of congregations or denominations'.[143] Under the influence of the Evangelical Revival, common life began to give way to individualism, church membership became a personal choice, involvement became optional. The nature of the understanding of the church changed from one in which the church determined the nature of community to one in which individual needs are met; and the nature of the church was largely determined by the nature of its environment, as happened with the shift to the 'social gospel' approach to church life. It was in this sense that the church became subject to the 'spirit of the age', and it was the age in which there was a movement away from individualism both in religion and politics; union was needed in order hold together the centrifugal forces of individualism.

Both Wilson and Currie argue that the ecumenical movement involves the surrender or compromise of distinctive principles. With the General and Particular Baptists it is difficult to determine who surrendered what to whom. The General Baptists surrendered their independence and denominational organisations, but what did the Particular Baptists surrender? Not their organisation, for they had little. The tactic of foregoing discussion of theological principles meant that doctrine was not addressed. Was the Union a 'fusion' in which General Baptist ecclesiology and practice was wedded to the Calvinism of the Particular Baptists? Or was it 'absorption' in which the General Baptist contribution was diluted to such an extent that it was as good as lost? Both Wilson and Currie point out that in mergers of this nature the concerns of the larger group or parent body come to dominate.[144] With

---

[140] Johnson, *The Dissolution of Dissent*, p. 119.

[141] William Bartlet, cited by Geoffrey F. Nuttall, *Visible Saints 1640–1660* (Oxford: Basil Blackwell, 1957), p. 75.

[142] Sellers, *Nonconformity*, pp. 23-24.

[143] Ward, *Religion and Society*, p. 71.

[144] Currie, *Methodism Divided*, p. 313; and Wilson, *Religion in Secular Society*, p. 155.

perhaps the exception of the newly created East Midland Baptist Association, the influence of the Connexion was simply overwhelmed in the merger.

While there is much to the theological convergence argument as the condition for reunion, it needs to be broadened out to take account of the practical and theological compromise involved. But the major weakness is that it does not address the enormous social and demographic changes that had taken place within in the Connexion between 1770 and 1891.

The Constituency Argument

In addition to the secularisation and theological reasons put forward as explanations of the passing of the Connexion, a further group of factors need to be taken into consideration. This may be termed the constituency argument. Put simply, it says that the constituency from which the Connexion recruited had contracted to such an extent that it was no longer able to sustain viable recruitment. Account also needs to be taken of changes in the recruitment strategy of the Connexion. As we have seen, the strength of the Connexion lay in two areas, the rural communities of the East Midlands, Lincolnshire and South Yorkshire, and the industrial villages and small towns of Leicestershire, Nottinghamshire and Derbyshire. This constituency was radically affected in two ways. First, framework knitting, a dominant industry of the area, experienced decline and underwent a process of mechanisation in the middle of the nineteenth century. This resulted in large unemployment and a profound economic and social disturbance for the knitters. The Connexion had initially recruited heavily from this community. The failure to recruit brought home to the Connexion by the mid-century membership crisis and the 1851 Religious Census coincides with the mechanisation of the framework knitting industry. In the second half of the century, there is in the literature of the movement no mention of the changes or difficulties this industry was experiencing. In addition to this, the second agricultural revolution of the 1860s and 1870s led to a massive depopulation of the land and re-distribution of labour which affected the Connexion significantly. John Clifford spoke of the villages decreasing in numbers, 'and this means that the churches have greater difficulty to subsist, and that their young people leave them for the towns... Small towns, i.e. towns of the middle size are either at a stand still or only increasing slowly...but in the largest towns the growth is extremely rapid'. He concluded by saying that the denomination 'that does not address itself with all its might to this question will be unequal to its work, and soon lose its place and power'.[145] We have already seen that with the exception of Nottingham and Leicester, towns which while expanding were by no means at the forefront of urban growth, the Connexion had not, in any significant way, established themselves in the new urban areas. In 1876, Clifford said that science was improving men and women out of the villages, machines did their work better and in less time, the churches were suffering as those with 'the best brains, and the most resolute will, are

---

[145] Clifford, 'General Baptists in 1871', *GBM* (1871), p. 276.

ready to leave the traditions and associations of the old home for the risks of the sea and the hazards of a crowded town', the effect of which was 'fewer members of our churches, fewer local preachers'.[146] The migration to the fast expanding new urban centres was, in effect, the demise of a major part of the Connexion's constituency. Currie, Gilbert and Horsley argue that 'Economic downturns...leave members with less resources to meet the cost of membership'. They continue,

> But economic downturns are less dangerous to church growth than the manifold social and personal factors conducive to a dissolution of the church-centred community. As the special connection between migration and membership termination shows, individuals often leave churches at the same time as they leave their homes or the area in which they have long lived; and the effect on membership retention of a change in personal life circumstances is similar to that of historical and social changes which tend to disturb the settled life of the section of the population into which any given individual may have been born.[147]

We find a correlation between periods of disturbance in the 1860s and 70s, and a concern about 'erasures', which to some extent is an indicator of migration. The number of erasures was attributed to severe revision of membership rolls, and the failure of members to join a New Connexion church on moving. This, together with the Connexion's lack of impact in the cities, meant that it was struggling to recruit.

To the constituency argument we can add another factor, that of redemption and lift. This phenomenon, first noticed by John Wesley, says that the effect of conversion is to move people up the social scale. Clifford observed the same thing:

> The lever of Christianity raises men in the social scale, creates an aversion to poverty, drives off the harpies of wretchedness, refines taste and inspires culture; and so it came to pass that the churches like the Primitive Methodists and Wesleyans, that began at the bottom are gradually lifted to the higher ranges of respectability and social influence, and toil, if at all, only spasmodically and by constraint work in the old and original workings.[148]

We have noted earlier concern that the Connexion was losing members as a result of social as well as geographical migration. The old and original workings were becoming exhausted. There was an increasing dependence on indirect recruitment from the Sunday school.[149] The new urban areas were as much a mission field as the work in India; in these areas, according to Currie, Gilbert, and Horsley, 'the

---

[146] John Clifford, *Religious Life in the Rural Districts of England* (London: Yates and Alexander, 1876), p. 6.

[147] Currie, Gilbert and Horsley, *Churches and Churchgoers*, p. 123.

[148] John Clifford, *The Salvation Army: Its Genesis, Aims, Principles, Methods and Results* (London: Griffiths, 1920), p. 9.

[149] John Clifford, 'The General Baptist Church in 1882', *GBM* (1882), p. 366.

preliminary work of Christianization and even religious socialisation had to start virtually from the beginning'.[150]

These changes overtook the Connexion at a late stage in its life, and it seems to have lacked the flexibility to make the necessary changes in order to address the new situation in which it found itself. The gradual erosion of that particular section of society from which the Connexion had drawn large numbers of its members, and the social migration of others from the remaining group, made the redrawing of boundaries through amalgamation with the Particular Baptists attractive.

The Common Agenda Argument

The fourth argument looks to the development of a common agenda within Nonconformity. A significant contribution enabling the fusion of the two bodies was the influence of various movements in which the two bodies worked together. As nineteenth-century Nonconformity began to move from defence to attack in relation to the Established Church and to address what it saw as evils within the culture, so a number of pan-denominational agencies came into being to further these various objectives. In Edward Miall's Anti-State Church Association, formed in 1844, 'the Baptists Particular and General, were decidedly the most numerous party in the Conference'.[151] Concern was expressed by some at the amount of Baptist and Independent representation at the expense of others.[152] The formation of the Evangelical Alliance in 1846 brought together a wide range of evangelicals from various traditions. For the Baptists it was an opportunity to discover how much they had in common. The re-founding of the London Baptist Association in 1865 under Spurgeon, William Brock and William Landels, embraced both General and Particular Baptists. General Baptists worked on equal terms without any question as to their theology. What united them was missionary endeavour, their aim being to plant one new church a year.[153] While the work of the London Baptist Association was not ecumenical activity as such, it allowed General and Particular Baptists to discover how much they had in common, and raise in the minds of many the question, 'What keeps us apart?'

This cooperative action in mission was seen again in the visits of Moody and Sankey and was lauded by Clifford.[154] In 1886, there was a joint session of the Baptist Union and the Congregational Union.[155] John Briggs lists a number of non-theological factors that helped to develop kinship amongst Baptists. Both groups supported the Bible Translation Society, there was the Baptist Total Abstinence

---

[150] Currie Gilbert and Horsley, *Churches and Churchgoers*, p. 85.

[151] *Baptist Reporter* (1844), p. 188.

[152] *Baptist Reporter* (1844), p. 188.

[153] Mike Nicholls, *C.H. Spurgeon the Pastor Evangelist* (Didcot: Baptist Historical Society, 1992), p. 106.

[154] 'How the revival works', *GBM* (1875), p. 25, and 'Lessons for the churches from the Revival', p. 161. Hayden, 'Baptists Covenants and Confessions', p. 29.

[155] Payne, *Baptist Union*, p. 123.

Association, the Hanserd Knollys Society, Augmentation Fund, National Association for Aged and Infirm Baptist Ministers, and the Board of Education. He makes the point that 'Support for ministers of both sections of the family increasingly involved some kind of subsidy of General Baptist work by Particular Baptists'.[156] The fraternal nature of the relationship extended, as we have seen, to the formation of a Midland Union. In the North it took the form of the General Baptist Northern Conference affiliating directly with the Baptist Union.[157] In 1864, J.H. Millard of Huntingdon, the secretary and energetic supporter of the Baptist Union, defined the main object of the Union as 'to bring the Baptist churches of this kingdom into closer and more loving fellowship with each other, to remove the barriers that may unnecessarily exist, to a more frequent and more fraternal intercourse, and to establish such relations amongst the brethren generally as shall enable them to co-operate more easily and fully in every good work'.[158] This growing fraternity, assisted by the work of the Baptist Union, raised questions about the continuation of separate identities. This, together with factors we have considered above, contributed to the decision of the New Connexion of General Baptists to forgo the more intimate fellowship of their Connexion and throw in their lot with their elder and larger brother.

Bryan Wilson says, 'The ritual dance of ecumenism emphasizes steps known as "drawing together" and "growing together". A close observer of the dance might notice that the gyrations and revolutions of some of the dancers are far more numerous in a short space of time than those of others'.[159] This was certainly the case with the Connexion as it moved toward union; there seems to have been far more concession and adaption on the part of the Connexion than on the part of the Particular Baptists. The transition from revival movement to denomination had been completed.

Conclusion: A Question of Identity

Looking at the accounts of reunion, one is tempted to wonder why it took so long once the distinctive conditions of emergence had been eroded. Why did the Connexion last as long as it did? The differences between General and Particular Baptists were not very great, they shared a common history, ecclesiology, and desire for the salvation of men and women. By the time of the 1851 Census a number of churches were content to describe themselves simply as 'Baptist', leaving historians with the difficulty of sorting out what kind of 'Baptist unspecified' they were dealing with. The various hues of Methodism were much more particular about their designation.

One reason for the persistence of the Connexion may lie in its strong sense of identity. There were a number factors that contributed to this. The Connexion

---

[156] Briggs, *English Baptists*, p. 130.
[157] Briggs, *English Baptists*, p. 135.
[158] *Baptist Reporter* (1864), p. 531.
[159] Wilson, *Religion in a Secular Society*, p. 224.

evolved from a relatively small number of churches that had in the early stages shared a socially similar background. By 1890, there were still only 192 churches, plus various branch works. There was in the Connexion a sense of intimacy and fellowship. This sense of belonging gave a coherence and boundary awareness but, as we have seen, that was breaking down by the middle of the century.

At the heart of the New Connexion's identity lay the experience and offer of 'free grace'. This set them apart from the Particular Baptists and their evangelical enthusiasm and Christology distinguished them from the Old General Baptists. With the advent of 'Fullerism' and its growing acceptance among Particular Baptists that distinctiveness was eroded, and the basis for the existence of the Connexion as a separate entity diminished. The evangelistic concern that had provided a sense of mission and oneness was lost in the growth of denominational activity.

The appeal to a Connexional structure also contributed to this sense of identity; the magazine, the foreign mission and the college were all dependent on central funding. The annual assembly and regional conferences gave a sense of identity that the more diverse Particular Baptists lacked. Although structurally a Connexion, the movement's ethos and practice were Independent. While connexionalism provided distinctiveness, the independence of local churches curtailed the ability of the New Connexion to take effective strategic decisions with respect to mission.

A move away from personal evangelism to institutional evangelism, a growing dependence on full-time ministry, a turn away from the world outside the church to the internal constituency of the Sunday school and church organisations for recruitment, are all indications of changes taking place within the movement. To these need to be added the influence of profound demographic changes in areas of New Connexion strength. As the concerns of revivalism waned and those of denominationalism came into the ascendency, so the need for protest and distinctivness, characteristic of the early stages of the movement, diminished.

By the 1880s and 90s the self-consciousness of previous generations was considerably weakened. Identity was found in the word 'Baptist' rather than the word 'General'. Falling numbers, the strength and development of the Baptist Union, the theological convergence between the two bodies, upward social mobility, a decline in the value and utility of religious functions, and a growing secularism, all contributed to something like an identity crisis. For over 100 years the New Connexion of General Baptists had been sufficiently secure in their convictions to maintain their identity. But as a result of changes within and without the movement that sense of historical continuity was weakened. The merger of the two bodies provided the opportunity for the formation of a new identity. So it was within the context of the Baptist Union and under the generic term 'Baptist' that spiritual fellowship and a new identity was sought.

Appendixes

Appendix 1

Annual Percentage Growth Rate: New Connexion, National Population and Sunday School

Table 1: 1770–1815

Year	New Connexion Membership	National Population	Sunday School
1770	0.00	Figures start 1801	Figures start 1841
1771	-12.66		
1772	-14.50		
1773	12.78		
1774	4.94		
1775	1.31		
1776	13.32		
1777	0.24		
1778	4.03		
1779	-0.29		
1780	3.59		
1781	3.50		
1782	0.81		
1783	0.75		
1784	9.37		
1785	6.62		
1786	7.58		
1787	4.58		
1788	5.48		
1789	7.38		
1790	1.83		
1791	3.41		
1792	0.88		
1793	1.85		
1794	5.13		
1795	0.06		
1796	1.86		
1797	2.87		
1798	3.24		
1799	-1.54		
1800	-0.15		
1801	5.33	0.80	
1802	4.35	0.84	

1803	2.61	1.15
1804	2.57	1.38
1805	5.81	1.50
1806	7.18	1.45
1807	7.28	1.39
1808	2.99	1.30
1809	6.70	1.31
1810	1.78	1.27
1811	2.74	1.31
1812	5.12	1.52
1813	2.85	1.60
1814	2.89	1.58
1815	3.52	1.66

Appendix 2
Annual Percentage Growth Rate: New Connexion, National Population and Sunday School
Table 2: 1816–1839

Year	New Connexion Membership	National Population	Sunday School
1816	5.23	1.68	Figures start 1841
1817	3.00	1.60	
1818	4.90	1.54	
1819	3.06	1.44	
1820	3.34	1.51	
1821	5.01	1.66	
1822	3.66	1.70	
1823	3.64	1.63	
1824	4.87	1.49	
1825	-0.56	1.39	
1826	0.79	1.32	
1827	6.16	1.31	
1828	3.34	1.41	
1829	4.76	1.36	
1830	4.28	1.32	
1831	0.94	1.35	
1832	1.27	1.20	
1833	2.22	1.13	
1834	3.48	1.30	
1835	9.40	1.35	
1836	-0.58	1.33	
1837	4.02	1.16	
1838	4.28	1.19	
1839	2.36	1.41	

Appendix 3

Annual Percentage Growth Rate: New Connexion, National Population and Sunday School
Table 3: 1840–1869

Year	New Connexion Membership	National Population	Sunday School
1840	3.13	1.34	
1841	5.65	1.20	31.27
1842	3.83	1.25	12.41
1843	4.85	1.27	4.73
1844	3.04	1.24	5.70
1845	0.68	1.37	-1.09
1846	4.93	1.44	2.70
1847	-3.99	1.26	-0.56
1848	0.42	1.33	-5.30
1849	-0.37	1.31	-0.78
1850	-0.53	1.30	3.52
1851	1.82	1.26	1.95
1852	1.21	1.11	9.24
1853	-1.49	1.10	1.19
1854	0.16	1.07	-4.06
1855	0.58	0.94	4.76
1856	-1.05	1.04	-2.52
1857	0.98	1.04	2.26
1858	0.80	0.88	2.67
1859	3.75	1.40	4.16
1860	1.35	0.61	1.65
1861	2.35	1.01	2.48
1862	4.01	1.21	-3.65
1863	0.71	1.07	4.74
1864	1.12	1.19	-0.04
1865	0.20	1.05	-4.12
1866	-1.06	1.19	2.39
1867	-1.68	1.05	3.16
1868	0.73	1.19	2.24
1869	-2.01	1.05	-0.13

Appendix 4

Annual Percentage Growth Rate: New Connexion, National Population and Sunday School
Table 4: 1870–1890

Year	New Connexion Membership	National Population	Sunday School
1870	3.95	1.19	8.76
1871	0.58	1.10	2.67
1872	0.05	1.31	1.25
1873	-2.56	1.17	-2.94
1874	7.97	1.31	-17.95
1875	-0.80	1.32	28.41
1876	6.78	1.17	6.26
1877	0.25	1.32	-1.47
1878	0.31	1.32	3.71
1879	1.81	1.17	0.69
1880	3.12	1.32	4.93
1881	1.32	1.13	-1.73
1882	3.19	1.22	13.42
1883	0.26	1.23	1.07
1884	0.25	1.22	3.85
1885	1.35	1.22	1.51
1886	0.24	1.22	2.56
1887	1.59	1.22	-6.63
1888	0.73	1.37	-0.81
1889	-0.04	1.36	-7.61
1890	-8.3	2.06	1.36

Appendix 5
Numerical Growth of the New Connexion

The following tables give the numerical growth of the New Connexion by county. Only those counties with a New Connexion interest are shown. It should be noted that the left hand vertical scale (number of members) varies considerably. The range of this scale varies with the number of churches in a county, in some counties there are only one or two churches. The scale on the right, the number of members of the whole Connexion, and does not vary, it is included in order that the development of the Connexion in a particular county may be seen in the context of the whole Connexion. The annual returns are not consistent in the way they record the London churches, towards the end of the period the county designation is replaced by London. For the sake of clarity and simplicity the majority of the London churches are included in the figures for Middlesex as they were in the county until the boundary changes of 1887.

Table 5: Numerical Growth of the New Connexion, 1770–1890

Year	Members	Year	Members
1770	1635	1794	3176
1771	1428	1795	3178
1772	1221	1796	3237
1773	1377	1797	3330
1774	1445	1798	3438
1775	1464	1799	3385
1776	1659	1800	3380
1777	1663	1801	3560
1778	1730	1802	3715
1779	1725	1803	3812
1780	1787	1804	3910
1781	1850	1805	4137
1782	1865	1806	4434
1783	1879	1807	4757
1784	2055	1808	4899
1785	2191	1809	5227
1786	2357	1810	5320
1787	2465	1811	5466
1788	2600	1812	5746
1789	2792	1813	5910
1790	2843	1814	6081
1791	2940	1815	6295
1792	2966	1816	6624
1793	3021	1817	6823

1818	7157		1855	17894
1819	7376		1856	17707
1820	7622		1857	17881
1821	8024		1858	18024
1822	8318		1859	18700
1823	8621		1860	18952
1824	9041		1861	19397
1825	8990		1862	20174
1826	9061		1863	20317
1827	9619		1864	20544
1828	9940		1865	20586
1829	10413		1866	20367
1830	10859		1867	20025
1831	10961		1868	20171
1832	11100		1869	19765
1833	11346		1870	20488
1834	11741		1871	20607
1835	12845		1872	20617
1836	12771		1873	20090
1837	13285		1874	21692
1838	13853		1875	21519
1839	14180		1876	22978
1840	14624		1877	23036
1841	15450		1878	23107
1842	16042		1879	23525
1843	16820		1880	24259
1844	17332		1881	24580
1845	17450		1882	25365
1846	18310		1883	25431
1847	17580		1884	25494
1848	17654		1885	25837
1849	17588		1886	25899
1850	17495		1887	26310
1851	17813		1888	26502
1852	18029		1889	26491
1853	17761		1890	24334
1854	17790			

Numerical Growth of the New Connexion, 1770–1890

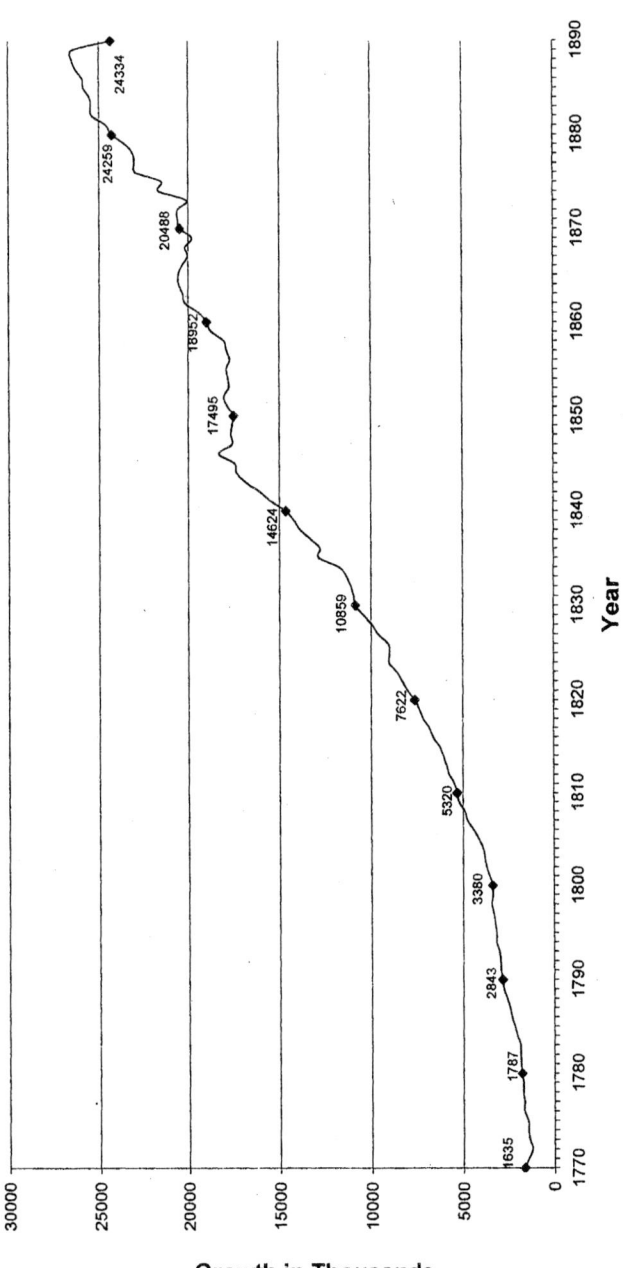

Year	Growth
1770	1635
1780	1787
1790	2843
1800	3380
1810	5320
1820	7622
1830	10859
1840	14624
1850	17495
1860	18952
1870	20488
1880	24259
1890	24334

Growth in Thousands

Appendix 6

Graphs Showing Numerical Growth of the New Connexion by County

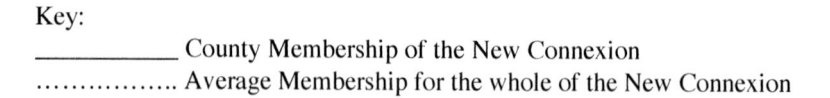

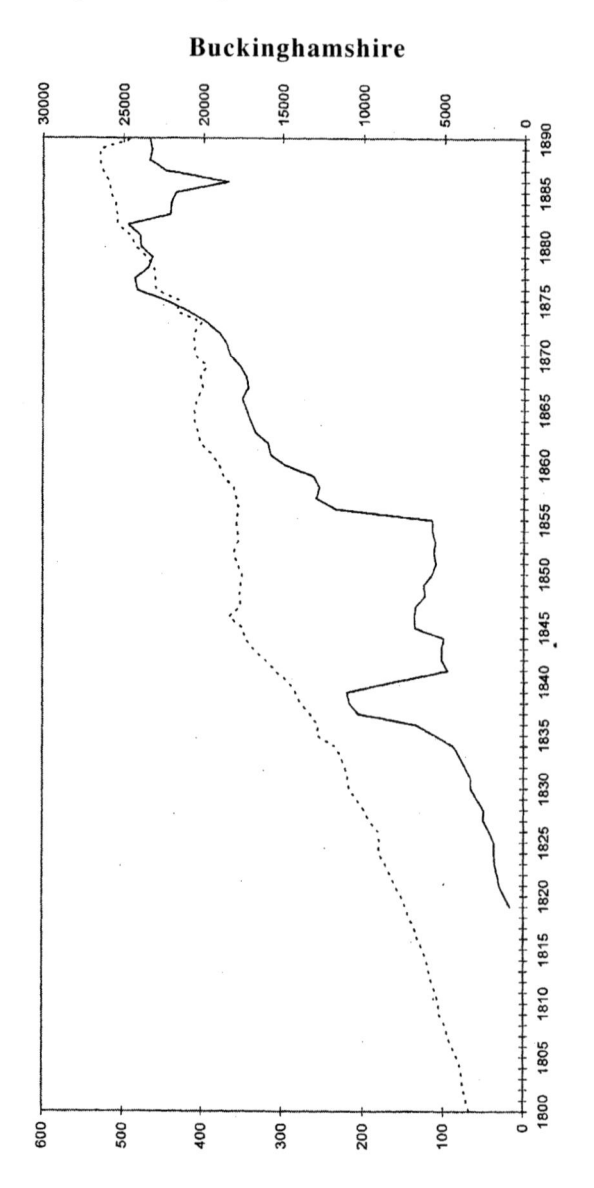

Key:
_____ County Membership of the New Connexion
.... Average Membership for the whole of the New Connexion

Buckinghamshire

Cambridgeshire

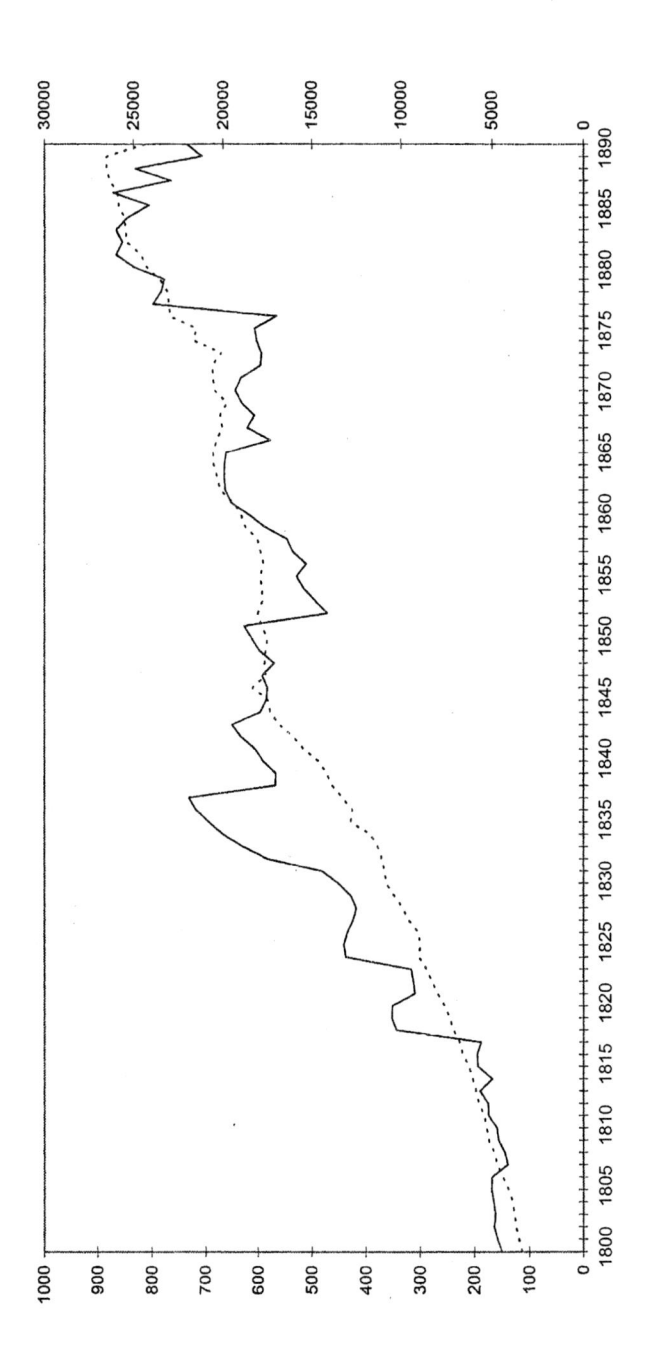

Cheshire

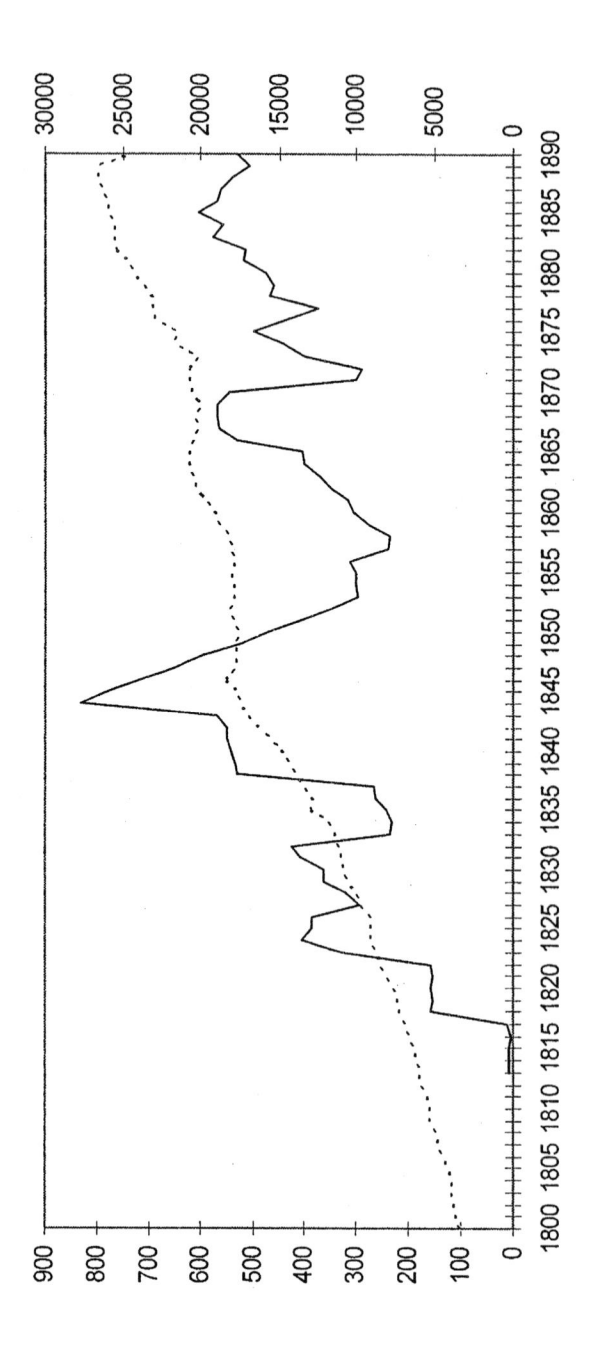

Derbyshire

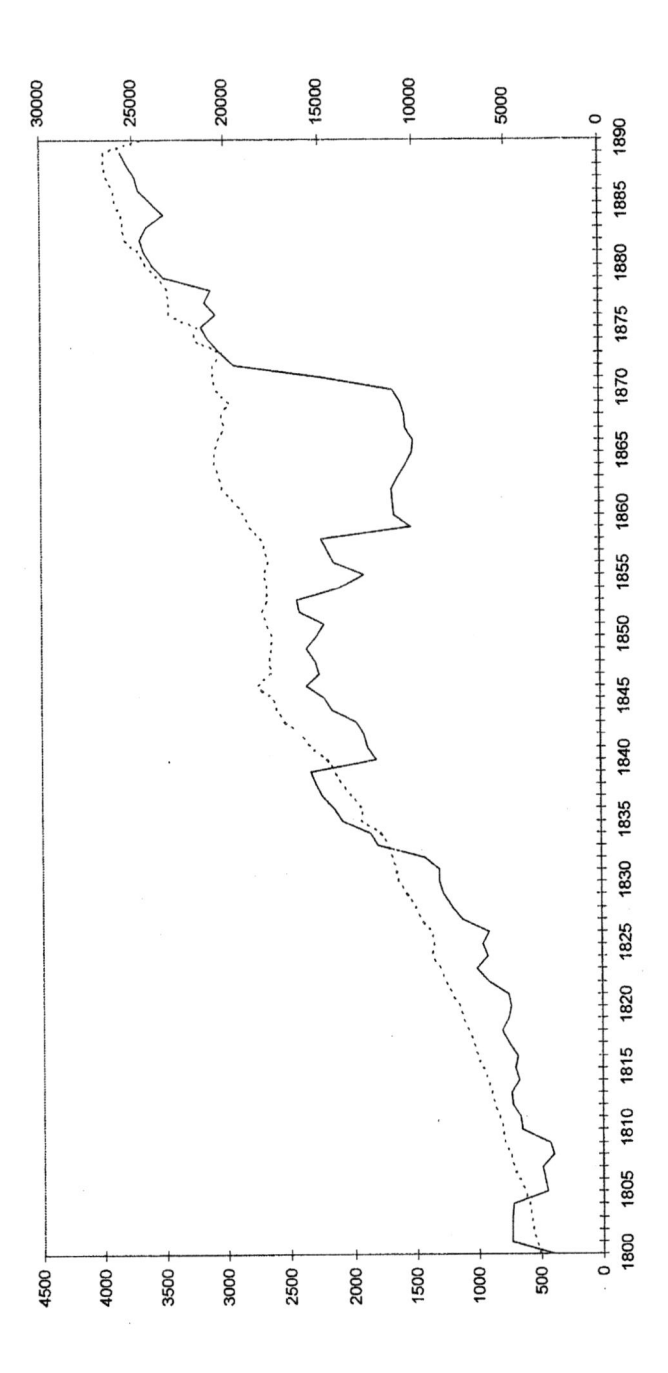

Hampshire

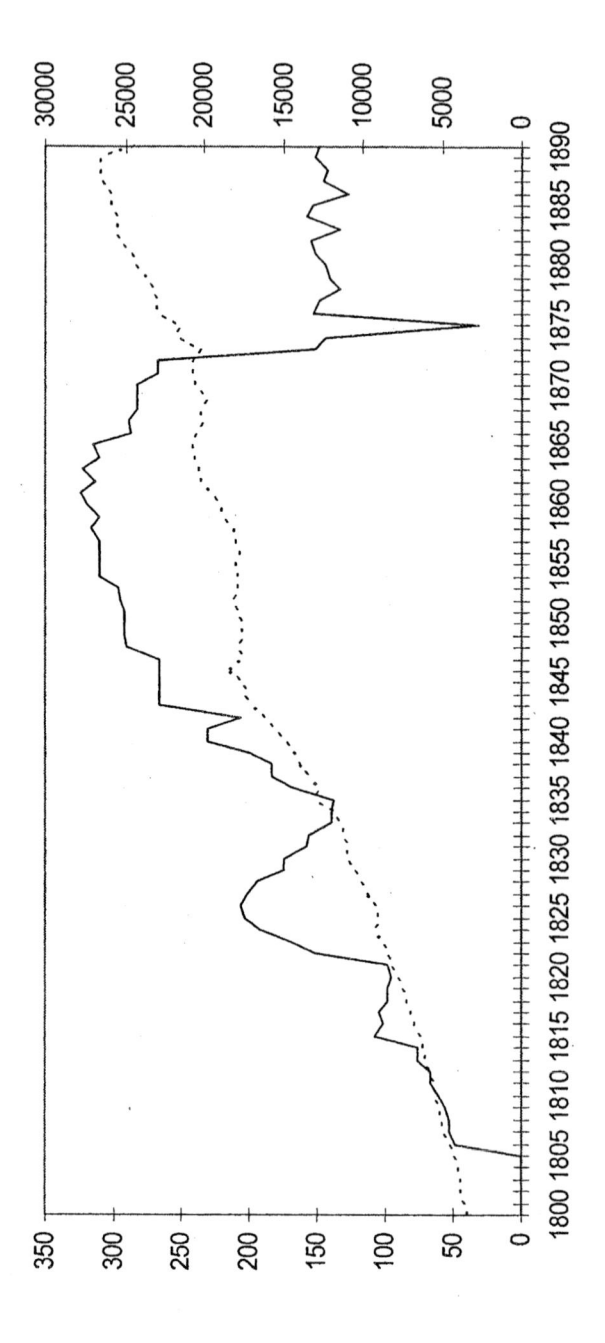

Hertfordshire

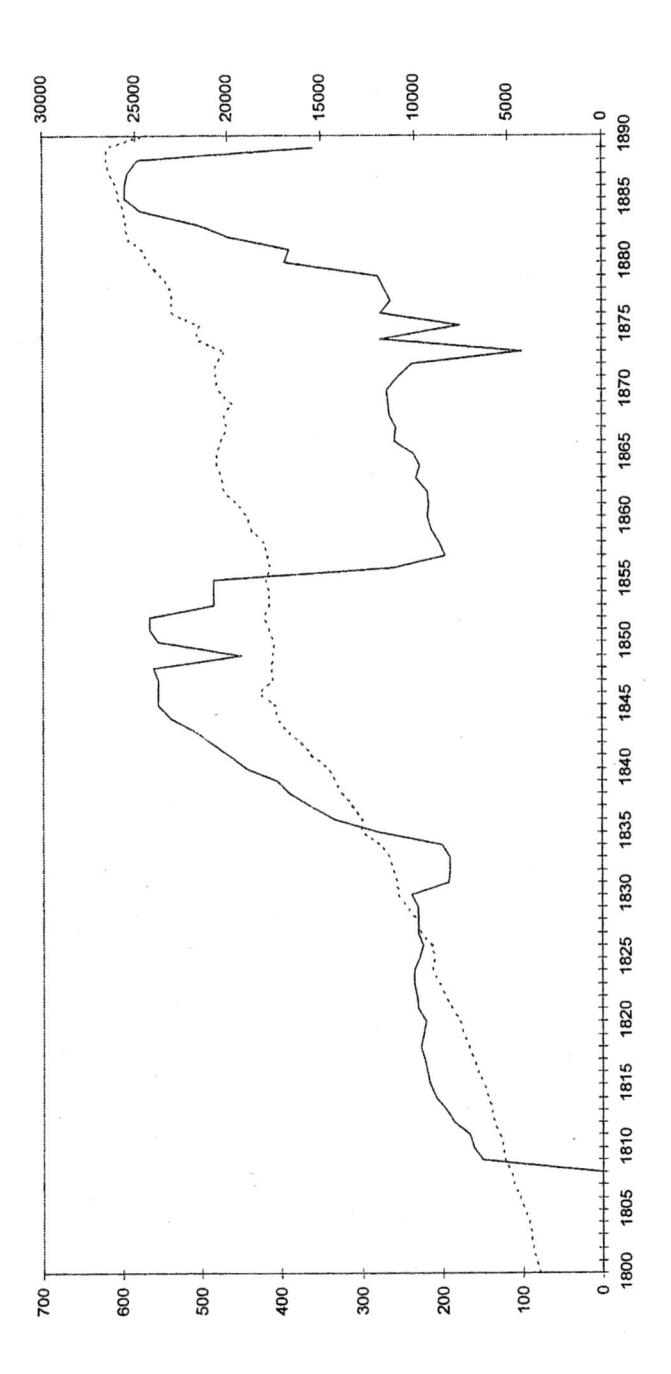

Huntingdonshire

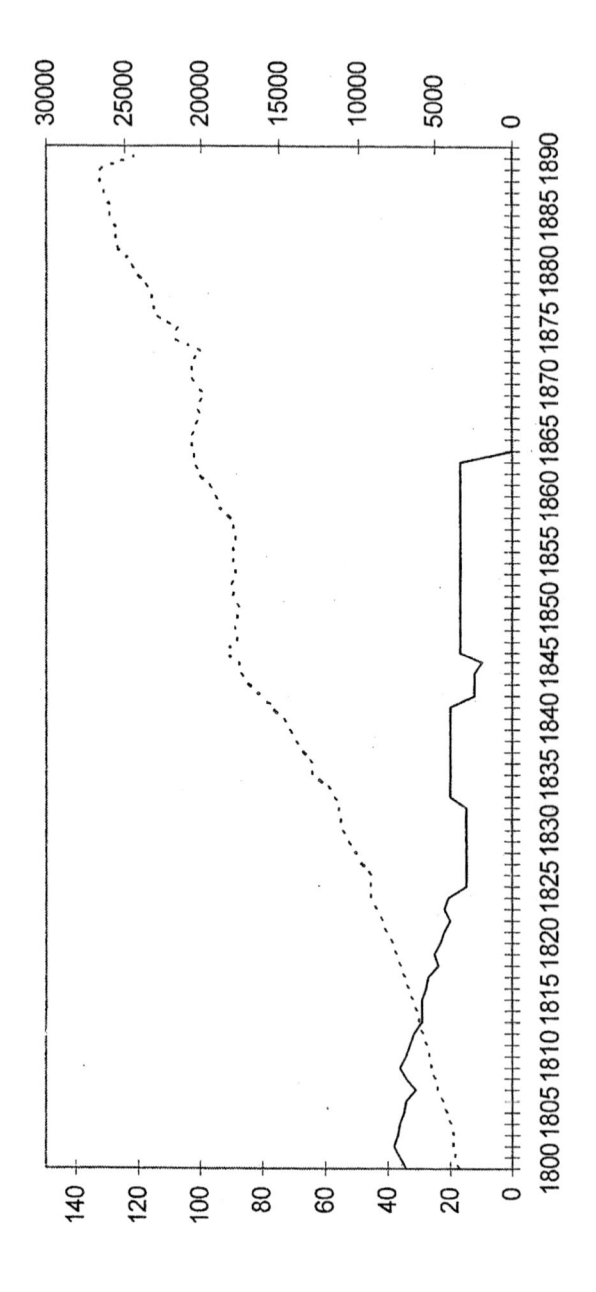

Appendixes 223

Isle of Wight

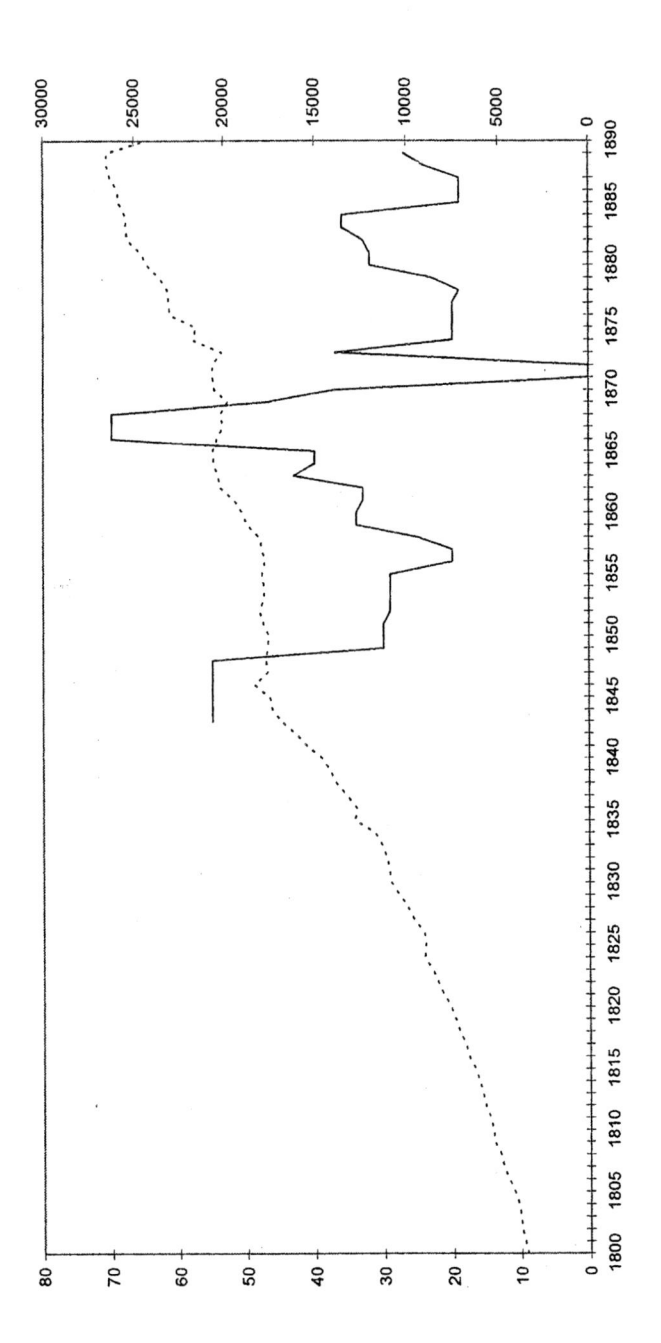

Kent

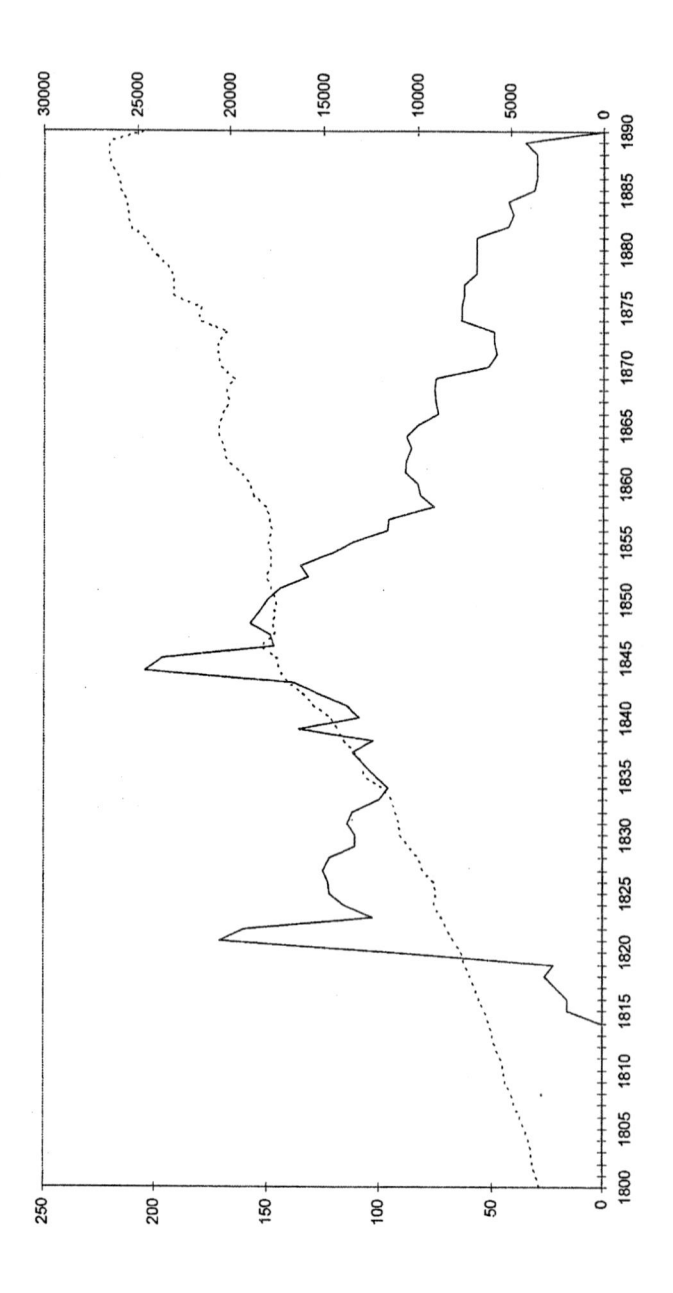

Appendixes 225

Lancashire

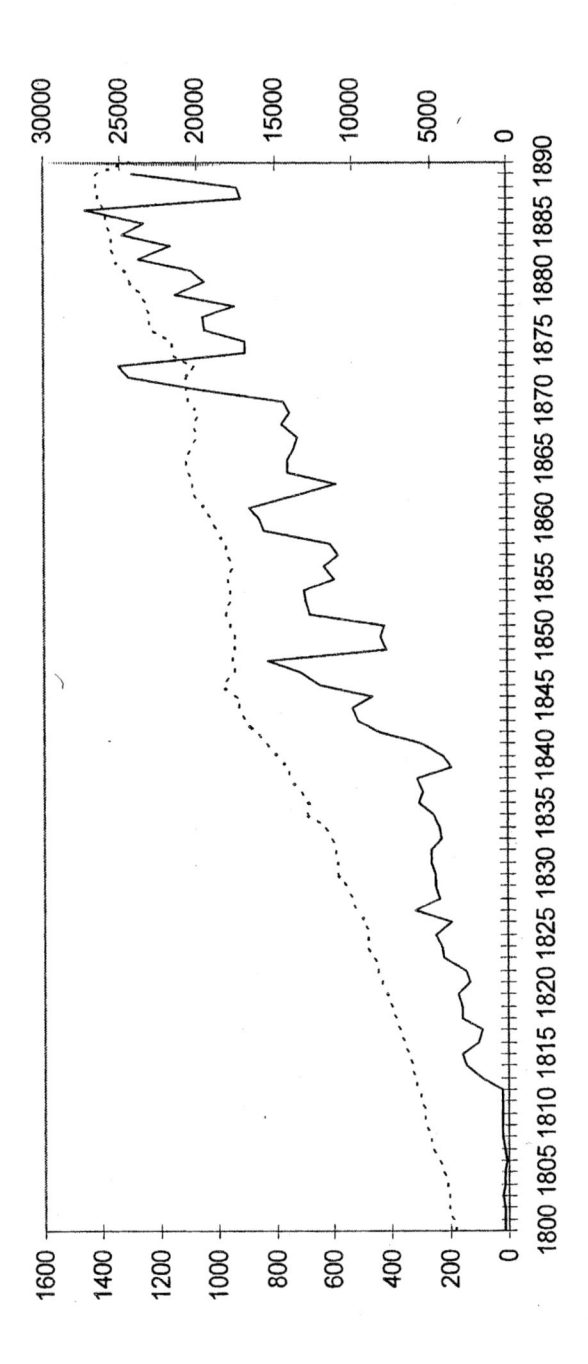

Leicestershire

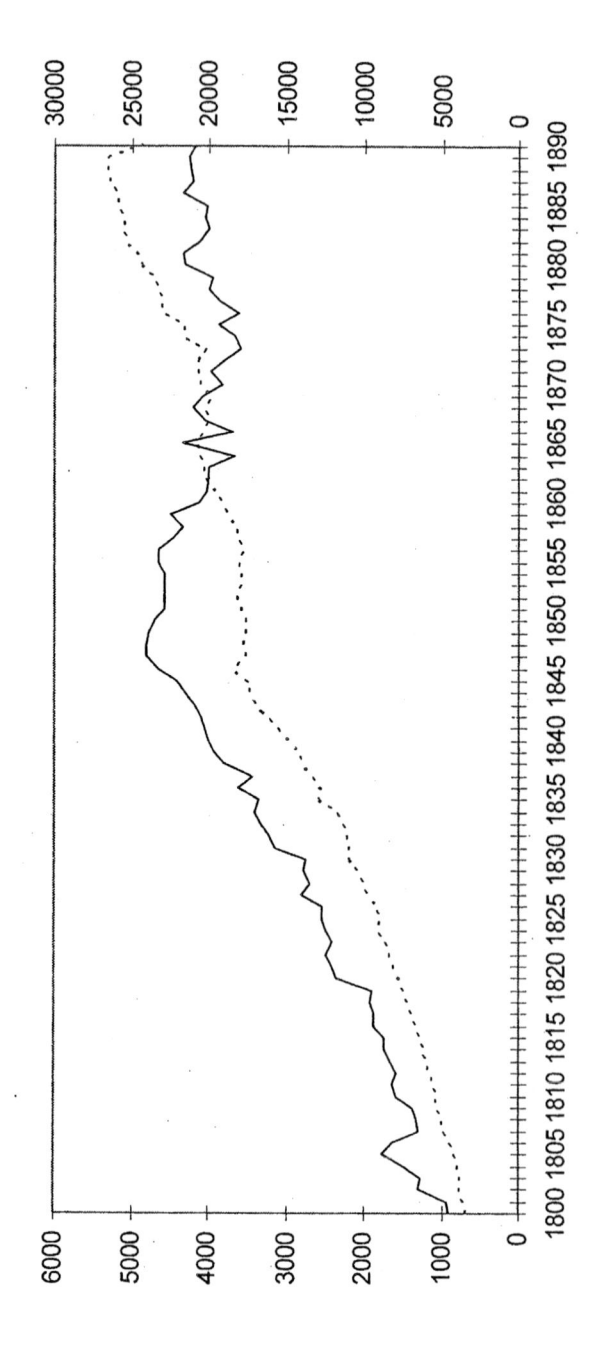

Lincolnshire

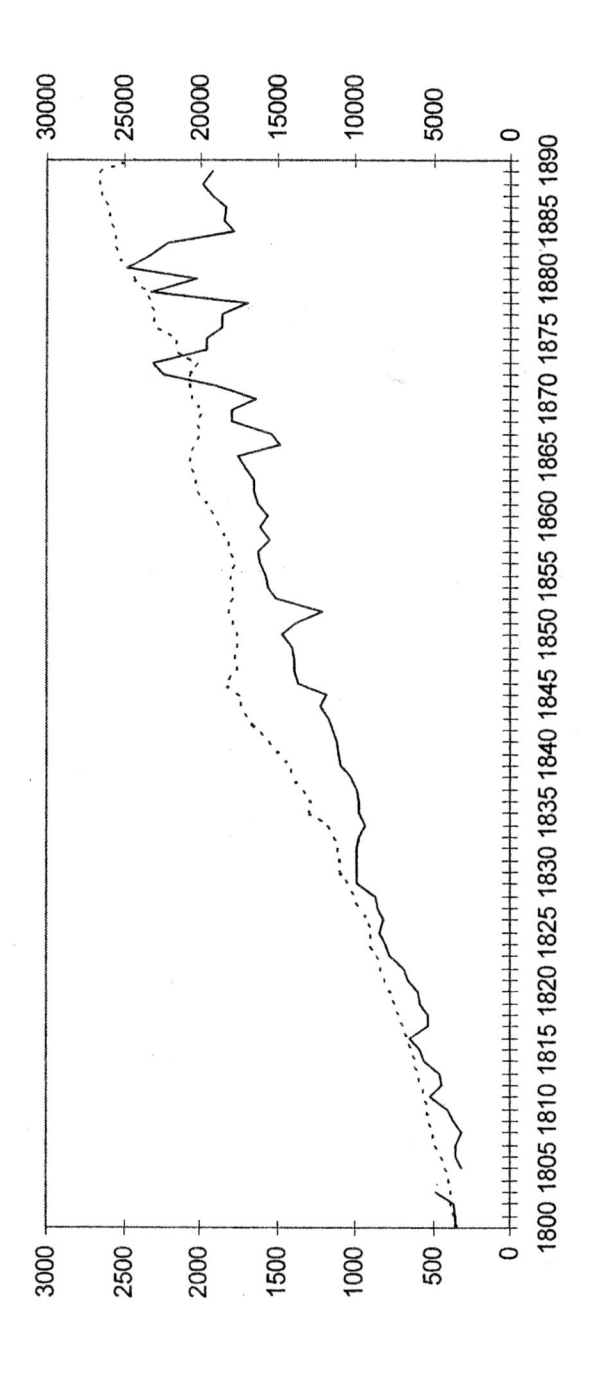

Middlesex

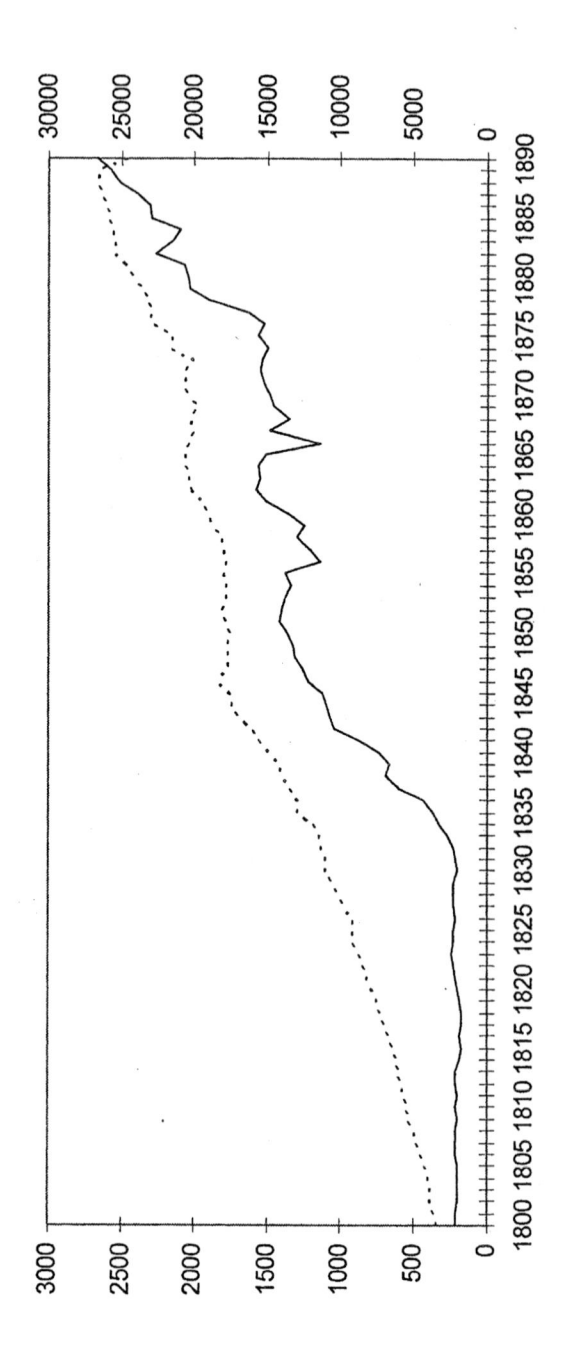

Norfolk

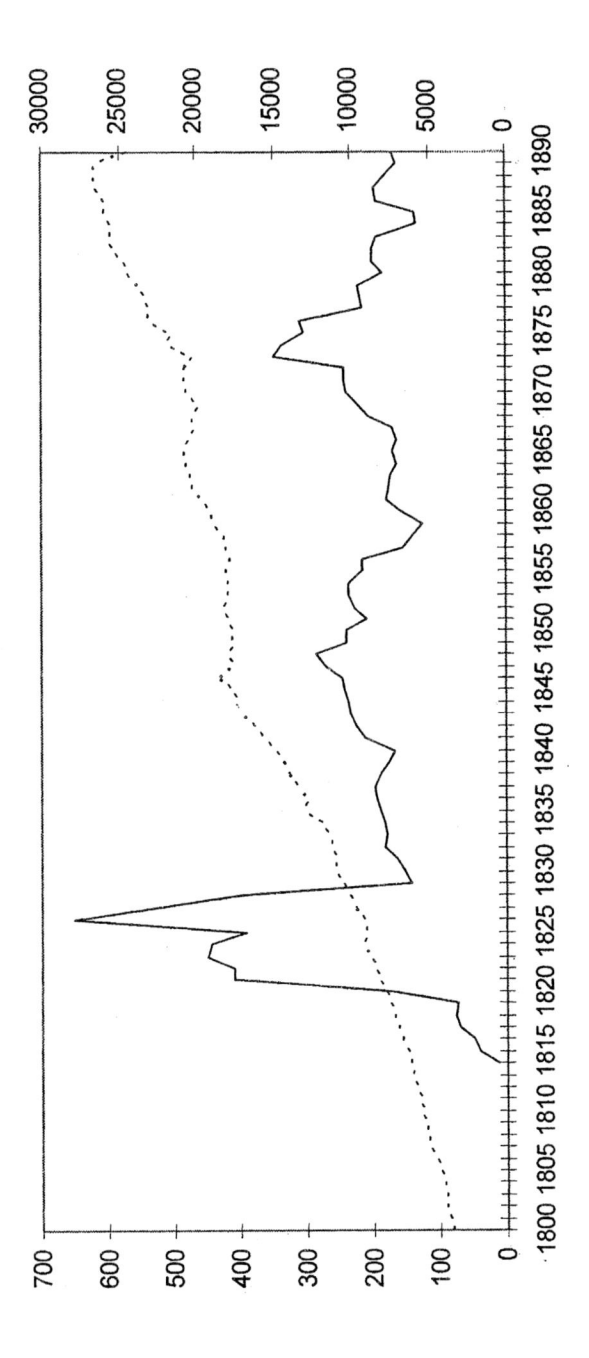

Northamptonshire

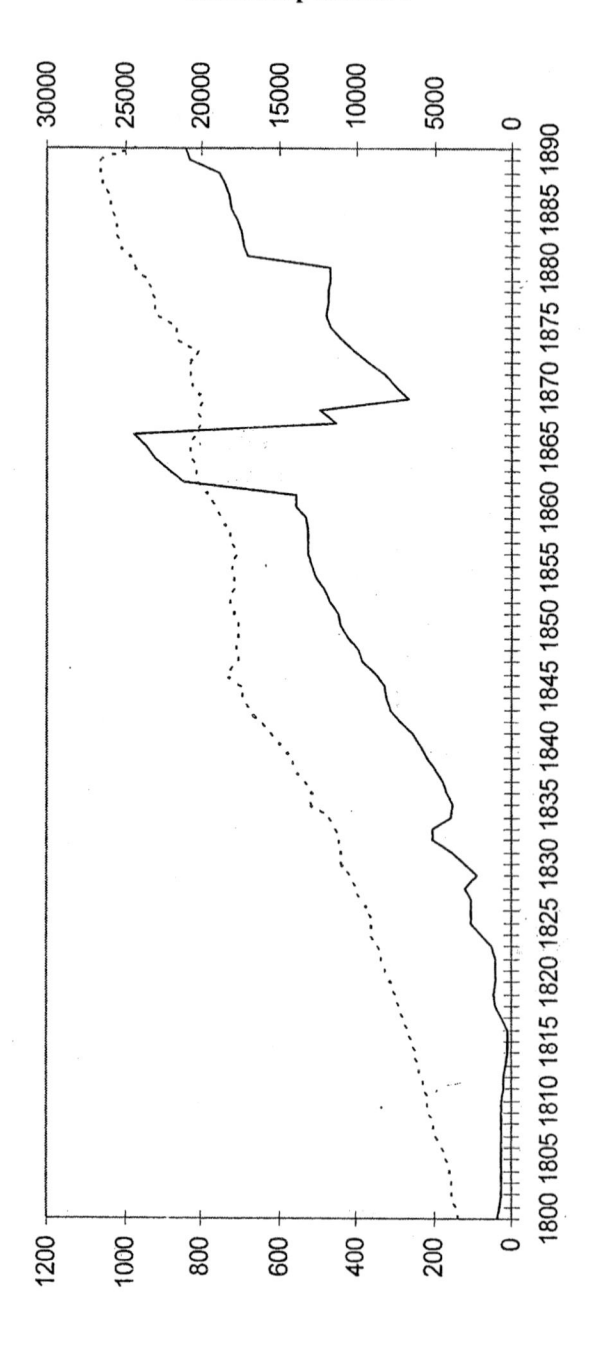

Nottinghamshire

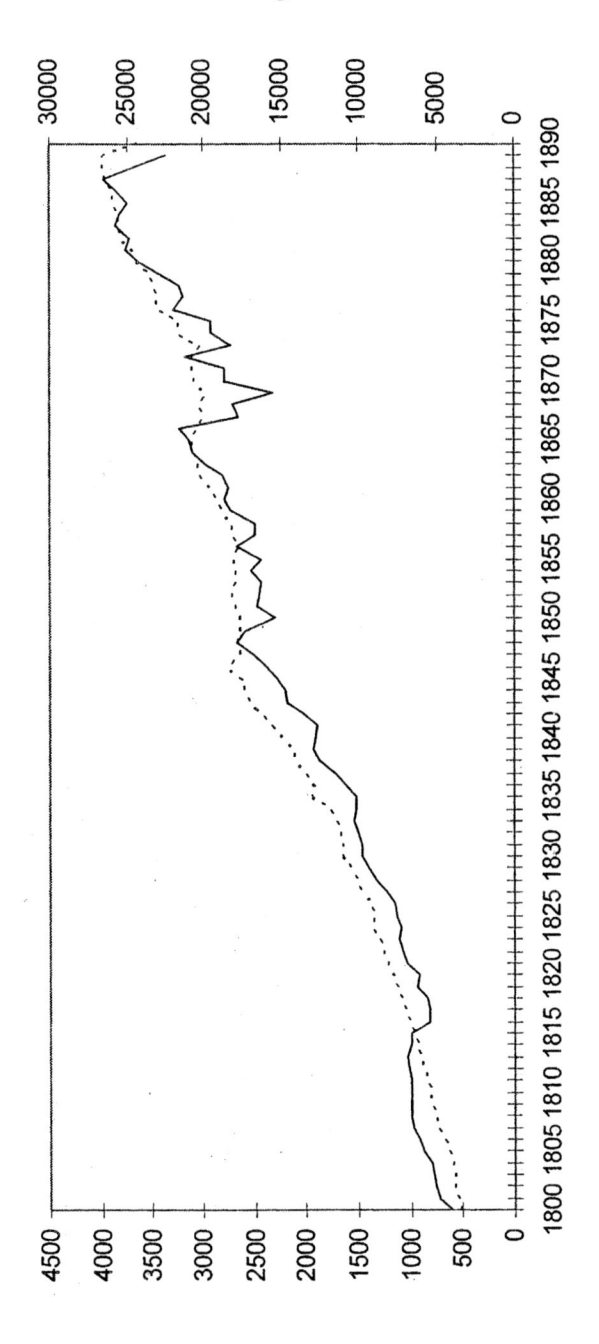

Rutland

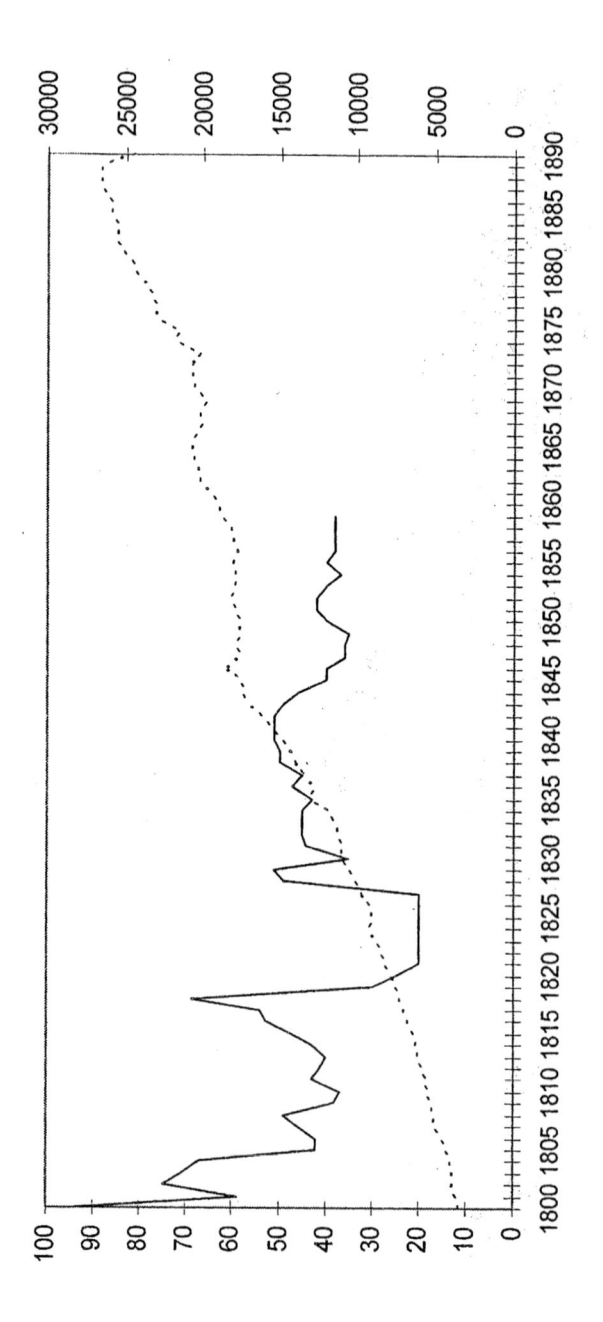

Scotland

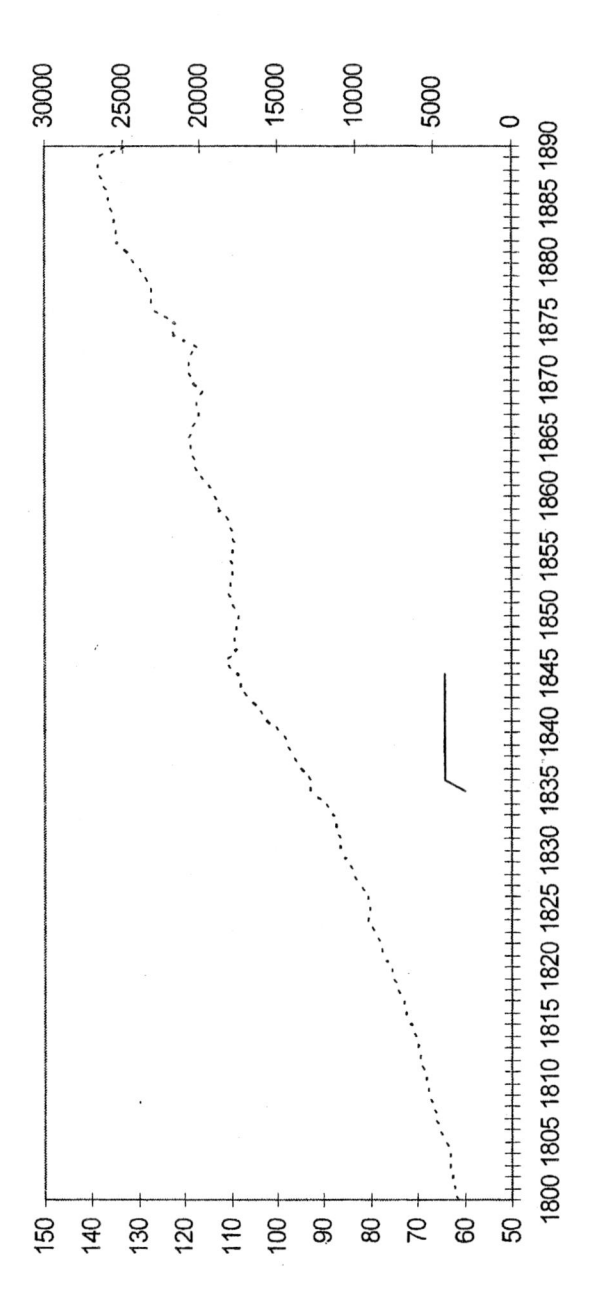

Suffolk

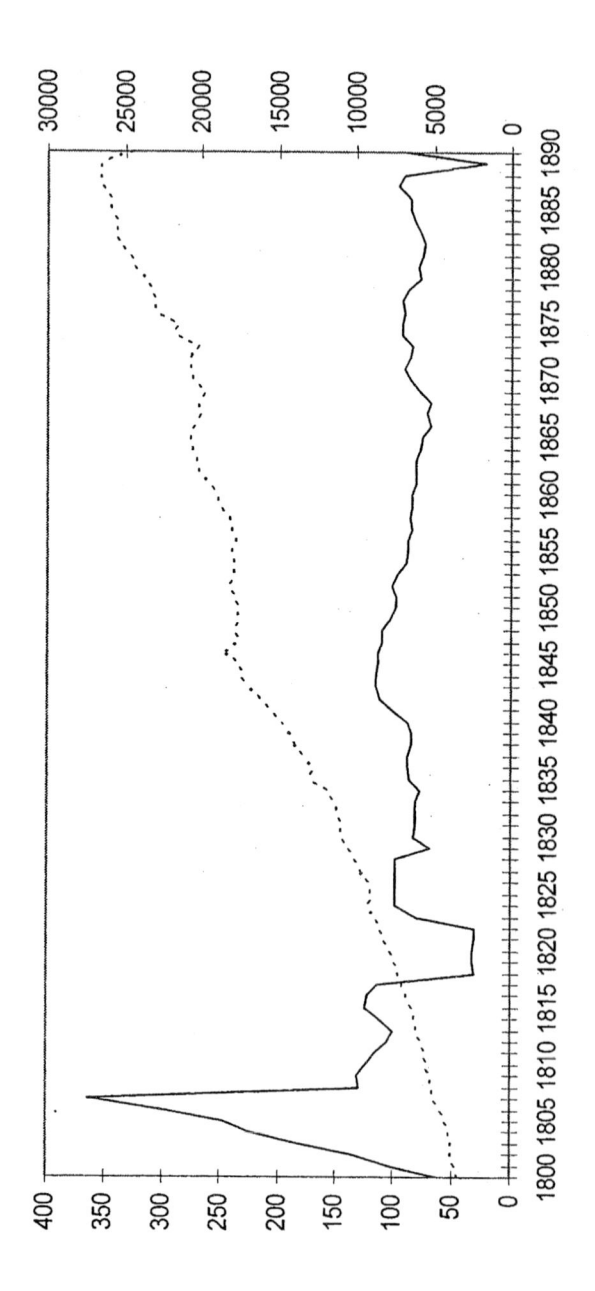

Appendixes 235

Staffordshire

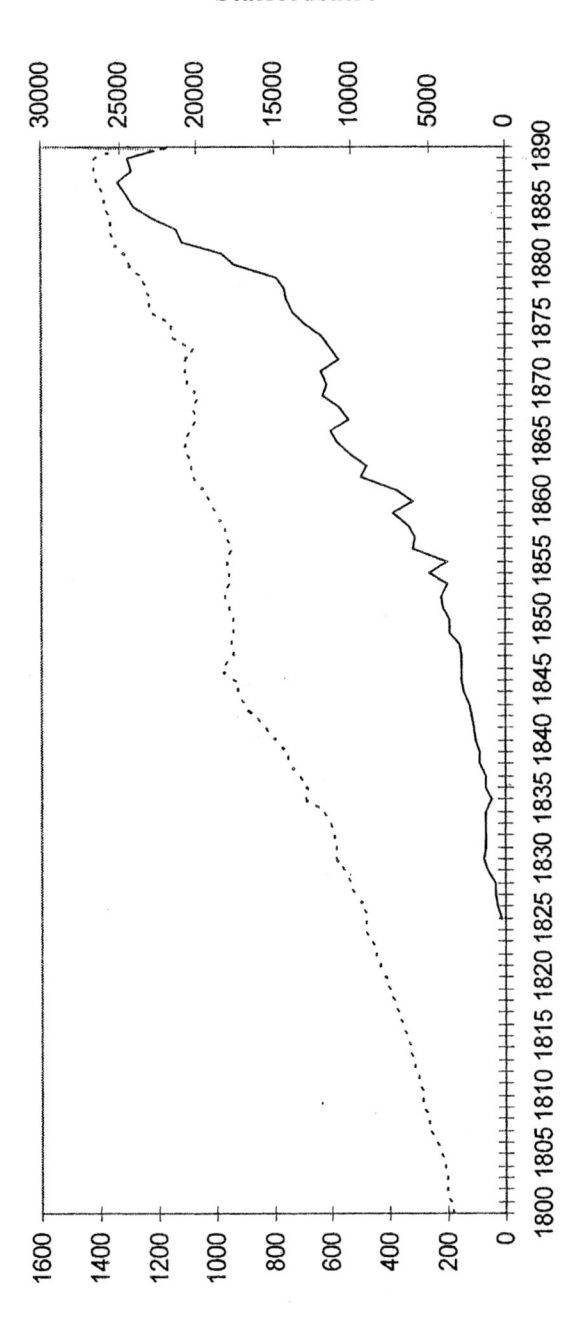

Warwickshire

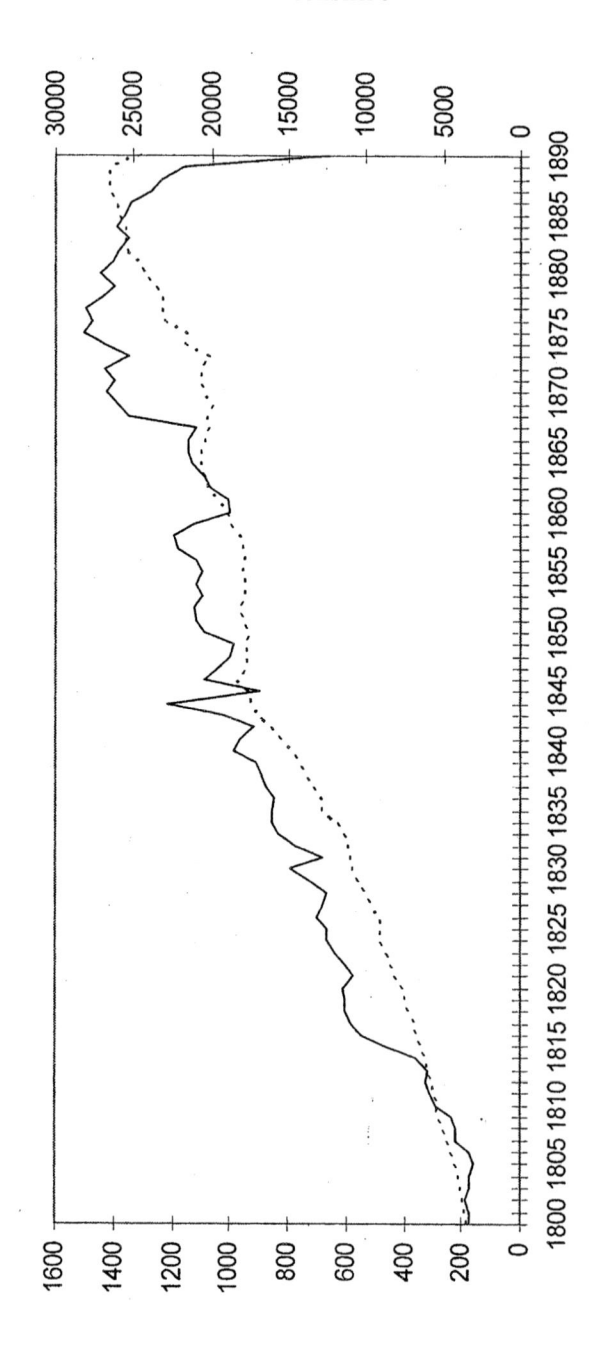

Wiltshire

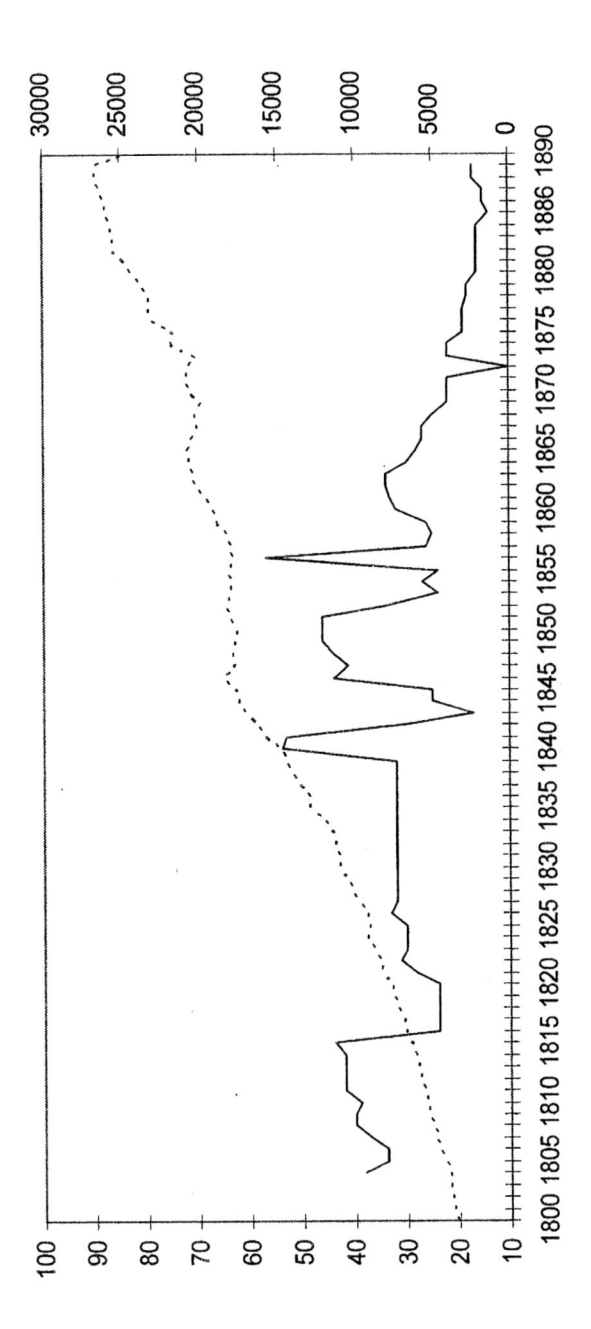

Worcestershire

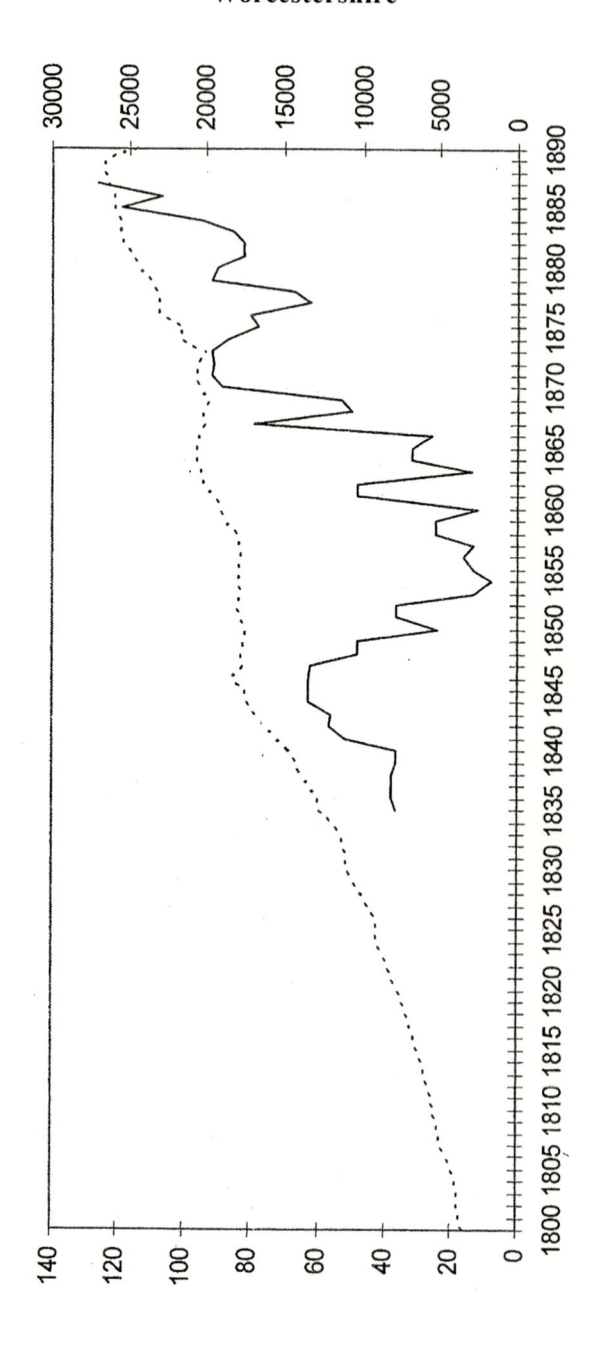

Yorkshire

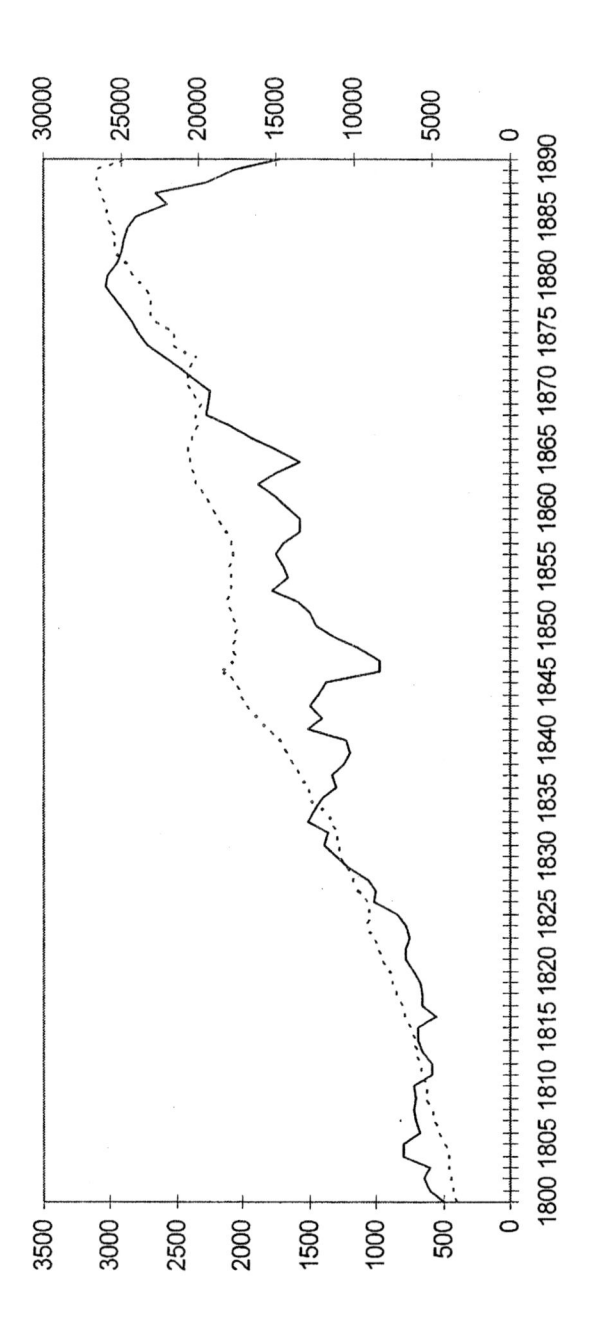

Appendix 7

Number of Baptisms per 1,000 Members. Age of Church by Size of Church

The following tables set out the number of baptisms per 1,000 members (a measure of recruiting efficiency), by the age of the church in years and size of membership. '**Age**' is the age of the church from its foundation, '**S**' is the size of the church in terms of membership.

1850	Age 0-10	Age 11-20	Age 21-30	Age 31-40	Age 41+
S1-49	4.82	2.41	3.72	8.41	1.38
S50-99	8.95	7.11	3.72	4.04	4.89
S100-149	6.76	2.52	1.25	5.04	4.49
S150-199	9.68	4.19	6.98	7.69	7.85
S200-299	2.87	—	7.33	2.92	5.10
S300-399	—	5.84	—	3.43	4.14
S400-499	11.19	—	—	3.61	3.80
S500-749	3.52	2.88	—	—	3.93
S750-999	—	—	—	—	1.71
S1000+	—	—	—	—	5.29

1860	Age 0-10	Age 11-20	Age 21-30	Age 31-40	Age 41+
S1-49	6.53	5.58	5.94	5.97	6.02
S50-99	9.34	—	9.34	5.87	8.61
S100-149	10.67	15.10	8.43	8.66	12.39
S150-199	25.00	—	2.50	—	5.53
S200-299	7.73	7.13	9.06	7.31	4.86
S300-399	15.62	—	8.75	—	4.75
S400-499	—	—	—	10.85	—
S500-749	6.16	—	—	6.88	8.85
S750-999	—	—	—	7.79	—
S1000+	—	—	—	—	7.38

1870	Age 0-10	Age 11-20	Age 21-30	Age 31-40	Age 41+
S1-49	1.16	2.92	5.42	5.62	1.00
S50-99	2.93	14.36	5.88	2.72	2.62
S100-149	1.29	—	11.48	2.32	5.58
S150-199	3.37	—	14.26	4.36	5.46
S200-299	3.76	—	1.53	5.61	5.09
S300-399	3.82	—	—	8.92	4.22
S400-499	4.59	—	—	2.64	5.23
S500-749	6.39	—	5.03	3.17	10.36
S750-999	—	—	—	5.88	5.69
S1000+	—	—	—	—	5.31

1880	Age 0-10	Age 11-20	Age 21-30	Age 31-40	Age 41+
S1-49	3.88	2.79	3.19	2.61	—
S50-99	4.59	—	7.45	3.47	3.65
S100-149	3.09	4.62	5.	—	3.14
S150-199	—	4.06	5.50	4.47	6.69
S200-299	2.42	—	9.92	10.92	2.97
S300-399	8.06	—	13.94	5.10	5.10
S400-499	—	—	—	3.63	5.05
S500-749	4.53	—	—	—	4.66
S750-999	6.70	—	11.03	—	7.09
S1000+	—	—	—	9.05	6.29

1890	Age 0-10	Age 11-20	Age 21-30	Age 31-40	Age 41+
S1-49	12.21	–	–	0.35	4.81
S50-99	–	6.06	5.04	15.35	2.19
S100-149	3.80	–	8.28	7.31	1.02
S150-199	9.16	–	4.37	5.17	6.40
S200-299	4.23	–	4.18	9.09	5.17
S300-399	1.23	–	9.05	3.23	4.54
S400-499	–	–	–	2.88	1.75
S500-749	3.34	–	–	–	5.58
S750-999	–	–	–	–	–
S1000+	–	–	4.98	4.46	4.51

It will be seen from the above that no clear pattern emerges as to a most efficient size or age for churches in terms of recruitment. The tendency for the younger smaller churches to be more efficient in the early part of the period shifts to the larger older churches in the latter part. When Joseph Fletcher suggested the most efficient size as one hundred to two hundred he was not too wide of the mark.[1] For a discussion on size and age as factors in growth see Dean R. Hoge and David A. Roozen, *Understanding Church Growth and Decline, 1950–1978*.[2]

---

[1] Joseph Fletcher, 'Church Leakage its causes and cure', *GBM* (1890), pp. 211, 214.
[2] Dean R. Hoge and David A. Roozen (eds), *Understanding Church Growth and Decline, 1950–1978* (New York: The Pilgrim Press, 1979, 2nd edn, 1981), p. 46

Select Bibliography

Manuscript Sources

Budge, Thomas, 'Records of the most Material affairs belonging to the Baptist Congregation at Melbourne in Derbyshire. Extracts from the Church Book 1774–1832', Unpublished MS. East Midland Baptist Archive

Taylor-Hall, S., 'Records of the First General Baptist Church in Derby', MS (1942), 1. East Midland Baptist Archive

Lincolnshire and Cambridgeshire Sunday School Union Minute Book, 31 July 1857–24 July 1913. Lincolnshire Record Office, 17/Bapt/3/

Minute Book of the Lancashire and Yorkshire Conference 1873–1892. Angus Library, Regent's Park College, Oxford

Non-parochial Registers. Public Record Office, London (Registrar General = RG)
  Gosberton RG4 2829
  Hinckley RG4 1435
  Fleckney RG4 1435
  Rothley and Sileby RG4 1307
  Wadsworth and Birchcliff RG4 2775

Church Books

Archdeacon Lane Minute Book, Leicester Record Office, N/B/179/101-8
  June 1806–June 1827, N/B/179/101
  July 1827–December 1840, N/B/179/102
  May 1831–December 1838, N/B/179/103
  January 1839–March 1848, N/B/179/104
  December 1840–June 1858, N/B/179/105
  April 1848–June 1863, N/B/179/106
  June 1858– December 1892, N/B/179/107
  June 1882– December 1885, N/B/179/108
  (Overlaps exist with some books)
Ashby and Packington Church Book. Leicester Record Office, N/9/1
The Church of Christ at Beeston denominated General Baptists (Nether Street)
  Book 1 1804–1837. Nottingham Record Office, BP/29/4
  Book 2 1837–1859. Nottingham Record Office, BP/29/5
  Book 3 1866–1874. Nottingham Record Office, BP/29/7
  Book 4 1884–1899. Nottingham Record Office, BP/29/8
Beeston Experience Books 1-6. Nottingham Record Office, BP10/14/1-6
Bourne Church Book 1703-1872. Bourne Baptist Church
Castle Donnington Baptist Church Books
  Book 1 17 June 1772–6 September 1807
  Book 2 20 June 1811–7 April 1816
  Book 3 5 May 1816–23 September 1821

Book 4 12 September 1830–27 December 1835
Book 5 25 January 1836–13 January 1845
Book 6 30 January 1845–19 April 1866
Book 7 5 May 1879–26 April 1896
Friar Lane Baptist Chapel Sunday School Records
  Book 1 1815–1828. Leicester Record Office, 15D/66/35
  Book 2 1828–1834. Leicester Record Office, 15D/66 /36
Gosberton Church Books. Lincolnshire County Archives.
  Book 1 1784-1836, 9/Bapt 1/1
  Book 2 1847-1878, 9/Bapt 1/3
  Book 3 1878-1896, 9/Bapt 1/4
Hyson Green, Palin Street, Nottingham, Church Book 1878–1897. Nottingham Record Office, NC/BP/38/1
Hinckley Baptist Church Book. Leicester Record Office
  Book 1 1816–1840, NB/142/1
  Book 2 1865–1881, NB/142/2
Minutes of Hugglescoote General Baptist Church. Leicester Record Office
  1823, NB/150/1-3.
Kegworth Church Book. Leicester Record Office, NB/159/1.
Leake and Wimeswold Church Book. Nottingham Record Office
  Book 1 1804–1819, BP/37/1
  Book 2 1833–1847, BP/37/2
Maltby Le Marsh Church Books. Lincolnshire County Archives
  Book 1 1773–1791, 16/Bapt/2
  Book 2 1791–, 16/Bapt /3
  Book 3 1854-1874, 16/Bapt /4
Market Harborough Church Book. Leicester Record Office, N/B/215/2
New Lenton General Baptist Church. Nottingham Record Office, NC/BP/10/5
General Baptist Preachers Union Minute Book 1849-1870. Nottingham Record Office, /BP/12/4
Retford and Gamston Church Book. Nottingham Record Office, BP/20/1-3
  Book 1 1843–1857, BP/20/2
  Book 2 1857–1893, BP/20/3
Spalding Church Book. Lincolnshire County Archives, 14 Bapt/1

Theses

F.M.W. Harrison, 'The Life and Thought of the Baptists of Nottinghamshire with Special Reference to the Period 1770–1913' (MPhil Thesis, University of Nottingham, 1972)

G. Jackson, 'The Evangelical Work of Baptists in Leicestershire 1740–1820' (MA Thesis, University of London, 1955)

John Lee, 'Baptists in Lancashire 1831–81' (PhD Thesis, University of Liverpool, 1970)

Select Bibliography 245

Michael R. Watts, 'John Clifford and Radical Nonconformity 1836–1923' (DPhil Thesis, University of Oxford, 1966)
Loren Craig Shull, 'The General Baptist Process: From Sect to Denomination' (DPhil Thesis, Southern Baptist Theological Seminary, 1985)

Published Sources
Primary Sources

Ambler, R.W. (ed.), 'Lincolnshire Returns of the Census of Religious Worship 1851', *Lincoln Record Society* 72 (Fakenham: Lincoln Record Society, 1979)
Clifford, John, *The Church of Christ: its Work Character and Message. An Address delivered at the dedication of Westbourne Park Chapel Sept 3rd* (London: Malborough, 1877)
— *The Inspiration and Authority of the Bible* (London: James Clarke, 2nd edn, 1895)
— *A New Testament Church in its Relation to the Need and Tendencies of the Age. A Statement made in connection with the laying of the memorial stone Westbourne Park Chapel July 10th 1876* (London: Yates and Alexander, 1876)
— *The Churches War with National Intemperance. A paper read at the conference of the British Total Abstinence Association held at Newcastle Oct 8th* (London: n.p., 1874)
— *Jesus and Modern Social Life* (London: Marlborough, 1872)
— *Thou Shalt not Hide Thyself. An Argument and an Appeal for the Cure of Britain's Intemperance* (London: W. Tweedie, 1877)
— *Religious Life in the Rural Districts of England* (London: Yates and Alexander, 1876)
— *The Salvation Army: Its Genesis, Aims, Principles Methods and Results* (London: Griffiths, 1920)
— *The Work of Christian Leaders* (London: Marlborough, 1879)
Cox, Samuel, *Expositions* (London: T. Fisher Unwin, 2nd edn, 1891)
— *The Hebrew Twins: A Vindication of God's Way with Jacob and Esau* (London: n.p., 1894)
— *The House and its Builder with other discourses* (London: n.p., 1889)
— *Salvator Mundi or is Christ the Saviour of All Men?* (London, 1877)
Deacon, Samuel, '*A Cabinet of Jewels*' (Barton Memorials, 1; London: Eliot Stock, Leicester: W. Buck, Winks and Son, 1889)
— *A Comprehensive Account of the General Baptists with respect to principle and practice in which are displayed their manner of Worship, Church order and Discipline. By a mechanic who was long conversant with them.* (Coventry, 1795)
Taylor, Dan., *The Consistent Christian or Truth, Peace, Holiness, Unanimity, Steadfastness and Zeal Recommended to Professors of Christianity. The Substance of Five Sermons by Dan Taylor to which is Prefixed a Brief account of the Authors removal from Wadsworth to Halifax* (Leeds, 1784)
— *A True Statement of the Leading Religious Sentiments of the New Connexion of General Baptists By a Friend to the Truth* (Dudley, 1824)

- *The Faithful and Wise Steward. An address to Young Ministers and Others at Conningsley in Lincolnshire* (Leeds: 1776)
- *The Mourning Parent Comforted* (n.pl., 1768)
- *The Nature and Importance of Preparatory Studies Prior to entering the Ministry* (London: n.p., 1807)
- *Our Saviour's Commission To His Ministers Explained and Improved: The Substance of a Sermon delivered at Canterbury and in Worship Street London. At the Administration of the Ordinance of Baptism* (Leeds: n.p., n.d.)
- *The Respective Duties of Ministers and People Briefly explained and Enforced. The Substance of Two Discourses, delivered at Great-Yarmouth, in Norfolk Jan. 9th, 1775 at the ordination of the Rev. Mr. Benjamin Worship, to the Pastoral Office* (Leeds, 1775)
- *A Sermon Occasioned by the Death of Mrs. Elizabeth Taylor who departed this life Oct 22nd 1793 in the 49th year of her age. With a short account of her life and a description of her character* (London, 1794)

Anonymous Published Material

A Brief Sketch of the Doctrine and Discipline of the General Baptist Churches, (Midland Tract Society: J.F. Winks. Leicester, n.d.). General Baptist Tracts CLIV No. 6, Angus Library, Regent's Park College, Oxford

Minutes of The General Baptist Association held at Boston Lincolnshire April 27-28 (1785)

Secondary Sources

[Anon.], *The History and Development of the Hosiery Industry in Leicestershire* (Huntingdon: Priory Press, 1990)

Ambler, R.W., *Lincolnshire Returns of the Census of Religious Worship 1851* (Lincoln Record Society ,72; Norfolk: Lincoln Record Society, 1979)

Arnold, Stuart, *Built upon the Foundation: Being the History of the General Baptist Church at Hucknall Nottinghamshire, 1849-1949* (Nottingham: Nottinghamshire. Newspapers, 1948)

Ashby, Douglas, *Friar Lane: The Story of Three Hundred Years* (London: Carey Kingsgate Press, 1951)

Bateman, Charles T., *John Clifford Free Church Leader and Preacher* (London: National Council of the Evangelical Free Churches, 1904)

Shipley, C.E., (ed.) *The Baptists of Yorkshire* (London: Kingsgate Press, 1912)

Beckett, J.V., 'The East Midlands from A.D. 1000', in Barry Cunliffe and David Hey (eds), *A Regional History of England* (London and New York: Longman, 1988)

Bebbington, D.W., *Evangelicalism in Modern Britain: A History from the 1730s to the 1980s* (London: Unwin Hyman, 1989)

Select Bibliography 247

— *The Nonconformist Conscience: Chapel and Politics 1870–1914* (London: George Allan & Unwin, 1982)
Berger, Peter L., *The Noise of Solemn Assemblies* (New York: Doubleday, 1961)
Best, Geoffrey, *Mid-Victorian Britain 1851–75* (Glasgow: Fontana, 11th edn, 1971)
Billington, R.J., *The Liturgical Movement and Methodism* (London: Epworth Press, 1969)
Binfield, Clyde, *So Down to Prayers: Studies in English Nonconformity 1780–1920* (London: Dent & Sons, 1977)
Briggs, J.H.Y., *The English Baptists of the Nineteenth Century* (A History of the English Baptists, 3; Didcot: Baptist Historical Society, 1994)
Briggs, John H.Y. and Ian Sellers, *Victorian Nonconformity* (Documents of Modern History; London: Edward Arnold, 1973)
Brown, Colin, *Philosophy and the Christian Faith* (London: IVP, 1969)
Brown, Kenneth D., *A Social History of the Nonconformist Ministry in England and Wales 1800–1930* (Oxford: Clarendon Press, 1988)
Brown, Raymond, *The English Baptists of the Eighteenth Century* (A History of the English Baptists, 2; London: Baptist Historical Society, 1986)
Byrt, G.W., *John Clifford: A Fighting Free Churchman* (London: Kingsgate Press, 1947)
Chamberlayne, John H., 'From Sect to Church in British Methodism', *British Journal of Sociology* 15 (1964), pp. 139-149
Church, Leslie F., *The Early Methodist People* (Fernley-Hartley Lecture; London: Epworth Press, 1948)
Cliff, Philip, *The Rise and the Development of the Sunday School Movement in England 1780–1980* (Redhill: National Christian Education Council, 1986)
Cook, Thomas, *Preacher Pastor Mechanic: Memoir of the late Mr. Samuel Deacon,— Nearly Forty Years Pastor and Fifty Years a Member of the General Baptist Church Barton Leicestershire* (Leicester: W. Buck late Winkes and Co., 1888)
Cooper, Thomas, *Life of Thomas Cooper written by Himself* (London, 1872)
Cosslett, Tess (ed.), *Science and Religion in the Nineteenth Century* (Cambridge: Cambridge University Press, 1954)
Court, W.H.B., *A Concise Economic History of Britain From 1750 to Recent Time* (Cambridge: Cambridge University Press, 1964)
Cragg, G.R., *The Church and the Age of Reason 1648–1789* (The Pelican History of the Church 4; Middlesex: Pelican, 1966)
Cross, F.L. (ed.), *Oxford Dictionary of the Christian Church* (Oxford: Oxford University Press, 2nd edn, 1978)
Currie, Robert, *Methodism Divided: A Study in the Sociology of Ecumenicalism* (London: Faber and Faber, 1968)
Currie, Robert, A. Gilbert and L. Horsley, *Churches and Churchgoers: Patterns of Church Growth in the British Isles since 1700* (Oxford: Clarendon Press, 1977)
Curtis, J., *A Topographical History of the County of Leicester: the ancient part compiled from Parliamentary and other documents and the modern for actual*

Survey by J. Curtis (Ashby-de-la-Zouch: W. Hextall/London: Sherwood, Gilbert & Piper, 1831)

Deacon, John, 'A History of the General Baptist Churches in the Counties of Leicester, Warwick, Derby, Nottingham, &c Usually denominated The New Connection', *General Baptist Magazine* (1798), pp. 157-190, 181-190, 225-230, 274-282, 322-326, 357-365, 404-408, 503-505; (1799) 20-25, 54-58, 150-155

Durkheim, E., 'The Social Foundations of Religion, Excerpts from E. Durkheim, The Elementary Forms of the Religious Life', in Rowland Robertson (ed.), *Sociology of Religion* (London: Penguin, 1971)

East, W.G. and G.H. Dury (eds), *The East Midlands and the Peak Regions of the British Isles* (London and Edinburgh: Thomas Nelson and Sons, 1963)

Elliott-Binns, L.E., *Religion in the Victorian Era* (London: Lutterworth, 1946)

— *The Early Evangelicals: A Religious Social Study* (London: Lutterworth, 1955)

Everitt, Alan, *The Pattern of Rural Dissent; the Nineteenth Century* (Department of English Local History Occasional Papers 2nd series; Leicester: University Press, 1972)

Felkin, W.A., *A History of the Machine-Wrought Hosiery and Lace Manufactures* (London: Longman Green, 1867)

Flinn, M.W., *British Population Growth 1700–1850* (London, Basingstoke: MacMillian Press, 1976)

Fuller, Andrew, 'Gospel Worthy of all Acceptation or the Duty of Sinners to Believe in Jesus Christ', in A.G. Fuller (ed.), *The Complete Works of Andrew Fuller with a Memoir of his Life* (3 vols; London: Henry G. Bohn, 1845)

Gay, John. D., *The Geography of Religion in England* (London: Duckworth, 1971)

Gilbert, A.D., *Religion and Society in Industrial England Church Chapel and Social Change 1740–1914* (London: New York: Longman, 1976)

Goadby, Bertha and Lilian Goadby, *Not Saints but Men or the Story of the Goadby Ministers* (London: Kingsgate Press, n.d.)

Godfrey, J.R., *Historic Memorials of Barton and Melbourne General Baptist Churches* (London: Buck/Leicester: Winks and Son, 1891)

Grant, J.W., *Free Churchmanship in England 1870–1940* (London: Independent Press, n.d.)

Hayden, Roger, 'Baptists Covenants and Confessions', in Paul S. Fiddes *et al.*, *Bound to Love* (London: Baptist Union, 1985), pp. 24-36

Harrison, F.W., *It All Began Here: The Story of The East Midland Baptist Association* (Worcester: East Midland Baptist Association, 1986)

Heasman, Kathleen, *Evangelicals in Action* (London: Geoffrey Bles, 1962)

Johnson, Mark D., *The Dissolution of Dissent, 1850–1918* (New York: Garland, 1987)

Kent, John H.S., *Holding the Fort: Studies in Victorian Revivalism* (London: Epworth Press, 1978)

Kruppa, Patrica Stallings, *Charles Haddon Spurgeon: A Preacher's Progress* (New York and London: n.p., 1982)

Lacqueur., T.W., *Religion And Respectability: Sunday Schools and the Working Class Culture, 1780–1850* (Yale: Yale University Press, 1976)
Lovegrove, Deryck W., *Established Church, Sectarian People: Itinerancy and the Transformation of English Dissent, 1780–1830*, (Cambridge: Cambridge University Press, 1988)
Marchant, James, *Dr. John Clifford* (London: Cassell, 1924)
McBeth, H. Leon, *The Baptist Heritage* (Nashville, TN: Broadman Press, 1987)
— *A Source Book for Baptist Heritage* (Nashville, TN: Broadman Press, 1987)
McGlothlin, W.J., *Baptist Confessions of Faith* (London: Baptist Historical Society, 1911)
McLeod, Hugh, *Class and Religion in the Late Victorian City* (London: Croom Helm, 1974)
— *Religion and the Working Class in Nineteenth Century Britain* (London: Macmillan, 1984)
McGavran, Donald, *Understanding Church Growth* (Grand Rapids, MI: Eerdmans, 1970)
Mitchell, B.R. and Deane Phyllis, *Abstract of British Historical Statistics* (Cambridge: Cambridge University Press, 1971)
Muelder, Walter, *From Sect to Church, Religion Society and the Individual: An Introduction to the Sociology of Religion* (New York: Macmillian, 11th edn, 1968)
Munson, James, *The Nonconformists: In Search of a Lost Culture* (London: SPCK, 1991)
Nicholls, Mike, *C.H. Spurgeon: The Pastor Evangelist* (Didcot: Baptist Historical Society. 1992)
Niebuhr, H. Richard, *The Social Sources of Denominationalism* (New York: Meridan, 1972)
Nuttall, Geoffrey F., *Visible Saints: The Congregational Way, 1640–1660* (Weston Rhyn: Quinta Press, 2nd edn, 2001).
Payne, E.A., *The Baptist Union: A Short History* (London: Carey Kingsgate Press, 1959)
Palmer, Marilyn, *Framework Knitting* (Aylesbury: Shire Publications, 1984)
Pike, J.G. (ed.), *Memoirs of Joseph Freestone late Pastor of the General Baptist Church Hinckley Written by himself with extracts form his letters* (London: n.p., 1823)
Pike, John and James Pike, *A Memoir and Remains of the Late Rev. John Gregory Pike*, (London: Jarrold and Sons, 1855)
Reardon, B.M.G., *Religious Thought in the Victorian Age: A Survey from Colleridge to Gore* (London: Longman, 1980)
Reynolds, Geoffrey G., *First Among Equals: A study of the basis of Association and Oversight among Baptist Churches Bath* (Bath: Berkshire, Southern and Oxfordshire and East Gloucestershire Baptist Associations, 1993)
Rowell, Geoffrey, *Hell and the Victorians* (Oxford: Clarendon Press, 1974)

Russell, Colin A., *Cross-Currents: Interactions Between Science and Faith* (Liecester: Inter-Varsity Press, 1985)

Sellers, Ian, *Nineteenth-Century Nonconformity* (London: Edward Arnold, 1977)

Shiner, Larry, 'The Meaning of Secularization', *International Year Book for the Sociology of Religion* 3 (1967), pp. 51-60

Snell, K.D.M., *Church and Chapel in the North Midlands: Religious Observance in the Nineteenth Century* (Department of English Local History Occasional Papers, 4th Series, No. 3; Leicester: Leicester University Press. 1991),

Stapleton, J., 'Evidence to Parliamentary Inquiry into the Condition of Framework Knitters 1845', in *The History and Development of the Hosiery Industry in Leicestershire* (Huntingdon: Priory Press, 1990)

Taylor, Adam, *The History of the English General Baptists: Part Second: The New Connexion of General Baptists* (London: T. Bore, 1818)

— *Memoirs of the Rev. Dan Taylor Late Pastor of the General Baptist Church Whitechapel, London. With extracts from his Diary, Correspondence and unpublished Manuscripts* (London, 1820)

— *Memoirs of Rev John Taylor Late Pastor of the General Baptist church at Queenshead, near Halifax Yorkshire. (Chiefly compiled from a manuscript written by himself)* (London, 1821)

Temple Patterson. A., *Radical Leicester: A History of Leicester 1780–1850* (Leicester: University College, 1954)

Thompson, David M., *Nonconformity in the Nineteenth Century* (London, Boston: Routledge & Kegan Paul, 1972)

Thompson, David M. 'Theological and Sociological Approaches to the Motivation of the Ecumenical Movement', in D. Baker (ed.), *Religious Motivation: Biographical and Sociological Problems for the Church Historian* (Studies in Church History, XV; Oxford: Basil Blackwell 1978), pp. 467-79

Thompson, E.P., *The Making of the English Working Class* (London: Penguin, 1963)

Townsend, Henry, *The Claims of the Free Churches* (London: Hodder and Stoughton, 1919)

Underwood, A.C., *A History of the English Baptists* (London: The Kingsgate Press, 1947)

Wagner, Peter, 'Guidelines for Making Basic Church Growth Calculations', in *Reporting Church Growth* (n.pl.: Fuller Evangelistic Association, 1977)

Walker, Michael J., *Baptists at the Table: The Theology of the Lord's Supper amongst English Baptists in the Nineteenth Century* (Didcot: Baptist Historical Society, 1992)

Ward, W.R., *Religion and Society in England 1780–1850* (London: B.T. Batsford, 1972)

— 'The Evangelical Revival', in Sheridan Gilley and W.J. Sheils (eds.), *A History of Religion in Britain* (Oxford: Blackwell, 1994), pp. 252-272

Watts, Michael R., *The Dissenters:*Volume 1. *From the Reformation to the French Revolution* (Oxford: Claredon Press, 1985)

— *The Dissenters:* Volume 2. *The Expansion of Evangelical Nonconformity* (Oxford: Clarendon Press, 1995)
Werner, Julia Stewart, *The Primitive Methodist Connexion* (n.pl.: The University of Wisconsin Press, 1984)
Wesley, John, *The Works of John Wesley,* Volume VII (London, 3rd edn, 1830)
Whale, J.S., *The Protestant Tradition: An Essay in Interpretation* (Cambridge: Cambridge University Press, 1955)
White, William, *History and Gazetteer and Directory of Nottinghamshire* (Sheffield, 1894)
— *History and Gazetteer and Directory of Leicestershire* (Sheffield, 1846)
— *White's 1856 Lincolnshire a reprint of the 1856 issue of History, Gazetter, and Directory of Lincolnshire* (Newton Abbot: David and Charles Reprints, 1969)
Whitley, W.T., *Minutes of the General Assembly of the General Baptist Churches in England: Vol. II, 1731–1811* (London: Carey Kingsgate Press, 1910)
Wilson, Bryan R., *Patterns of Sectarianism Organisation and Ideology in Social and Religious Movements* (London: Heinemann, 1967)
— *Religion in a Secular Society: A Sociological Comment* (London: G.A. Watts, 1966)
Wood, H.G., *Belief and Unbelief since 1850* (Cambridge: Cambridge University Press, 1955)
Wood, J.H.A., *A Condensed History of the General Baptists of the New Connexion* (London: Simpkin, Marshall/Leicester: J.F. Winks, 1847)
Yinger, J. Milton, *Religion, Society and the Individual: An Introduction to the Sociology of Religion* (New York: Macmillian, 11th edn, 1968)

Articles, Periodicals and Papers

Ambler, R.W., 'Building up the Walls of Zion: The development of the New Connexion of General Baptists in Lincolnshire, 1770–1891' (paper delivered at the University of York Conference 'Church and People in Britain and Scandinavia', 6-19 April 1995)
— 'Ranters to Chapel Builders: Primitive Methodism in the South Lincolnshire Fenland c.1820–1875', in W.J. Sheils and Diana Wood (eds), *Voluntary Religion* (Oxford: Basil Blackwell, 1986), pp. 319-331
Elliott, Malcolm, 'Belief and Disbelief in Victorian Leicester', *The Leicester Archaeological and Historical Society: Transactions* 56 (1982), pp. 88-96
Head, P., 'Putting out in the Leicester Hosiery Industry in the Middle of the Nineteenth Century', *Transactions of the Leicestershire Archaeological and Historical Society* 37 (1963), pp. 44-59
Inglis, K.S., 'Patterns of Religious Worship in 1851', *Journal of Ecclesiastical History* XI (1960), pp. 74-86
Johnson, Benton, 'A Critical Appraisal of the Church-Sect Typology', *American Sociological Review* 22 (1957), pp. 88-92

Lee J.M., 'The Rise and Fall of a Market Town: Castle Donnington in the Nineteenth Century', *The Leicestershire Archaeological and Historical Society Transactions* 22 (1957), pp. 53-79

Lovegrove, Deryck, 'Idealism and Association in Early Nineteenth Century Dissent', in W.J. Sheils and Diana Wood (eds), *Voluntary Religion* (Oxford: Basil Blackwell, 1986), pp. 303-317

Martin, D.A., 'The Denomination', *The British Journal of Sociology* 13 (1962), pp. 1-14

Nuttall, Geoffrey, F., 'Assembly and Association in Dissent, 1687–1831', in G. Cumming and D. Baker (eds), *Councils and Assemblies* (Studies in Church History, 7; London: Cambridge University Press, 1971), pp. 289-309

— 'Northhamptonshire and the Modern Question: a turning-point in eighteenth-century Dissent', *Journal of Theological Studies* 16.1 (1965), pp. 101-123

— 'The Rise of Independency in Lincolnshire', *The Journal of the United Reformed Church History Society* 4.1 (1987), pp. 35-50

Pfautz, Harold W., 'The Sociology of Secularization: Religious Groups', *American Journal of Sociology* 41 (1956), pp. 121-128

Royal, Stephen A., 'The spiritual destitution is excessive—the poverty overwhelming: Hinckley in the mid nineteenth century', *Leicestershire Archaeological and Historical Society Transactions* 54 (1980), pp. 51-60

Walsh, John, 'Religious Societies Methodist and Evangelical, 1738–1800', in W. J. Sheils and Diana Wood (eds), *Voluntary Religion* (Oxford: Basil Blackwell, 1986), pp. 279-302

Watts, M., '"The Hateful Mystery": Non-conformists and Hell', *Journal of the United Reformed Church History Society* 2.8 (October, 1981), pp. 248-258.

Welch, Edwin, 'The Origins of the New Connexion of General Baptists in Leicestershire', *Transactions of the Leicestershire Archaeological and Historical Society* 69 (1995), pp. 57-70

Transactions of the Baptist Historical Society and the Baptist Quarterly

'Minutes of the Monthly Conferences', *Transactions of the Baptist Historical Society* 5 (1916–1917), pp. 35-42, 115-126

Avery, W.J., 'The Late Midland College', *Baptist Quarterly* 1 (1922–23), pp. 220-222, 263-269, 327-336

Beckwith, Frank, 'Dan Taylor (1738–1816) and Yorkshire Baptist Life', *Baptist Quarterly* 11 (1938–39), pp. 297-306

Betteridge, Alan, 'Barton in the Beans, Leicestershire: A Source of Church Plants', *Baptist Quarterly* 26.2 (April, 1995), pp. 70-79

Brachlow, Stephen, 'Puritan Theology and General Baptist Origins', *Baptist Quarterly* 31.4 (October, 1985), pp. 179-194

Brown, Kenneth D., 'The Baptist Ministry of Victorian England and Wales: A Social Profile', *Baptist Quarterly* 32.3 (July, 1987), pp.105-120

Foreman. H., 'Baptists Provision for Ministerial Education in the 18th Century', *Baptist Quarterly* 27.8 (October, 1978), pp. 320-327
Harrison, F.M.W., 'Approach of the New Connexion General Baptists to a Midland Industrial Town', *Baptist Quarterly* 33.1 (January, 1989), pp. 16-19
— 'The Nottinghamshire Baptists: Rise and Expansion', *Baptist Quarterly* 25.2 (April, 1973), pp. 59-73
'The Nottinghamshire Baptists: Polity', *Baptist Quarterly* 25.5 (January, 1974), pp. 212-231
— 'The Nottinghamshire Baptists: Mission, Worship, Training', *Baptist Quarterly* 25.7 (July, 1974), pp. 309-328
Hastings, F.G., 'The Passing of St. Mary's Gate Derby', *Baptist Quarterly* 9 (1938–39), pp. 45-49
Lovegrove, Deryck, 'Particular Baptist Itinerant Preachers during the Late 18th and Early 19th Centuries', *Baptist Quarterly* 28.3 (July, 1979), pp. 127-139
Nuttall, Geoffrey F., 'Calvinism in Free Church History', *Baptist Quarterly* 22.8 (October, 1968), pp. 418-428
— 'Questions and Answers: An Eighteenth-Century Correspondence', *Baptist Quarterly* 25.2 (April, 1977), pp. 83-90
— 'Baptist Churches and their Ministers in the 1790s: Rippon's Baptist Annual Register', *Baptist Quarterly* 30.8 (1984), pp. 383-387
Stroud. W.S., 'John Clifford', *The Baptist Quarterly* 6 (1932–33), pp. 305-311
Taylor, Rosemary, 'Early Baptist Periodicals 1790–1865', *Baptist Quarterly* 27.2 (April, 1977), pp. 50-82
Thompson, David M., 'John Clifford's Social Gospel', *Baptist Quarterly* 31.5 (January, 1986), pp. 199-217
Walker, Michael J., 'Presidency of the Lord's Table among Nineteenth-Century English Baptists', *Baptist Quarterly* 32.5 (January, 1988), pp. 208-223

Index

Abingdon Association of Particular Baptist Churches, the 175
Abolition Act, the (1868) 90
absenteeism 70, 71, 137
Abstinence Society, the 91
academies
   Academy (General Baptist) 55, 101, 157-62, 172
   General Baptist College, Chilwell, Nottingham 29, 181, 183, 187, 193, 206
   Midland Baptist College, the 161, 194
   Wisbech Academy 160
activism 9
Adult Bible Classes 111
Aged Ministers' Fund, the 53
agnosticism 32
Alford 99
Allerton 123
Ambler, R.W. 14, 125
American General Association of General Baptists 2
An Orthodox Creed 174
Anglicanism 146
Anglicans 88, 90
Anglo-Catholicism 179
Angus, Joseph 161
annual association/assembly 49-53
antinomianism 11
Anti-State Church Association, the 90, 204
anti-trinitarian Anabaptists 6
Archdeacon Lane, Leicester 39, 60, 62, 65, 66, 80, 84, 87, 89, 93, 103, 114, 164
Arianism 6, 7, 10, 11, 17
Arminianism 4, 22, 135
Arminians 181
Arnold 128
Ashby 65
Ashby and Packington 22, 92, 93, 102, 146
Ashby, Douglas 93
Ashby-de-la-Zouch 163, 185
Ashford 43

atonement 10, 12, 13, 17, 27, 183, 193
   general atonement 9
   limited atonement 6
   vicarious atonement 6
Augmentation Fund, the 205
Austin, brother 163
Austrey 102, 146, 160
Avery, W.J. 162, 198

Badderley, brother 145, 151
Baines, William 89
Bairstow, John 98
Bakewell, brother 54, 151
Band of Hope, the 92, 93
baptism 3, 9, 11, 13, 61-64, 66, 85, 86, 109, 132, 134, 135, 136, 137, 138, 141, 183, 193
   believer's baptism 6, 9, 37, 187
   immersion 13, 61, 62, 64, 65
   infant baptism 3
Baptist Missionary Society, the 21, 56, 176, 177, 192
Baptist Total Abstinence Association, the 93, 204-205
Baptist Union Augmentation Fund, the 164
Baptist Union Corporation, the 195
Baptist Union, the 22, 28, 48, 67, 92, 174, 176, 182, 187, 189, 190, 191, 192, 193, 195, 199, 204, 205, 206
Baptist World Alliance, the 140
Baptists 2, 6, 10, 24, 26, 29, 37, 38, 42, 45, 48, 62, 63, 65, 71, 93, 116, 121, 143, 155, 161, 162, 168, 169, 176, 177, 181, 182, 183, 184, 185, 197, 199, 200, 201, 204, 205, 206
Barass, Thomas 127
Barton group of churches 19, 37, 41-42, 45, 46, 98, 101-102
Barton in the Beans, Leicestershire 10, 16, 36n, 99, 102, 121, 145, 147, 152, 160, 196
Barton preachers 115
Barwell, William 76
Baxter Gate, Loughborough 160
Baxter, Richard 21

Beardsall, Francis 58, 92
Bebbington, D.W. 15, 140
Beckett, J.V. 127
Beeby, Elizabeth 76
Beer, brother 149
Beer, sister 149
Beeston group, the 100
Beeston, Nottingham 60, 100
Belfast 33
benevolent societies 167
Bennett, brother 54
Bennett, J. 53
Berg, J. Van Den 25
Bessels Green, Kent 36n
Bible Translation Society, the 204
biblical criticism 28-30
  higher criticism 32
biblicism 14-16
Biffin, John 134
Birchcliffe 37, 50, 98, 99, 155, 158
Birmingham 106, 134, 182, 183, 192
Birstall 8
bishops 174
Bissell, John 25, 27, 81, 171
Board of Education, the 205
Board of Reference for Pastors and Churches, the 151
Booth, Samuel 191, 198
Boston, Lincolnshire 3, 36n, 38, 51, 158, 163, 196
Bosworth 163n
Bourne, Lincolnshire 40, 98, 127, 129, 145, 146, 156, 164, 195
Boyce, Gilbert 3, 10, 17, 175
Bradford 112
Brampton, William 159, 177
Brand, William 150, 153, 163, 165, 166
Briggs, John H.Y. 1, 2, 38, 64, 67, 91, 155, 167, 174, 178, 187, 201, 204
Brine, John 176
British Association of the Promotion of Temperance, the 92
Brittain, John 36
Brock, William 204
Brotherhood movement, the 138
Broughton 102
Brown, Callum G. 121
Brown, Hugh Stowell 200
Brown, Kenneth D. 162, 164
Brown, Raymond 1
Buckley, Mr 87
Bunting, Jabez 171

Burgess, Mr 79
Burgess, W. 46
Burnley 99, 196
Burns, Dawson 91, 92, 192, 193, 194
Burns, Jabez 92, 121, 179, 183
Burns, Mrs Dawson 91
Burrows, Mr 133
Burton on Trent 176
Butler, Bishop 20

Calvinism 6, 8, 13, 21 44, 132, 181, 183, 185, 187, 188, 189, 193, 195, 196, 199, 201
  high-Calvinism 11, 174, 176, 180, 199
  moderate Calvinism 180, 181
  rigid Calvinism 21, 174
Calvinists 22, 56, 186
  moderate Calvinists 21
camp meetings 129
Cannon Street, Birmingham 56
Card, Nathaniel 91
Carley Street, Leicester 60, 82
Carlile, Mrs 92
Carlton 128
Carroll, J.W. 88
Castle Donnington, Leicestershire 36n, 46, 47, 49, 54, 55, 58, 59, 60, 64, 83, 85, 88, 100, 102, 121, 145, 147, 148, 149, 150, 151, 152, 153, 163, 165, 166, 179, 183, 195
Castle Gate, Nottingham 148
Castle Hedingham 36n
Cauldwell 102, 176
Chapel Building Fund, the 184
Chapel Lane, Whitechapel 51, 52, 53
Chartism 75, 82
Chartists 75, 81, 82, 121
Chesham 103, 180
children 135
Chilwell, Nottingham 100, 161
China 124
Christian Endeavour 140
Christianization 204
Christological controversy (1970s) 196
Christology 6, 7, 11, 12, 13, 190
Church Lane Meeting House, Whitechapel, London 36, 43
church meeting 44-45, 165, 166
Church of England 69, 70, 71, 83, 84, 86, 88, 89, 90, 195
church rates 88-90

Index

Clapham Sect, the 88
Clark, Mr 175
Clarke, C. 123, 185
Cliff, Philip 112
Clifford, John 2, 24, 30, 31, 32, 33, 34, 63, 64, 85, 86, 87, 88, 91, 93, 94, 111, 112, 113, 115, 116, 122, 123, 124, 128, 134, 136, 137, 138, 139, 140, 141, 157, 161, 162, 169, 170-73, 179, 184, 186, 193, 194, 195, 196, 198, 199, 201, 202, 203, 204
Clowes 129
collectors 148
Coltman, George 132, 136, 185
conference 45-48
  Cheshire and Lancashire Conference, the 47
  Derbyshire Conference 47
  Leicester Conference 47, 48, 146, 152, 167
  London Conference 47
  Midland Conference, the 137, 145, 169, 185, 196
  Northern Conference 205
  Nottingham Conference 47
  Warwickshire Conference 47
  West Midland Conference (General Baptist) 192
  Yorkshire Conference 47, 122
Confession of Faith (1785) 18
Congregational colleges 183
Congregational Union 204
Congregationalists 2, 10, 14, 23, 26, 201
Coningsby 10, 145
connexionalism 59-61, 206
conversion 9, 14, 17, 18-19, 49, 103, 141
Cook, Mrs Thomas 94
Cook, Thomas 59, 62, 94, 105, 166, 167, 190, 192
Cooke, Mrs 183
Cooper, Thomas 75, 121
Corn Laws, the 81, 82
Corporation Act, the (1661) 69
Countess of Huntingdon 41
covenant 42
Cox, Samuel 26, 27, 28, 29, 31, 32
creeds 200
Creighton (a Methodist) 62
Crofts, brother 150

Currie, Robert A. 96, 103, 109, 138, 142, 197, 198, 201, 203

Dalton, J.J. 164
Dart, W.F. 141, 142
Darts, Mr 164
Darwin, Charles 30, 31
Davies, Thomas Witton 162
Daybrook, Nottingham 109
Deacon, Mr 164
Deacon, Frederick 105
Deacon, John 1, 41, 42, 69, 70
Deacon, Samuel 1, 10, 11 16, 17, 19, 20, 36n, 148, 149, 192
deacons 144, 147, 148-50, 166
Deal, Kent 36n
Declaration of Principle, the 187, 190
Denominational Fund 66
denominationalism 61, 137, 157, 172, 206
Derby 40, 65, 74, 99, 106, 163, 169, 176, 192
Derby General Baptist Religious Tract Society, the 54
Derby Road, Nottingham 180
Derbyshire 41n, 72, 73, 74, 121, 127, 184, 202
Derry, John 145
Dissent 6, 20, 44, 71, 72, 73, 74, 86, 90, 95, 160
  New Dissent 25, 71
  Old Dissent 1, 10, 11, 69, 70, 71
  Protestant Dissent 95
  Victorian Dissent 1
Dissenters 6, 69, 70, 83, 89, 98
Dixon, Mrs 147
Dixon, Stephen 41, 42
Dobney, Henry Hamlet 26
Doddridge, Philip 11
Donisthorpe, Joseph 101
Dorcas Societies 85, 167
Dossey, John 3
Dow 129
Downgrade controversy, the 28, 199
Duffield 40
Duke of Portland 73
Dury, G.H. 127
Dyson, Watson 191

East Midland Baptist Association 196, 202
East Midlands 2, 92, 127, 164, 196, 202

ecclesiology 44, 201
ecumenism/ecumenicalism 197 204, 205
Education Act, the (1870) 114
Education Society, the 104, 160, 161
elders 144, 147-48, 152, 153, 165, 174
elect, the 6
election 44
Elliott, Malcolm 34
Elliott-Binns, L.E. 31, 25
Ellis, James 164
Enclosure Acts, the 74, 83
Enlightenment, the 15
Epworth 41n
Essex 7, 43
Established Church, the 32, 204
Evangelical Alliance, the 92, 95, 132, 185, 204
Evangelical Arminianism 20
Evangelical Nonconformity 30, 84
Evangelical Revival, the 1, 2, 5, 8-9, 10, 13, 11, 15, 19, 20, 24, 27, 28, 40, 43, 62, 156, 157, 158, 172, 176, 197, 201
Evangelicalism 141, 179, 180, 187
Evangelicals 29, 182, 204
    Protestant Evangelicals 199
evangelism 11, 16, 104, 107, 109-15, 122, 123, 172, 206
    personal evangelism 123
Everitt, Alan 72, 73
Ewald, Heinrich 29
Eythorn 36n

faith 18-19
    justification by faith 8, 11, 13, 190
Fall, the 12
Farmer, T. 150
Felkin, William A. 59, 60, 73, 75, 165
Fenn, James 36n
Finn (Chartist leader) 82
Fleckney, Leicestershire 74, 132
Fleet 38, 46
Fletcher, Joseph 28, 63, 137
Fletcher, R.J. 191
Folds, Richard 158
Foreign Missionary Society 123
Fowkes, Mary 100
Fowkes, William 100
Framework Knitters Friendly and Relief Society of the Town and the County of Leicester, the 80

framework knitters/knitting 25, 73-75, 79, 80, 81, 82, 83, 84, 85, 202
Free Churches 86, 125
Free Churchmen 88
free grace 16-20
Freestone, Joseph 21
Friar Lane, Leicester 1, 63, 79, 84, 91, 93, 113
Frith, William 76
Fuller, Andrew 21, 56, 176, 177, 199
Fullerism 178, 206
Fullerites 22

Gamston 3, 9, 10, 39, 131
General Baptist Academy, Mile End, London 4, 183
General Baptist Assembly 7, 36, 37, 43, 49, 175, 180
General Baptist Association, the 7, 179, 182, 191, 194, 196, 198
General Baptist Conference 196
General Baptist Gospel Mission and Preachers' Institute, the 169
General Baptist Home Missionary Society, The 54, 58, 104, 105
General Baptist Institute, the 170
General Baptist Missionary Society, the 55, 56-57, 181, 192
General Baptist Preachers Union, the 131, 167
General Baptists 2, 3, 6-8, 9, 10, 11, 14, 17, 21, 23, 29, 31, 37, 40, 42, 43, 44, 48, 49, 50, 51, 56, 59, 62, 69, 82, 87, 91, 92, 101, 104, 106, 108, 105, 121, 128, 131, 135, 138, 143, 145, 147, 148, 150, 154, 155, 158, 174, 175, 176, 177, 178, 179, 180, 181, 182 183, 184, 186, 187, 188, 189, 190, 191, 192, 193, 195, 198, 199, 200, 201, 204, 205, 206
General Baptists of Lincolnshire 42, 43
Gilbert, A.D. 69, 70, 71, 84, 94, 96, 103, 109, 113, 135, 137, 138, 203
Gill, John 176
Gill, T. 123
Gladstone, W.E. 88, 92
Glover, John 183
Goadby, Bertha 29
Goadby, Frederick W. 127, 186
Goadby, John 159
Goadby, Joseph Jr 108
Goadby, Joseph Sr 21, 60, 65, 99, 108, 159, 163

Index

Goadby, Lilian 29
Goadby, Thomas 14, 24, 28, 29, 30, 31, 32, 81, 83, 115, 124, 127, 128, 162, 200
Goddard, J. 100
Godfrey, J.R. 41n, 70, 192, 193
Godkin, H. 125
Good, Lucy 134
Gore, Charles 195
Gosberton, Lincolnshire 40, 43, 141, 142, 157, 164
Gothard, brother 151
Great Yarmouth 15
Green, Frances 65
Greenwood, James 146, 156
Griffiths, Foulkes, 198
Grimley, John 36n
Gunn, George 134

Hackney Phalanx, the 88
Halifax 3, 46, 50, 51, 71, 80, 99, 100, 106, 155, 163
Hall, Robert 21, 80, 81, 82
Halsted 36n
Hanserd Knollys Society, the 205
Harrison, F.M.W. 1, 29, 84, 160, 167, 183
Harvey Lane, Chapel, Leicester 81
Haslam, John 191
Hayden, Roger 179
Hayworth 8
Head, Peter 74
Heasman, Kathleen 95
helps 147-48
Heptonstall 9
Hickling, George 36n
Hinckley 21, 74, 75-80, 102, 105, 148, 160
Hinton, John Howard 177, 179, 180, 181
Hirchin, William 134
Hodges, brother 168
holiness 40
Home Mission 104, 121
Home Mission Building Fund, the 193
Home Mission Society (Particular Baptist) 104, 105
Hopkinson, James 91
Horsley, L. 96, 103, 109, 138, 203
Hose, Leicestershire 52
Hucknall 99
Huddersfield 191

Hugglescote 39, 71, 102, 103, 146, 148, 183, 186
Hull, S. 65
Hunter, Hugh 90, 171
Huntingdon 205
hymns 20
Hyson Green, Nottingham 131, 195

Ibstock 160
Ilkeston 64, 65, 100
Ilkeston and Smalley 102
Ilkins, Mr 64
Independency 2, 43, 58, 201
independency/local autonomy 44, 48, 67
Independents 10, 37, 38, 65, 145, 206
individualism 88, 95, 123, 201
Ingham, Benjamin 41n
Ingham, Jeremy 158
Ingham, Mr 163
Ingham, Richard 57, 159, 171
itinerancy 96, 98, 101-102, 105
Itinerant Fund, the 53, 54, 104
Ivimey, Joseph 177

Jackson, George 51, 108, 143, 144
Jamaica 48
Jarman, John 148, 149
Jarrom, Joseph 58, 159, 160, 171
Johnson, Mark 132
Jones, J.A. 157
Jones, J.C. 63
Jones, R.C. 192
Jones, W. 112

Kegworth, Leicestershire 36n, 45, 80, 85, 102, 143, 149, 152, 165
Kendrick, William 41, 42, 147
Kenny, Richard 185
Kent 7, 37, 43
Kent, John 94, 199
Kiddall, J. 89
Killingholme 43
Kirkby-Woodhouse 99, 100, 102
Kirton in Lindsey 43
Knott, John 36n
Kruppa, Patricia 95

Lancashire 187, 200
Landels, William 204
lay leaders 37
lay leadership 151

lay ministry 166-70
lay preaching 169, 172
laying on of hands 154-57, 175
laymen 157
lay-preachers 101
Leake 131
Leake and Wimeswold 102
Lee, John 44, 200
Lee, R.S. 197
Leeds 54
Leicester 34, 68, 72, 74, 80, 81, 94, 106, 128, 161, 169, 181, 192, 202
Leicester and Leicestershire Political Union, the 81
Leicester Association 171
Leicester Corporation, the 81
Leicester Working Men's Anti-Corn Law Association, the 82
Leicestershire 37, 41n, 65, 72, 73, 74, 106, 108, 121, 127, 143, 169, 184, 202
Lenton, Nottingham 100, 128
Liberalism 141
Liberation Society, the 90
liberty 90
Lilly, W.S. 32
Lincoln 3, 192
Lincolnshire 2, 9, 37, 38, 42, 46, 53, 54, 73, 90, 99, 104, 126, 127, 164, 167, 175, 202
Lincolnshire and Cambridgeshire General Baptist Sunday School Union, the 109
Lincolnshire Association 3, 10, 17, 37
liturgy 141
Liverpool 54, 169
London 37, 50, 51, 52, 55, 100, 101, 104, 106, 112, 128, 140, 143, 158, 159, 161, 169, 175, 177, 178, 180, 182
London Baptist Association 119, 137, 170, 204
Long Eaton 196
Long Whatton 102
Longford 36n, 51, 102, 143
Lord's Supper 62, 64-66, 69, 92, 93, 99, 149, 152, 153, 154, 156, 165
Loughborough Educational Society, the 172
Loughborough, Leicestershire 36n, 102, 104, 122, 146, 161, 185
Louth 89
Lovegrove, Deryck 101

Luddism 75
Lux Mundi 195
Lynch, T.T. 26

Mabbs, Goodeve 128
Mablethorpe 94
Maltby Le Marsh, Lincolnshire 43, 94, 99, 151, 185
Manchester 70, 92, 93, 111, 169
Mann, Horace 121
Manning, James 121
Mansfield Road, Nottingham 26, 27, 85, 141, 180
March, W. 136, 137
Market Harborough 14, 39, 65, 94
Markings, John 98
Marsh, W. 116
Marshall, W. 122, 167, 168, 170
Martin, D.A. 176
Marylebone, London 91
Matthews, T.W. 142, 184
Maurice, F.D. 27
McLeod, Hugh 20, 70, 141
Mee, Thomas 144
Megg, Jane 134
Melbourne 100, 102, 144, 163, 192
Melbourne, Derbyshire 150
Melbourne, Leicestershire 36n, 39, 51, 71
membership 40, 45, 61, 62, 63, 103, 135, 137, 138, 140, 175
closed membership 135
Mennonites 7
messengers 182
Methodism 3, 5, 8-9, 12, 37, 38, 39, 40, 41, 42, 44, 45, 46, 62, 98, 125, 134, 142, 171, 205
Methodist Church 197
Methodist Revival 4
Methodists 3, 9, 21, 44, 108, 121, 136, 143, 168
Metropolitan Sunday School Union, the 112
Metropolitan Tabernacle, the 30, 65, 169
Miall, Edward 88, 89, 90, 204
Middlesex 43
Midland Association (Particular Baptist) 192
Midland Baptist Union, the 121, 184, 205
Midland churches 67
Midland group, the 99, 101

Midlands, the 42, 75, 88, 124, 131, 136, 160, 161
Mile End, London 159
Mill Lane, Ashby 99
Millard, J.H. 205
Miller, Jarvis 53
ministerial income 162-65
ministers 144-47, 154, 157, 166
ministry 156
mission 85
missionary societies 195
Moody, Dwight L. 116, 117, 129, 133, 134, 204
Moravians 42, 147
Morton 98
Moss, brother 176
Munson, James 197
Murch, William Harris 180
Murray, H.R. 200
Mursell, James Phillip 88, 181
mysticism 197

National Association for Aged and Inform Baptist Ministers, the 205
National Temperance League, the 91
Nether Street, Beeston, Nottingham 131, 160
New Connexion Home Mission Society, the 166
New Lenton, Nottingham 27, 39, 62, 88, 132, 133
Newberry, J. 53
Newbold, B. 148
Newcastle-upon-Tyne 41n
Newman, brother 94
Niebuhr, Richard 86, 115, 144
Nonconformists 29, 90, 92, 117, 122, 197
Nonconformity 1, 53, 69, 73, 84, 87, 88, 90, 95, 122, 124, 157, 163, 198, 204
North of England 131, 134
Northamptonshire 167
Northowram 2
Norton, brother 150
Nottingham 27, 33, 49, 72, 74, 105, 117, 127, 162, 169, 180, 182, 183, 191, 192, 202
Nottingham General Baptist Preachers Union, the 109, 168, 169
Nottingham University 161
Nottinghamshire 1, 72, 73, 74, 84, 121, 128, 167, 184, 202

Nuneaton 77

Old General Baptists 67, 144, 147, 190, 206
Oldershaw, Joseph 54, 166
open communion 187
ordination 150-62, 172
Orissa 177
Orissa Mission, the 123, 124, 193
Orton, T. 60, 66
Osborn, Elizabeth 134
Oxford 144
Oxford Movement/Tractarians, the 31, 88, 157

Packington 19, 99, 163n
Paedobaptists 65
Parman, Charles 36n
Parmone, William 71
Particular Baptist colleges 183
Particular Baptists 2, 8, 9, 13, 18, 20, 21, 22, 23, 24, 26, 49, 56, 62, 63, 64, 67, 69, 81, 84, 92, 95, 104, 121, 135, 142, 144, 145, 148, 150, 161, 173, 174, 175, 176, 177, 178, 179, 180, 182, 183, 184, 185, 186, 190, 191, 193, 195, 198, 199, 199, 201, 204, 205, 206
particular redemption 6
pastors 144-47, 148, 151, 152, 153, 156
Patterson, A. Temple 81, 82, 89
Payne, Ernest A. 1, 21, 178, 180, 196, 199, 200
Pearce, Samuel 56
Pegg, James 145, 159, 177
Perkins, Thomas 36n
Peto, Morton 30
Pickering, brother 151
Pickering, N. 36n, 99
Pickering, T. 99
Pickering, William 57
Picknance, George 155
pietism 197
Pike, E.C. 22, 136, 161
Pike, J.B. 146, 182
Pike, J.C. 22
Pike, J.G. 22, 38, 53, 56, 59, 60, 65, 83, 119, 129, 131, 163, 171, 176, 177, 179
Pleasant Sunday Afternoon services 138
Ploughwright, john 167
Pollard, brother 51

Poole, Henry 36n
Portsea, Hampshire 176
Praed Street, London 91, 122, 139, 140
Presbyterians 10, 14, 92
Primitive Methodism 101, 108, 131
Primitive Methodists 106, 107, 129, 131, 203
Prospect Place, Nottingham 131
Protestantism 90
Protestants 26
Proud, Joseph 175
Pudsey, Yorkshire 42
Puseyism 86

Quakers 10, 91
Queenshead, Yorkshire 40, 79, 98, 100, 155
Quordon 102

Radford 128
Rakow, Poland 6
Rawdon Baptist College 29
Reardon, B.M.G. 28
regeneration 13, 49
Regent's Park College 22, 161
   Stepney Academy/College 22, 26, 161
Religious Census (1851) 72, 121, 124, 202, 205
renewal 49
Retford and Gamston, Nottinghamshire 164
Retford, Nottingham 39, 99, 131, 187
revival 131, 132
Revival, the (1859) 134, 185
Revival, the (1874) 134
revivalism 91, 129-35, 137, 206
revivals 134, 135
Reynolds, Geoffrey R. 175
Richardson, W. 116, 169
Riddels, Harriet 134
Roman Catholic Church 90
Roman Catholics 69, 86
Romanticism 195
Roozen, D.A. 88
Rose, Henry 161
Rothley 102
Rowe, Mr 183
rulers 147
Rushall 86
Rushbrooke, J.H. 140
Rutland 167
Ryde, Isle of Wight 26

Saint Mary's, Nottingham 128
Salisbury, James 33, 186
salvation 11, 12, 13, 18, 122, 178
sanctification 12
Sankey, Ira D. 116, 129, 134, 204
Sarjant, S.C. 161
Savil, Thomas 148
Sawley 179
science 30-35
Scotland 131, 134
Second London Confession 175, 176
secularisation 95, 197, 202
secularism 30-35, 197, 198
Seeds, Matilda 62
Sellers, Ian 38, 91, 112, 120, 140, 178, 201
Serampore 21, 177
Seven Oaks, Kent 52, 155
Sharpe, Thomas 19
Sheffield 54, 72
Shepshead, Leicestershire 79, 86
Shibden, Yorkshire 71
Shore 99
Shull, Loren 2
Simpson family 99
sin 6
Six Articles, The 11-14, 18, 21, 36, 49, 62, 63, 159, 190, 192
Skinner, Larry 197
Small, J.H. 148
Smalley, Derbyshire 56, 86, 100, 160
Smedley, J. 100
Smith, A. 60
Smith, F. 100
Smith, Francis 19, 36n
Smith, Mary 133
Smith, Mr 64
Smith, Robert 158
Smith, William 36n
Smyth, John 147
Snenton 128
social migration 83-88
Socinianism 6, 7, 10, 11, 17
Socinians 185
Southwark, London 36n
Sozzini, Faustus 6
Spalding 192
Spurgeon, C.H. 30, 65, 95, 187, 189, 190, 200, 204
St Mary's Baptist Church, Norwich 65
Stanger, John 36n
Stapleton, John 79
Stayleybridge 101

Index

Steane, Edward 180
Stevenson, E. 167
Stevenson, John 160, 161
Stevenson, R.W. 29
Stevenson, T. Sr 114
Stevenson, T.R. 134
Stevenson, Thomas 60, 65, 160, 161, 164
Stevenson, Thomas Sr 104, 105, 106
Stevenson, W.R. 127, 137, 141
Stone, S.M. 178
Stoney Street, Nottingham 53, 91, 109, 117, 167
Stovel, Charles 187
strict communion 187
Stroud, W.S. 194
Summers, W. 36n
Sunday schools 57, 109-15, 138, 206
Sussex 7, 43
Sutterton, Leicestershire 177
Sutterton, Lincolnshire 146
Sutton Bonnington 102
Sutton Coldfield 163
Syme, G.A. 180

Tarratt, John 36n, 151, 155
Taylor, Adam 1, 4, 9, 11, 14, 22, 38, 49, 51, 54, 57, 98, 115, 158, 159
Taylor, brother 151
Taylor, Dan 2, 3-5, 7, 8, 9, 10, 11, 12, 14, 15, 16, 17, 18, 21, 24, 36, 37, 38, 40, 42, 43, 44, 46, 50, 51, 61, 67, 98, 100, 102, 103, 115, 143-44, 145, 146, 147, 155, 158, 159, 163, 170-71, 175, 196
Taylor, David 41
Taylor, James 74, 82, 105
Taylor, John 4, 8, 9, 41, 46, 47, 71, 79, 98, 99, 100, 155, 158, 165
Taylor, Michael 196
Taylor, Mrs Dan 24
teachers 147, 148
teetotalism 91
temperance 91-95
Temperance Convocation, the 92
Temple, Frederick 32
Test Act, the (1673) 69
Tetley, W.H. 191
Thompson, David M. 139, 198
Thompson, Mr 155
Thompson, William 3, 36n, 163
Thurlaston 102
Tilson, William 133

Toleration Acts, the (1689) 69, 998
Tract and Lord's Day School Society, and Juvenile Magazine, the 54
Trinity, the 6, 7
Tunnicliff,, Jabez 92
Tydd St. Giles 94
Tyndall, John 32

Underwood, A.C. 1, 199
Underwood, William 23, 29, 84, 109, 111, 113, 117, 156, 161, 180, 181, 182, 191
union of General and Particular Baptists (1891) 162, 173, 174-206
union of Particular Baptists (1812 and 1832) 177-80, 181
Unitarianism 10
United Kingdom Alliance, the 91, 92
United Kingdom Band of Hope Union 92
University of London 194

Venn, Hervey 11
Village Mission, the 105
voluntaryism 176

Wadsworth, Yorkshire 3, 36n, 50, 51
Wagner, Peter 119
Walker, Michael 156
Wall, William 3
Wallis, John 156
Wallis, Joseph 30, 161
Walsall 191, 195
Ward, W.R. 129, 201
Ward, William 177
Warner, Martha 76
Watts, Isaac 11
Watts, Michael R. 2, 73
Werner, Julia Stewart 101
Wesley, Charles 8
Wesley, John 3, 4, 8, 9, 19, 20, 39, 41, 42, 98, 143, 144, 171, 203
Wesleyan Methodist Church 124
Wesleyans 23
West Country 7
West Indies 124
West Retford 48
West Riding of Yorkshire 2
Westbourne Park, Paddington 63, 87, 139, 140, 170
Westminster Confession, the 14
White, Edward 26
Whitechapel, London 8

Whitefield, George 8, 11, 41n, 42
Whitley, W.T. 1, 43, 178
Whittlesea 161
Wilders, John 159, 160
Wilkin, David 36n
Williams, Charles 190, 200
Wilson, Bryan 5, 8, 55, 158, 186, 197, 198, 199, 201, 205
Wimeswold 131
Winks, Joseph F. 2, 22, 54 81, 82, 89, 121
Wirksworth 121
Wisbech 43, 159, 175
Wolvey 102
Wood, H.G. 31
Wood, J.H. 1, 41, 42, 49, 58, 131, 159

Woodhouse 131
Woodhouse Eaves 102
Woodly, Henry 134
Wootan, Mr 143
Wooton, Ben 150
Wooton, Mr 165
Worksop 128
Worship, Benjamin 15, 16

Yarmouth 43
Yates, Thomas 121, 146
Yinger, J. Milton 158
Yorkshire 37-41, 46, 47, 53, 71, 79, 100, 101, 123, 126, 127, 128, 144, 152, 158, 163, 196
   South Yorkshire 2, 124, 202

Studies in Baptist History and Thought

(All titles uniform with this volume)
Dates in bold are of projected publication
Volumes in this series are not always published in sequence

David Bebbington and Anthony R. Cross (eds)
Global Baptist History
(SBHT vol. 14)

This book brings together studies from the Second International Conference on Baptist Studies which explore different facets of Baptist life and work especially during the twentieth century.

2006 / 1-84227-214-4 / approx. 350pp

David Bebbington (ed.)
The Gospel in the World
International Baptist Studies
(SBHT vol. 1)

This volume of essays from the First International Conference on Baptist Studies deals with a range of subjects spanning Britain, North America, Europe, Asia and the Antipodes. Topics include studies on religious tolerance, the communion controversy and the development of the international Baptist community, and concludes with two important essays on the future of Baptist life that pay special attention to the United States.

2002 / 1-84227-118-0 / xiv + 362pp

John H.Y. Briggs (ed.)
Pulpit and People
Studies in Eighteenth-Century English Baptist Life and Thought
(SBHT vol. 28)

The eighteenth century was a crucial time in Baptist history. The denomination had its roots in seventeenth-century English Puritanism and Separatism and the persecution of the Stuart kings with only a limited measure of freedom after 1689. Worse, however, was to follow for with toleration came doctrinal conflict, a move away from central Christian understandings and a loss of evangelistic urgency. Both spiritual and numerical decline ensued, to the extent that the denomination was virtually reborn as rather belatedly it came to benefit from the Evangelical Revival which brought new life to both Arminian and Calvinistic Baptists. The papers in this volume study a denomination in transition, and relate to theology, their views of the church and its mission, Baptist spirituality, and engagements with radical politics.

2007 / 1-84227-403-1 / approx. 350pp

July 2005

Damian Brot
Church of the Baptized or Church of Believers?
A Contribution to the Dialogue between the Catholic Church and the Free Churches with Special Reference to Baptists
(SBHT vol. 26)
The dialogue between the Catholic Church and the Free Churches in Europe has hardly taken place. This book pleads for a commencement of such a conversation. It offers, among other things, an introduction to the American and the international dialogues between Baptists and the Catholic Church and strives to allow these conversations to become fruitful in the European context as well.
2006 / 1-84227-334-5 / approx. 364pp

Dennis Bustin
Paradox and Perseverence
Hanserd Knollys, Particular Baptist Pioneer in Seventeenth-Century England
(SBHT vol. 23)
The seventeenth century was a significant period in English history during which the people of England experienced unprecedented change and tumult in all spheres of life. At the same time, the importance of order and the traditional institutions of society were being reinforced. Hanserd Knollys, born during this pivotal period, personified in his life the ambiguity, tension and paradox of it, openly seeking change while at the same time cautiously embracing order. As a founder and leader of the Particular Baptists in London and despite persecution and personal hardship, he played a pivotal role in helping shape their identity externally in society and, internally, as they moved toward becoming more formalised by the end of the century.
2006 / 1-84227-259-4 / approx. 324pp

Anthony R. Cross
Baptism and the Baptists
Theology and Practice in Twentieth-Century Britain
(SBHT vol. 3)
At a time of renewed interest in baptism, *Baptism and the Baptists* is a detailed study of twentieth-century baptismal theology and practice and the factors which have influenced its development.
2000 / 0-85364-959-6 / xx + 530pp

Anthony R. Cross and Philip E. Thompson (eds)
Baptist Sacramentalism
(SBHT vol. 5)
This collection of essays includes biblical, historical and theological studies in the theology of the sacraments from a Baptist perspective. Subjects explored include the physical side of being spiritual, baptism, the Lord's supper, the church, ordination, preaching, worship, religious liberty and the issue of disestablishment.
2003 / 1-84227-119-9 / xvi + 278pp

Anthony R. Cross and Philip E. Thompson (eds)
Baptist Sacramentalism 2
(SBHT vol. 25)
This second collection of essays exploring various dimensions of sacramental theology from a Baptist perspective includes biblical, historical and theological studies from scholars from around the world.
2006 / 1-84227-325-6 / approx. 350pp

Paul S. Fiddes
Tracks and Traces
Baptist Identity in Church and Theology
(SBHT vol. 13)
This is a comprehensive, yet unusual, book on the faith and life of Baptist Christians. It explores the understanding of the church, ministry, sacraments and mission from a thoroughly theological perspective. In a series of interlinked essays, the author relates Baptist identity consistently to a theology of covenant and to participation in the triune communion of God.
2003 / 1-84227-120-2 / xvi + 304pp

Stanley K. Fowler
More Than a Symbol
The British Baptist Recovery of Baptismal Sacramentalism
(SBHT vol. 2)
Fowler surveys the entire scope of British Baptist literature from the seventeenth-century pioneers onwards. He shows that in the twentieth century leading British Baptist pastors and theologians recovered an understanding of baptism that connected experience with soteriology and that in doing so they were recovering what many of their forebears had taught.
2002 / 1-84227-052-4 / xvi + 276pp

Steven R. Harmon
Towards Baptist Catholicity
Essays on Tradition and the Baptist Vision
(SBHT vol. 27)
This series of essays contends that the reconstruction of the Baptist vision in the wake of modernity's dissolution requires a retrieval of the ancient ecumenical tradition that forms Christian identity through rehearsal and practice. Themes explored include catholic identity as an emerging trend in Baptist theology, tradition as a theological category in Baptist perspective, Baptist confessions and the patristic tradition, worship as a principal bearer of tradition, and the role of Baptist higher education in shaping the Christian vision.
2006 / 1-84227-362-0 / approx. 210pp

Michael A.G. Haykin (ed.)
'At the Pure Fountain of Thy Word'
Andrew Fuller as an Apologist
(SBHT vol. 6)
One of the greatest Baptist theologians of the eighteenth and early nineteenth centuries, Andrew Fuller has not had justice done to him. There is little doubt that Fuller's theology lay behind the revitalization of the Baptists in the late eighteenth century and the first few decades of the nineteenth. This collection of essays fills a much needed gap by examining a major area of Fuller's thought, his work as an apologist.
2004 / 1-84227-171-7 / xxii + 276pp

Michael A.G. Haykin
Studies in Calvinistic Baptist Spirituality
(SBHT vol. 15)
In a day when spirituality is in vogue and Christian communities are looking for guidance in this whole area, there is wisdom in looking to the past to find untapped wells. The Calvinistic Baptists, heirs of the rich ecclesial experience in the Puritan era of the seventeenth century, but, by the end of the eighteenth century, also passionately engaged in the catholicity of the Evangelical Revivals, are such a well. This collection of essays, covering such things as the Lord's Supper, friendship and hymnody, seeks to draw out the spiritual riches of this community for reflection and imitation in the present day.
2006 / 1-84227-149-0 / approx. 350pp

Brian Haymes, Anthony R. Cross and Ruth Gouldbourne
On Being the Church
Revisioning Baptist Identity
(SBHT vol. 21)

The aim of the book is to re-examine Baptist theology and practice in the light of the contemporary biblical, theological, ecumenical and missiological context drawing on historical and contemporary writings and issues. It is not a study in denominationalism but rather seeks to revision historical insights from the believers' church tradition for the sake of Baptists and other Christians in the context of the modern–postmodern context.

2006 / 1-84227-121-0 / approx. 350pp

Ken R. Manley
From Woolloomooloo to 'Eternity': A History of Australian Baptists
Volume 1: Growing an Australian Church (1831–1914)
Volume 2: A National Church in a Global Community (1914–2005)
(SBHT vols 16.1 and 16.2)

From their beginnings in Australia in 1831 with the first baptisms in Woolloomoolloo Bay in 1832, this pioneering study describes the quest of Baptists in the different colonies (states) to discover their identity as Australians and Baptists. Although institutional developments are analyzed and the roles of significant individuals traced, the major focus is on the social and theological dimensions of the Baptist movement.

2 vol. set 2006 / 1-84227-405-8 / approx. 900pp

Ken R. Manley
'Redeeming Love Proclaim'
John Rippon and the Baptists
(SBHT vol. 12)

A leading exponent of the new moderate Calvinism which brought new life to many Baptists, John Rippon (1751–1836) helped unite the Baptists at this significant time. His many writings expressed the denomination's growing maturity and mutual awareness of Baptists in Britain and America, and exerted a long-lasting influence on Baptist worship and devotion. In his various activities, Rippon helped conserve the heritage of Old Dissent and promoted the evangelicalism of the New Dissent

2004 / 1-84227-193-8 / xviii + 340pp

Peter J. Morden
Offering Christ to the World
Andrew Fuller and the Revival of English Particular Baptist Life
(SBHT vol. 8)
Andrew Fuller (1754–1815) was one of the foremost English Baptist ministers of his day. His career as an Evangelical Baptist pastor, theologian, apologist and missionary statesman coincided with the profound revitalization of the Particular Baptist denomination to which he belonged. This study examines the key aspects of the life and thought of this hugely significant figure, and gives insights into the revival in which he played such a central part.
2003 / 1-84227-141-5 / xx + 202pp

Peter Naylor
Calvinism, Communion and the Baptists
A Study of English Calvinistic Baptists from the Late 1600s to the Early 1800s
(SBHT vol. 7)
Dr Naylor argues that the traditional link between 'high-Calvinism' and 'restricted communion' is in need of revision. He examines Baptist communion controversies from the late 1600s to the early 1800s and also the theologies of John Gill and Andrew Fuller.
2003 / 1-84227-142-3 / xx + 266pp

Ian M. Randall, Toivo Pilli and Anthony R. Cross (eds)
Baptist Identities
International Studies from the Seventeenth to the Twentieth Centuries
(SBHT vol. 19)
These papers represent the contributions of scholars from various parts of the world as they consider the factors that have contributed to Baptist distinctiveness in different countries and at different times. The volume includes specific case studies as well as broader examinations of Baptist life in a particular country or region. Together they represent an outstanding resource for understanding Baptist identities.
2005 / 1-84227-215-2 / approx. 350pp

James M. Renihan
Edification and Beauty
The Practical Ecclesiology of the English Particular Baptists, 1675–1705
(SBHT vol. 17)

Edification and Beauty describes the practices of the Particular Baptist churches at the end of the seventeenth century in terms of three concentric circles: at the centre is the ecclesiological material in the Second London Confession, which is then fleshed out in the various published writings of the men associated with these churches, and, finally, expressed in the church books of the era.

2005 / 1-84227-251-9 / approx. 230pp

Frank Rinaldi
'The Tribe of Dan'
A Study of the New Connexion of General Baptists 1770–1891
(SBHT vol. 10)

'*The Tribe of Dan*' is a thematic study which explores the theology, organizational structure, evangelistic strategy, ministry and leadership of the New Connexion of General Baptists as it experienced the process of institutionalization in the transition from a revival movement to an established denomination.

2006 / 1-84227-143-1 / approx. 350pp

Peter Shepherd
The Making of a Modern Denomination
John Howard Shakespeare and the English Baptists 1898–1924
(SBHT vol. 4)

John Howard Shakespeare introduced revolutionary change to the Baptist denomination. The Baptist Union was transformed into a strong central institution and Baptist ministers were brought under its control. Further, Shakespeare's pursuit of church unity reveals him as one of the pioneering ecumenists of the twentieth century.

2001 / 1-84227-046-X / xviii + 220pp

Karen Smith
The Community and the Believers
A Study of Calvinistic Baptist Spirituality in Some Towns and Villages of Hampshire and the Borders of Wiltshire, c.1730–1830
(SBHT vol. 22)
The period from 1730 to 1830 was one of transition for Calvinistic Baptists. Confronted by the enthusiasm of the Evangelical Revival, congregations within the denomination as a whole were challenged to find a way to take account of the revival experience. This study examines the life and devotion of Calvinistic Baptists in Hampshire and Wiltshire during this period. Among this group of Baptists was the hymn writer, Anne Steele.
2005 / 1-84227-326-4 / approx. 280pp

Martin Sutherland
Dissenters in a 'Free Land'
Baptist Thought in New Zealand 1850–2000
(SBHT vol. 24)
Baptists in New Zealand were forced to recast their identity. Conventions of communication and association, state and ecumenical relations, even historical divisions and controversies had to be revised in the face of new topographies and constraints. As Baptists formed themselves in a fluid society they drew heavily on both international movements and local dynamics. This book traces the development of ideas which shaped institutions and styles in sometimes surprising ways.
2006 / 1-84227-327-2 / approx. 230pp

Brian Talbot
The Search for a Common Identity
The Origins of the Baptist Union of Scotland 1800–1870
(SBHT vol. 9)
In the period 1800 to 1827 there were three streams of Baptists in Scotland: Scotch, Haldaneite and 'English' Baptist. A strong commitment to home evangelization brought these three bodies closer together, leading to a merger of their home missionary societies in 1827. However, the first three attempts to form a union of churches failed, but by the 1860s a common understanding of their corporate identity was attained leading to the establishment of the Baptist Union of Scotland.
2003 / 1-84227-123-7 / xviii + 402pp

Philip E. Thompson
The Freedom of God
Towards Baptist Theology in Pneumatological Perspective
(SBHT vol. 20)

This study contends that the range of theological commitments of the early Baptists are best understood in relation to their distinctive emphasis on the freedom of God. Thompson traces how this was recast anthropocentrically, leading to an emphasis upon human freedom from the nineteenth century onwards. He seeks to recover the dynamism of the early vision via a pneumatologically-oriented ecclesiology defining the church in terms of the memory of God.

2006 / 1-84227-125-3 / approx. 350pp

Philip E. Thompson and Anthony R. Cross (eds)
Recycling the Past or Researching History?
Studies in Baptist Historiography and Myths
(SBHT vol. 11)

In this volume an international group of Baptist scholars examine and re-examine areas of Baptist life and thought about which little is known or the received wisdom is in need of revision. Historiographical studies include the date Oxford Baptists joined the Abingdon Association, the death of the Fifth Monarchist John Pendarves, eighteenth-century Calvinistic Baptists and the political realm, confessional identity and denominational institutions, Baptist community, ecclesiology, the priesthood of all believers, soteriology, Baptist spirituality, Strict and Reformed Baptists, the role of women among British Baptists, while various 'myths' challenged include the nature of high-Calvinism in eighteenth-century England, baptismal anti-sacramentalism, episcopacy, and Baptists and change.

2005 / 1-84227-122-9 / approx. 330pp

Linda Wilson
Marianne Farningham
A Plain Working Woman
(SBHT vol. 18)

Marianne Farningham, of College Street Baptist Chapel, Northampton, was a household name in evangelical circles in the later nineteenth century. For over fifty years she produced comment, poetry, biography and fiction for the popular Christian press. This investigation uses her writings to explore the beliefs and behaviour of evangelical Nonconformists, including Baptists, during these years.

2006 / 1-84227-124-5 / approx. 250pp

July 2005

Other Paternoster titles
relating to Baptist history and thought

George R. Beasley-Murray
Baptism in the New Testament
(Paternoster Digital Library)

This is a welcome reprint of a classic text on baptism originally published in 1962 by one of the leading Baptist New Testament scholars of the twentieth century. Dr Beasley-Murray's comprehensive study begins by investigating the antecedents of Christian baptism. It then surveys the foundation of Christian baptism in the Gospels, its emergence in the Acts of the Apostles and development in the apostolic writings. Following a section relating baptism to New Testament doctrine, a substantial discussion of the origin and significance of infant baptism leads to a briefer consideration of baptismal reform and ecumenism.

2005 / 1-84227-300-0 / x + 422pp

Paul Beasley-Murray
Fearless for Truth
A Personal Portrait of the Life of George Beasley-Murray

Without a doubt George Beasley-Murray was one of the greatest Baptists of the twentieth century. A long-standing Principal of Spurgeon's College, he wrote more than twenty books and made significant contributions in the study of areas as diverse as baptism and eschatology, as well as writing highly respected commentaries on the Book of Revelation and John's Gospel.

2002 / 1-84227-134-2 / xii + 244pp

David Bebbington
Holiness in Nineteenth-Century England
(Studies in Christian History and Thought)

David Bebbington stresses the relationship of movements of spirituality to changes in their cultural setting, especially the legacies of the Enlightenment and Romanticism. He shows that these broad shifts in ideological mood had a profound effect on the ways in which piety was conceptualized and practised. Holiness was intimately bound up with the spirit of the age.

2000 / 0-85364-981-2 / viii + 98pp

July 2005

Clyde Binfield
Victorian Nonconformity in Eastern England 1840–1885
(Studies in Evangelical History and Thought)
Studies of Victorian religion and society often concentrate on cities, suburbs, and industrialisation. This study provides a contrast. Victorian Eastern England—Essex, Suffolk, Norfolk, Cambridgeshire, and Huntingdonshire—was rural, traditional, relatively unchanging. That is nonetheless a caricature which discounts the industry in Norwich and Ipswich (as well as in Haverhill, Stowmarket and Leiston) and ignores the impact of London on Essex, of railways throughout the region, and of an ancient but changing university (Cambridge) on the county town which housed it. It also entirely ignores the political implications of such changes in a region noted for the variety of its religious Dissent since the seventeenth century. This book explores Victorian Eastern England and its Nonconformity. It brings to a wider readership a pioneering thesis which has made a major contribution to a fresh evolution of English religion and society.
2006 / 1-84227-216-0 / approx. 274pp

Edward W. Burrows
'To Me To Live Is Christ'
A Biography of Peter H. Barber
This book is about a remarkably gifted and energetic man of God. Peter H. Barber was born into a Brethren family in Edinburgh in 1930. In his youth he joined Charlotte Baptist Chapel and followed the call into Baptist ministry. For eighteen years he was the pioneer minister of the new congregation in the New Town of East Kilbride, which planted two further congregations. At the age of thirty-nine he served as Centenary President of the Baptist Union of Scotland and then exercised an influential ministry for over seven years in the well-known Upton Vale Baptist Church, Torquay. From 1980 until his death in 1994 he was General Secretary of the Baptist Union of Scotland. Through his work for the European Baptist Federation and the Baptist World Alliance he became a world Baptist statesman. He was President of the EBF during the upheaval that followed the collapse of Communism.
2005 / 1-84227-324-8 / xxii + 236pp

Christopher J. Clement
Religious Radicalism in England 1535–1565
(Rutherford Studies in Historical Theology)
In this valuable study Christopher Clement draws our attention to a varied assemblage of people who sought Christian faithfulness in the underworld of mid-Tudor England. Sympathetically and yet critically he assess their place in the history of English Protestantism, and by attentive listening he gives them a voice.
1997 / 0-946068-44-5 / xxii + 426pp

July 2005

Anthony R. Cross (ed.)
Ecumenism and History
Studies in Honour of John H.Y. Briggs
(Studies in Christian History and Thought)

This collection of essays examines the inter-relationships between the two fields in which Professor Briggs has contributed so much: history—particularly Baptist and Nonconformist—and the ecumenical movement. With contributions from colleagues and former research students from Britain, Europe and North America, *Ecumenism and History* provides wide-ranging studies in important aspects of Christian history, theology and ecumenical studies.

2002 / 1-84227-135-0 / xx + 362pp

Keith E. Eitel
Paradigm Wars
The Southern Baptist International Mission Board Faces the Third Millennium
(Regnum Studies in Mission)

The International Mission Board of the Southern Baptist Convention is the largest denominational mission agency in North America. This volume chronicles the historic and contemporary forces that led to the IMB's recent extensive reorganization, providing the most comprehensive case study to date of a historic mission agency restructuring to continue its mission purpose into the twenty-first century more effectively.

2000 / 1-870345-12-6 / x + 140pp

Ruth Gouldbourne
The Flesh and the Feminine
Gender and Theology in the Writings of Caspar Schwenckfeld
(Studies in Christian History and Thought)

Caspar Schwenckfeld and his movement exemplify one of the radical communities of the sixteenth century. Challenging theological and liturgical norms, they also found themselves challenging social and particularly gender assumptions. In this book, the issues of the relationship between radical theology and the understanding of gender are considered.

2005 / 1-84227-048-6 / approx. 304pp

July 2005

David Hilborn
The Words of our Lips
Language-Use in Free Church Worship
(Paternoster Theological Monographs)
Studies of liturgical language have tended to focus on the written canons of Roman Catholic and Anglican communities. By contrast, David Hilborn analyses the more extemporary approach of English Nonconformity. Drawing on recent developments in linguistic pragmatics, he explores similarities and differences between 'fixed' and 'free' worship, and argues for the interdependence of each.
2006 / 0-85364-977-4

Stephen R. Holmes
Listening to the Past
The Place of Tradition in Theology
Beginning with the question 'Why can't we just read the Bible?' Stephen Holmes considers the place of tradition in theology, showing how the doctrine of creation leads to an account of historical location and creaturely limitations as essential aspects of our existence. For we cannot claim unmediated access to the Scriptures without acknowledging the place of tradition: theology is an irreducibly communal task. *Listening to the Past* is a sustained attempt to show what listening to tradition involves, and how it can be used to aid theological work today.
2002 / 1-84227-155-5 / xiv + 168pp

Mark Hopkins
Nonconformity's Romantic Generation
Evangelical and Liberal Theologies in Victorian England
(Studies in Evangelical History and Thought)
A study of the theological development of key leaders of the Baptist and Congregational denominations at their period of greatest influence, including C.H. Spurgeon and R.W. Dale, and of the controversies in which those among them who embraced and rejected the liberal transformation of their evangelical heritage opposed each other.
2004 / 1-84227-150-4 / xvi + 284pp

Galen K. Johnson
Prisoner of Conscience
John Bunyan on Self, Community and Christian Faith
(Studies in Christian History and Thought)
This is an interdisciplinary study of John Bunyan's understanding of conscience across his autobiographical, theological and fictional writings, investigating whether conscience always deserves fidelity, and how Bunyan's view of conscience affects his relationship both to modern Western individualism and historic Christianity.

2003 / 1-84227- 151-2 / xvi + 236pp

R.T. Kendall
Calvin and English Calvinism to 1649
(Studies in Christian History and Thought)
The author's thesis is that those who formed the Westminster Confession of Faith, which is regarded as Calvinism, in fact departed from John Calvin on two points: (1) the extent of the atonement and (2) the ground of assurance of salvation.

1997 / 0-85364-827-1 / xii + 264pp

Timothy Larsen
Friends of Religious Equality
Nonconformist Politics in Mid-Victorian England
During the middle decades of the nineteenth century the English Nonconformist community developed a coherent political philosophy of its own, of which a central tenet was the principle of religious equality (in contrast to the stereotype of Evangelical Dissenters). The Dissenting community fought for the civil rights of Roman Catholics, non-Christians and even atheists, on an issue of principle which had its flowering in the enthusiastic and undivided support which Nonconformity gave to the campaign for Jewish emancipation. This reissued study examines the political efforts and ideas of English Nonconformists during the period, covering the whole range of national issues raised, from state education to the Crimean War. It offers a case study of a theologically conservative group defending religious pluralism in the civic sphere, showing that the concept of religious equality was a grand vision at the centre of the political philosophy of the Dissenters.

2007 / 1-84227-402-3 / x + 300pp

Donald M. Lewis
Lighten Their Darkness
The Evangelical Mission to Working-Class London, 1828–1860
(Studies in Evangelical History and Thought)
This is a comprehensive and compelling study of the Church and the complexities of nineteenth-century London. Challenging our understanding of the culture in working London at this time, Lewis presents a well-structured and illustrated work that contributes substantially to the study of evangelicalism and mission in nineteenth-century Britain.
2001 / 1-84227-074-5 / xviii + 372pp

Stanley E. Porter and Anthony R. Cross (eds)
Semper Reformandum
Studies in Honour of Clark H. Pinnock
Clark Pinnock has clearly been one of the most important evangelical theologians of the last forty years in North America. Always provocative, especially in the wide range of opinions he has held and considered, Pinnock, himself a Baptist, has recently retired after twenty-five years of teaching at McMaster Divinity College. His colleagues and associates honour him in this volume by responding to his important theological work which has dealt with the essential topics of evangelical theology. These include Christian apologetics, biblical inspiration, the Holy Spirit and, perhaps most importantly in recent years, openness theology.
2003 / 1-84227-206-3 / xiv + 414pp

Meic Pearse
The Great Restoration
The Religious Radicals of the 16th and 17th Centuries
Pearse charts the rise and progress of continental Anabaptism – both evangelical and heretical – through the sixteenth century. He then follows the story of those English people who became impatient with Puritanism and separated – first from the Church of England and then from one another – to form the antecedents of later Congregationalists, Baptists and Quakers.
1998 / 0-85364-800-X / xii + 320pp

Charles Price and Ian M. Randall
Transforming Keswick
Transforming Keswick is a thorough, readable and detailed history of the convention. It will be of interest to those who know and love Keswick, those who are only just discovering it, and serious scholars eager to learn more about the history of God's dealings with his people.
2000 / 1-85078-350-0 / 288pp

Jim Purves
The Triune God and the Charismatic Movement
A Critical Appraisal from a Scottish Perspective
(Paternoster Theological Monographs)
All emotion and no theology? Or a fundamental challenge to reappraise and realign our trinitarian theology in the light of Christian experience? This study of charismatic renewal as it found expression within Scotland at the end of the twentieth century evaluates the use of Patristic, Reformed and contemporary models (including those of the Baptist Union of Scotland) of the Trinity in explaining the workings of the Holy Spirit.
2004 / 1-84227-321-3 / xxiv + 246pp

Ian M. Randall
Evangelical Experiences
A Study in the Spirituality of English Evangelicalism 1918–1939
(Studies in Evangelical History and Thought)
This book makes a detailed historical examination of evangelical spirituality between the First and Second World Wars. It shows how patterns of devotion led to tensions and divisions. In a wide-ranging study, Anglican, Wesleyan, Reformed and Pentecostal-charismatic spiritualities are analysed.
1999 / 0-85364-919-7 / xii + 310pp

Ian M. Randall
One Body in Christ
The History and Significance of the Evangelical Alliance
In 1846 the Evangelical Alliance was founded with the aim of bringing together evangelicals for common action. This book uses material not previously utilized to examine the history and significance of the Evangelical Alliance, a movement which has remained a powerful force for unity. At a time when evangelicals are growing world-wide, this book offers insights into the past which are relevant to contemporary issues.
2001 / 1-84227-089-3 / xii + 394pp

Ian M. Randall
Spirituality and Social Change
The Contribution of F.B. Meyer (1847–1929)
(Studies in Evangelical History and Thought)
This is a fresh appraisal of F.B. Meyer (1847–1929), a leading Free Church minister. Having been deeply affected by holiness spirituality, Meyer became the Keswick Convention's foremost international speaker. He combined spirituality with effective evangelism and socio-political activity. This study shows Meyer's significant contribution to spiritual renewal and social change.
2003 / 1-84227-195-4 / xx + 184pp

July 2005

Geoffrey Robson
Dark Satanic Mills?
Religion and Irreligion in Birmingham and the Black Country
(Studies in Evangelical History and Thought)
This book analyses and interprets the nature and extent of popular Christian belief and practice in Birmingham and the Black Country during the first half of the nineteenth century, with particular reference to the impact of cholera epidemics and evangelism on church extension programmes.
2002 / 1-84227-102-4 / xiv + 294pp

Alan P.F. Sell
Enlightenment, Ecumenism, Evangel
Theological Themes and Thinkers 1550–2000
(Studies in Christian History and Thought)
This book consists of papers in which such interlocking topics as the Enlightenment, the problem of authority, the development of doctrine, spirituality, ecumenism, theological method and the heart of the gospel are discussed. Issues of significance to the church at large are explored with special reference to writers from the Reformed and Dissenting traditions.
2005 / 1-84227330-2 / xviii + 422pp

Alan P.F. Sell
Hinterland Theology
Some Reformed and Dissenting Adjustments
(Studies in Christian History and Thought)
Many books have been written on theology's 'giants' and significant trends, but what of those lesser-known writers who adjusted to them? In this book some hinterland theologians of the British Reformed and Dissenting traditions, who followed in the wake of toleration, the Evangelical Revival, the rise of modern biblical criticism and Karl Barth, are allowed to have their say. They include Thomas Ridgley, Ralph Wardlaw, T.V. Tymms and N.H.G. Robinson.
2006 / 1-84227-331-0

July 2005

Alan P.F. Sell and Anthony R. Cross (eds)
Protestant Nonconformity in the Twentieth Century
(Studies in Christian History and Thought)
In this collection of essays scholars representative of a number of Nonconformist traditions reflect thematically on Nonconformists' life and witness during the twentieth century. Among the subjects reviewed are biblical studies, theology, worship, evangelism and spirituality, and ecumenism. Over and above its immediate interest, this collection provides a marker to future scholars and others wishing to know how some of their forebears assessed Nonconformity's contribution to a variety of fields during the century leading up to Christianity's third millennium.
2003 / 1-84227-221-7 / x + 398pp

Mark Smith
Religion in Industrial Society
Oldham and Saddleworth 1740–1865
(Studies in Christian History and Thought)
This book analyses the way British churches sought to meet the challenge of industrialization and urbanization during the period 1740–1865. Working from a case-study of Oldham and Saddleworth, Mark Smith challenges the received view that the Anglican Church in the eighteenth century was characterized by complacency and inertia, and reveals Anglicanism's vigorous and creative response to the new conditions. He reassesses the significance of the centrally directed church reforms of the mid-nineteenth century, and emphasizes the importance of local energy and enthusiasm. Charting the growth of denominational pluralism in Oldham and Saddleworth, Dr Smith compares the strengths and weaknesses of the various Anglican and Nonconformist approaches to promoting church growth. He also demonstrates the extent to which all the churches participated in a common culture shaped by the influence of evangelicalism, and shows that active co-operation between the churches rather than denominational conflict dominated. This revised and updated edition of Dr Smith's challenging and original study makes an important contribution both to the social history of religion and to urban studies.
2006 / 1-84227-335-3 / approx. 300pp

July 2005

David M. Thompson
Baptism, Church and Society in Britain from the Evangelical Revival to *Baptism, Eucharist and Ministry*

The theology and practice of baptism have not received the attention they deserve. How important is faith? What does baptismal regeneration mean? Is baptism a bond of unity between Christians? This book discusses the theology of baptism and popular belief and practice in England and Wales from the Evangelical Revival to the publication of the World Council of Churches' consensus statement on *Baptism, Eucharist and Ministry* (1982).

2005 / 1-84227-393-0 / approx. 224pp

Martin Sutherland
Peace, Toleration and Decay
The Ecclesiology of Later Stuart Dissent
(Studies in Christian History and Thought)

This fresh analysis brings to light the complexity and fragility of the later Stuart Nonconformist consensus. Recent findings on wider seventeenth-century thought are incorporated into a new picture of the dynamics of Dissent and the roots of evangelicalism.

2003 / 1-84227-152-0 / xxii + 216pp

Haddon Willmer
Evangelicalism 1785–1835: An Essay (1962) and Reflections (2004)
(Studies in Evangelical History and Thought)

Awarded the Hulsean Prize in the University of Cambridge in 1962, this interpretation of a classic period of English Evangelicalism, by a young church historian, is now supplemented by reflections on Evangelicalism from the vantage point of a retired Professor of Theology.

2006 / 1-84227-219-5

Linda Wilson
Constrained by Zeal
Female Spirituality amongst Nonconformists 1825–1875
(Studies in Evangelical History and Thought)

Constrained by Zeal investigates the neglected area of Nonconformist female spirituality. Against the background of separate spheres, it analyses the experience of women from four denominations, and argues that the churches provided a 'third sphere' in which they could find opportunities for participation.

2000 / 0-85364-972-3 / xvi + 294pp

Nigel G. Wright
Disavowing Constantine
*Mission, Church and the Social Order in the Theologies of
John Howard Yoder and Jürgen Moltmann*
(Paternoster Theological Monographs)

This book is a timely restatement of a radical theology of church and state in the Anabaptist and Baptist tradition. Dr Wright constructs his argument in dialogue and debate with Yoder and Moltmann, major contributors to a free church perspective.

2000 / 0-85364-978-2 / xvi + 252pp

Nigel G. Wright
Free Church, Free State
The Positive Baptist Vision

Free Church, Free State is a textbook on baptist ways of being church and a proposal for the future of baptist churches in an ecumenical context. Nigel Wright argues that both baptist (small 'b') and catholic (small 'c') church traditions should seek to enrich and support each other as valid expressions of the body of Christ without sacrificing what they hold dear. Written for pastors, church planters, evangelists and preachers, Nigel Wright offers frameworks of thought for baptists and non-baptists in their journey together following Christ.

2005 / 1-84227-353-1 / xxviii + 292

Nigel G. Wright
New Baptists, New Agenda

New Baptists, New Agenda is a timely contribution to the growing debate about the health, shape and future of the Baptists. It considers the steady changes that have taken place among Baptists in the last decade – changes of mood, style, practice and structure – and encourages us to align these current movements and questions with God's upward and future call. He contends that the true church has yet to come: the church that currently exists is an anticipation of the joyful gathering of all who have been called by the Spirit through Christ to the Father.

2002 / 1-84227-157-1 / x + 162pp

Paternoster:
thinking faith

Paternoster
9 Holdom Avenue,
Bletchley,
Milton Keynes MK1 1QR,
United Kingdom
Web: www.authenticmedia.co.uk/paternoster

July 2005